Battered Women and Feminist Lawmaking

Battered Women & Feminist Lawmaking

Elizabeth M. Schneider

Yale University Press / New Haven and London

Designed by Nancy Ovedovitz and set in Minion
type by Tseng Information Systems. Printed in the
United States of America by R. R. Donnelley & Sons,
Harrisonburg, Virginia.

Library of Congress Cataloging-in-Publication Data
Schneider, Elizabeth M.
Battered women and feminist lawmaking /
Elizabeth M. Schneider.
p.   cm.
Includes bibliographical references and index.
ISBN 0-300-08343-2 (alk. paper)
1. Abused women — Legal status, laws, etc. — United
States.   2. Family violence — Law and legislation —
United States.   3. Feminist jurisprudence — United
States.   I. Title.
KF9322. S36   2000
362.82'92 — dc21   00-036784

A catalogue record for this book is available from
the British Library.

The paper in this book meets the guidelines for
permanence and durability of the Committee on
Production Guidelines for Book Longevity of the
Council on Library Resources.

10   9   8   7   6   5   4   3   2   1

For Harry M. Schneider

for Anna and Matthew Schneider-Mayerson

for Tom Grunfeld

and in memory of Natalie Usdan Schneider

Contents

Acknowledgments

The ideas that I examine in this book emerged from my legal work at the Center for Constitutional Rights from 1973 through 1980, and in a series of articles beginning in 1978. Various aspects of my work on feminist lawmaking and permutations of my argument concerning the link between violence and equality have developed over the years in legal advocacy work on domestic violence, in teaching at Brooklyn Law School and Harvard Law School, in many articles, and in talks at many conferences, law schools, and forums.

Many people have given me tremendous support and encouragement. Martha Minow's friendship and belief in the importance of the project have kept me going during many hard times. Susan N. Herman, Minna Kotkin, Stacy Caplow, and Nan Hunter, extraordinarily supportive friends and colleagues at Brooklyn Law School, have daily cheered me on, read many drafts, and helped me think through many problems. My dear friends Betty Levinson, Carol Oppenheimer, Sylvia Law, Elinor Langer, Connie Brown, Janet Benshoof, and Judith Levin have helped me in innumerable ways. Linda Kerber's careful reading of the entire manuscript gave me the benefit of her tremendous knowledge, fine editorial judgment, and good sense. Clare Dalton, Linda Gordon, and Mary Haviland read through early drafts and provided thoughtful comments; Sara Blackburn helped me edit an early draft. The comments of anonymous reviewers improved the manuscript.

I have been lucky to be part of a supportive community at Brooklyn Law School. My colleagues, especially Margaret Berger, Eve Cary, Joe Crea, Mary Jo Eyster, Betsy Fajans, Mollie Falk, Linda Feldman, Nancy Fink, Maryellen Fullerton, Marsha Garrison, Beryl Jones, Bailey Kuklin, Michael Madow, Gary Minda, Sam Murumba, Arthur Pinto, Jennifer Rosato, Tony Sebok, Larry Solan, Jane Stevens, Sue Susman, Aaron Twerski, Marilyn Walter, Spencer

Weber Waller, Steven Winter, David Yassky, Carol Ziegler, and Victor Zonana, have helped me in various ways. At Harvard Law School, Martha Minow, Frank Michelman, Todd Rakoff, Duncan Kennedy, Jim Vorenberg, Betsy Bartholet, Gary Bellow, Chris Desan, Chris Edley, Martha Field, Gerry Frug, Danny Greenberg, Lani Guinier, Phil Heymann, Mort Horwitz, Randy Kennedy, Charles Ogletree, Joe Singer, Abbe Smith, Carol Steiker, Henry Steiner, Bernie Wolfman, Lucie White, David Wilkins, and Debbie Anker helped to make my visits enjoyable and stimulating; Martha Minow, Joe Singer, and Mira Judith Minow Singer gave me a home away from home. I have learned from a community of dedicated activists, lawyers, and legal scholars who have worked on issues of violence against women, including Kathy Abrams, Marina Angel, Mary Becker, Julie Blackman, Cynthia Grant Bowman, Sue Bryant, Sarah Buel, Charlotte Bunch, Naomi Cahn, Donna Coker, Rhonda Copelon, Kimberlé Crenshaw, Karen Czapanskiy, Clare Dalton, Alisa Del Tufo, Rebecca Dobash, Russell Dobash, Mary Ann Dutton, Martha Fineman, Anne Flitcraft, Marie Fortune, Ann Ganley, Martha Garcia, Sally Goldfarb, Julie Goldscheid, Barbara Hart, Mary Haviland, Ann Jones, Nancy Lemon, Betty Levinson, Christine Littleton, Holly Maguigan, Martha Mahoney, Isabel Marcus, Peter Margulies, Joan Meier, Anne Menard, Sue Osthoff, Ellen Pence, Cookie Polan, Jody Raphael, Judith Resnik, Beth Richie, Cookie Ridolfi, Jenny Rivera, Susan Schechter, Ann Shalleck, Reva Siegel, Esta Soler, Evan Stark, Nadine Taub, Kate Waits, Laurie Woods, Ellen Yaroshefsky, and Joan Zorza.

The human and intellectual roots of this book are deep. As an undergraduate at Bryn Mawr College and a graduate student at the London School of Economics, I first explored the interrelationship between social theory and social-movement practice with Richard Bernstein, Peter Bachrach, and Ralph Miliband; each of their voices is in these pages. At the Center for Constitutional Rights, I learned about the visionary possibilities of lawmaking: Rhonda Copelon, Nancy Stearns, Arthur Kinoy, Morton Stavis, and Peter Weiss taught and inspired me; their voices are here as well. Norman Dorsen and the Arthur Garfield Hays Civil Liberties Fellowship Program at New York University School of Law gave me a community in which to explore these issues as a law student; Frank Askin and Jonathan Hyman at the Constitutional Litigation Clinic at Rutgers Law School–Newark gave me a community in which to explore these issues as a law teacher. I am grateful for all these experiences.

Many colleagues gave me the opportunity to develop this material, and to present parts of this work at various conferences, forums, and law schools over many years. June Zeitlin asked me to prepare a report on domestic violence legal advocacy for the Ford Foundation, which was the genesis of this book; Helen Neuborne continued to involve me in discussion of these issues at Ford. Karl Klare and Frank Michelman first brought me to South Africa to work with South African lawyers and judges on the South African Constitution; Joanne Fedler brought me back to South Africa to teach and learn from many inspiring South African domestic violence activists and lawyers; Christina Murray, Cathi Albertyn, Dennis Davis, and the United States Information Service in South Africa facilitated many South African conversations. These experiences highlighted the need to understand violence within a framework of equality. Regina Graycar and Michael Coper invited me to Australia, where I presented parts of this book and benefited from conversations with colleagues at the University of Sydney and Australian National University Law Schools. I have learned from audiences at Harvard Law School, Vanderbilt University, Northeastern University Law School, Columbia Law School, Boston University Law School, Georgetown University Law School, University of Pittsburgh Law School, University of Pennsylvania Law School, Vermont Law School, Albany Law School, University of Maine Law School, University of Hong Kong Law School, Pennsylvania State University, Columbia University Seminar on Women and Society, Law and Society Annual Meetings, and Association of American Law Schools Annual Meetings. I am especially grateful to the many law students who have worked closely with me over many years, provided invaluable research assistance, and enriched my thinking—Kristin Bebelaar, Jodi Golinsky, Pamela Garas, Tracy Peterson, Ami Mehta, Joan Erskine, Alexandra Derian, Nicole Scarmato, Theresa Quinn, Catherine Paszkowska, Lina Del Plato, Suzanne Brackley, Stephanie Manes, and Jennifer Toritto—and to students in my classes who have discussed these issues with me and challenged my ideas. Harold Mayerson and Stella Taylor helped take loving care of our children, which enabled me to work. Without Charles Krause, my talented and devoted assistant, who has done amazing work on endless drafts with extraordinary cheer, this book would not have been completed. Sara Robbins, Linda Holmes, and other members of the Brooklyn Law School Library staff have been extraordinarily helpful and patient with my extensive research needs. Deans David G. Trager and Joan G. Wexler of Brooklyn Law School generously supported my work over many years with summer research grants.

John Covell of Yale University Press believed in this project from the first and has been a supportive and enthusiastic editor. His excitement for and commitment to the book has made all the difference. Jenya Weinreb has been the manuscript editor I have long dreamed of. I have been incredibly lucky to work with both of them.

My parents, Harry and Natalie Usdan Schneider, raised me to fight for the rights of women and to seek justice. They have been my first and foremost supporters in every way. My father's deep commitment to helping others and providing loving care as a doctor set an early and lifelong example for me. Although my mother passed away while I was writing this book, her determination, energy, and spirit live on in my work and in her grandchildren. My children, Anna and Matthew, inspire me daily with their wonderful inquisitiveness, openness, boundless love, and intelligence. Tom Grunfeld's love, wisdom, kindness, generosity, patience, and belief in me and in the importance of my work have grounded, nurtured, and sustained me. To all of them, I dedicate this book, with my deepest thanks and heartfelt love.

Portions of Chapter 3 are adapted from "The Dialectic of Rights and Politics: Perspectives from the Woman's Movement," 61 *New York University Law Review* 589 (1986) and "Markets and Women's International Human Rights," 25 *Brooklyn Journal of International Law* 141 (1999). Chapter 4 is adapted from "Particularity and Generality: Challenges of Feminist Theory and Practice in Work on Woman-Abuse," 67 *New York University Law Review* 520 (1992). Chapter 5 is adapted from "Feminism and the False Dichotomy of Victimization and Agency," 38 *New York Law School Law Review* 387 (1993). Chapter 6 is adapted from "The Violence of Privacy," 23 *Connecticut Law Review* 973 (1991). Part of Chapter 7 has been published as "Hearing Women Not Being Heard: On Carol Gilligan's *Getting Civilized* and the Complexity of Voice," 63 *Fordham Law Review* 17 (1994). Portions of Chapter 8 have been published in "Equal Rights to Trial for Women: Sex Bias in the Law of Self-Defense," 15 *Harvard Civil Rights–Civil Liberties Law Review* 623 (1980); "Describing and Changing: Women's Self-Defense Work and the Problem of Expert Testimony on Battering," 9 *Women's Rights Law Reporter* 195 (1986); and "Resistance to Equality," 57 *University of Pittsburgh Law Review* 477 (1996). Portions of Chapter 10 have been published as "Engaging with the State about Domestic Violence: Continuing Dilemmas and Gender Equality," 1 *Georgetown Journal of Gender and Law* 173 (1999); "Introduction: The Promise of the Violence Against Women Act of 1994," 4 *Journal of Law and Policy* 371 (1996);

and "The Civil Rights Remedy of the Violence Against Women Act: Legislative History, Policy Implications and Litigation Strategy," 4 *Journal of Law and Policy* 427 (1996). Chapter 11 is adapted from "What Happened to Public Education About Domestic Violence?" in *Postmortem, the O. J. Simpson Case: Justice Confronts Race, Domestic Violence, Lawyers, Money and the Media* (Jeffrey Abramson, ed., 1996). Chapter 12 is adapted from "Violence Against Women and Legal Education: An Essay for Mary Joe Frug," 26 *New England Law Review* 843 (1992). All these chapters have been revised for this book.

I

Domestic Violence as a Social and Legal Problem

1

Introduction: Battered Women, Feminist Lawmaking, and Equality

In the late 1960s a movement of feminist activists and lawyers began to bring the problem of woman abuse to public attention. At that time, there was no legal recognition of a harm of violence against women by intimates — today known as domestic violence. It simply didn't exist in the legal vocabulary.[1] In 1992, the United States Supreme Court recognized the pervasiveness and severity of intimate violence for the first time in *Planned Parenthood v. Casey*, and in 1994 Congress passed the Violence Against Women Act. This book is about the process of feminist legal advocacy and lawmaking on intimate violence that has led the Supreme Court, other courts, Congress, and state legislatures to recognize this harm.

Planned Parenthood v. Casey is widely known as the decision in which the Supreme Court narrowly upheld constitutional protection for women's right to reproductive choice, not as a case about intimate violence. But the restrictive Pennsylvania abortion statute challenged in *Casey* included a mandatory "spousal notification" provision. Battered women's advocacy organizations argued that enforcement of this provision would mean that women who faced intimate violence, and who could not tell their partner that they were pregnant without fear of harm, would be unable to freely exercise their reproductive choice. The Court struck down this provision as unconstitutional on these grounds.

In its decision, the Court described the problem of domestic violence, drawing on a startling statistical picture:

- In an average 12-month period in this country, approximately two million women are the victims of severe assaults by their male partners. In a 1985 survey, women reported that nearly one of every eight husbands had assaulted their wives during the past year. The [American Medical Association] views these figures as "marked underestimates," because the nature of these incidents discourages women from reporting them, and because surveys typically exclude the very poor, those who do not speak English well, and women who are homeless or in institutions or hospitals when the survey is conducted. According to the AMA, "researchers on family violence agree that the true incidence of partner violence is probably *double* the above estimates; or four million severely assaulted women per year."

• Studies on prevalence suggest that from one-fifth to one-third of all women will be physically assaulted by a partner or ex-partner during their lifetime. . . . Thus on an average day in the United States, nearly 11,000 women are severely assaulted by their male partners. Many of these incidents involve sexual assault. . . . In families where wife-beating takes place, moreover, child abuse is often present as well.

• Other studies fill in the rest of this troubling picture. Physical violence is only the most visible form of abuse. Psychological abuse, particularly forced social and economic isolation of women, is also common.

• Many victims of domestic violence remain with their abusers, perhaps because they perceive no superior alternative. . . . Many abused women who find temporary refuge in shelters return to their husbands, in large part because they have no other source of income. . . . Returning to one's abuser can be dangerous. Recent Federal Bureau of Investigation statistics disclose that 8.8 percent of all homicide victims in the United States are killed by their spouses. . . . Thirty percent of female homicide victims are killed by their male partners.[2]

The statistics that the Court recited, though horrifying, were not news. Feminists in the United States had argued for more than two centuries that women's legally sanctioned subordination within the family denied them equality and citizenship. They saw intimate violence as an important vehicle of this subordination, for, as Wendy Williams put it, it involves the "ultimatum: do as I say, . . . subordinate yourself to me, or you will be injured."[3] Feminists claimed that domestic violence threatened not only women's right to physical integrity and perhaps even life itself, but women's liberty, autonomy, and equality. Yet it was only in the late 1960s that any aspect of this link between violence and equality began to be reflected in law and culture.

Since then, the rebirth of a women's rights movement in the United States has had a substantial impact in shaping social attitudes and defining public issues. Law has been a critical component of this process of change, and feminist lawyers have played a central role in shaping it. Feminist activists and lawyers have challenged assumptions about gender roles, the family, and the workplace. Through a process of feminist lawmaking they have given name and visibility to harms experienced by women, such as intimate violence and sexual harassment, that were previously buried by cultural complicity.

The development of a battered women's movement has been one of the most important contributions of the women's rights struggle. This movement created the theoretical concept of battering, and the issue has now moved from social invisibility as a "private problem" to an important public concern. There is hardly a day when a story on some aspect of domestic violence does not appear in the media. The O. J. Simpson case, with its subtext of battering, held public attention for several years. There has been an explosion of innovative activist and advocacy efforts in both state and federal legislative arenas. Organizations have founded shelters or networks of "safe homes," set up telephone hotlines, challenged police practices that fail to intervene effectively to assist battered women, drafted legislation to protect women through civil orders of protection as well as criminal and tort remedies, and developed programs to work with battering men. Lawsuits and legislation have produced improved police and court practices. Activists have developed teen-dating violence programs and special law school and medical school courses. Government reports, legal and social-science literature, and media coverage have proliferated. Advocates and scholars continue to formulate new legal approaches to violence against women. Work in the United States is linked to a feminist human rights campaign on gender violence around the world.

Nevertheless, this many-faceted barrage of activity has not achieved linear, ascending progress; instead, the result has been complex change, partial inroads, and deep resistance. In this book I examine both accomplishments and contradictions through the lens of feminist legal advocacy efforts on violence against women in the United States.

Feminist legal arguments about gender violence have developed from feminist insights about the way heterosexual intimate violence is part of a larger system of coercive control and subordination; this system is based on structural gender inequality and has political roots. The source of insight about the connection between lived personal experience and structural power relations was the notion that "the personal is political." In the context of intimate

violence, the impulse behind feminist legal arguments was to redefine the relationship between the personal and the political, to definitively link violence
and gender.

Although there have been dramatic strides in the way the law on intimate violence has incorporated these insights, in the process of lawmaking, feminist ideas about the relationship between violence and gender have
been simultaneously transformed, depoliticized, subverted, and contained:
the broader link between violence and gender inequality that animated them
has, to a large degree, been lost, or at least undermined. For example, widespread use of the term "battered woman syndrome" has reinscribed notions
of female pathology, provocation, and victim blaming into legal discourse.
In the very process of change, systemic analysis of gendered violence consistently meets with ambivalence and resistance. Each step forward provokes
efforts to dilute and contain the original theoretical framework.

I have been deeply involved in the work of the movement that I describe. I
first became concerned with the problem of violence against women through
my work as a lawyer on issues of legal treatment of battered women who,
having defended themselves against their assailants, faced problems of gender
bias in the criminal law. I have continued to work on these issues in a variety of
capacities: in teaching, writing, legal advocacy, and public education; in preparing a report for the Ford Foundation on legal reform efforts for battered
women; in training judges and lawyers about issues of gender and violence;
and in working to integrate issues of gender generally, and gender violence
in particular, into legal education. I have also done work internationally on
these issues, most recently and intensely with feminist lawyers, activists, and
judges in South Africa. These experiences as activist, lawyer, and theorist have
given me a wide vantage point to critically evaluate feminist lawmaking on
domestic violence.

My work has explored the social and political meaning of legal claims
in feminist struggle, and particularly within the battered women's movement. This work on rights claims began with the development of a theoretical framework that I have called the "dialectical interrelationship between
rights and politics." The assertion of legal claims and claims of rights has
been shaped by political struggle. Legal argumentation and the articulation of
rights reveal tensions and contradictions that sharpen political analysis and
move it forward; these theoretical insights must be integrated into practice

in order to reshape it. I emphasize the need for close attention to the inter-relationship between theory and practice in our understanding of the complexity of women's lives and in the articulation of women's experiences into legal claims.

This theoretical perspective on the relationship between law and social movements shapes this book. The book examines concrete ways in which this dialectical interrelationship operates in feminist lawmaking on battering. It analyzes how the articulation of rights has exposed tensions and paradoxes in feminist legal strategies and visions, but has also clarified issues and sharpened debate. In both content and structure, the book reflects this dialectical relationship between theory and practice.

Now is a time of enormous challenge and opportunity for work on male battering of women. The passage of the Violence Against Women Act and the introduction in Congress of a second Violence Against Women Act have given broad national attention to this issue. Stories of women murdered by battering men continue to receive widespread publicity. Grants of clemency to battered women who killed their abusers have attracted much media attention. In states where restraining-order legislation or the mandatory arrest of batterers has strengthened legal remedies, the percentage of batterings that are reported has increased dramatically. Nevertheless, women who seek help often face "mutual restraining orders" or arrest along with their abusers. And at the same time that legal reform efforts have expanded, public response to clemency efforts has rekindled a national debate on issues of violence against women and women's "retaliation." Anita Hill's experience in alleging sexual harassment against Supreme Court nominee Clarence Thomas, and other more recent, highly publicized sexual harassment cases have underscored the tenacity of views of women as unreasonable and provocative. The current right-wing backlash on such issues as the Violence Against Women Act contests claims of the seriousness of the problem.

The challenge for feminist lawmaking is profound. Feminist legal theorists and practitioners must confront the theoretical implications of strategic choices and the strategic implications of theoretical choices in women's rights litigation, and in legal work on battering particularly. I have argued that the task for feminist lawyers is both to describe and allow for change: to describe a legal problem for women—describe it in detail and in context—and translate it to unsympathetic courts in such a way that it is not misheard and at the same time does not remain static. Feminist lawmakers must develop legal theory and practice that are accurate to the realities of women's diverse experiences but that also take account of complexity and allow for change.

Although this book grew out of this dialectical understanding of the relationship between law and social movements, it has developed far beyond this framework in two important respects. First, I now see law in a more complex, fluid, and multifaceted way. Law is made, and operates, in many sites and in many different ways; it does not exist outside culture but is reflected in popular consciousness, where it takes on a wide range of cultural forms and produces cultural meanings. Law is made, and works, both on the level of "grand" theory and visionary conceptualization and on the "ground" level in practice, not only in major law reform litigation but in individual cases. Yet I still believe that law can be a means of defining and redefining selfhood, of perceiving and reconceiving experience, and that law reform can express new collective identities and needs and manifest a sensitivity to those needs.

Second, I now more deeply understand that even if feminist lawyers describe women's experiences and get the description right, positive change will not necessarily ensue. The process of change is chaotic and uneven; the constitution of women as legal subjects, and the social and legal construction of the problem of domestic violence, are multifaceted; the hurdles of containment and subversion in legal discourse are substantial. As the saying goes, change may simultaneously involve one step forward and two steps backward.

The first section of the book describes the history and early experience of the battered woman's movement, the feminist vision that drove it, and social construction of the problem of domestic violence. It then turns to the theoretical framework of feminist lawmaking. I situate this analysis in feminist legal work and strategy on domestic violence, detail the history of feminist lawmaking on domestic violence, and explore new legal descriptions of violence as gendered that draw on feminist insights concerning gender and violence. I examine aspirations and contradictions of feminist lawmaking in examples of battered women in court and women's international human rights.

In the second section of the book, I explore three core theoretical dilemmas in this framework of feminist analysis on battering: notions of how to define abuse and identity of battered women, which raise issues of what I call particularity and generality in feminist legal theory and practice; of how to describe the complexity of battered women's experiences; and of concepts of domestic violence as private. I explore how these three theoretical tensions emerge and reemerge in different aspects of feminist lawmaking.

In the third section of the book, I examine feminist lawmaking "on the ground." Here, I describe how assertion of legal claims and incorporation of feminist arguments into legal discourse reveal both possibilities and limitations of the vision of gender violence. I look at how legal discourse has opened up the possibility of political "conversation" and transformative experience, and how this process of transformation, containment, and subversion of feminist insights has occurred. I detail generic issues that shape the translation of these insights into law, the incorporation of battered women's experiences and stories into law, the processing of these experiences into "cases," the rejection of battered women's experiences as an authoritative source of legal knowledge, consequent reliance on "experts" and the construction of expert testimony, the role of lawyers, and the meaning of process. I then turn to a closer examination of these themes in two contexts: battered women who have committed homicide in defending themselves against assault, and battered women who are mothers.

The final section of the book focuses on feminist lawmaking and social change—on aspirations for, limits of, and possibilities for transformation. It begins with a chapter on the dilemmas of feminist law reform that "engages" with the state, focusing on criminal prosecution and the civil rights remedy of the Violence Against Women Act of 1994, which makes "gender-motivated violence" a civil rights violation. (As this book went to press in May 2000, the U.S. Supreme Court held this civil rights remedy unconstitutional on commerce clause grounds in *Brzonkala v. Morrison*.) I then explore the intersection between lawmaking and education, examining various ways in which lawmaking on domestic violence affects public education and, conversely, education on domestic violence affects lawmaking, focusing on the O.J. Simpson trials and my class on battered women and the law at Harvard Law School. I conclude with the need to reaffirm the original vision of violence and gender equality that animated activist and legal work and to implement this vision in the various aspects of lawmaking that I have described.

This book is about both activism and jurisprudence. Legal advocacy for battered women has much to teach us about legal theory, and legal theory has much to teach us about advocacy and activism. The book crosses these conventional boundaries, weaves back and forth between theory and practice, and examines recurring dilemmas in feminist lawmaking from various and overlapping vantage points. I speak to many audiences: people who work on issues of gender discrimination; activists and legal advocates for battered women; social, political, and legal theorists; judges, legislators, and policy makers; and all those concerned with the relationship between law, gender, violence, and social change.

This book is also about pain—the pain of violence and the violence of law. bell hooks's important insight, that the liberatory dimensions of theory grow out of pain and struggle, is profoundly applicable to the story I tell.[4] The pathbreaking legal argumentation, legal reform efforts, and legal theory that I describe here have been a way to articulate and remedy the pain of far too many women. The inspiring, creative, and committed work of battered women, activists, advocates, and lawyers for battered women around the world has made feminist lawmaking possible.

2

The Battered Women's Movement and the Problem of Domestic Violence

Here goes.

Broken nose. Loose teeth. Cracked ribs. Broken finger. Black eyes. I don't know how many; I once had two at the same time, one fading, the other new. Shoulders, elbows, knees, wrists. Stitches in my mouth. Stitches in my chin. A ruptured eardrum. Burns. Cigarettes on my arms and legs. Thumped me, kicked me, burned me. He butted me with his head. He held me and still butted me; I couldn't believe it. He dragged me around the house by my clothes and by my hair. He kicked me up and he kicked me down the stairs. Bruised me, scalded me, threatened me. For seventeen years. Hit me, thumped me, raped me. Seventeen years. He threw me into the garden. He threw me out of the attic. Fists, boots, knee, head. Bread knife, saucepan, brush. He tore out clumps of my hair. Cigarettes, lighter, ashtray. He set fire to my clothes. He locked me out and he locked me in. He hurt me and hurt me and hurt me. He killed all of me. Bruised, burnt and broken. Bewitched, bothered and bewildered. Seventeen years of it. He never gave up. Months went by and nothing happened, but it was always there — the promise of it. . . .

For seventeen years. There wasn't one minute when I wasn't afraid, when I wasn't waiting. Waiting for him to go, waiting for him to come. Waiting for the fist, waiting for the smile. I was brainwashed and braindead, a zombie for hours, afraid to think, afraid to stop, completely alone. I sat at home and waited. I mopped up my own blood. I lost all my friends, and most of my teeth. He gave me a choice, left or right; I chose left because he broke the little finger on my left hand. Because I scorched one of his shirts. Because his egg was too hard. Because the toilet seat was wet. Because because because. He demolished me. He destroyed me. And I never stopped loving him. I adored him when he stopped. I was grateful, so grateful, I'd have done anything for him. I loved him. And he loved me.

—Roddy Doyle, *The Woman Who Walked into Doors*, 175 (1996)

Nearly 1.9 million women are physically battered in the United States each year. The Federal Bureau of Investigation estimates that almost fourteen hundred women, about 9 percent of all murders, were killed by their spouses or partners in 1996 alone.[1] The statistics are numbing. A colleague of mine, after seeing a televised public service announcement on battering featuring photographs of women bruised and beaten, said to me: "I didn't know this is what they looked like."

Battering fits within a larger picture of abuse of power. The "power and control wheel" developed by the Domestic Abuse Prevention Project in Duluth identifies interrelated dimensions of physical abuse, economic abuse, coercion and threats, intimidation, emotional abuse (using isolation, minimizing, denying, and blaming), and abusing male privilege. Men who batter are frequently described as romantic, charming, controlling, seductive, jealous, and possessive. They want control over "their" women.

Violence researcher Evan Stark has observed that battering should be understood as both "the pattern of violent acts and their political framework, the pattern of social, institutional, and interpersonal controls that usurp a woman's capacity to determine her destiny."[2] Feminist legal scholar Donna Coker explains the link between the physical fact of battering and these controls in the following way:

> Battering may be experienced as a personal violation, but it is an act facilitated and made possible by societal gender inequalities. The batterer does not, indeed could not, act alone. Social supports for battering include widespread denial of its frequency or harm, economic structures that render women vulnerable, and sexist ideology that holds women accountable for male violence and for the emotional lives of families, and that fosters deference to male familial control. Batterers often use the political and economic vulnerability of women to reinforce their power and dominance over particular women. Thus, their dominance, or their attempts at dominance, are frequently bolstered by stigmatization of victims through the use of gender social norms that define the "good" woman (wife/mother). Batterers also take advantage of the vulnerabilities of their victims, such as the victim's economic dependence on the batterer or on the state, her status as an illegal immigrant, her alcohol or drug dependency, or her responsibility to provide and care for children. Battering also increases women's social and economic vulnerability. Battered women lose jobs, education opportunities, careers, homes, and savings. They may also lose relationships with family and friends that might otherwise provide material aid.

Women become homeless as a result of battering, their homelessness is made more difficult to remedy because they are battered, and they are more vulnerable to further battering because they are homeless. Women on the run, avoiding a batterer, are unable to stay long in one place, unable to participate fully in job training programs and housing programs, and unable to wait out the long lists required for government-sponsored childcare. Women involved with someone who batters find their efforts at economic self-sufficiency sabotaged.[3]

Historical Perspectives

Anglo-American common law originally provided that a husband, as master of his household, could subject his wife to corporal punishment or "chastisement" if he did not inflict permanent damage upon her. During the nineteenth century, an era of feminist activism for reform of marriage law, English and U.S. authorities declared that a husband no longer had the right to chastise his wife. Yet for more than a hundred years after courts rejected the right of chastisement, the American legal system continued to treat what was then called wife beating differently from other cases of assault and battery. Authorities denied that a husband had the right to beat his wife, but they rarely intervened in cases of marital violence. Men who assaulted their wives were often granted formal and informal immunities from prosecution, in order to protect the privacy of the family and to promote "domestic harmony."[4] In the 1960s, with the rebirth of an active women's movement in the United States, feminists again began to challenge this concept of family privacy; the new consciousness created by these efforts provided an arena in which hidden "private" violence became more and more visible.

Domestic violence is known in almost every culture throughout history.[5] Roman society treated a wife as the property of her husband, and she was therefore subject to his control. According to early Roman law, a man could beat, divorce, or murder his wife for offenses committed by her that affected his honor or jeopardized his property rights. Enforcement of these rights of control was a private matter.[6] In the fifteenth century, the Catholic Church endorsed the Rules of Marriage, which permitted a husband to be the judge of his wife and to beat her with a stick if she committed an offense. To the church, wife beating showed the husband's concern for the wife's soul.[7] The prevailing law of England gave a husband the legal right to beat his wife in order to maintain family discipline. According to Blackstone, a widely read nineteenth-century writer of legal treatises, husband and wife were one, and that one was the husband.

The work of feminist historians Linda Gordon and Elizabeth Pleck and feminist legal historian Reva Siegel has provided an important historical perspective on the problem of domestic violence in the United States. Gordon and Pleck have written historical analyses of laws, public attitudes, and campaigns concerning domestic violence. Siegel's work analyzes historical changes from the perspective of reforms in women's legal status, and closely examines issues of race and class. As a result of their work, we have textured and sophisticated historical perspectives on domestic violence, which I draw on in this section.

English law and Blackstone's commentaries on it had considerable influence over early American legal thought and shaped the development of the American legal system. Yet there were other influences as well. The Puritans abhorred woman abuse, because they perceived it as a threat to order and stability. During the mid-seventeenth century, the Massachusetts Bay and Plymouth Bay colonies enacted laws that prohibited wife abuse, although they were not strictly enforced; colonial courts preferred to reconcile couples even when there were complaints of abuse.[8] Courts would also order runaway wives to return to the family home.

The principles reflected in Blackstone's commentaries were deeply embedded in English law; these principles were affirmed in much of America. Courts applied the rationales of English common law, emphasizing the importance of family autonomy and privacy by refusing to invade the marital relationship except when the husband exceeded the bounds of "moderate chastisement." Thus in 1824, the Supreme Court of Mississippi granted a husband the right to "chastise" his wife. The court limited the punishment to "moderate chastisement" but suggested that a man should not be subjected to "vexatious prosecutions" by his wife for exercising that right, and that courts should not reveal private conduct to the public.[9] In 1836, a New Hampshire court held that a wife who did not submit to the legitimate authority of her husband and who manifested characteristics "unbecoming a lady" could not obtain a divorce. The court also indicated that "a woman who provoked her husband's anger, and who refused to remain silent in the face of his temper, deserved any abuse inflicted upon her as a result of her disobedience and had no cause for complaint." Because the husband was head of the household and the law made the husband responsible for his wife's debts, crimes committed in his presence, and torts, the law gave him authority to control her actions. Reflecting the social ambivalence that continues today, the New Hampshire court concluded that "although society condemned the husband's unmanly conduct in beating his wife, it abhorred even more the wife's unseemly rebellion against the proper exercise of his authority."[10]

Domestic violence became a subject of reform in the late nineteenth century from two distinct activist perspectives. Temperance campaigners viewed it as inextricably linked to the evils of alcohol and sought prohibition in order to protect abuse victims. Feminists as well as social purist reformers argued that the physical and sexual abuse of women stemmed from a husband's rights of ownership of his wife's body and campaigned for emancipation to remove that privilege.[11] The feminist campaign for divorce employed the recounting of graphic stories about wife beating. Some leaders in the fight for women's rights addressed wife beating as a political struggle, primarily by publicizing cases involving women of substantial social standing. In Gordon's words, "Feminists sheltered runaway wives, organized concerning particular divorce and child-custody cases, and held public meetings on egregious cases of injustice, and they used these cases to argue for women's rights to divorce and to vote."[12]

Siegel explains the interplay between the temperance and feminist perspectives in the following way:

In 1848, when the woman's rights movement held its first convention, it denounced the common-law doctrines of marital status in a formal Declaration of Sentiments:

"He has made her, if married, in the eye of the law, civilly dead.

He has taken from her all right in property, even to the wages she earns.

. . . In the covenant of marriage she is compelled to promise obedience to her husband, he becoming, to all intents and purposes, her master — the law giving him power to deprive her of her liberty, and to administer chastisement." . . .

The woman's rights movement differed from the temperance movement, both in its diagnosis of family violence and in the social remedies it proposed. As the Declaration of Sentiments illustrates, the chastisement prerogative figured prominently in the feminist movement's first challenge to the marital-status rules of the common law. Woman's rights advocates protested the hierarchical structure of marriage; and, as they did so, they attacked the chastisement prerogative as a practical and symbolic embodiment of the husband's authority over his wife. The woman's rights movement thus broke with the temperance movement by depicting wife beating as a symptom of fundamental defects in the legal structure of marriage itself. The movement's 1848 Declaration of Sentiments identified chastisement as part of a political system of male dominance, an analysis that feminists continued to elaborate in the ensuing decades.[13]

Gordon suggests that wife beating was an issue that influenced the nineteenth-century women's rights movement, but it was addressed primarily indirectly, through campaigns for temperance, child welfare, and social purity, and only marginally through direct lobbying for legislative or judicial reforms regarding wife beating. She notes that "putting a temperance frame around criticisms of male behavior allowed feminists to score points obliquely, without attacking marriage or men in general. Male brutality, not male tyranny, was the target. The problem came from exceptional, 'depraved' men, not the male gender as a norm."[14]

By the late nineteenth century, public and judicial opinion had begun to shift. By the 1870s, there was no judge or treatise writer in the United States who recognized a husband's prerogative to chastise his wife. As Siegel recounts: "Thus, when a wife beater was charged with assault and battery, judges refused to entertain his claim that a husband had a legal right to strike his wife; instead they denounced the prerogative and allowed the criminal prosecution to proceed. In several states, legislatures enacted statutes specifically prohibiting wife-beating; three states even revived corporal punishment for the crime, providing that wife beaters would be sentenced to the whipping post." In 1871, both Alabama and Massachusetts judicially abrogated a husband's right to abuse his wife physically. The Alabama court held that husband and wife were equal, and that each was endowed with civil and political rights and public privileges. In Massachusetts, the court indicated that even a drunken or insolent wife deserved protection from her husband's abuse. Siegel observes: "Thus as the American legal system repudiated the husband's prerogative to chastise his wife, it did begin to respond differently to wife beating—yet did not adopt policies calculated to provide married women much relief from family violence. Women of the social elite might escape husbands who beat them by obtaining a divorce, if they were not deemed blameworthy, and if they were willing to subject themselves and their children to the economic perils and social stigma associated with single motherhood. Women of poorer families might have a husband fined, incarcerated or perhaps even flogged, if they were willing to turn him over to a racially hostile criminal justice system. The law thus provided relief to some battered wives, but the majority had little recourse against abusive husbands."[15] Gordon maintains that by the late nineteenth century, wife beating was not accepted as a right, and was effectively illegal in most states.

The concept of companionate marriage undermined the authority-based conception of marriage in which the chastisement prerogative was rooted. Siegel notes that "the repudiation of chastisement precipitated a shift in the rules and rhetoric of laws regulating interspousal violence—giving rise to a new doctrinal regime couched in discourses of affective privacy that preserved, to a significant degree, the marital prerogative that chastisement rules once protected. . . . Judicial concerns about privacy were class-salient, invoked to protect propertied men from regulatory oversight in ways they were not invoked to protect the poor."[16] These new discourses of affective privacy, combined with the abrogation of chastisement, led to judicial rationales of privacy and immunity for non-intervention in woman abuse. Siegel relates:

> Thus, judges seeking to explain the modified structure of marital status law increasingly drew upon gender concepts of the industrial era to depict the law of marriage in more contemporary and socially credible terms. Rather than represent marriage in the biblical discourse of "one flesh," as a hierarchical relation that "merged" the wife into husband, courts instead discussed marriage as it was understood in nineteenth-century America: as a companionate relationship based on an affective bond that flourished best in a sphere separate from civil society. And, over the decades, the idiom of marital status law shifted, with tropes of interiority (describing feelings and spaces) progressively supplanting tropes of hierarchy. Judges even discussed the privacy of the marital relationship by invoking heavily curtained windows of the sort fashionable in the late nineteenth century: Reasoning in this idiom of interiority, a court would not hear a wife's suit for damages against a husband who assaulted her because public policy counseled that "it is better to draw the curtain, shut out the public gaze, and leave the parties to forget and forgive." The transformation in the discourse of marital status was far-reaching in scope, affecting its rhetoric and rule structure. Once, the common law had vested a husband with the right to command his wife's obedience, by physical chastisement if necessary, and had vested him with property rights in the economic value of her "services," but now courts represented marriage as an affective relationship uniquely unsuited to regulation by law.[17]

Gordon tells us that in the early twentieth century, as the family court system developed, judges assumed that family preservation was necessary and that abuse could be cured or corrected. Courts discouraged separation and divorce, sometimes even to the point of judicial coercion of abuse victims: badgering wives into withdrawing complaints, denying their petitions for financial support from husbands, or assigning cases to a social service organization. These courts often failed to provide a battered woman with physical protection after she filed a complaint, which increased the possibility of retaliatory assault from her abuser.

But women who were beaten experienced a "right" to protection as a complex issue. Gordon posits the reasons for their contradictory perceptions:

> Many women clients did not seem to believe that they had a "right" to freedom from physical violence. When social workers expressed disgust at the way they were treated, the clients sometimes considered that reaction naive. They spoke of the inevitability of male violence. Their refusal to condemn marital violence in moral terms must be interpreted carefully. It did not mean that these women were passive or accepted beatings. They often resisted assault in many ways: fighting back, running away, attempting to embarrass the men before others, calling the police. And they did express moral outrage if their men crossed some border of tolerability. There is no contradiction here. The language of absolute "rights" is only one legitimate approach to self-defense. In a patriarchal system there were neither institutions nor concepts defending absolute rights, but rather custom and bargaining. Because the client women did not conduct a head-on challenge to their husband's prerogatives does not mean that they liked being hit or believed that their virtue required accepting it.
>
> What was new in the nineteenth-century middle-class reform sensibility was the notion that wife-beating was entirely intolerable. Family reformers proposed, like abolitionists toward slavery and prohibitionists toward drink, to do away with physical violence in marriage altogether. . . . By contrast, many poor battered women had a more complex view of the problem than their benefactors: welcoming all the help they could get in their individual struggles against assault, they also needed economic help in order to provide a decent family life for children. Given a choice, they might have preferred economic aid to prosecution of wife-beaters.[18]

Gordon argues that social and economic circumstances shaped battered women's complex experiences of their situation:

In their complaints against husbands we see women's implicit construction of a "right," an entitlement to protection. It was a claim women began to make only when they had some reasonable expectation that they could win—otherwise strategies other than head-on confrontation with a husband's prerogatives were more effective.

Women's invention of a right not to be beaten came from a dialectic between changing social possibilities and aspirations. When women's best hope was husbands' kindness, because they were economically dependent on marriage, they did not protest violations of their individual rights but rested their case on their importance as mothers. As women's possibilities expanded to include wage-earning, remarriage after divorce, birth limitation and aid to single mothers, their best hopes escalated to include escape from marital violence altogether.[19]

In a fascinating dimension of her study, Gordon observes that the most striking and consistent aspect of women's complaints up to the 1930s was that they focused on husbands' non-support rather than abuse and, in that way, sought support from social control agencies without directly challenging male authority. She suggests that "women's complaints about wife-beating escalated just as feminism was at its nadir"; after the 1930s most women clients complained directly rather than indirectly about wife-beating. Gordon posits an economistic interpretation:

> Wife-beating accusations stood out even more because of the virtual disappearance of non-support complaints. This striking inverse correlation between non-support and wife-beating complaints stimulates an economistic hypothesis: economic dependence prevented women's formulation of a sense of entitlement to protection against marital violence, but it also gave them a sense of entitlement to support; by contrast, the growth of a wage labor economy, bringing unemployment, transience, and dispersal of kinfolk, lessened women's sense of entitlement to support from their husbands, but allowed them to insist on their physical integrity. It is a reasonable hypothesis that the Depression, by the leveling impact of its widespread unemployment, actually encouraged women regarding the possibilities of independence.[20]

Gordon also describes dimensions of the battering relationship that persist today. She notes that although the "first-wave" women's movement had asserted women's rights to personal freedom even in marriage, it had not provided any institutional vehicles to assist poor women to secure and defend that right, "a power which was necessary for women really to believe in their own entitlement."[21] Until the revival of feminism and the establishment of battered women's shelters in the 1970s, wife-beating victims had only three resources: their own individual strategies of resistance; the help of relatives, friends, and neighbors; and the intervention of child welfare agencies. The first two were easily outweighed by the superior power of husbands, and the third was often of no help.

Contemporary Development of a Battered Women's Movement

Elizabeth Pleck observes that virtually no public discussion of wife beating took place from the beginning of the twentieth century until the mid-1970s:

> Wifebeating was called "domestic disturbance" by the police, "family maladjustment" by marriage counselors and social caseworkers. Psychiatry, under the influence of Helene Deutsch, regarded the battered woman as a masochist who provoked her husband into beating her. In the *Journal of Marriage and the Family,* the major scholarly journal in family sociology, no article on family violence appeared from its founding in 1939 until 1969.
>
> Very few modern novels contained scenes of marital violence. . . . Newspapers did not begin to report on abuse of wives until 1974. The next year, however, women activists organized conferences in several cities to establish shelters for battered women, demand arrest of wife beaters by the police, and draft new legislation. In 1977, the *New York Times* carried forty-four articles on wife beating, ranging from stories about hotlines and shelters to the trials of women who had murdered their assaultive husbands.[22]

It took the rebirth of feminism in the 1960s for the "rediscovery" of battering.[23] With a new spotlight on intimate violence and the ensuing development of a battered women's movement, many reforms designed to protect women from marital violence have been secured.

In both England and the United States, the focus of feminist consciousness-raising about domestic violence was on intimate violence in the context of heterosexual relationships. The term first used to describe the problem was "wife-abuse," which revealed that it was viewed primarily through the lens of a marital relationship. Domestic violence was seen as part of the larger problem of patriarchy within the marital relationship.

Feminist activism around issues of domestic violence was highly diffuse and took many different forms. One focus was the development of battered women's "refuges," "shelters," or "safe houses." These houses, women-run and women-centered, were established to give battered women a place to go when they left a violent home, and to provide safety for them and their children. The idea of temporary residences for battered women was devised by a group of women in London who established a neighborhood center, Chiswick, that offered child care and a refuge for homeless women; many of those who needed the help of the center were women who had been abused. Police, social workers, social service agencies, and doctors wouldn't help them, but Chiswick admitted any woman who wanted to stay. Soon, women began to arrive from all over, and the center received wide publicity. Other shelters were set up around the country.

Many Americans visited the English shelters during their first years. In the United States, however, the only available models were safe houses for the wives of alcoholics. One of the first American shelters for battered women was Women's Advocates in St. Paul, Minnesota, founded in 1974 by Women's Advocates, a consciousness-raising group that had previously written a divorce rights handbook and organized a phone service to provide legal information to women. When battered women called the group's telephone hotline for assistance, they were housed at first in the staff's own apartments, then in a one-bedroom apartment, then in the dining room of a private home, and then in a three-story, five-bedroom house. Eventually, a twenty-four-hour crisis telephone operated from the house, which could accommodate twelve women and their children at a time. There was a paid staff as well as volunteers, but Advocates operated as a collective and divided administrative responsibilities; they opposed hiring professionally credentialed staff. Pleck quotes a founder of the shelter as saying, "A shelter is not a treatment center, residents are not described as clients, battering is not described as a syndrome. Women are not thought of as victims except as victims of a crime requiring redress."[24]

Battered women's organizations were important sites of political activism and organizing—in communities, college campuses, and national women's rights organizations. As statewide task forces and national coalitions were formed, the battered women's movement began to shape public debate.

The theoretical approach to battering that developed from the battered women's movement was explicitly political. Its dimensions were not made explicit; they were never listed as part of a social program but functioned as precepts of activist literature and work. First, "battered women" were set forth as a definable group or category, with battering regarded within the larger context of "power and control"; physical abuse was a particular "moment" in a larger continuum of "doing power," which might include emotional abuse, sexual abuse and rape, and other maneuvers to control, isolate, threaten, intimidate, or stalk. Battering, and the problem of power and control, were understood within a systemic framework as part of the larger dilemma of gender subordination, which included gender role socialization; social and economic discrimination in education, workplace, and home; and lack of access to child care. Battered women and battered women's experiences were the focal point of strategies for change; battered women were viewed as "sisters," actors, participants in a larger struggle. Their needs for safety, protection, refuge, and social and economic resources drove the movement.

In her book on the early contributions of the battered women's movement, Susan Schechter describes the political content of the movement. "Feminists," she says, "defined violence against women as a political problem to be solved with political solutions." She cites the movement's commitment to women's self-determination, self-organization, and democratic participation. Within the shelters, Schechter says, "women have learned to think differently about male-female relationships, sex-roles and the meanings behind the violence." She quotes one woman's expression of this change: "Do or die I will raise my children with the understanding that no matter how much or what kind of physical abuse man has perpetrated on his subordinates, it is not and cannot be used to make another being do what you want them to do, nor is it humane to use another person as a punching bag, to take your frustrations out on." She tells us that activists had learned that "violence restricts women's ability to move freely and confidently into the world and therefore hinders their full development. The fear of violence robs women of possibilities, self-confidence, and self-esteem. In this sense, violence is more than a physical assault; it is an attack on women's dignity and freedom." She concludes that "the movement [has] . . . challenged the idea that the family is always a safe haven from a brutal world. . . . The seemingly private sphere of the family and the public sphere of social and worklife will never be quite so separate again. . . . Male privilege and domination are further eroded as violence is redefined from appropriate chastisement directed toward an inferior, to criminal abuse. This radical redefinition signifies how deeply male domination, even within its hidden bastion, is under attack."[25]

Today, some of this has changed. In the United States, the trend within battered women's organizations has been toward a service orientation and away from explicitly feminist organizing. Although many groups that began as feminist organizations are still actively involved in battered women's work, many newer groups that have organized around battering see themselves primarily as service providers. They do social service work and perceive battered women as "clients," not "sisters" — as persons to be helped, not participants in a larger struggle.

The Challenge to Feminist Perspectives

The battered women's movement defined battering within the larger framework of gender subordination. Domestic violence was linked to women's inferior position within the family, discrimination within the workplace, wage inequity, lack of educational opportunities, the absence of social supports for mothering, and the lack of child care. Traditionally, however, intimate violence had been viewed from a psychological perspective. This approach, which predated the feminist analysis of the 1960s, had been concerned with how violence is linked to specific pathology in the individual's personality traits and psychological disorders.[26]

Significantly, even since the advent of the battered women's movement, this psychological perspective has not focused primarily on the pathology of male batterers. Although violent men are commonly labeled "sick" or "emotionally disturbed," in the public mind this perspective of pathology focuses largely on the woman who is battered. Those who are battered and who remain in battering relationships are regarded as more pathological, more deeply troubled, than the men who batter them. Some psychiatrists have attributed domestic violence to the victim's inherent sexual and biological problems, or regarded battering as related to women's masochism, a construct within which women are seen first to provoke battering and then to remain in battering relationships.

More recently, this psychological perspective has been stoked by a public perception of "battered woman syndrome," a term originally coined by feminist psychologist Lenore Walker as a clinical description of certain psychological effects that the trauma of battering produces in women.[27] Paradoxically, "battered woman syndrome" is now used as a catch-all phrase by the media and in courtrooms to describe a great range of issues: a woman's prior responses to violence and the context in which those responses occurred; the dynamics of the abusive relationship; a subcategory of post-traumatic stress disorder; or woman abuse as a larger social problem.[28] Employing "battered woman syndrome" as an explanatory framework shifts the focus of the violent act to the woman, and the use of "syndrome" suggests that it is she who is emotionally or mentally impaired.

A second perspective, a sociological approach, rests on the premise that social structures affect people and their behaviors. This approach, which exploded as a focus of research on battering in the early 1980s, focuses on the problem of family violence—the way the institution of the family is set up to allow and even encourage violence among family members. Proponents of this view look at violence as a result of family dysfunction and examine how all participants in the family may be involved in perpetuating the violence.[29]

Research on family violence further deflected attention from the crucial link to gender, and shifted focus onto research tools that deeply challenged feminist approaches. In a review of the family violence literature in 1983, Wini Breines and Linda Gordon perceived the dangers in this approach: "First, all violence must be seen in the context of wider power relations; violence is not necessarily deviant or fundamentally different from other means of exerting power over another person. Thus, violence cannot be accurately viewed as a set of isolated events but must be placed in an entire social context. Second, the social contexts of family violence have gender and generational inequalities at their heart. There are patterns to violence between intimates which only an analysis of gender and its centrality to the family can illuminate."[30]

Yet one of the consequences of this shift to family violence theory has been the move to gender-neutral explanations, highlighting the long-standing and continuing debate surrounding the question whether women are as violent as men. Some researchers, notably Murray Straus and Richard Gelles, have resuscitated the view that violence against husbands is as prevalent as violence against wives.[31] Spousal violence has been said to be symmetrical in its extent, severity, intentions, motivational contexts, and even its consequences. Prominent violence researchers R. Emerson Dobash and Russell Dobash, along with many others, have rebutted these arguments, saying that women use violence primarily in self-defense.[32] They describe the view that women are as violent as men in the following way:

> Proponents of this position typically cite statistics that show women's frequency of violence against intimates to be about the same as men's frequency of

violence against intimates. Studies showing that women often aggress against their partners first, without provocation or retaliation, are consistently cited, and now that data are available on lesbian battering, these data are being used to bolster the claim that "women do it too." All of this evidence together supposedly undermines the feminist theory of domestic violence, which advocates of the "women are as violent as men" position portray as unitary and invariable, although they also usually pay lip service to the contributions feminist theorists have made in advancing our field.

A careful review of the extant data collected by both feminist and nonfeminist researchers, for instance, reveals that men are more likely than women to be victims of violent crimes. At the same time, however, women are more likely than men to be injured or killed by an intimate partner. That women are sometimes violent in intimate relationships does not diminish the importance of discerning the role gender plays in the etiology of domestic violence. When women use violence against their partners, they are not behaving "like men." A glaring error in the "women are as violent as men" position is that it holds male behavior as normative and evaluates female behavior in terms of this male standard. Yet as [researchers] show, the violent behavior of women is both quantitatively and qualitatively different from the domestically violent behavior of men. Their research documents gender differences in intimate violence.

This is not to say that individual factors are irrelevant or insignificant in the etiology of domestic violence. [Researchers] have made a strong case for the inclusion of individual variables, such as head injuries and personality disorders, in any theoretical account of domestic violence. However, feminist theory does not preclude an examination of individual factors, just as such an examination does not lessen the need for an analysis of the role of gender. Indeed, given [that] the possibility of incurring a head injury as well as the likelihood of being diagnosed with a specific personality disorder are also gendered phenomena, we are reminded again of the centrality of the gender variable.[33]

These rebuttals notwithstanding, the "women are as violent as men" perspective has had considerable impact on public consciousness through the news media, as well as on academic and clinical thinking. In fact, both psychological and sociological perspectives have done much to shape the context of research and the nature of public views of violence. Evan Stark has observed: "For fifty years or more, the realities have been concealed behind images that alternately 'pathologize' family violence or else 'normalize' it, making it seem the inevitable byproduct of some combination of predisposition—because the abuser was mistreated as a child, for example—and environmental 'stress.'

The use of violence is abstracted from its political context in gender and generational struggles, and its varied meanings in different cultures and classes are simply glossed over. Static conceptions posit aggression as inherent in (male) human nature or as inevitable given poverty, 'violence prone' cultures or personalities, and intergenerational transmission." Advocates of psychological and sociological perspectives recognize the significance of the "alternate" perspective and acknowledge that both psychological and social factors are significant variables. Yet both these approaches minimize the role and the impact of gender and are grounded in gender-neutral explanations.[34]

Claire Renzetti, a sociologist who has written extensively on domestic violence, observes that there is "an important battle being waged over the nature of women's behavior and its role in woman abuse." Right-wing organizations such as the Independent Women's Forum have challenged feminist interpretations of battering, placing op-ed pieces and editorials in prominent newspapers and magazines across the United States. Renzetti concludes that "this is a battle whose outcome has serious consequences for battered women, especially in terms of our society's institutionalized responses to their behavior. Battered women's survival strategies increasingly are being stigmatized, and, worse, criminalized."[35]

Renzetti also notes that "the social construction of intimate violence as a problem involves not only drawing attention to the phenomenon, but also characterizing its essential nature, by portraying particular cases as typical. Although the media plays a central role in the typification process, reporters and commentators inevitably draw on the work of academics and experts in the field." With the support of academic researchers writing from the "women are as violent as men" perspective, the media has increasingly used such high-profile cases as the Lorena Bobbitt and O. J. Simpson cases to socially construct an image of battered women as culpable partners.[36]

This politicization of social "knowledge" by "experts" on battering has a long history. In 1983 Evan Stark and Anne Flitcraft identified "the sudden social science concern with family violence in the 1980's" as part of the "same self-righteous puritanism that reappears in the very upper-class campaign to abolish 'sin' (prostitution, alcoholism, 'dirty homes' and wife beating) among the working classes." They argued that "just behind the cycle of concern about abuse lies a new ideological affinity between those who document the evils at the heart of family life, those who 'treat' these evils, and those who, like the

ideologues supporting the current Family Protection Act, would unhesitat-
ingly restore traditional patriarchal authority whatever the costs in individual
freedom, an alliance between those who locate the principles of violence in
'private' life and those who would leave violence against women to private
solutions."[37] Contested sources of knowledge about battering highlight the
deeply political nature of the descriptive stakes.

Reconceiving Gender Violence

Work on issues concerning battered women is now at a turning point. Some
reforms have been institutionalized, and the problems of battered women
have achieved credibility and visibility. To some degree, a public dimension to
the problem is now recognized. Although federal, state, and private resources
devoted to these reform efforts have increased substantially, they are still
minimal, and the culture of female subordination that supports and maintains abuse has undergone little change. At the same time, there is a serious
backlash to these reform efforts, and many of the reforms that have been accomplished are in jeopardy.

Today, then, there are profound contradictions. Domestic violence has been
widely recognized as a "social problem"; President Clinton has brought battered women's advocates to the White House. Stories about battered women,
shelters, homicides, and police and judges who fail to enforce protective
orders appear in newspapers and magazines and on television and radio.
Public service announcements on television dramatize the seriousness of the
problem and affirm the public's responsibility to report it. October has been
officially named Domestic Violence Awareness Month. There is a federal Office of Violence Against Women in the Justice Department. But the issue of
domestic violence has been decontextualized from the larger issue of gender subordination that animated the movement. Elizabeth Pleck has observed
that today, "as in the nineteenth century, feminism questioned the nature of
the family and espoused greater options for women. Nonetheless, for reform
on behalf of abused women to succeed, feminism — a controversial ideology —
had to be tamed."[38]

Domestic violence is now treated as a problem in isolation, with neither history nor social context. It is viewed as though it can be "solved" or "treated"
through legal remedies or mediation or therapy alone, without considering

the issues of women's equality and gender subordination. In this way, the concept of battering has been unmoored from its historical roots of gender subordination and feminist activism.

Paradoxically, it is the exciting development of an explicitly feminist international human rights campaign on gender violence that has garnered worldwide attention. This campaign, which began in a series of conferences in the 1990s and led to the Beijing Declaration and Platform for Action in 1995, continues today and has mobilized women around the world. This human rights framework places women at the center, defines the problem of intimate violence as "gender violence," and recognizes the indivisibility of violence, reproductive choice and sexual equality, workplace discrimination, wage equity, child care, and health care. Consequently, the rallying cry for many feminists who continue to do trailblazing work on battering in the United States has been, as women's international human rights scholar Rhonda Copelon has put it, to "bring Beijing home,"[39] to reshape domestic violence work in this country with the explicitly feminist political and expansive social vision that first inspired the issue's advocates.

3

Dimensions of Feminist Lawmaking on Battering

As a college student in the 1960s, active in civil rights struggles and other political work and studying political science and social theory, I saw examples from the civil rights movement of lawyers using the law to advance political efforts. I became actively involved in the women's movement, and my experience as an activist gave me the impetus to attend law school. It was 1970, and efforts to reshape the law to include women's experiences were just beginning. If women were to secure the protection of the law, women with a feminist perspective would have to become lawyers.

Between 1971 and 1980, I was lucky to work at the Center for Constitutional Rights in New York (first as a law student and then as a lawyer). The Center was founded by Arthur Kinoy, William Kunstler, and Morton Stavis, lawyers who played an important role in the civil rights movement. Center lawyers had a long history of using the law to effect social change and working to expand the law to reflect the experience of those whom it had previously excluded. In the early 1970s, women lawyers on the Center's staff began work on women's rights issues. Nancy Stearns, Rhonda Copelon, Janice Goodman, and I worked primarily on these issues. We were part of a network of feminist litigators around the country who attempted to use our experience as women, as activists, and as lawyers to reshape the law by including women's perspective. We worked in a wide variety of legal areas: pregnancy discrimination, employment discrimination, reproductive rights, and violence against women, as lead counsel and sometimes in an amicus curiae capacity. We worked with other lawyers to analyze problems from a feminist perspective and to translate our analysis into legal argumentation to be presented to the courts. We also were involved in a wide range of other activities, such as legislative reform, public speaking, political organizing, and outreach work.

At the Center, we used the law to capture a vision and to build community. We saw the role of law in a political context: we asserted rights not simply to advance legal argument or to win a case but to express the politics, vision, and demands of a social movement, and to assist in the political self-definition of that movement. We understood that winning legal rights would not be meaningful without political organizing and education to ensure the enforcement of those rights. Lawmaking could be constitutive and creative; it could have political meaning independent of its success or failure in the courts.

State v. Wanrow is a case that is an important example of feminist lawmaking and of the way in which legal argumentation that expresses the concerns of a social movement can assist in its political development.[1] In *Wanrow,* a jury had convicted Yvonne Wanrow, a Native American woman, of second-degree murder for shooting and killing William Wesler, a white man whom she believed had tried to molest one of her children. Wesler had entered her babysitter's home uninvited when Wanrow and her children were there. Wanrow, who at the time had a cast on her leg and was using crutches, claimed that, based on her perceptions of the danger created by Wesler, she had acted in self-defense. She maintained that she had information leading her to believe that Wesler had a history of child molestation and had previously tried to molest one of her children. The trial court, however, instructed the jury to consider only the circumstances "at or immediately before the killing" when evaluating the gravity of the danger the defendant faced. The trial court also instructed the jury to apply the equal-force standard, whereby the person claiming self-defense can respond only with force equal to that which the assailant uses. Wesler, however, had not been carrying a gun.

Center lawyers became involved in the case on appeal to the Washington Supreme Court. After reading the trial transcript, my colleague Nancy Stearns and I realized that the judge's instructions had prevented the jury from considering Yvonne Wanrow's state of mind, as shaped by her experiences and perspective as a Native American woman, when she confronted Wesler. The jury had not been presented with evidence concerning the general lack of police protection in such situations, the pervasiveness of violence against women and children, the effect on Wanrow of her belief that Wesler was a child molester, Wanrow's lack of trust in the police, and her belief that she could successfully defend herself only with a weapon. Moreover, the judge's instructions directed the jury to apply the equal-force standard and prevented them from considering Wanrow's perspective when it evaluated her claim of self-defense. Our decision to challenge gender bias in the law of self-defense—as reflected in the judge's instructions—was formed from our conviction that Yvonne Wanrow's perspective as a Native American woman had been excluded from the courtroom.

We developed a legal argument for women's "equal right to trial," which maintained that the law of self-defense was biased against women. The argument was based on our knowledge of the particular problems that women who killed men faced in the criminal justice system: the prevalence of homicides committed by women in circumstances of male physical abuse or sexual assault; the different circumstances in which men and women kill; stereotypes and other misconceptions in the criminal justice system that brand women who kill as "crazy"; the deeply ingrained problems of domestic violence, physical abuse, and sexual abuse of women and children; the physical and psychological barriers that prevent women from feeling capable of defending themselves; and stereotypes of women as unreasonable. If the jury did not understand Yvonne Wanrow's experience and the way it shaped her conduct, then it could not find her conduct to have been reasonable and therefore an appropriate act of self-defense.

On appeal, Wanrow's conviction was reversed. In a plurality opinion, the Washington Supreme Court held that the trial court's instructions violated Washington law in three ways.[2] First, the instruction that limited the jury's consideration to the circumstances "at or immediately before the killing" misconstrued Washington law. Properly construed, state law allowed the jury to consider Wanrow's knowledge of the deceased's reputation, any prior aggressive behavior, and all other prior circumstances, even if that knowledge had been acquired long before the killing.[3] Second, the instruction concerning equal force misstated state law and denied Wanrow equal protection: "The impression created—that a 5′4″ woman with a cast on her leg and using a crutch must, under the law, somehow repel an assault by a 6′2″ intoxicated man without employing weapons in her defense, unless the jury finds her determination of the degree of danger to be objectively reasonable—constitutes a separate and distinct misstatement of the law and, in the context of this case, violates the respondent's right to equal protection of the law."[4] Third, the trial court had failed to direct the jury to consider the reasonableness of Wanrow's act from Wanrow's perspective, or, in other words, "seeing what [s]he sees and knowing what [s]he knows."[5] The court affirmed a standard of self-defense based on the individual defendant's perception, as required by

Washington law, and underscored the need for this standard by recognizing the existence of sex bias in the law of self-defense generally: "The respondent was entitled to have the jury consider her actions in the light of her own perceptions of the situation, including those perceptions which were the product of our nation's 'long and unfortunate history of sex discrimination.' Until such time as the effects of that history are eradicated, care must be taken to assure that our self-defense instructions afford women the right to have their conduct judged in light of the individual physical handicaps which are the product of sex discrimination. To fail to do so is to deny the right of the individual woman involved to trial by the same rules which are applicable to male defendants." [6]

The political insights into sex bias in self-defense that helped explain Yvonne Wanrow's situation arose out of legal formulation and argumentation. But the legal argument concerning the "equal right to trial" grew out of a political analysis of gender discrimination that the legal team developed, discussed, and applied to the particular case. It brought together diverse strands of feminist analysis and theory concerning gender bias in the criminal justice system.

This legal argumentation reflected a perspective that feminist activists and lawyers, many of them organizing defense committees around the cases of specific women defendants, were beginning to articulate. Aspects of this argument were being asserted in other courts, in such cases as those of Inez Garcia and Joan Little.[7] Feminist writers were beginning to explore these issues as well.

In this sense, the legal formulation not only grew out of political analysis but also pushed the political analysis forward. The particular legal focus on gender bias in the law of self-defense, and on what had been asserted as the absence of a women's perspective in the courtroom, clarified feminist analysis of the problems facing women who kill. It explained why both women defendants and the lawyers representing them were more likely to perceive these cases as appropriate for (and thus claim) insanity or impaired-mental-state defenses rather than self-defense. Beginning to talk about the possibility of self-defense raised a set of important issues about women's own sense of their experiences; women could not claim self-defense and present those claims to lawyers until they believed that they had "selves" to defend. Both women defendants and their lawyers were not likely to argue self-defense because they could not perceive the women's actions as reasonable. At the same time, the idea that women had psychological claims to self-defense opened up the possibility that they would be able to claim self-defense in law. The legal formulation thus moved the political work to a different level; it posed the political questions of what a woman's perspective might be, whether there was a distinct women's perspective, and what equal treatment would look like. It focused further legal work on the disparate hurdles that limited women defendants' choice of defense—particularly the various ways women's experiences were excluded from the courtroom—and laid the foundation for remedial political and legal strategies.

What has subsequently become known as "women's self-defense work"—legal reform and legal advocacy on the hurdles that women defendants face concerning choice of defense—is now an established area of both feminist litigation and legal scholarship. It has been applied primarily in cases of women who are battered and who have been charged with assault or homicide for killing their batterers.[8]

Many courts have now accepted the view that there is gender bias in the law of self-defense. Yet ongoing legal work in this area teaches us new lessons. Judges have considerable difficulty in genuinely "hearing" and taking in women's experiences, and consequently in modifying the law to take them into account. Some judges that have applied the understanding reflected in the argument for equal right to trial have unwittingly recreated the very sex stereotypes of female incapacity that women's self-defense work was intended to overcome. This process of containment and subversion of feminist insights in law is complex. But these new dilemmas of feminist theory, and indeed, even the process of subversion, can help to deepen understanding, clarify issues, sharpen debate, and strengthen advocacy.

Wanrow exemplifies the way that legal formulation of rights emerging from political analysis and practice can be expressive. The assertion of legal argumentation can flow from political analysis and then become the basis for a more self-reflective and nuanced political analysis. Legal formulation can be part of an ongoing process of politics. The rights claim is a "moment" in that process, in which the political vision emerges from within the claim of rights.

The work of the Center for Constitutional Rights in *Wanrow*, as in many other cases, is an example of feminist theory in practice. Legal argumentation and theory emerges from political experience and articulation; this legal theory in turn serves to refine and sharpen political insights and to clarify tensions in the political struggle; the political struggle is reassessed in light of the legal theory; and political insight goes on to reshape legal theory. The process continues. This creative, dynamic, and expressive process is at the heart of feminist lawmaking.

The Theory and Process of Feminist Lawmaking

Lawmaking has been a crucial part of the work of the battered women's movement. Feminist lawmaking on battering has built on the experiences of battered women and has sought to transform law in light of this experience. This process of lawmaking, legal and legislative advocacy, legal reform, representation of individual battered women, and representation of battered women's organizations has reflected core assumptions concerning the link between gender and violence

Feminist lawmaking is what Robert Cover has called "jurisgenerative" — lawmaking that seeks to transform social meaning.[9] Lawmaking can express the fundamental aspirations and vision of a social movement. Claims of rights for battered women have emerged from the political perspectives of the battered women's movement and have generated a visionary jurisprudence that transforms intimate relationship into a framework of women's equality and full citizenship. Assertion of rights can move a political struggle forward by revealing theoretical contradictions and dilemmas in political vision. Feminist lawmaking on battering has revealed fundamental issues of definition, identity, and strategy concerning the problem of woman abuse. It has exposed the complexity of cultural and legal descriptions of battered women's experiences, and has highlighted tensions in the concepts of public and private. The assertion of rights claims may assist in the growth of legal and political consciousness and simultaneously reveal the limitations of legal change.

Feminist lawmaking on battering must be understood in the context of the battered women's movement. The interrelationship between law and social-movement practice that I describe is grounded in a view of the dialectical nature of consciousness and social change, and the dialectical interrelationship between rights and politics. Lawmaking and rights assertion can be understood as forms of the philosophical concept of praxis: the unity of theory and action, the active role of consciousness and subjectivity in shaping both theory and practice, and the dynamic interrelationship that results. Lawmaking can be constitutive, creative, and, as legal scholar Karl Klare puts it, an expression of "the embeddedness of action-in-belief and belief-in-action."[10]

Although lawmaking and rights discourse can sometimes appear to be distinct from politics and an obstacle to political growth, lawmaking in general and claims of rights in particular can be part of a larger process of political struggle.

The concept of dialectics has shaped much of contemporary social theory. Dialectical approaches emphasize the idea of process—the process, connection, and opposition of dualities—and look for subsequent change and transcendence. One "moment" gives rise to its own negation, and, in the words of philosopher Richard Bernstein, "out of this negativity, another 'moment' emerges which at once negates, affirms, and transcends the original 'moment.'"[11] Thus, an idea may be both what it appears to be and something else at the same time; an idea may contain the seeds of its own contradiction, and ideas that appear to be in opposition may really be connected. At any given "moment," ideas may appear to be connected or in opposition, because this connection or opposition exists in only one stage of a larger process. The dialectical process is not a mechanical confrontation of an opposite from outside, but an organic emergence and development of opposition and change from within the "moment" or idea itself.

I view feminist lawmaking and the assertion of rights linked to feminist activism through the lens of the dialectical relationship of rights and politics. Over the past few decades, feminist theoretical work in a range of disciplines has made important contributions to the development of social and political theory. Some of this work has emphasized dialectical change and the relationship between theory and practice, thereby enriching social perspectives on law and perceptions of rights. My experience with feminist legal practice shapes my view of the dialectical nature of lawmaking and rights discourse— the way lawmaking can creatively express as well as constrain political vision.

Although feminist theoretical perspectives are diverse, feminist theory is generally characterized by a focus on dialectical process and the interrelationship of theory and practice.[12] As embodied in the feminist adage "the personal is political," feminist theory emphasizes the value of direct experience as the place where theory should begin. The realm of personal experience, the "private," which has always been trivialized as unworthy of serious scrutiny, particularly for women, is an appropriate and important subject of public inquiry; "private" and "public" worlds are inextricably linked. The tradition of consciousness-raising as feminist method flows from this insight; learning begins with the individual and personal (the private), moves to the

general and social (the public), and then reflects back on itself with heightened consciousness through shared group process.[13] Consciousness-raising
is a form of praxis; it transcends the dichotomy between theory and practice. Consciousness-raising starts with personal and concrete experience, inte-
grates this experience into theory, and then, in effect, reshapes theory based
on experience and experience based on theory. Theory expresses and grows
out of experience, but it also relates back to that experience for further re-
finement, validation, or modification.

Consciousness-raising suggests an approach to social change that recognizes dynamic tension, reflection, and sharing as essential aspects of growth.
Feminist theory has historically valued this process, which starts with experience, generalizes through self-reflection and evaluation, and then returns
to experience. This dialectical process transcends the oppositions of self and
other, public and private, individual and community, and is simultaneously
grounded in an understanding that any connection between these apparent
dualisms will be only partial and tentative, and that distinctions will again
emerge.

Feminist theory seeks to reveal the social dimension of individual experience and the individual dimension of social experience. It values the dynamic
interrelationship of the individual and community. In the words of feminist
theorist Kathy Ferguson, "Feminist discourse and practice entail a struggle
for individual autonomy that is with others and for community that embraces
diversity— that is, for an integration of the individual and the collective in an
ongoing process of authentic individuation and genuine connectedness."[14]

The fact that this process begins with the self, and then connects to the
larger world of women, is important. For feminists, theory is not "out there,"
but rather is based on the concrete, daily, and "trivial" experiences of individuals and emerges from the shared experiences of women talking. And because feminist theory grows out of direct experience and consciousness actively asserting itself, it emphasizes context and affirms the importance of
identifying experience and claiming it for one's own.

Recognizing the links between individual change and social change means
going beyond theory and understanding the importance of political activity.
In this way, theory emerges from practice and practice then informs and reshapes theory. Because of its dialectical cast, feminist theory encompasses
a notion of process that encourages a grounded and reflective appreciation

of this interrelationship between theory and practice—its possibilities and limits, visions and defeats.

A dialectical perspective sees lawmaking, rights, and politics as part of a dynamic, complex, and multifaceted process in which lawmaking and rights discourse can simultaneously advance and obscure political vision. Lawmaking can be at once expressive, transformative, and problematic, for as poverty lawyer Edward Sparer observed, "as much as rights are instruments of legitimizing oppression, they are also affirmations of human values. . . . As often as they are used to frustrate social movement, they are also among the basic tools of social movement."[15] Many years ago, legal scholar Duncan Kennedy suggested that "embedded in the rights notion is a liberating accomplishment of our culture: the affirmation of free human subjectivity against the constraints of group life, along with the paradoxical countervision of a group life that creates and nurtures individuals capable of freedom."[16] This notion of paradox, of the seeming contradiction of two opposites that are really interconnected, is critical to the dialectical perspective I offer.

Critical scholars have emphasized appropriate caution concerning the role of law and the use of rights discourse to further political struggle, and I share this concern. Lawmaking and the assertion of rights must be understood as part of a larger process of change; a political struggle may be so fixed on lawmaking, rights discourse, or winning rights in courts that it will not move beyond rights and will paralyze political debate and growth. Legal discourse can be either a means to articulate new values and political vision or an alienated and artificial language that constricts political debate. How a social-movement group decides to use law and rights claims and to place this use of law in a broader context can affect the ability of rights discourse to aid political struggle. Legal discourse and rights claims can play a role in forming political consciousness that can be useful in the development of a social movement.

Exploration of the role of feminist lawmaking must take account of the many dimensions of law. First there is its concrete and material impact—the actual effect it has on people's lives. Then there is its symbolic level—the role that law plays in expressing, embodying, and shaping social messages. Law must also be understood as having a role in constructing social and cultural life and producing cultural meanings and identities. Feminist legal scholar Kathryn Abrams observes that "law . . . performs a function analogous to that of political rhetoric or the imagery of popular culture: it characterizes groups in ways that ultimately filter into popular understandings and counteract or reinforce the assumptions and stereotypes that already exist."[17]

Rights language can express human and communal values; it can be a way for individuals to make their voices heard, to assert or develop a sense of self, and for individuals and groups to experience a collective identity. Rights discourse can also have a dimension that underlines the interdependence of autonomy and community. The assertion of rights can deeply affect consciousness — the way that law can give individuals a sense of self-definition, connect an individual to a larger group and community, and express the vision of a political struggle or social movement, particularly during the early development of a movement. Law shapes and is shaped by a sense of individual and communal self; new claims are articulated because individuals and groups see themselves in a new way. The articulation of new claims can also assist individuals and groups to see themselves in a new way.

Law affects public consciousness in many ways. It reflects the process of social change in society, as litigants, lawyers, advocates, judges, and jurors respond to new social currents within the larger society, but it also shapes those currents. Litigants and lawyers may experience, characterize, or imagine harms in a new way and present them to courts in a new framework. Judges and jurors can understand harms with altered perceptions because of how they are presented. Law can play a role in legitimating and giving voice to new and "outsider" experiences and perspectives; it can also subvert and contain this process of giving voice. Feminist lawmaking on domestic violence must be analyzed on these multiple levels.

The Experience of Feminist Lawmaking

The development of a "second wave" of a women's rights movement in the late 1960s led to a dramatic increase in the use of law by feminist lawyers as a vehicle of social change. In many areas, women's rights were articulated for the first time, and traditional legal concepts were redefined. This process of feminist lawmaking has significantly shaped the development of law over the past thirty years and has had a substantial impact on public consciousness concerning issues of gender.

Feminist focus on notions of rights has a long and distinguished history in the United States.[18] In 1848, the women's rights convention at Seneca Falls issued a Declaration of Sentiments and passed resolutions that set forth a platform on women's rights. This first wave of feminism sought to enhance women's access to political and economic opportunity by challenging laws that denied women the right to vote and barred them from various occupations. For example, the struggle to win passage of the Nineteenth Amendment drew its power from illuminating women's right to vote. These rights claims grew out of early feminist political analyses, which saw women's exclusion from public and political life as central to their continued subordination. Spurred by the explosion of the second wave of feminist consciousness in the 1960s, women's rights have been claimed in an expanded variety of contexts.

A claim of right can make a political statement and transmit a powerful message concerning what feminist legal scholar Frances Olsen has called "the kind of society we want to live in, the kind of relations among people we wish to foster, and the kind of behavior that is to be praised or blamed. It is a moral claim about how human beings should act toward one another." [19] For individuals, a claim of right can be an assertion of one's self-worth and an affirmation of one's moral value and entitlement.

The women's rights movement has had an important affirming and individuating effect on women's consciousness. The articulation of women's rights provides a sense of self and distinction of individual women, while at the same time supplying an important sense of collective identity. Through this articulation, women's voices are heard in a public forum and afforded a legal vehicle for expression.

Rights claims not only define women's individual and collective experience, they also actively shape public discourse. Claims of equal rights and reproductive choice, for example, have provided a framework of empowerment. Before the 1970s women as a class were not included within the reach of the Fourteenth Amendment. [20] By claiming rights, women asserted their intention to be taken seriously in society. This "liberal" assertion of rights gave women the "audacity" to compare themselves with men. [21] They could now claim that they were *entitled* to the equal protection of the law, not just permitted to seek it. [22] Women's interests, previously relegated to the private sphere and therefore outside the public protection of the law, now received the protection of the Constitution. [23] On an ideological level, rights claims reinforced that the personal is political, changing previously private concerns into public ones that needed to be taken seriously by the society at large.

The public nature of women's rights assertion is especially significant because of the private nature of discrimination against women. The locus of women's subordination is frequently the private and individual sphere—the home and family—and is thus perceived as isolated and experienced in isolation. The way women are socialized in our culture may encourage them to feel individual fault rather than to identify a systemic pattern of social discrimination. Thus, public claims of legal rights do more than simply put women's sense of self into the personal moral equation. The assertion of rights claims and the use of rights discourse help women to overcome the pervasive sense of privatization and personal blame that has perpetuated women's subordination in public and private spheres alike. Rights claims assert women's selfhood collectively, thereby giving them a sense of group identity and pride; they make manifest the fact that women can act and claim their place in history.[24]

Many women lawyers who have focused on women's rights work—like myself—entered law school during the second wave of feminism or were drawn into the women's movement during law school. We have articulated rights claims in a dual capacity, as lawyers and as activists. Lawyering was not "other" to us, but rather a deepening process of identification, self-reflection, and connection with others (both women clients and lawyers), which mirrored the experience of the movement itself. This process made lawyering in such cases as *Wanrow* particularly intense. It shaped the way women lawyers perceived legal problems, the insights women litigators brought to sex-discrimination cases, and the strategies women litigators developed to handle these cases.[25]

Consequently, feminist lawmaking generally has involved the use of experience as a starting point and guide, the creative use of both political and social contexts, and the exploration of the human impact and context of the case in concrete terms. Much of this litigation has used amicus curiae briefs to present these broader perspectives in order to ensure that women's voices are heard in court.[26]

Although legal rights rhetoric can be abstract, a good deal of feminist lawmaking has succeeded in concretizing women's experience and emphasizing women's specificity and particularity. Women's rights litigation began the process of shaping the law of equality to reflect women's diverse perspectives. Women's rights discourse has linked the specific experience of women with the universal claim of rights—a potentially radical and transforming notion.

The advocacy process itself has also had a significant effect in mobilizing women for political action. For women who have historically been excluded from public life and political action, activity in the public sphere helps to transcend the dichotomy of public and private. It also helps women learn skills that are necessary to organize and mobilize political support. In this sense, the struggle for rights has enabled women to become more politically active and to gain power.

At the same time, the women's movement's experience with rights has suffered from serious problems. First, the idea of rights or equal rights has not captured the scope of the feminist program. Although women's rights have been perhaps "too much" for society, in a sense they have been "too little" for the women's movement. Feminists understand that genuine equality for women will not be achieved simply by winning rights in court; equality requires profound social reconstruction of gender roles within the workplace, the family, and the larger society. Rights claims do not effectively challenge existing social structures and social relations and seek to transform them. Reflecting on the experience of claiming reproductive rights, feminist scholar Rosalind Petchesky observes: "Rights are by definition claims staked within a given order of things. They are demands for access for oneself, or for 'no admittance' to others; but they do not challenge the social structure, the social relations of production and reproduction. The claim for 'abortion rights' seeks access to a necessary service, but by itself it fails to address the social relations and sexual divisions around which responsibility for pregnancy and children is assigned."[27]

Second, the articulation of a right can, despite a movement's best efforts, put the focus of immediate political struggle on winning the right in court. Thus, even if one is concerned with and understands the need for social reconstruction, it is hard simultaneously to sustain an understanding of short-term goals. The concreteness and immediacy of legal struggle tends to subsume the more diffuse role of political organizing and education. For this reason, the use of rights and lawmaking in general have been viewed with considerable ambivalence.

Third, because women's rights formulations oblige the state to act, serious questions about the appropriate role of the state in the context of women's rights have emerged. Women's rights litigators argue that by fighting for women's rights in the courts, they do not exclusively rely on the state. Nevertheless, feminist skepticism about the state's willingness or ability to help women understandably heightens many women's reservations about feminist law reform efforts, in both the courts and the legislatures.

When I first explored the dialectical relationship of feminist lawmaking and the impact of rights on feminist struggle, assertion of rights claims concerning battering was one of several areas I briefly examined. In the mid-1980s, I saw the assertion of legal claims concerning battering as an important example of how rights assertion might advance "political conversation" concerning women's rights and gender equality.[28] Legal claims concerning battering had exposed new harms, expanded public understanding by labeling what was previously private as public, manifested a shared political understanding which reflected the view that women needed to be free from sexual subordination and violence, and made important statements concerning women's autonomy. I noted that articulation of these claims had raised serious questions about how to view the state and the need for a feminist theory of the state; and that the claims had identified some shared experience of battered women and highlighted issues that revealed systemic patterns of gender subordination and lack of resources, as opposed to individual "bad men." I suggested that rights assertion concerning battering had facilitated more discerning analysis within the battered women's movement as to whether a particular reform helps to strengthen an analysis of sex discrimination within the family, rather than individual victimization, and to challenge the public-private dichotomy. Legal claims of battering seemed to have a particularly "political" dimension and to particularly reflect the politics of the movement, and I raised the question of why this might be so: because the political message and demand of the claims were narrow, because the claims had done well in courts, or because legal claims concerning battering were at an early stage of development. My interest in exploring these questions has generated this book.

Battering: Articulating, Litigating, and Reinterpreting Rights

Claims regarding women's right to be free from battering did not begin in the 1960s. Linda Gordon has detailed the experiences of battered women in the early twentieth century who, through their interactions with social workers, began to define an affirmative entitlement not to be hit. Gordon has subsequently suggested that these stories of battered women "show how deeply notions of rights were at times able to intensify and solidify their grievances and sense of purpose in taking action against them." [29]

Gordon is interested in exploring "how forms of resistance emerge from a variety of historical influences: what conditions are necessary for an extremely subordinated group to talk of rights?" She notes that "these battered women present a good example for examination because they are in a uniquely difficult position. Disproportionately poor and oppressed, they were also unusually isolated in their victimization because wife beating occurs in private and because they had to deal with a dominant culture that has rendered this problem unspeakable." [30]

Gordon examines how the very discovery or invention of family violence in the 1870s was conditioned by the women's rights movement. The women's movement looked at violence shaped by the temperance movement and the feminist campaign for divorce. Feminists also saw violence within a child-raising discourse in which the harm to the mother was inextricably linked with harm to the child. She observes that "when feminists condemned wife beating they did so in a chivalric mode, positioning women as vulnerable and men who would abuse their wives as monstrous and depraved, lacking in true manhood. Some spoke of a woman's ownership of her body, but not of her right to freedom from violence." Gordon suggests that it was not until after 1930 that a new tactic was discernable in women's struggles against abusive men and women's complaints to social workers. "This new discourse claimed an entitlement to absolute freedom from physical molestation and was grounded in terms of a 'right.' . . . [It] meant that clients felt entitled to ask for help in leaving their abusive marriages." She explores how the assertion of rights emerged from "changing social possibilities and aspirations" but led to many forms of resistance as women met obstacles in enlisting assistance from social workers and police, fighting with their partners, and seeking to end their marriages. [31]

Gordon suggests that rights claims concerning battering seem to emerge under conditions of social and economic possibility: assertion of rights claims were avoided while social and economic conditions made it difficult for married women to become independent of their husbands. At the same time, she concludes that talk of rights was problematic and did not capture the complexity of women's experiences and needs. Rights talk seemed to fit with absolute claims—no physical coercion, for example—which did not reflect the constrained life experiences of many women "for whom putting up with a husband's fists might not be worse than the poverty and loss of one's children attendant to separation," or who "might have preferred economic aid to prosecution of wife beaters."[32] Gordon's historical perspective and insight on rights assertion by battered women are useful in considering contemporary developments of rights claims concerning battering.

From the beginning of the battered women's movement in the 1960s, legal work played an important role in activist efforts on battering. Activists saw the law as a necessary and important tool in obtaining safety and protection for battered women. It was also an essential way in which the battered women's movement asserted "claims" and defined the social problem of intimate violence. Many local legal groups and national organizations were formed to do legal work and advocacy on issues of violence against women, including the National Center on Women and Family Law in New York and the Center for Women's Policy Studies in Washington, D.C. The focus of much of this work was the development or expansion of legal remedies to protect women and stop the abuse and to assert battered women's right to be free from violence.

One of the first and most important legal issues that came to the fore was the failure of police to protect battered women from assault. In the early 1970s, class-action lawsuits were filed in New York City and Oakland, California, which challenged police's failure to arrest batterers. This litigation raised the dramatic notion that domestic violence was criminal, sanctionable activity that was a harm against the "public," the state, not just an individual woman, and should be treated the same as an assault against a stranger. The New York case, *Bruno v. Codd,* was the focus of much national attention.[33] Development of injunctive remedies to keep the batterer away, known as civil protective or restraining orders, was also an important area of work. These orders were first sought in the late 1960s, and during the late 1960s and early 1970s many states passed statutes to provide for civil protective remedies.

Since that time, domestic violence has been the focus of an extraordinary degree of legal activity in the context of both law reform and litigation. New state statutes have required mandatory arrest by the police, developed complex civil protection order provisions, and enacted special rules regarding child custody where there is evidence of domestic violence. Federal legislation, such as the Violence Against Women Act of 1994, which was passed as part of the Violent Crime Control and Law Enforcement Act of 1994, asserts federal power to remedy violence.[34] Feminist advocates on battering have begun to draw important interconnections between battering and economic discrimination and poverty, linking issues of homelessness, insurance, work-

place violence, and immigration to battering. In conjunction, they are propos-
ing new federal and state legislative initiatives and working to protect battered
women's interests in current welfare "reform" legislation.[35] Much of this law
reform activity and litigation has been premised on the link between gender
discrimination and violence.

Struggles over meaning in law are important sites of definition and resistance. We live within particular cultures that reflect both legal structures and
legal interpretation. Women's lives, culture, and law are in a state of continuing interaction. As feminist legal scholar Martha Mahoney explains, "Cultural
assumptions about domestic violence affect substantive law and methods of
litigation in ways that in turn affect society's perceptions of women; both law
and societal perceptions affect women's understanding of our own lives, relationships and options; our lives are part of the culture that affects legal interpretation and within which further legal moves are made."[36] Historically,
serious harm to women has resulted from the ways law and culture have dis-
torted women's experiences. Feminist lawmaking seeks to transform the way
both law and culture describe these experiences.

Descriptions of legal process and legal images of battered women convey
particular political meanings. Feminists have long struggled over the characterization of the problem as "domestic violence," "family violence," "spouse
abuse," and "woman abuse," and recognized that each of these terms is limited, problematic, and provides only a partial description.[37] The proliferation
of procedural remedies for woman abuse that have been developed over the
past thirty years also reflects a range of meanings. Although orders of protection— injunctive orders that a woman who is battered can get from a court
to stop a man from beating her or to restrict his activity— are now available, they are only pieces of paper and may be rendered ineffective by lack
of police enforcement. Criminal statutes provide for arrest of batterers, either
for a violation of protective orders or for felonies generally. Tort remedies
have developed as a result of the abolition of interspousal immunity, so that
a woman can now sue her battering husband for money damages. More private and informal processes such as mediation are being used on family law
issues, despite criticism by advocates who believe that these tactics hurt battered women who are disadvantaged with respect to power, money, and resources, and signal that battering is an individual woman's private problem.
More recently, violence against women has been defined as a more explicitly
"public" harm, as a civil rights violation, as an international human rights

violation, and as a form of involuntary servitude. New anti-stalking laws have expanded the definition of the harm of battering by criminalizing threats of violence and harassment.

Various forms of legal process define the harm of battering differently and convey particular messages about its social impact. Naming is a form of claiming—claiming identity, claiming experience, claiming rights. The names that are used define the claims that are made. Naming also operates as what Siobhan Lloyd has called "a political breaking of silence."[38] The meaning of the name matters. Making battering a crime against the state has a broader social and more public meaning than granting an individual order of protection. Defining battering as a civil rights violation reflects a different set of social meanings than an individual ruling. Defining battering in the more general context of stalking, or as a violation of international human rights, conveys a different social message than a restraining order. At the symbolic level, this proliferation of process has been important. The development of legal process can shape social consciousness by identifying and redefining harm, breaking down the public-private dichotomy, and legitimizing the seriousness of the problem.

Three categories of feminist legal descriptions are particularly significant: first, what I call "broad" descriptions of battering—descriptions that attempt to capture interrelated aspects of coercion, power, and control and are not limited to physical abuse; second, descriptions of battering that I call "political"—which use conventional statist imagery to detail the experience of battering; and third, descriptions that explicitly link violence, gender, and women's equality.

Characterizations of battering by feminists early in the development of the battered women's movement explicitly articulated a broad view of violence—a notion of violence as a "moment" in, or part of, a troubled relationship of power and control. This view has been strongly contested by those who view male violence from a psychological or sociological perspective. Nevertheless, several theoretical characterizations develop this conceptual framework and detail this process more fully: "coercive control," "separation assault," loss of "self," and stalking.[39] Each of these descriptions includes aspects of physical violence within a larger social framework. Each regards physical violence along a larger continuum—as part of a broader process of threats, emotional humiliation, terrorism, and "doing power."

Evan Stark describes the framework of "coercive control" as emphasizing the batterer's pattern of coercion and control rather than his violent acts or their effect on the psyche of the victim. Stark's description draws on the traditional feminist interpretation of intimate violence: "The coercive control framework shifts the basis of women's justice claims from stigmatizing psychological assessments of traumatization to the links between structural inequality, the systemic nature of women's oppression in a particular relationship, and the harms associated with domination and resistance as it has been lived." The framework emphasizes "restrictions on 'liberty,' highlighting a class of harms that extends beyond psychological or physical suffering to fundamental human rights."[40] Deprivation of liberty results from a process of ongoing intimidation, isolation, and control.

Martha Mahoney describes battering in terms of the concept of "separation assault," the way the woman's effort to assert her independence in the form of separation triggers battering. Mahoney maintains that the struggle for power and control is at the heart of the battering relationship. At the moment of separation or attempted separation—for many women the first encounter with the authority of law—the batterer's quest for control often becomes acutely violent and potentially lethal. Separation assault is "the particular assault on a woman's body and volition that seeks to block her from leaving, retaliate for her departure, or forcibly end the separation."[41] Mahoney emphasizes that naming "separation assault" as the harm is crucial to a broader understanding of power and control:

> As with other assaults on women that were not cognizable until the feminist movement named and explained them, separation assault must be identified before women can recognize our own experience and before we can develop legal rules to deal with this particular sort of violence. Naming the particular aspect of the violence then illuminates the rest. For example, the very concept of "acquaintance rape" moves consciousness away from the stereotype of rape (assault by a stranger) and toward a focus on the woman's volition (violation of her will, "consent"). Similarly, by emphasizing the urgent control moves that seek to prevent the woman from ending the relationship, the concept of separation assault raises questions that inevitably focus additional attention on the ongoing struggle for power and control in the relationship.[42]

Charles Ewing has also defined the impact of battering broadly—emphasizing its psychological impact on the woman. He has emphasized the degree to which battering shatters a woman's core sense of self. The sense of self he describes is not just the concept of self, normally equated only with physical life and bodily integrity, but also includes "those psychological functions, attributes, processes and dimensions of experience that give meaning and value to physical existence." [43] The harm to the woman is thus existential—the destruction of identity and selfhood.

The articulation of stalking as a crime similarly reflects a broadening understanding of violence against women. Stalking first came to public attention in the context of threats of violence against, and harassment of, celebrities. Stalking is now widely understood as a pattern of threatening and harassing behavior that is part of a larger pattern of assertion of power and control linked with physical violence. Statutes that criminalize stalking have now been passed in all fifty states and the District of Columbia. [44]

Some articulations of violence rest on analogies to explicitly political formulations. These include domestic violence explained as terrorism, torture, involuntary servitude, and a form of private tyranny. [45] Significantly, these formulations underscore the problem of woman abuse as political, and identify the underlying issues of liberty, autonomy, and women's citizenship, which have become important in feminist social theory. This use of deliberate statist imagery highlights the degree to which intimate violence is understood within a broader public-private dichotomy, and challenges this dichotomy to describe the "personal" and "domestic" problem of intimate violence as a problem of public dimension—a harm that we recognize as a serious public, national, and indeed international problem. The seriousness of the loss of freedom, liberty, basic human rights, privacy, and autonomy that results from woman abuse may seem invisible in the case of an individual family and relationship. Yet these harms are given a new meaning when they are presented within a framework of citizenship and political rights.

Intimate violence has often been trivialized because of its location in personal relationships. As Reva Siegel describes the traditional view, "intimacy occurs in a domain having no bearing on matters of citizenship." [46] Significantly, when this relationship is taken out of its "family" or "private" context and characterized within these more "public" generic frameworks, such as torture, terrorism in the home, a regime of private tyranny, being held hostage, involuntary servitude, hostile domestic environment, or a human rights violation, which have been advocated by feminist legal scholars, the moral and political dimensions of domestic violence move into sharper focus. [47]

The formulation of violence against women as a civil rights violation began in the 1980s. It was premised explicitly on the link between violence and gender, on violence as a violation of the fundamental right to equality, and on an understanding of violence as both reflecting and affecting women's subordination. State civil rights statutes had been used sporadically for harms of woman abuse, so activists argued for the idea of a federal civil rights statute. The Violence Against Women Act contains a civil rights provision that explicitly links violence to gender inequality, although the Supreme Court is determining its constitutionality.[48] Similarly, we see the use of an equality framework in the international human rights concept of "gender violence."

These "broad," "political," and "gendered" definitions of violence reflect the richness of feminist legal interpretations of battering, the expressive dimensions of these rights claims. These new theoretical frameworks have shaped the important work of feminist lawmaking on battering.

Battered Women in Court: Rights "on the Ground"

What anthropologist Sally Merry has called the "culturally productive role of law—the ways in which law produces cultural meanings and identities as an aspect of its power"—is an important aspect of feminist lawmaking. The language and categories of law that are mobilized and shaped by social movements can be powerful even when litigants do not win any cases, for law can nonetheless "provide the language and the locale for resistance."[49] I turn now to examples of different ways law can provide this "language" and "locale" for resistance, first "on the ground" and then on the level of "grand theory."

Merry's ethnographic study of the treatment of domestic violence in courts in Hawaii details the multiple and contradictory experiences and meaning of rights assertion "on the ground." Merry explores the "everyday meanings of rights for people not trained in the law." She describes "the way that rights are commonly used as the basis of claims for help or definitions of self in relation to others," examines how rights are "acquired through school, media discussions of law and rights and encounters with law," and looks at "rights talk as it appears in everyday experience and speech rather than the formal vocabulary of rights in legal discourse."[50]

Merry studied a small town in Hawaii that, since the early 1980s, has developed an increasingly activist, feminist approach to domestic violence. Here, as in many settings around the United States, courts have seen an "astronomical increase" in the number of cases coming before them since 1990, both in

family court as victims seek protective orders and in criminal court as batterers are criminally prosecuted. Women are more inclined to turn to the legal
system for help, and police and prosecutors are more active in making arrests and pressing charges. Laws on intimate violence have been strengthened,
including an increase in criminal penalties. Local feminists concerned with
violence against women have staffed a shelter, developed a violence control
program for men, and formed a support group for women. Many convicted
batterers and men subject to restraining orders are mandated by the court to
attend the violence control program.

Merry concludes that the cases that come to court have had a considerable
impact on the participants' understanding of themselves, violence, and the
role of law; these cases in courts "redefine gender roles." The experiences in
court and "messages communicated . . . about rights, about themselves and
about their relationships to the law are very different" for women and for men.
"The court becomes a place for women to turn for protection rather than
a place that reinforces male authority. For men, it is a place of alienation, a
disruption of their sense of the social support for male authority."[51]

An important theme that emerges from Merry's study is the sharp contrast
between the women's and the men's experiences of the role of law and the
different messages that are communicated. The "women's support group is
organized around the trope of empowerment, in which women are encouraged to see the law as a source of help and support while they gather strength
from others in the same position," while "the men's program adopts the trope
of the school and the prison, requiring attendance, demanding homework
and threatening jail for failure to attend." Furthermore, "the discourse of the
court denaturalizes domestic violence. As judges, attorneys, and advocates
talk about domestic violence, it slips from the unseen to the seen, from the
natural to the cultural. Actions that were part of the 'normal' order of family
relationships acquire new names, such as abuse. And abuse, unlike the violence embedded in patriarchal authority, is reconstituted as crime."[52]

Legal discourse in court also "reveals a cultural transformation in the meanings of violence against women." For example, "in the past . . . there was generally little support for leaving the man from either the woman's family or her
husband's family. . . . It took the political activities of feminists, the creation
of a shelter, and the support of the judiciary and the police to generate the
massive increase in the number of women asking the courts for help." Merry
notes that "through participation in court-hearings and a court-mandated

batterers' treatment program, men and women learn a new language. Terms such as male privilege, emotional abuse, psychological battering, economic abuse, intimidation and the importance of cool-downs become part of their everyday talk about human relations. Although the court does not produce this new language and cultural understanding, it authorizes it and backs it with the legitimate force of the state."[53]

But at the same time that rights claims in this context provide this transformative possibility, Merry emphasizes the practical limitation of rights assertion for many battered women. Assertion of rights requires that women take action to end the relationship, when what they may really want is the "connection but without the violence": "In order to escape the violence, they must also end the connection, but they may end up replacing it with a new dependence on the state in the form of the courts and the welfare system. For many women, the violent partner is also someone they love and someone on whom they depend for sex and for economic support. . . . The dilemma the woman faces as she turns to the legal system for help is that she is encouraged to leave the man."[54] If a woman is to act on the help offered by the legal system, she must be willing to send him to jail, sever her relationship with him, and risk his violence when he is released. If she repeatedly calls the police and presses charges, then withdraws and refuses to prosecute, the courts and police become frustrated, ignore her complaints, and may also ignore the complaints of other women.

A woman who is able to make the break faces considerable danger: "She is offered, instead of subordination to patriarchal authority in a violent relationship, the promise of liberal legalism: a self protected by legal rights, able to make autonomous decisions, as long as she is willing to sever the relationship with the man, or at the least, risk making him very angry by filing charges against him or testifying against him. Not only is this a difficult decision but it is also a dangerous one. Men are most likely to be violent to women after the women have left them. The men rely on the old strategy of achieving connection through violence, putting the women in considerable danger, which the law can do little to mitigate."[55] In addition to emotional pressure, this requirement of "severance" poses enormous material problems for many battered women. Merry reports: "Since [these women] are typically poor, young, relatively uneducated and caring for small children, they are dependent on their husbands as well as welfare for support. Moreover, many wish to hold on to the man. . . . The legal system recognizes that violent men very often hit their wives again, and returning women to the same situation poses a substantial risk of further violence to them." Rights assertion may also involve women's separation from their children, which is frequently a battered woman's greatest fear: women "risk having their children removed by the child protective services. . . . Thus, acknowledging the violence by asking the legal system for help or by fighting back, risks another loss of connection, that with the children. . . . The message is that maintaining connections requires accepting violence." [56]

Merry concludes that the courts convey messages about violence and connection that have quite different implications for men and women. "While men are told that violence earns them separation . . . women are encouraged in the support group to form other kinds of connections besides those premised on violence. One of the new connections proffered is with the legal system. The law expects women to leave the violent partner in order to earn its full support. Thus, women are encouraged to reconstitute themselves not as selves defined by relationships but as selves connected to the law, with rights defined by the legal system." [57]

The problem is that this "connection" with the legal system is inadequate. This "promise of liberal legalism" is disconnected from the realities of women's lives. Legal intervention alone cannot do the job. Legal intervention may provide women certain protection from battering, but it does not provide women housing, support, child care, employment, community acceptance, or love. It also does not deal with the economic realities of life. "Women often find themselves in the awkward position of going to court, getting a no-contact restraining order, getting the man out of the house, and then needing money from him and watching him give it to another girlfriend, or finding that her own kin group doesn't support her for kicking him out." [58]

The contradiction is profound. The rights claim in law is inevitably limited in practice, but it also has transformative dimensions:

> The law provides a place to contest relations of power, but it also determines the terms of the contest. Its ideology, its representation of the problem and its solution, dominates as wife battering is defined as a matter of individual rights not to be hit rather than as a violation of a collective community need for peace.
>
> On the other hand, what is novel in this situation is the expansion of [the] self to battered women. The rights-bearing self fundamental to social contract

theory has not always been extended to include all humans. Through domestic violence interventions, this self is extended to poor women who have often been denied this legally protected self.[59]

Merry's work powerfully identifies a critical dilemma of feminist lawmaking on battering and presents the conflict between rights assertion in theory and the meaning of rights assertion "on the ground." Rights assertion may provide transformative possibilities, messages about gender role socialization, experiences of individual agency and resistance, legal consciousness, psychological assertion, "selfhood," and development. At the same time, however, rights assertion has an individualizing dimension, may require the battered woman to separate from the batterer, and cannot do the job of providing safety and security. It cannot help a battered woman to change her life once the law has intervened.

Gender Violence: Rights as "Theory"

International human rights work on gender violence provides an example of rights claims as grand theory. Compared with the history of women's rights struggles in the United States and around the world, the development of feminist approaches to international human rights is a recent phenomenon, but women's international human rights work has enriched and internationalized feminist legal theory, discourse, and law reform.[60] Women's international human rights work challenges our more conventional understandings of women's rights and provides new opportunities for feminist legal work generally, and particularly on woman abuse. Most important, this work demonstrates the liberatory possibilities of rights claims.

Over the past twenty years, legal work on issues of women's international human rights has exploded. This work has particularly focused on questions of what is now called "gender violence." Activist efforts by women around the globe have led to important women's international conferences in Nairobi in 1985 and in Beijing in 1995, and in 1994 resulted in the appointment of a United Nations Special Rapporteur on Violence, Radhika Coomaraswamy, who has issued reports on violence against women around the globe. Countries must now include reports on women's rights within general human rights reports to the United Nations and other international bodies. The development of women's international human rights is an important example of the dialectical dimensions of rights claims in envisioning new political possibilities.

Serious questions, however, have been raised about the meaning of these claims. There has been widespread criticism of the lack of concrete results of women's international human rights advocacy. The U.N. Commission on the Status of Women has recommended that a Special Session in June 2000 conduct a "high-level review" of the Nairobi plan adopted at the 1985 World Conference to Review and Appraise the Achievements of the U.N. Decade for Women and of the Beijing Platform of Action from the Fourth World Conference on Women in 1995, to focus on the need for more U.N. resources and reallocation of resources to women's rights.[61] In 1999, Coomaraswamy issued a report criticizing governments for "lack of strategies of implementation on commitments to eradicate violence." Although she observes that many countries have "acknowledged domestic violence as an important human rights issue," she concludes that states have "overwhelmingly" failed in their international obligations to prevent, investigate, and prosecute domestic abuse. Hilary Charlesworth, a leading feminist legal scholar on women's international human rights, concurs, concluding that "the human rights system appears to have learned that the art of politically correct rhetoric is an effective tool in silencing potential critics. It finds it very hard, however, to institute significant change."[62]

Nevertheless, women's international human rights and related issues of globalization raise crucial questions for theory and practice, and they should be understood from a dialectical perspective. First, feminist challenge to the dichotomy of public and private is expanded by experiences of globalization. There is an extraordinary proliferation of all sorts of non-state groupings, subnational groupings based on regional and ethnic identity, as well as international regulatory agencies. This requires us to understand much more about the interrelationship between public and private. In international human rights work we are also examining broader notions of state responsibility and complicity. This important theoretical development has consequences for international law, for feminist law reform, and for legal theory.

Second, this work highlights the indivisibility of violence, reproductive choice and sexual equality, workplace conditions, wage equity, child care and health care, and economic and social rights. Over the past several years I have done legal work in South Africa assisting lawyers and judges with the development of the new South African Constitution and training lawyers, judges, and advocates in issues of violence against women. The struggle to have social and economic rights included in their Constitution was extraordinary; in the end, these rights, not just civil and political rights, were explicitly incorporated into the South African Constitution. The particular situation of women's rights within the framework of international human rights and globalization underscores the need for economic and social rights to be integrated into this broader perspective. Economic and social rights guarantees are an important antidote to the problems of both women's international human rights and globalization.

Globalization also presents concrete opportunities for connection. The internationalization of this work has already had a considerable political and psychological impact. The concept of an international "non-governmental organization" did not exist twenty-five years ago. Globalization and internationalization, then, provide an extraordinary opportunity for change.

Technology underscores this opportunity. The Internet has made information about faraway places accessible. In preparation for a workshop on domestic violence that I was to conduct in South Africa, for example, I was able to obtain activist materials from South Africa through an online organization, Women's Net, that linked women's organizations throughout the world. It collected documents, programs for action, and lists of organizations, and it provided extraordinary access to information. The new possibilities of internationalism that flow from this technology cannot be minimized.

The concept of universal human rights also enriches simple domestic understandings of rights. In South Africa I participated in a workshop assisting local activists to document cases of woman abuse as international human rights violations. One of the things we talked about was what difference it made to women who were already doing activist work on violence against women within South Africa under South African law to perceive these issues within a framework of international human rights. For these women, the concept of universalization was implicit in the notion of international human rights and connected their experience in South Africa with struggles of women around the world. The concept of international human rights took what was previously understood as trivial and invisible and gave it larger meaning; it transformed simple domestic rights claims into "human rights" claims and "international" claims. Power and organizing potential are inherent in experiencing oneself as linked to what Aihwa Ong has called a "strategic sisterhood of women activists around the globe." [63]

This international work also has transformative potential for activist work within North America. Legal treatment of pregnant workers in the *maquiladora*, U.S. manufacturing export zones in northern Mexico, has received considerable international human rights attention. In the United States, exclusion of pregnant women from workplaces because of reproductive hazards is not new. Pregnancy exclusion and even forced sterilization policies have been widespread. Many years ago I was involved with litigation challenging the sterilization policy at the American Cyanamid plant in West Virginia, and despite the Supreme Court's subsequent decision in *Johnson Controls*,[64] U.S. workplaces continue to have exclusionary policies respecting reproduction. What difference does it make to have these issues raised in a global context? In the United States we have not had large protests or activist efforts concerning reproductive hazards in the workplace for many years, so global pressure could make a big difference. Another example is international human rights concern about the use of the "honor" defense in Muslim countries to punish, control, and kill women who have been adulterous or promiscuous.[65] Yet in the United States, the analogous "defense" has a long history; only a few years ago it was the basis for a Maryland judge's expression of empathy for a man who had killed his wife after finding her in bed with another man.[66] If part of what happens as a result of the internationalization of global problems is a renewed attention to these issues both domestically *and* around the world, so much the better.

These understandings of a new "publicness," of a new internationalism, of perspectives on woman abuse that cross borders, are important. Through lawmaking on international human rights we have broadened our vision, deepened our understanding of the links between gender and violence, and reshaped feminist analysis. This work has given us a sense of new and renewed possibilities for activism. Ideally, these efforts can strengthen both our international work and our understanding of the inextricable link between violence and equality in the United States.

II

Theoretical Dimensions of Feminist Lawmaking on Battering

4

Defining, Identifying, and Strategizing

In the next three chapters I examine theoretical dimensions of feminist law-making on battering. I begin in this chapter with definitional themes concerning woman abuse. Questions of how intimate violence is defined raise crucial issues of theory and practice for work on woman abuse and reveal a paradox in feminist theory: feminist theoretical work must simultaneously be "particular," in documenting the experiences of women who are battered by men, and "general," in linking violence against women to women's subordination within society and to wider social problems of abuse of power and control.[1] I use the term "particularity" here to mean the importance of accurately describing and detailing the complexity of women's experiences; in the context of woman abuse, this means understanding the dimensions of the problems of intimate violence that are unique to women. At the same time, we must explore the "general" dimensions of woman abuse: first, that it is a facet of women's subordination in society; and second, that it is linked to larger problems of societal violence.

This argument concerning the importance of linking particularity with generality is likely to be viewed as controversial, perhaps even heretical. Feminist theory has largely been premised on a notion of women's particular and unique experiences—a "particularity" strand of analysis which denies, sometimes even rejects, the "general," because the general is viewed as based on male experience. This tendency toward particularity is reflected in the theoretical framework of gender subordination, and thus understood (although contested) as gender-specific. The early stages of the battered women's movement recognized a strategic need for certain definitional categories and certain characterizations of battered women's experiences which were useful; it is now unsettling to challenge these familiar categories and characterizations.

Feminist legal theory has also correctly focused on the specificity of women's situated experience; indeed, recent criticism of essentialism — the claim that there is one single "woman's" experience — underscores the importance of particularity in descriptions of "women's" experiences.[2]

My approach resonates with feminist legal theorists and others working within the pragmatic legal tradition who have explored the importance of context, articulated the need for a self-reflective, woman-centered stance that simultaneously moves beyond women's experiences, and identified the inter-relationship between the particular and the general.[3] I recognize that a danger in moving away from particularity toward generalization is that the specificity and richness of women's situated experience may be lost in the process; proposed reforms or theories premised on more general understandings may thus become irrelevant or inaccurate. Thus, for good reason, generalization, or what I call the move to generality, has been viewed as suspect. However, exclusive focus on particularity is problematic and limits the development of richer feminist theory and practice.

Making the link between the particular and the general is vital, for as we honestly explore the deeply particular aspects of women's experiences, we are faced with theoretical contradictions that force us to confront more general issues. This relationship between particularity and generality is dialectical. The particular illuminates the general, and the general then provides context and depth to our understanding of the particular. The effort to link the particular with the general is also a moral stance, for it reflects the value of both acknowledging situatedness (women's experience with abuse) and seeking commonality with other experiences of violence.

The Concept of "Battered Woman"

Ever since the women's movement first articulated the concept of battering, feminists have grappled with the issue of what the "problem" should be called. Each of the possible terms — wife abuse, spouse abuse, domestic violence, intimate violence, wife battering, or woman abuse — reflects a different perception of battering. Is the critical determinant marriage, gender, familial relationship, intimacy, or physical violence? The most common term is "battering," a harm experienced by women that had been unnamed, but it now also describes a person, a "battered woman." Yet this term, which we now take for granted, raises critical questions of definition and strategy.

In contrast with other descriptions of harm to women, "battered woman" describes the victim and focuses on her qualities. A woman is or is not a "battered woman." The phrase is reductive in that it implies the total life experience of the particular woman: a "battered woman" can be no more than a woman who has been battered. Yet significantly, women who have experienced abuse resist applying the term "battered woman" to themselves, whether they are calling hotlines, seeking shelter, going to court to obtain temporary restraining orders, going to emergency rooms, or talking with other women. For example, Susan Schechter has reported that in her work with battered women in shelters and in hospital emergency rooms, most women who had been battered were reluctant to identify themselves as "battered women" and frequently rejected the application of the term to themselves.[4]

This reluctance suggests that the term "battered woman" has a restrictive meaning—a meaning that defines a woman exclusively in terms of her battering experience. It also suggests that the term carries a negative connotation from which an individual woman may wish to distance herself: a "battered woman" is someone else, not me. Compare the static term "battered woman" with the phrase "woman who has been sexually harassed" or even "woman who has been raped." These terms describe a woman who has been subjected to an external harm: they focus on the problem of the harm—sexual harassment or rape—and leave the woman intact. In contrast, "battered woman" does not capture the range and complexity of a woman's experiences beyond the facts of abuse. The term makes her the problem, not her experiences. We reinforce this interpretation by talking about the "problems of battered women," rather than focusing on the problem of male violence or male battering of women, or men who assert and use violence as a means of control.

Advocates often suggest a more accurate, less totalizing description: "a woman who has (or had) a relationship with a battering man."[5] This phrase evokes an image of the woman as survivor of a relationship with a controlling man, who exists independently of this relationship, rather than defining her by the behavior of the man with whom she has a relationship. In 1992 two leading battered women's advocates, Ann Jones and Susan Schechter, wrote a book to assist women in relationships with controlling men and gave it the title *When Love Goes Wrong*. Recent work on battering, then, emphasizes women's survival skills and resources and purposely characterizes battered women not as victims but as survivors.[6]

The totalizing impact of the term "battered woman" may also be grounded in negative social stereotypes that accompany the description of battering. Public experience of the term "battered woman" has been shaped by association with the concept of "battered woman syndrome," primarily in criminal trials involving battered women who have fought against their abusers. In many such cases, experts have testified that there is a "battered woman syndrome," which has been commonly understood to define battered women as suffering from a kind of helplessness that renders them incapable of leaving their abusers. Thus, the term "battered woman" conjures up images of helplessness and defeat rather than survival and resistance. Neither the term itself, then, nor the social meaning of the term, accurately captures the complexity of women's experiences with abuse.

Battered Women and Essentialism

Just as the term "battered woman" is static and incomplete, so too is the notion that one paradigmatic "battered woman" exists. Feminist legal theorists are now sensitive to the problem of essentialism. Over the past several years, important developments within feminist legal theory have challenged the notion of a single feminist perspective. Many feminist critics have written powerfully about the way the notion of womanhood has been described as a single uniform experience, thereby excluding a multiplicity of experiences based on race, class, ethnicity, age, sexual orientation, and other dimensions.[7] Postmodern theory intersects with this analysis in challenging the meaning of any unitary concept of "woman." Denise Riley, for example, argues that one is not born a woman but "becomes" a woman. Notions of indeterminacy, of paradox, of mobile subjectivities, of performativity have shaped recent theoretical work on gender.[8] Thus an important theme of feminist lawmaking has been: Is there such a category as "battered woman?" Is the term "battered woman" inherently problematic because of its essentializing nature?

Here I assume a pragmatic stance on the issue of gender. Feminist theory on domestic violence should take as a given the centrality of gender, but should not focus on gender in a unidimensional way. Battered women are not all similarly situated; pressures shaping their experiences are linked to the specific dynamics of the community in which the abuse occurs. Efforts to assist battered women must be tailored to meet their diverse needs.

One popular misconception concerning the problem of woman abuse is that most women who are battered are poor or are women of color. To the contrary: battering cuts across class, racial, and ethnic lines.[9] Although, within the battered women's movement, work to protect women from battering has largely been shaped by the experience and understanding of white women, battered women's advocates and women of color have done considerable work to expand definitions and perspectives to include women of color who have been battered.[10]

The intersection of racism and sexism exacerbates many of the problems commonly faced by white women in a battering relationship. The racial bias inherent in the housing market, for example, and the disparity between the earning power of black and white women, intensify the difficulties that confront a woman of color who is attempting to leave a battering relationship. As Kimberlé Crenshaw recounts, a worker in a shelter serving a predominantly black population reported that nearly 85 percent of her clients returned to the battering relationship because of the difficulties posed by finding housing and employment. Crenshaw suggests that although violence is a common issue among women, it usually occurs within a context that varies according to the race, class, and other social characteristics of the woman.[11]

Apart from the difficulties of finding housing and employment, institutional racism and its impact on communities of color is an acute dilemma for the battered woman who identifies her experiences not only as an abused individual, but as an abused person who is a member of an abused community. Crenshaw documents her frustrating search for statistics about battering and race, a process which led her to conclude that the pressure to minimize or suppress information about the prevalence of domestic violence in the African American community may reflect a desire to maintain community integrity and to discourage the perception of black men as uncontrollably violent. Beth Richie voices similar concerns about negative perceptions of the black community and the community's reluctance to lend them credibility. She observes that battered black women are often caught in the "trap called loyalty." In such a climate, "disclosure is so easily confused with treason!"[12]

Richie notes that the African American community, which has experienced violence at the hands of the criminal justice system, has found it deeply problematic to turn to this same system "as a vehicle for protection and problem resolution." Angela Harris suggests that black women are likely to view the criminal justice system with suspicion because of its historical tendency to "ignore violence against [black] women while perpetrating it against [black] men." As one counselor reported: "Not only do we fear that we will be mistreated by the institutions, but that our men will be also. We want the violence in our homes to stop but we do not want to contribute in any way to the unjust treatment of our race or ethnic community."[13]

Counselors who work within the Asian community note a special reluctance to report battering. This reluctance, they posit, partly reflects an imperative to avoid bringing shame on the family.[14] Other counselors who work within Latino communities report a similar concern about focusing shame on the family, which contributes to the tendency to keep information about battering private.[15]

The plight of battered immigrant women who lack American citizenship or proper legal status tragically dramatizes how the context in which abuse occurs affects battered women's options. They are constrained not only by their gender but by their illegal status, so the power their husbands wield over them is even greater than it would be otherwise. The potential for abuse is all too obvious. One Chinese immigrant reported that her battering husband threatened, "You do exactly what I say, or I'll call immigration." A counselor recounted the experience of another woman "who has been hospitalized . . . but she keeps coming back to him because he promises he will file for her. . . . He holds that green card over her head." Although laws now give women the opportunity to self-petition for their immigration status, the coercion can be severe and the bureaucratic hurdles difficult to overcome.[16] Battered women from other countries also seek asylum in the United States on grounds of gender-based persecution.[17]

These diverse experiences of battering highlight the importance of taking the critique of essentialism seriously. Understanding the power dynamics of gender subordination is crucial, but the model of battering we construct must be tempered with a recognition of other forces that shape the battering relationship. At the same time, these diverse experiences suggest the need for a form of "strategic essentialism"—recognition of an important commonality to women's experiences of battering in response to postmodern and essentialist challenges.[18] Linda Gordon observes that this commonality has material dimensions and is not simply cultural: "Women do not need a conceptual breakthrough from patriarchal culture, as was necessary for them to want to vote, in order to dislike being hit. The problem of wife-beating is an example of the importance of the body and a reminder not to be so threatened by charges of essentialism that we forget physicality."[19] The shared experience of

women's physical abuse and pain provides a concrete basis for the commonality of woman battering.

Battering as Physical Abuse

The definitions of battering that social scientists traditionally have adopted
focus on physical abuse, and for strategic purposes battered women's activists
have often adopted these definitions as well. A battered woman is a woman
who is hit or hurt repeatedly, or against whom weapons are used; definitions
of battering may involve the amount, type, frequency, or intensity of the hitting, or link hitting with rape or other forms of sexual abuse, or with other
types of violence.[20]

Feminists' theoretical work on battered women traditionally stresses male
domination within the marital relationship and concepts of male ownership
of women in marriage as the basis for woman abuse.[21] In the early stages of ar-
ticulating the experiences of battered women and translating them into legal
claims, it was important to emphasize the physical dimension of the abuse.
Asserting physical harm established and legitimized the notion that women
were subjects of abuse and that physical battering was something serious and
unique that happened to women.[22] Society would be willing to redress de-
monstrable physical injury.

In spite of this strategic focus, feminists did not intend to limit the concept
of abuse to solely physical harm. The broader description of battering relationships is premised on an understanding of coercive behavior and of power
and control— including a continuum of sexual and verbal abuse, threats,
economic coercion, stalking, and social isolation—rather than "number of
hits."[23] Many women report that the emotional abuse is more scarring. The
experiences of a woman in one of Liz Kelly's studies illustrate the inadequacy
of the word "battering" to describe abusive behavior that encompassed more
than severe physical violence: "What he did wasn't exactly battering but it was
the threat. I remember one night I spent the whole night in a state of terror,
nothing less than terror all night. . . . And that was worse to me than getting
whacked." Kelly's research demonstrated the pervasiveness of the tendency to
identify battering by the quantifiability and frequency of physical acts, particularly among those experiencing the abuse. Many of the women refused to
define their experiences as domestic violence as long as the abuse remained
infrequent.[24]

As feminist lawmaking on battering continues to develop, practical experience blurs the distinction between physical abuse and other aspects of the battering relationship. First, it is now widely recognized that within intimate relationships there is a significant overlap between physical abuse and sexual abuse.[25] Second, experience with battering men who have joined groups to treat their battering suggests that even men whose physically abusive behavior has been modified and who have stopped hitting do not stop harassing, threatening, and controlling women.[26] Third, the recognition of battering within lesbian and gay male communities, and of the battering of elderly persons, further expands our understanding of battering as part of larger problems of power and control within intimate relationships.

The initial feminist vision of battering recognized physical, sexual, verbal, and emotional abuse as integrally interrelated aspects of the exertion of power and control. But recognizing that physical abuse does not exist in isolation, and defining battering as part of an ongoing continuum, have complex ramifications. Although this revised definition of battering more authentically describes the actual experiences of women who are beaten (who frequently describe the threats and verbal abuse as more devastating than the physical), it complicates the strategic argument that women who have been physically battered are a distinct group with unique problems. By collapsing the distinction between physical abuse and other forms of abuse within intimate relationships, women who are battered become like other women, like everyone else. Acknowledging battering as part of a continuum forces us — jurors in self-defense cases involving battered women, judges in restraining-order cases, legislators, and the general public — to confront our fantasies of the family as a haven. If battering is perceived not simply as physical abuse but as an issue of power and control, it threatens our traditional notions of the family even more profoundly. It is far easier to distance ourselves when the issue is physical abuse rather than personal domination, which may feel uncomfortably close to home.

Thus, paradoxically, redefining battering as an issue of power and control contradicts the strategic necessity of establishing woman abuse as a particular and unique harm (and a basis for legal claims), justifying special legal recognition. Although the expanded understanding is truer to women's experiences of abuse and to feminist *theoretical* conceptions of battering, it is risky because it heightens the likelihood of *practical* problems — judicial and societal denial of, and distancing from, battering generally because of the pain involved in acknowledging that issues of power and control are troublingly characteristic of all intimate relationships. The particularity that makes battering legally cognizable thus limits the generality that reflects a more complex, but more accurate, vision of battering relationships. This generality is often too threatening for society to acknowledge.

Battering as Sexism

Historically, feminists have identified battering as a problem of sexism, of male domination within heterosexual relationships, shaped by the institution of marriage. Battering was viewed as a natural extension of notions of women as male property within the marital relationship. Over the past several years, the recognition of the problems of lesbian battering, and battering within gay male relationships, has challenged this view of battering as unique to heterosexual relationships.[27] Recent exploration of the problem of elder abuse has further expanded feminists' understanding of battering.

Including this broader range of experiences in which abuse takes place complicates the traditional heterosexist framework of woman abuse. First, it redefines battering as an issue of power and control generally, rather than an issue of particular or even exclusive male power and control. This definition has the potential to strengthen individual psychological and sociological perspectives that focus on "family violence" — perspectives that feminist activists and academics have criticized as inadequate.[28] Including other battering relationships in an expanded definition is also problematic because it suggests and reinforces an individual psychological, "anger-management" perspective on battering instead of an explicitly feminist perspective. In any case, both in theory and in practice, acknowledging lesbian, gay male, and elder abuse affects definitions of battering.

This notion of sexual symmetry or gender neutrality has had a widespread impact on legal reforms, particularly in the area of criminal justice. For example, mandatory arrest laws, which were intended to *protect* battered women from abusive partners, are now commonly framed in gender-neutral language and have produced skyrocketing arrest rates of battered women themselves. Even though the evidence in these cases almost always indicates that the women arrested were acting in self-defense, they are often criminally charged and sentenced to jail or treatment programs.[29] Battered women who kill must claim they are "true victims"; greater availability of services for battered woman are used against them. In addition, long-standing efforts by men to claim that battered women's shelters or services should be available to men have been given new life.[30]

A theoretical framework that recognizes the primacy of gender need not exclude other factors. Sexual orientation, race, class, and age ought to be recognized as interconnected variables that affect both the perpetuation of violence and institutional and governmental responses.

Lesbian and Gay Male Battering

The mainstream domestic violence movement has long operated from a heterosexist perspective. Ironically, although lesbian activists were among the first to work with battered women, the general perception of a battering problem within the lesbian community itself came much later.[31] Gay men, who have not been as widely involved in the domestic violence movement, have had even more difficulty acknowledging these problems.[32] As a result, comparatively little has been written about lesbian battering, and even less has been written about gay male battering. Several reasons might explain this dearth of research. Just as communities of color put a premium on loyalty, lesbian and gay male communities, which have been the objects of severe and sometimes violent discrimination by the society at large, wish to protect the fragile credibility they have worked so hard to earn in the public mind. In addition, lesbian and gay male communities are reluctant to dispel certain internal utopian myths about same-sex relationships by admitting that lesbians and gay men are sometimes in as much danger from partners as they are in a homophobic world. Third, the problem of lesbian and gay male battering, like battering among all groups, disturbingly highlights the capacity for all intimate relationships to descend into violence.[33]

When the violent partner is a woman or the victim is a man, the traditional model that defines domestic violence as a way of maintaining patriarchal control within the nuclear family unit is thrown into question. The perception of battering as men using violence to control women, or women and children, within the dominant nuclear family structure fails to explain satisfactorily the incidence of lesbian and gay male battering, which appears to occur at rates approximately equal to violence in heterosexual relationships.[34] Although some legal theorists have attempted to explain lesbian or gay male battering by attributing it to the violence of heterosexual role-playing, lesbian and gay male relationships do not fit neatly into traditional gender roles.[35] In fact, some observers have argued that the characterization of lesbian violence as part of "butch-femme" dual role-play may represent an effort within the lesbian community to avoid the reality of violence even in "feminist" lesbian relationships. Moreover, rigid gender roles by themselves do not explain heterosexual battering. Commentators suggest that it is when women attempt to challenge these roles that the violence erupts. It is the attempt to threaten the superiority of the more powerful partner, not the presence of rigid gender roles in and of themselves, that provides the catalyst for heterosexual battering.[36]

The phenomenon of lesbian battering relationships, then, compels an expansion of the traditional concept of battering. Ruthann Robson has suggested that "'dominance' is a hetero-relational concept that may not be applicable to lesbian relationships." In seeking to develop a lesbian legal theory of battering, she rejects heterosexist formulations embedded in mainstream feminist legal theories. Instead, she argues that the legal community should recognize lesbian relationships and protect battered lesbians, while understanding that lesbian relationships cannot be neatly analogized to heterosexual relationships. Such analogies only serve to victimize lesbians further by obliterating their distinct sexuality and community.[37]

Other theorists seek to resolve the inconsistencies between the traditional heterosexual paradigm and the realities of lesbian and gay male battering relationships by focusing on the use of power and control in all intimate relationships as the root of relational violence in general. From this perspective, the assertion of male power within the historical medium of the heterosexual family is therefore only a single — although the most common — manifestation of the use of violence to control partners in intimate relationships.[38]

Problems in recognizing and describing lesbian battering may stem from the many important differences between lesbian and heterosexual battering relationships. Lesbians face serious discrimination in the legal system, so for survivors of lesbian battering, such issues as custody, shared property rights, and protection from the batterer pose substantial problems.[39] The complexity of feelings that lesbian victims of battering have toward their batterers is evident in the first-person literature about the experience, where lesbians have often been freer to detail their stories. In lesbian battering cases, the batterer is often physically smaller than the abused partner, and thus volunteers may make the mistake of assuming that the violence is mutual because both women claim to have been abused.[40] In addition, volunteers who telephone a house where violence often occurs in a lesbian relationship cannot assume that the woman's voice on the line is that of the victim.

Without expanding our definitions of battering beyond the traditional heterosexual framework, it will be impossible to reach out to and assist battered lesbians and gay men in the community. Women who work in the shelter movement already worry about "lesbian baiting." Lesbians who are battered are sometimes denied shelter outright; at times, they choose not to seek shelter because of homophobic attitudes that proliferate among shelter workers or other shelter residents.[41] Understanding the experiences of lesbian and gay male abuse is an important step toward a comprehensive redefinition of battering relationships.

Elder Abuse

Elder abuse has been brought to public scrutiny as another manifestation of "family violence." As with lesbian and gay male battering, elder abuse is not necessarily grounded in the phenomenon of men beating women, so it, too, challenges the idea that sexism is the root of battering. The director of a family shelter in Illinois remarked: "When everyone began looking at domestic violence, they started with child abuse, then woman abuse. The third phase is elder abuse." [42]

The literature concerning the problem remains limited, and theoretical models on elder abuse continue to develop.[43] As with woman abuse, studies are complicated by the fact that elder abuse is vastly underreported. A House of Representatives Committee on Aging Report estimated that 5 percent of the elderly population experiences abuse, but that only one in eight cases is reported. In one survey, only 14 percent of the reports of abuse were made by the elderly person — an indication both of the reluctance to implicate family members, who in the majority of the cases of elder abuse are the perpetrators, and of the social isolation of the elderly.[44]

One of the major issues in the literature examining elder abuse has been the definition of the term "abuse." Unlike models of woman battering, which historically have tended to focus on physical violence, models of elder abuse almost always adopt a continuum, which includes physical, psychological, and financial abuse. Abuse of the elderly thus ranges from the extremely violent cases of beating and murder reported in the news, to the more common-place occurrences of threatening behavior, confining the elderly to a chair or a room, depriving the person of care, or forcing medicine or food on the person.[45]

Like all intrafamily violence, elder abuse is a complex phenomenon that results from the interaction of many factors. It often develops around a relationship where the elderly person is bound to the caregiver by physical dependency and where the caregiver is emotionally and financially dependent on the aged person.[46] The abuse that occurs in these situations is closely related to the kind of internal stress endemic to such family relationships. Elder abuse bears a particular resemblance to woman abuse, for both involve a long-term intimate relationship between two adults. In addition, elder abuse sometimes is the continuation of woman abuse.[47] Studies report that most victims of elder abuse are women.[48]

Particularity and Generality: Implications for Feminist Theory and Practice

The definitional questions concerning woman battering that I have raised here are complex and have profound implications for feminist theory and practice on intimate violence. Battering and abuse extend beyond heterosexual relationships, in particular, to intimate relationships, in general. Yet feminist activists and lawyers must continue to affirm the particular experience of woman abuse, shaped by understandings of male domination in heterosexual relationships, while expanding our understanding of abuse to perceive the ways in which power and control operate in all intimate relationships. The situations described here provide us with opportunities to deepen our theoretical understanding and broaden our practical experience of the problem of abuse. We need not deny the particular urgency of the feminist critique in order to recognize the broader range of situations in which battering occurs. Recognition of both particularity and generality can reshape our theoretical framework.

These problems of definition highlight the complex dimensions of feminist lawmaking as an effort to both describe and change—to describe the experience of woman battering accurately and simultaneously to be able to translate it to courts. Although the battered women's movement has had to demonstrate distinctive aspects of the problem of physical battering of women in order to establish battered women as a legal and social construct—a group that can assert and claim legal rights—these characterizations of distinctiveness have not explained fully the complex experiences of battering and have constrained feminist analysis. Expanding our vision will allow us to understand what is distinctive about battered women's experiences and also to see these experiences in the larger and more general context of violence between intimates.

While the development of a distinct legal construct concerning male battering of women has been theoretically important and strategically necessary, moving to the more general level of violence between intimates and women's subordination can illuminate theoretical and strategic issues that advance our work. Paradoxically, this very emphasis on particularity, on the distinctiveness of battered women's experiences, has had an unintended effect of compounding the problems of battered women because we have insufficiently connected battered women's experiences both to the larger and more general problems of women and to those of violence between intimates.

Focusing simultaneously on particularity and generality does not mean denying the distinctiveness of women's experiences with woman abuse; it means a richer and more detailed description of women's diverse and particular problems, an acknowledgment of abuse as part of a general continuum of violence between intimates, and an understanding of the way particular experiences of woman abuse are shaped by gender, by gender roles, by more general experiences of motherhood, by unequal and constrained relationships with men, and by general societal attitudes toward women.

In practice, we can see the unintended consequences of this emphasis on particularity for public policy on woman abuse. In the media and in legal and legislative arenas, the problems that battered women face are viewed in isolation; they are rarely linked to gender socialization, women's subservient position within society and the family structure, sex discrimination in the workplace, economic discrimination, problems of housing and lack of child care, lack of access to divorce, inadequate child support, problems of single motherhood, or lack of educational and community support. The focus is still on the individual woman and her "pathology" instead of on the batterer and the social structures that support the oppression of women and that glorify or otherwise condone violence. For these reasons, we must place battering in context and link woman abuse to more general issues of gender subordination, power relationships, and violence between intimates. If we confront these issues of definition, identity, and strategy, and are clearer in our descriptions of experience—acknowledging both a richer "particularity" of woman abuse and a more inclusive "generality" of gender subordination and intimate violence— feminist lawmaking will be more effective in making change.

5

Beyond Victimization and Agency

Since the late 1960s, feminist activists and lawyers have attempted to transform societal understandings and to shape legal definitions of several interrelated harms against women: woman abuse, rape, sexual harassment, and pornography. These areas of feminist lawmaking, premised on a theoretical framework of gender subordination in which women have been viewed as primarily victims, have been highly controversial.[1]

The theme of feminism as victimization dominates contemporary popular culture.[2] Although feminist legal struggles take place on many diverse fronts, anti-pornography work has historically captured a disproportionate share of media attention.[3] The important issues of sexual harassment, given new life in the early 1990s by the Anita Hill–Clarence Thomas hearings and "date rape,"[4] have also attracted public attention to women's claims of gender subordination, and have been perceived as portraying women as victims. Feminist work has also often been shaped by an incomplete and static view of women as either victims or agents; this false dichotomy between women's victimization and women's agency is a central tension within feminism.

The disabling dichotomy between notions of women's victimization and agency manifests itself in diverse areas of feminist legal theory and practice. Consider pornography. For Catharine MacKinnon and other "porn-suppression" feminists, "sexuality is a realm of unremitting unequalled victimization for women. Pornography appears as the monster that made this so."[5] Anti-pornography ordinances developed several years ago by Catharine MacKinnon, Andrea Dworkin, and others emphasized this exclusivity of women's victimization. Other groups of feminists organized to refute the MacKinnon-Dworkin assertions and argued that "women are agents and not merely victims, who make decisions and act on them and who desire, seek out and enjoy sexuality."[6]

Today we see a backlash against aspects of feminism that focus on women as victims, and an intensification of the rhetoric of victim versus agent. Charges of "victim feminism" have been leveled by conservative and right-wing women's organizations such as the Independent Women's Forum.[7] Several years ago this backlash was fueled by such books as Katie Roiphe's *The Morning After* and Naomi Wolf's *Fire With Fire*, which attacked victim feminism and received extraordinary media attention.[8] These authors criticize feminist work on date rape, sexual harassment, and anti-pornography as victim feminism and offer "power feminism" — premised on women's individual agency, choice, and exercise of responsibility—as an alternative.[9] Roiphe and Wolf argue that feminist emphasis on victimization in these contexts reinforces sex-stereotypical views of woman as fragile and passive. But their complaint of victim feminism and their solution of power feminism are simplistic, for they fail to grapple with the systemic nature of women's subordination and women's active efforts to resist it. They also demonstrate a lack of compassion for women, particularly for those who are not sufficiently privileged to assert power feminism. Their work underscores the fundamental inadequacy of *either* victimization *or* agency (reconceived as "victim feminism" or "power feminism") to capture the complexity of struggle in women's lives, and highlights how this false dichotomy leads to problematic extremes.[10]

Victimization claims are deeply embedded in our culture and viewed with intense ambivalence. Martha Minow has observed that, on the one hand, victimization claims make powerful appeals for sympathy, solidarity, compassion, and attention; on the other hand, they are regarded as attempts to avoid responsibility, to suppress the societal and structural dimensions of discrimination, to emphasize a fixed and limited sense of identity, and to undermine personal strength and capacity.[11] These contradictions of victimization are particularly profound in the area of gender. Victim claims for women are often the only way that women are heard,[12] yet they trigger entrenched stereotypes of passivity and purity, as well as strong feelings of protectiveness and deep resentment. Concepts of agency are also limited and problematic. Traditional views of agency are based on notions of individual choice and responsibility, individual will, and action—perceptions of atomized individuals, acting alone, unconstrained by social forces, unmediated by social structures and systemic hardship.[13] Agency rhetoric and "power feminism" have mass appeal; consider the National Rifle Association's effort to sell guns to women by using advertisements telling women "how to choose to refuse to be a victim."[14] This rhetoric urges us to believe that women are victims by choice, despite the realities of gendered violence.

Women's victimization and agency are each understood to exist as the absence of the other — as if one must be either pure victim or pure agent — when in fact they are profoundly interrelated. Martha Mahoney criticizes "prevailing social and legal concepts of agency," which suggest that "agency does not mean acting for oneself under conditions of oppression; it means being without oppression, either having ended oppression or never having experienced it all. This all-agent or all-victim conceptual dichotomy will not be easy to escape or transform."[15]

Neither victimization nor agency should be glorified, understood as static, viewed in isolation, or perceived as an individual or personal issue, because gender subordination must be understood as a systemic and *collective* problem — one in which women experience both oppression and resistance. This emphasis on victimization has shaped feminist lawmaking in many areas. Martha Fineman has observed that this resurgence of victimization-agency rhetoric has an overly personal, "self-help" dimension, and has minimized such systemic problems as economic discrimination, single motherhood, and welfare.[16] Vicki Schultz and Carlin Meyer have similarly argued that claims of sexual harassment in the workplace have been culturally interpreted as more in the realm of the sexual (individual) than the workplace (material and collective).[17]

The battered women's movement has begun to grapple with this victim-agent dichotomy. The phrase "battered woman survivor" is often used instead of "victim," and along with this rhetorical change has come a developing literature concerning battered woman survivors.[18] Many resource materials on battered women now emphasize the strengths of battered women who struggle to survive, protect themselves, and keep their families functioning. Yet battered women continue to suffer from the rigid dichotomy of being described either as victims or as irrational agents.

The victim-agent dichotomy has shaped legal work on battering in crucial and deleterious ways. Women who have been battered are required to leave these relationships in order to gain the protection of the law; women who have been battered are also viewed as inherently "unreasonable." I explore these issues and then turn to legal and cultural efforts to reinterpret battered women's variable responses to abuse as forms of resistance. This process of reinterpretation can help us to describe more accurately the complexity of battered women's experiences.

Requiring Battered Women to Leave

Themes of victimization and agency and the vacillation between these extremes pervade feminist lawmaking on issues of violence against women. We can see this in public attitudes toward battered women who kill and battered women who are mothers, who are viewed as exclusively responsible for the harms their children face, without any understanding of their own victimization. Courts may deny these mothers custody of their children or terminate their legal rights because the legal system views them as passively having failed to protect their children from abuse, even when they may have made active efforts to do so. The common view is that a battered woman should somehow have left the violent relationship and that if she didn't leave, anything that happened was her fault. The lurking question behind any public or private discussion of battered women is "Why didn't she leave?"

Focusing on why the woman doesn't leave leads to troubling results.[19] Asking the question places responsibility on the woman. It reflects a tendency to want battered women to assume responsibility, to take control, to act as agents and simply reject their victimization, and it puts the women's conduct under scrutiny, rather than placing the responsibility on the battering man. Many battered women, however, cannot leave. Leaving provides battered women no assurance of separation or safety; the stories of battered women who have been hunted down across state lines and harassed or killed are legion.[20] Much abuse can be viewed as what Martha Mahoney has called "separation attack" — beatings that are provoked by the woman's threat or assertion of independence, or actual separation from the man.[21] For many women, leaving only intensifies the risk of harm. Many women who are battered have little money, no child care, no employment; they may be financially and emotionally dependent on the men who batter them; they believe that it is better to stay with the men because of their children; or they don't want to leave because they love the men and want to maintain whatever intimacy and sense of connection they can. Women have been socialized to stay in the family—to keep the family together no matter what. Many battered women report that they want what Christine Littleton has called "safe connection": for the relationship to continue but the battering to stop.[22]

Instead of asking "Why doesn't the woman leave?" we should ask "Why do men batter?" or perhaps, more significantly, "Why does society tolerate men who batter?" The emphasis on the woman's leaving trivializes the woman's victimization, the physical harm that she has suffered, and the trauma that she has experienced; it also reflects no understanding of the complexity of the relationship, the risk of death she might face in leaving, and the social, psychological, and economic factors that impede her. Moreover, as Mahoney has observed, "emphasizing a particular form of agency—exit—renders invisible all the other active efforts that the woman may have made to protect herself and her children. If exit remains a focal point, we fail to examine a more important act of agency—staying—and the tremendous will, strength and determination that may accompany such a decision."[23]

Asking "Why doesn't she leave?" hypocritically denies cultural socialization that trains young girls and women to think of marriage and family as the measure of success, to "stand by her man" and keep the marriage together no matter what, and blames the woman if the marriage fails. Asking "Why doesn't she leave?" also assumes a false black-and-white model of human relationship, of simple right and wrong, condemning the woman for seeking to maintain connection. If we are honest with ourselves concerning the painful contradictions and compromises involved in all intimate relationships—summed up by the title of Peter Kramer's book *Should You Leave?*—our own experiences might be a source of identification with, rather than distance from, the experiences of women who are battered.

Where each individual draws the line depends on context, on the nature of our human, economic, and social dependence, on the existence of and relationship with children, on social supports, and on the degree to which we perceive that there are realistic options. Battered women's experiences must be understood within the context of the power imbalance and compromise inherent in all intimate relationships. Asking why battered women stay, rather than what makes batterers abuse, prevents us from having to examine the messiness of our own intimate relationships.

When people become victims, become "battered woman," claim sexual harassment, or claim discrimination generally, they assume superhuman dimensions and thus become the focus of unrealistic expectations. Because one is claiming to be harmed, to be in need of special protection, one's life and conduct become open to scrutiny. Think of Anita Hill. Others who observe the spotlighted situation compare themselves to this projected image and then presume to judge it from the safety of their own protected position. In this regard, requiring a battered woman to leave her batterer is a projection of a higher standard of conduct; it reflects a process of shielding oneself and one's own behavior, of asserting "this is not me." If instead we were able to acknowledge the human connection, to see the similarities between this woman's situation and our own experience, to understand the commonality of sexual subordination and the complexity and compromise involved in all intimate relationships, we could understand why a woman who had a relationship with a battering man might choose to remain, struggle, and actively strategize to stay safe, but still want the battering to stop. We might be more accepting of the complex circumstances of women who are battered and better able to devise compassionate and responsive strategies to help.

The Biased Concept of Reasonableness

There is deep gender bias in the concept of reasonableness.[24] This issue first emerged in the context of battered women who faced homicide or assault charges for killing or injuring their assailant and who argued that they acted in self-defense. Self-defense is premised on the idea of reasonableness, so a battered woman who claims that she acted in self-defense must show that she acted reasonably. Early work on women's self-defense argued that reasonableness was a gendered concept because only men were viewed as reasonable — women were viewed as inherently unreasonable — and that these views had long been part of the common law. As a consequence of this bias, women were less likely to successfully plead self-defense and had been relegated to pleas of temporary insanity or manslaughter. Feminist legal scholars have also examined the problems of reasonableness in other contexts, such as sexual harassment.[25]

An overwhelming majority of cases in which courts have addressed issues of women's self-defense have involved battered women charged with killing men who battered them. The problems were heightened in cases of battered women who killed their assailants, where myths and misconceptions of battered women as "crazy" or "provocative" made them seem particularly unreasonable. The primary legal issue that emerged, relating to gender bias in the law of self-defense, was the admissibility of expert testimony on battering. The content of much of this testimony focused solely on what became known as "battered woman syndrome"—the psychological impact of the battering on the woman—rather than on her prior responses to violence (such as seeking to protect herself or avoid the violence altogether), on the unresponsiveness of police or health professionals, and on the broader social context of economic resources, family, children, or religion, which constrained her choices. The strategy of admitting expert testimony on battering was developed by feminist lawyers to explain the common experiences and impact of repeated abuse on battered women first in self-defense cases and later in many other cases. A significant number of legal victories have been won in admission of this testimony. In 1984, for example, the New Jersey Supreme Court ruled that this testimony was admissible in *State v. Kelly.*[26] Despite my own involvement in developing the theoretical framework of these cases, I have been concerned with the contradictory implications of the use of expert testimony.

The perspective leading to testimony on battered woman syndrome reflected ongoing tensions and paradoxes within women's self-defense work. Conceived of as a way to remedy the unequal treatment of women resulting from the application of male norms and standards in the criminal justice system, women's self-defense work was intended to assist women to speak in their own voices in the courtroom, and to describe the variety and complexity of their experience. It aimed to expand the legal options available in defending women against charges of homicide or assault beyond the traditional pleas of insanity and incapacity. Expert testimony on battered woman syndrome was developed to explain the common experiences of repeated assault on battered women, and its impact. The goal was to assist the jury and the court in fairly evaluating the reasonableness of the battered woman's action. The notion of expert testimony was predicated on an assumption that battered women's voices either would not be understood or were not strong enough to be heard alone in the courtroom.

Examination of these cases involving battered women has underscored the complexity of the task of expanding defense options for battered women. The cases have demonstrated the tenacity of sex-stereotyping: despite the purposes of this legal strategy, old stereotypes of incapacity have been replicated in a new form. Lawyers who have submitted testimony have primarily focused on the passive, victimized aspects of battered women's experiences—their "learned helplessness"—rather than explaining homicide as a woman's necessary choice to save her own life. Judges and jurors hear this testimony within this context of passivity and victimization. Even the term "syndrome" (and the psychological description of battered women that predominates in "battered woman syndrome") conjures up images of a psychological defense—a separate defense based on an impaired mental state.

Expert testimony on battering has now been used in many different kinds of cases—such as custody and termination of parental rights, in which battering is an issue. It has also been used in many cases where there is a need to explain battered women's actions in a context that might otherwise make these actions inexplicable—such as where a woman has decided to "recant" her prior testimony in support of criminal prosecution of the batterer and change her story because she is afraid for her safety and the safety of her children.[27] Although the development of expert testimony on battering has been critical in assisting battered women to have their experiences and claims heard in court, the content of this testimony has often been problematic. Expert testimony that emphasizes, or is understood to emphasize, only the helplessness or victimization of battered women is necessarily incomplete because it does not address the crucial issue of the particular woman's action, or her agency—namely, how that battered woman acted to save her own life.

In self-defense cases we can see this dilemma concretely. Judges and juries evaluating the self-defense claims of battered women who have killed their batterers are looking at women who have been both victims and actors. In spite of their victimization, these women have mobilized their resources to keep themselves and their children alive, and they ultimately acted to protect themselves. But this emphasis on victimization has the potential to drive lawyers and judges into stereotypical thinking, which might prevent them from understanding the reasonableness of the individual battered woman's act.

As a lawyer, I have argued that in order to present an appropriate explanation of her act, defense lawyers representing a battered woman who has killed her assailant must be sensitive to both victimization and agency; the woman's action has to be put in the context of her own victimization. But while an appreciation of women's experiences as victims is necessary, an exclusive focus on women's victimization is limiting because it ignores women's active efforts to protect themselves and their children, and to mobilize their resources to survive. An exclusive focus on women's agency, reflected in the emphasis on why a woman had not left the battering relationship, is shaped by liberal visions of autonomy and individual control and mobility, which are equally unsatisfactory without the larger social context of victimization.

Both fail to take account of the oppression and resistance that women experience daily in their ongoing relationships. Portrayal of women as *solely* victims or agents is neither accurate nor adequate to explain the complex realities of women's lives.

Judicial and public perception of battered woman syndrome as a form of incapacity has thus had problematic consequences for battered women in many circumstances. But when battered woman syndrome is presented or heard in a way that sounds like passivity or incapacity, it does not address the basic fact of the woman's action and contradicts a presentation of reasonableness. Indeed, the overall impact of the stereotype of battered woman syndrome may be to limit rather than expand the legal options of women who cannot conform to this stereotype. Many women's actions are likely to depart significantly from both the traditional "male" model of self-defense and the passive "battered woman" model because the women are too assertive, aggressive, or insufficiently remorseful. Judges are then not likely to recognize the need for expert testimony. Jury verdicts in battered women cases underscore the difficulty that jurors have in seeing battered women as reasonable. Women are seen as too strong or "together" to fit the definition of victim, particularly when public perceptions of battering are shaped by battered woman syndrome as a kind of learned helplessness. Because racial stereotypes of cultural aggression or passivity exacerbate these problems, women of color may face special hurdles.[28]

The concept of women's reasonableness faces resistance in other contexts. Parallel developments can be seen in the law of sexual harassment. Although some courts have now adopted a "reasonable-woman" standard on the theory that women's experiences with sexual harassment are so distinct that they cannot apply the generic legal standard of reasonableness, feminist scholars have disagreed as to whether this is a good idea or whether it will similarly stereotype women.[29] In the summer of 1991 the movie *Thelma and Louise* ignited public debate about violence against women and the appropriateness of women's violent responses, and suggested a vast gender gap between women and men on these issues.[30] That fall, Anita Hill alleged that Judge Clarence Thomas had sexually harassed her, and the Senate Judiciary Committee held a four-day hearing. Although many feminists were hopeful that these proceedings would educate the public about the issue of sexual harassment, the pernicious use of sexist and racist stereotypes that unfolded during the hearing demonstrated the public — and senatorial — resistance to the notion of women as reasonable.[31] Anita Hill, calm and composed, was viewed either as too remote or as delusional, while Clarence Thomas, who exploded in rage before the committee, was viewed as forceful and reasonable.[32]

Continuing public resistance to the concept of a woman's reasonableness underscores the long-term nature of feminist legal work; feminist legal advocates may have underestimated the psychological barriers to seeing women as reasonable. The enormous credibility problems that women face as complainants and witnesses seem almost insurmountable. Yet adopting a separate standard of reasonableness, either for battered women in particular, for victims of sexual harassment, or for women in general, remains problematic. There is no single "reasonable woman," and adopting a separate standard for battered women in particular or women in general will penalize women's varied experiences and women's departures from a stereotypical male norm.[33] It is important to challenge the concept of reasonableness in general and to ensure that it includes the wealth of both women's and men's individual experiences.

Reinterpreting Battered Women's Agency

Although notions of victimization and agency seem embedded in both legal and cultural images of battered women, it is crucial to understand that these concepts are socially constructed and that women's experiences can be envisioned and interpreted in a different way. Linda Gordon's historical examination of battered women's efforts to assert their own interests in the late nineteenth and early twentieth centuries is instructive in this regard. In seeking to understand battered women's actions and their formation of ideas in responding to abuse, Gordon raises key questions concerning the social construction of women's victimization, women's agency, and women's resistance to abuse. She stresses that any concept of autonomy or agency must be understood as shaped by social forces, and that forms of "agency are endlessly variable." At the same time, she cautions against romanticizing responses of resistance, for "concepts like agency and resistance do not mean victory: nor should they work to soften the ugly and painful history of victimization." She emphasizes that "resistance is itself an interpretation, a construction, one participated in by the historian and reader, as certainly as by the wife-beating victim herself."[34]

Gordon's insights suggest the subtlety of the themes of agency and resistance and raise important issues with respect to feminist lawmaking generally. A more textured analysis of the interrelationship between women's oppression and acts of resistance to abuse is crucial: we must seek both to understand the social context of women's oppression, which shapes women's choices and constrains women's agency and resistance, and to examine manifestations of women's agency and resistance more contextually. This means rejecting simple dichotomies and accepting contradiction and ambiguity in women's lives. As Kathryn Abrams has argued, feminist legal work should seek "more complex, contingent accounts of gender discrimination and women as subjects."[35]

Feminist legal scholarship provides promising examples of such efforts. Dorothy Roberts' work on motherhood and crime details the meaning of both oppression and resistance, exploring the possibility of "resistance theory that restores the critical return of human agency, while recognizing the constraints of structure." She examines these issues in the context of crimes involving women's failure to mother, exploring how the criminal law both enforces the subordinating aspects of motherhood and punishes women's resistance to their political situation as mothers. Angela Harris has identified the complex dynamics of victimization and agency in communities of color: "Black women have simultaneously acknowledged their own victimization and the victimization of black men by a system that has consistently ignored violence against women by perpetrating it against men." Martha Mahoney has thoughtfully explored the interrelationship between oppression and resistance for battered women, examining the concept of exit in battering and sexual harassment as an example of the limited notion of agency.[36]

Battered women, activists, and theorists criticize the way legal images of battered women frequently depict them as passive in the face of abuse if they have not left the relationship. Women who are battered may be unable to bring a battering relationship to an end, but they may be constantly planning and asserting themselves — strategizing, in ways that are carefully hidden from the batterer, to contribute to their own safety and to that of their children. They may be negotiating and carefully hiding small but important acts of independence so as to mitigate "separation assault." They may be gathering information, seeking money and support to assist them when they leave, and succeeding in breaking away only after multiple attempts.

Kathryn Abrams describes these actions as a form of what she calls "resistant self-direction." She says: "A woman who exhibits independence within, or seeks to extricate herself from, an abusive relationship may be met with domestic violence. The ways in which women respond to these challenges often constitute a form of self-direction or an effort to negotiate gender-based obstacles in order to achieve these larger goals. These responses, however, do not always involve explicit confrontation; therefore they are not always recognized as forms of resistance or manifestations of agency." She argues that this is a mistake: "These aspects of battered women's self-direction need to be recognized as a form of agency. They permit battered women to protect their children, to preserve specific portions of their lives, and in some cases, to exit their abusive relationships. These examples of battered women's self-direction also reflect agency's variable, context-specific, nonunitary character. A woman's self-assertion may be prominent in some contexts of her life and virtually absent in others. Examined across time, or in different areas of a woman's life, it may present a multi-faceted picture of her ability to direct her course."[37] Yet as she suggests, this notion of self-direction as a form of agency is more partial and variable than the unitary, all-or-nothing agency of liberal theory.

This more complex vision of agency will be difficult to capture in law, but it presents a crucial challenge for feminist lawmaking. Like historians and readers, lawyers and clients are participants in interpretation of facts and legal arguments that can construct and reconstruct our understandings of agency. In litigation and law-reform contexts, lawyers and advocates must examine, unearth, and describe aspects of battered women's lives that constitute dimensions of self-direction, which an emphasis on exit has rendered invisible. They also must emphasize broader problems of contradiction and complexity, and shifting combinations of choice and restriction within which these actions take place.[38]

At the same time, it is critical that these more complex accounts of human nature and agency should not be limited to lawmaking, but should be integrated into popular and legal debates as well. Lawmaking is shaped by culture, and culture shapes lawmaking. In order to make the experiences of women who have been battered understandable and to shape the thinking of both legal decision makers and the broader public, it is important to emphasize these issues in the particular contexts of battered women, but to draw parallels between battered women's experiences and more general dilemmas of social constraint and choice. Recognition of the existence of both choice and constraint in women's lives, and description of this complexity in both law-making and culture, can move us beyond the dichotomy of victimization and agency that has impeded justice for battered women.

6

The Violence of Privacy

Historically, male battering of women was untouched by law, protected as part of the private sphere of family life. This rhetoric of privacy, the "veil of relationship," has been the most important ideological obstacle to legal change and reform.[1] Since the battered women's movement in this country has made issues of battering visible, battering is no longer perceived as a purely private problem and has taken on the dimensions of a public issue. The explosion of legal reform and social service efforts — the development of battered women's shelters and hotlines, and new legal remedies developed for battered women — has been premised on the idea of battering as a public harm. Nevertheless, widespread resistance to acknowledging battering as a public issue continues.

Concepts of privacy permit, encourage, and reinforce violence against women. The notion of marital privacy has been a source of oppression to battered women and has helped to perpetuate women's subordination within the family. The idea of privacy continues to pose a challenge to theoretical and practical work on woman abuse. The ideological tenacity of conceptions of battering as "private" is revealed in the meanings of "public" and "private" in American family life; in the Supreme Court's decision in *Deshaney v. Winnebago County Department of Social Services*;[2] in the inadequacy of legal reform efforts to date; and in tensions that persist within the battered women's movement.

Meanings of Private and Public in the Family

The dichotomy of "public" and "private" has shaped our understandings of gender. The traditional notion of separate spheres is premised on a dichotomy between the private world of family and domestic life (the "women's sphere"), and the public world of marketplace (the "men's sphere").[3] In 1982 Nadine Taub and I examined the difference between the role of law in the public sphere and its role in the private sphere.[4] In the public sphere, sex-based exclusionary laws join with other institutional and ideological constraints to limit women's participation directly. In the private sphere, the legal system operates more subtly: the law claims to be absent in the private sphere, and historically it has refused to intervene in ongoing family relations. We described the traditional role of privacy in family law in the following way:

> Tort law, which is generally concerned with injuries inflicted on individuals, has traditionally been held inapplicable to injuries inflicted by one family member on another. Under the doctrines of interspousal and parent-child immunity, courts have consistently denied recoveries for injuries that would be compensable but for the fact that they occurred in the private realm. In the same way, criminal law declined to punish intentional injuries to family members. Common law and statutory definitions of rape in many states continue to carve out a special exception for a husband's forced intercourse with his wife. Wife beating was initially omitted from the definition of criminal assault on the ground that a husband had the right to chastise his wife. Even today, after courts have explicitly rejected the definitional exception and its rationale, judges, prosecutors, and police officers decline to enforce assault laws in the family context.[5]

Some aspects of this legal system have changed today—there is no longer interspousal immunity, and marital rape has been recognized—but the vestiges of these rationales continue in the law. Although a dichotomous view of the public sphere and the private sphere has some heuristic value and considerable rhetorical appeal, the dichotomy is overdrawn. The notion of a sharp demarcation between public and private has been widely rejected by feminist and critical scholars.[6] In practice, no realm of personal and family life exists totally separate from the reach of the state. The state defines both the family, the so-called private sphere, and the market, the so-called public sphere; "private" and "public" exist on a continuum.

Consequently, in the sphere of domestic and family life, purportedly immune from law, the law is always being applied, though selectively. "Privacy" is selectively invoked as a rationale for immunity in order to protect male domination. For example, when the police do not respond to a battered woman's call for assistance, or when a civil court refuses to evict her assailant, the woman is relegated to self-help, while the man who beats her receives the law's tacit encouragement and support.[7] Legislative and prosecutorial efforts to control women's conduct during pregnancy in the form of "fetal" protection laws—premised on the notion that women's childbearing capacity, and pregnancy itself, subject them to public regulation and control—provide another example. A pregnant battered woman may face criminal prosecution for drinking liquor, but a man who batters her does so with impunity.[8]

The rhetoric of privacy that has isolated the female world from the legal order sends a message to the rest of society. It devalues women and their functions and says that women are not important enough to merit legal regulation:

> This message is clearly communicated when particular relief is withheld. By declining to punish a man for inflicting injuries on his wife, for example, the law implies she is his property and he is free to control her as he sees fit. Women's work is discredited when the law refuses to enforce the man's obligation to support his wife, since it implies she makes no contribution worthy of support. Similarly, when courts decline to enforce contracts that seek to limit or specify the extent of the wife's services, the law implies that household work is not real work in the way that the type of work subject to contract in the public sphere is real work. These are important messages, for denying woman's humanity and the value of her traditional work are key ideological components in maintaining women's subordinate status. The message of women's inferiority is compounded by the totality of the law's absence from the private realm. In our society, law is for business and other important things. The fact that the law in general claims to have so little bearing on women's day-to-day concerns reflects and underscores their insignificance. Thus, the legal order's overall contribution to the devaluation of women is greater than the sum of the negative messages conveyed by individual legal doctrines.[9]

The concept of privacy has historically been viewed as problematic by feminist theorists. Privacy rests on a division of public and private that has been oppressive to women and has supported male dominance in the family. The concept reinforces the idea that the personal is separate from the political; privacy also implies a realm that should be kept secret. Privacy inures to the benefit of the individual, not the community. The right of privacy has been viewed as a passive right, one which says that the state cannot intervene.[10]

Nevertheless, privacy is important for all people—particularly women.[11] It provides an opportunity for individual self-development, for individual decision making, and for protection against endless caretaking. Rights to autonomy, equality, liberty, and freedom of bodily integrity are central to women's independence and well-being. For women who have been battered, these aspects of privacy are particularly relevant. Remedies for intimate violence must preserve opportunities for safety, seclusion, intimacy, and individual decision making.

Definitions of "private" and "public" in any particular legal context can and do constantly shift. Their meanings are based on social and cultural assumptions of what is valued and important, and these assumptions are deeply gendered. Thus, the interrelationship between what is understood and experienced as "private" and what is understood and experienced as "public" is particularly complex in the area of gender, where the rhetoric of privacy masks inequality and subordination. The decision about what we protect as private is a political decision that always has public ramifications.[12]

Privacy and Denial

Although battering has evolved from a private to a more public issue, the depth of social resistance to change cannot be minimized. The concept of battering is deeply threatening. It strikes at our most fundamental assumptions about the nature of intimate relations and the safeness of family life. The concept of male battering of women as a private issue exerts a powerful ideological pull on our consciousness; by seeing woman abuse as private, we affirm it as a problem that is individual and involves only a particular intimate relationship, for which there is no social responsibility to remedy. We need to deny its seriousness and pervasiveness in order to distance ourselves from the possibility of it in our own lives, to deny the interconnectedness of battering with so many other aspects of family life and gender relations. As a result, instead of focusing on the batterer, we focus on the battered woman, scrutinize her conduct, examine her pathology, and blame her for remaining in the relationship, in order to maintain our denial and our failure to confront the more basic and disturbing issues of power and control in intimate relationships. Focusing on the woman, not the man, perpetuates the power of patriarchy. Denial supports and legitimates this power, and the concept of privacy is a key aspect of this denial.

This process of denial takes many forms and operates on many levels. Men deny battering in order to protect their own privilege.[13] Women need to deny the pervasiveness of the problem so as not to link it to their own lives. Individual women who are battered tend to minimize the violence in order to distance themselves from some internalized negative concept of a "battered woman." I see denial in the attitudes of jurors, who try to remove themselves from the experiences of the battered and think "this could never happen to me; if it did, I would handle it differently."[14] I see denial in the public engagement in the 1988 case involving Hedda Nussbaum and Joel Steinberg, which focused on Nussbaum's complicity for the death of their child and involved feminists in active controversy over the boundaries of victimization.[15] The reports of the many state task forces on gender bias in the courts have painstakingly recorded judicial attitudes of denial.[16] Clearly, there is serious denial on the part of state legislators, members of Congress, and members of the executive branch who do not discuss battering as a public issue. In battering, we see both the power of denial and the denial of power. The concept of privacy is an ideological rationale for this denial and serves to maintain it.

For these reasons, the concept of privacy has encouraged, reinforced, and supported violence against women. Privacy says that violence against women is immune from sanction, that it is acceptable and part of the basic fabric of American family life. Privacy says that what goes on in the violent relationship should not be the subject of state or community intervention. Privacy says that battering is an individual problem, not a systemic one. Privacy operates as a mask for inequality, protecting male violence against women.

Shifting Parameters of Private and Public for Battered Women

As work on battered women has evolved, social meanings of what is private and public, and the relationship between them, have become more complex. Traditionally, battering was viewed as within the private sphere of the family, and therefore unprotected by law. Yet, as Martha Minow has suggested, this social failure to intervene in battering on grounds of privacy should be seen not as separate from the violence, but as part of the violence: "When clerks in a local court harass a woman who applies for a restraining order against the violence in her home, they are part of the violence. Society is organized to permit violence in the home; it is organized through images in mass media and through broadly based social attitudes that condone violence. Society permits such violence to go unchallenged through the isolation of families and the failures of police to respond. Public, rather than private, patterns of conduct and morals are implicated. Some police officers refuse to respond to domestic violence; some officers themselves abuse their spouses. Some clerks and judges think domestic violence matters do not belong in court. These failures to respond to domestic violence are public, not private, actions."[17]

Although social failure to respond to problems of battered women has been justified on grounds of privacy, this failure to respond is an affirmative political decision that has serious public consequences. The rationale of privacy masks the political nature of the decision. Privacy thus plays a particularly pernicious role in supporting, encouraging, and legitimizing violence against women and other battered partners or family members. The state actively permits this violence by protecting the privileges and prerogatives of the batterer and failing to protect the battered women, and by prosecuting battered women for homicide when they act to protect themselves. These failures to respond, or selective responses, are part of "public patterns of conduct and morals."[18]

As legal reform efforts for battered women have developed, the border between public and private, concerning issues of battered women, has shifted. In some sense, the public dimension of the problem has expanded. Courts have rendered legal decisions holding police officers liable for money damages for failure to intervene to protect battered women; we have experienced an explosion of state legal remedies to protect battered women; and advocates have secured federal legislation to assist battered women in implementing remedies. These gains suggest at least a recognition by governmental bodies, speaking with a public voice, that they must acknowledge and address the problem. Some of the rhetoric surrounding issues of battering has shifted from the language of private to the language of public.

Yet, on the level of practice, it is questionable which remedies, if any, are likely to provide real protection for those women who are abused, or leverage to change their lives. Some aspects of the legal process may be significant because it may be important for a battered woman to be able to state in a public forum what happened, and to be taken seriously by the judge. But none of these legal processes—not orders of protection, nor arrest alone—protect the woman, change her partner's intimate behavior, or create life support and alternatives to enable her to be safe. In addition, because most women who are abused in any of these contexts lack legal representation, meaningful access to these remedies is severely limited, especially for women without financial means.

Even as legal remedies and public perceptions have changed, the notion of family violence as relegated to the private sphere was given additional support by the Supreme Court's 1989 decision in *DeShaney v. Winnebago County Department of Social Services*. In *DeShaney*, the Court held that the state had no affirmative responsibility to protect a child who had been permanently injured as a result of abuse committed by his custodial father, even when the state had been investigating the child abuse for several years. The majority opinion reflects a crabbed view of the world that reasserts a clear distinction between public and private: family violence is private and therefore immune from state scrutiny because, implicitly, the state had no business to be there in the first place and no responsibility to intervene at all. *DeShaney* has been interpreted by courts around the country to limit police liability in civil suits brought by battered women.[19]

The tension between public and private also is evident in the issue of what legal processes are available to battered women, and what the social meaning of those processes is to battered women and to society at large. For example, civil remedies known as restraining orders, or orders of protection, are court orders with flexible provisions that a battered woman can obtain to stop a man from beating her, prevent him from coming to the house, or evict him from the house. Criminal statutes provide for the arrest of batterers, either for beating or for violation of protective orders.[20] Although serious problems in the enforcement and implementation of these orders remain, the fact that these formal legal processes exist is evidence of a developing understanding of the public dimension of the problem. By giving battered women remedies in court, the need for public scrutiny, public control, and public sanction has at least theoretically been acknowledged. In addition, some states impose marriage license fees to generate funds for battered women's services, thus making a statement about the public impact of purportedly private conduct as well as implying an ideological link between marriage and violence. Some of these state statutory provisions have been challenged by battering men.[21]

At the same time that these remedies have been developing, a move toward more private and informal processes, notably mediation, has been under way. Most battered women's advocates are critical of mediation, because they believe that informal modes of dispute resolution substantially hurt battered women who are disadvantaged with respect to power, money, and resources. Mediation is viewed as signaling that battering is the women's individual "problem" that should be "worked out," and that the state has no role in it. The general mood in legal circles that favors alternative dispute resolution has helped to legitimate mediation and obscure its problematic implications in this context. The move to mediation and other more informal processes can also be understood as a reflection of the low priority that the law accords family issues generally, and battered women's problems in particular.[22]

Criminal remedies for battering, particularly mandatory arrest provisions, are now widespread. Activists have argued that criminal remedies generally, and mandatory arrest in particular, send a clear social message that battering is impermissible, and that because criminal remedies are prosecuted by the state, they give more public force to the sanction. Yet even civil remedies, such as orders of protection and tort suits brought by individual women against batterers, send a social message. The lawsuits use formal court processes and are subject to public scrutiny, and the legal decisions they produce make a public statement. Tort actions in particular may carry a greater social meaning in light of the demise of interspousal immunity, the social dimension of the claimed harm, and the affirmative nature of the claim for damages.[23] Other examples of alternative procedural frameworks that have a public meaning include the articulation of battering as a civil rights violation, as an international human rights violation, and as involuntary servitude.[24] There is a fundamental contradiction, however, in the gap between the articulation of these approaches on the "grand" level of theory and their implementation on the "ground" level of practice. Here, both theory and practice necessarily reflect our fundamental ambivalence about privacy.

Reva Siegel's documentation of the historical evolution of legal rationales concerning domestic violence supports this view of social ambivalence toward, and tenacity of, privacy rationales in legal reform. She suggests that although treatment of domestic violence in the law has moved from a rule of chastisement to views that protect domestic violence as within the "veil of privacy," this reform of legal status has largely legitimated violence, made it more palatable and more invisible. Even reforms that appear to revise the law dramatically, such as the Violence Against Women Act of 1994, contain the seeds of ambivalence toward violence that characterize what she calls "prerogative and privacy." Siegel's work underscores the importance of critical analysis of the inevitable role of privacy in shaping legal reform on domestic violence.[25]

At the same time, the development of more formal processes has promoted public education and helped to redefine violence as a public issue. Because of the availability of these legal remedies, more court proceedings take place, and participants, judiciary, court personnel, and public are educated about the problem of domestic violence. Public participation in these disputes may well have contributed to changing attitudes concerning the acceptability of violence against women.[26] The media frequently focus on court cases, producing many newspaper articles and television programs about cases involving violence against women.[27] Further, analysis of the actual implementation of these legal remedies, and of the failure of the courts to enforce their provisions, has been widely publicized in many state reports on gender bias and has expanded the educational process within the states.

The development of these more formal processes has also been important to battered women themselves. One empirical study of battered women's experiences in obtaining restraining orders in New Haven, Connecticut, concluded that temporary restraining orders help battered women in ways other than increasing police responsiveness or deterring violent men; "the process is (or can be) the empowerment." The authors of the study, Molly Chaudhuri and Kathleen Daly, stress that "this occurs when attorneys listen to battered women, giving them time and attention, and when judges understand their situation, giving them support and courage." They also observe: "As important, although unfortunately less frequent, women's empowerment can occur when men admit to what they have done in a public forum. Such conversations and admissions can transform the violence from a private familial matter, for which many women blame themselves, to a public setting where men are made accountable for their acts." [28]

The New Haven study underscores the importance of legal representation, another issue that reveals the tension between public and private. Although battered women now have remedies that are available to them "on the books," they have no assured access to lawyers to represent them. Many battered women cannot afford to hire a lawyer. Moreover, few lawyers are sensitive to their particular problems. State statutory schemes do not provide for counsel; indeed, many of the protective-order statutes specifically provide the option for battered women to represent themselves.[29] Battered women's advocates—formerly battered women or shelter workers themselves, usually without formal legal training—are now the link between battered women and the legal system, as well as between battered women and the child welfare and social service systems. For battered women, access to advocates shapes their satisfaction with the legal process.[30]Although battered women's advocacy has played a critical role for battered women and has contributed a woman-centered form of representation, it is necessarily limited. Even what may appear as the narrowest legal question concerning restraining orders may involve complex legal issues that affect divorce, support, and custody. Lack of skilled legal representation to assist in these necessarily interrelated matters has a deleterious impact on battered women's lives and safety.

None of the plethora of new state and federal legal remedies provide free counsel, so battered women's advocates assist many battered women who would not otherwise have had legal representation. Many battered women cannot use these legal remedies. If counsel were required but not provided by the state, those battered women who could not pay for representation would be severely disadvantaged. Only the provision of free counsel who are knowledgeable about these issues would make a substantial difference. Thus, although in theory more formal legal process for battered women might be preferable, in practice, under the present conditions of scarce legal resources and cutbacks in legal services, it may not be realistic.

Finally, the complex interrelationship between the private and the public can be seen within the battered women's movement itself. Remember that the terms "woman abuse" and "battered woman" did not exist before the movement developed. As Nancy Fraser has observed, "Linguistically, [wife beating] was classified with the disciplining of children and servants as a 'domestic,' as opposed to a 'political' matter." Feminist activists in the battered women's movement named the problem in a different way; they claimed that battering was not a personal, domestic problem but a systemic, political problem. Fraser notes that feminist redefinition of battered women's needs transcended the "conventional separation of sphere": "In order to be free from dependence on batterers, battered women needed not just temporary shelter but also jobs paying a 'family wage,' day care and affordable permanent housing."[31]

The battered women's movement, then, began with a clearly political and public agenda. Battered women were viewed primarily not as individual victims, but as potential feminist activists. Activists organized battered women's shelters, which functioned as woman-centered refuges as well as sites of consciousness-raising; the organization of shelters was non-hierarchical and egalitarian, and many formerly battered women went on to become counselors or advocates. Many battered women who blamed themselves for having been abused developed a more political perspective and began to identify with other women rather than with the men who battered them.[32]

As woman abuse became a more legitimate political issue, battered women's organizations and shelters began to receive government funding.

Fraser recounts that "a variety of new, administrative constraints ranging from accounting procedures to regulation, accreditation and professionalization requirements were imposed."[33] Many organizations began to develop a service perspective rather than to consider themselves activists. This had a substantive impact on the earlier, more explicitly political vision:

> As a consequence, publicly funded shelters underwent a transformation. Increasingly, they were staffed by professional social workers, many of whom had not themselves experienced battery. Thus, a division between professional and client supplanted the more fluid continuum of relations that characterized the earlier shelters. Moreover, many social work staff have been trained to frame problems in a quasi-psychiatric perspective. This perspective structures the practices of many publicly funded shelters even despite the intentions of individual staff, many of whom are politically committed feminists. Consequently, the practices of such shelters have become more individualizing and less politicized. Battered women tend now to be positioned as clients. They are only rarely addressed as potential feminist activists. Increasingly, the language game of therapy has supplanted that of consciousness raising. And the neutral scientific language of "spouse abuse" has supplanted more political talk of "male violence against women." Finally, the needs of battered women have been substantially reinterpreted. The very far-reaching earlier claims for the social and economic prerequisites of independence have tended to give way to a narrower focus on the individual woman's problems of "low self esteem."[34]

The battered women's movement has thus experienced the tension between a systemic "public" definition of the problem and an individualistic "privatized" vision. Within the movement and within the service and advocacy community, internal pressures propel the move to a more privatized definition and experience of battering. Claims of privacy encourage a focus on the individual, and they discourage collective definition, systemic analysis, and consequent social responsibility. This tendency has also affected public definitions of battering. The phenomenon of denial, which functions to keep individuals from acknowledging battering as a potential ingredient of all intimate relationships, is at work here as well.

Concepts of public and private have thus had a considerable impact on feminist lawmaking on battering. Rationales invoking privacy pervade and constrain feminist lawmaking. Privacy rhetoric continues to shape law reform and activism in a subtle but powerful way.

Implementing Feminist Lawmaking

7

Battered Women, Feminist Lawmaking, and Legal Practice

The process of legal reform on issues of domestic violence has taken place within the large-scale conceptualization of new legal remedies based on new social perceptions of domestic violence. It also occurs "on the ground," in the translation of these approaches into legal claims in everyday cases involving legal representation of battered women. In this chapter I examine generic aspects of this process of translation, and the barriers to battered women's voices being heard in the law.

In theory, feminist lawmaking on battering is a process by which women's experiences with battering are translated into law. But this oversimplified statement presents many problems: the first is the conceptual and epistemological question of who women are, who battered women are, and whether there is some distinct or common experience that battered women share. Assuming that the answer to this last question is a qualified and strategic yes — that women do lead what Martha Fineman has called "gendered lives"[1] — the translation of these experiences into legal claims faces many hurdles. The process of social, cultural, and legal construction of battered women in law, which makes it difficult for battered women's experiences to be reflected in law, is complex and is only beginning to be detailed.

The Complexity of Incorporating Women's Experiences into Law

Feminist lawmaking involves describing, but what experience or experiences of women are being described? The move within feminist legal practice to incorporate women's experiences, fundamental to feminist legal theory, intersects with the jurisprudential move to what has, somewhat self-consciously, now been termed the move to "narrative," to law as a form of storytelling. Storytelling—using the "stories" of clients as the essential factual matrix of the case—has always been an essential part of good lawyering, and narrative accounts of battered women's experience have historically been incorporated into feminist lawmaking. The move to narrative in legal scholarship has strengthened this theme in legal reform work on battered women. State task force reports on gender bias have also been a rich source of stories and experiences about violence.[2] This work has, in turn, had an impact on legal practice, for many younger lawyers who have read these articles and reports, or who have been exposed to law school clinics, courses, or advocacy programs, now explicitly use and reflect the experiences of battered women in their own lawyering.[3]

This proliferation of legal exposure to, and experience with, issues of battering has affected the resolution of cases from the highest to the lowest level of judicial decision making. At the highest level, we have *Planned Parenthood v. Casey,* the Supreme Court's 1992 decision on abortion, in which the Court's conclusion—that Pennsylvania's spousal notification rule was unconstitutional—was shaped by a view of the relationship between marriage, abuse, and notification, and a broad understanding of the coercive dimension of violence in heterosexual relationships, which had been presented in amicus curiae briefs emphasizing battering.[4] In many other cases in the Supreme Court and in state and federal courts, issues that affect battered women have been carefully presented in amicus briefs in order to educate the court.[5] Nevertheless, it is questionable whether the stories of "outsiders" generally, or women in particular, can ever really be heard. If "different" perspectives are reflected in the lawmaking process, does the translation of those experiences into the legal system disqualify and subvert them?

Even if we consider battered women's voices to be distinct, many obstacles impede women from easily expressing themselves and having their voices heard in society and, by implication, in law. Carol Gilligan identifies some of the issues that may make it difficult for women to be heard. For Gilligan, Anita Hill's testifying against Clarence Thomas was a profound historical moment. Gilligan remembers "listening to Anita Hill—hearing her, and *then hearing her not being heard.*" Gilligan's story of Anita Hill is a parable for the problems of "second-stage" feminism, in particular, and for feminist lawmaking in general. The first stage is to recognize women's different voice, or voices, and to make it possible for these voices to be heard. The second stage is to recognize all the ways women's voices can be heard and yet not *really* heard — to identify what I call the complexities of voice.[6]

In law, women's voices have only just begun to be heard. They have had an impact on reshaping the law in such areas as violence against women, employment discrimination, family law, and reproductive rights. An explosion of feminist legal scholarship has explored issues affecting women in almost every area of the law. Women are entering the legal profession in droves, and there are now two women on the Supreme Court. The evolution of feminist legal theory and practice has meant that a wide range of women's experiences are now brought into the open. Experiences that were previously invisible — rape, intimate violence, sexual harassment, incest — are now made visible. But this visibility does not mean that women are really being listened to, or that the listener (or society at large) gets the point.

Progress has been made, then, in incorporating women's voices into law, but these voices may not really be heard. The first reason why it is difficult for women's voices to be heard is that there many "different voices." Feminist activists and scholars now recognize a wide range of theoretical perspectives, feminisms, and feminist strategies.[7] The development of a strong multicultural feminist community, broad critiques of feminist essentialism, and attention to issues of race, ethnicity, class, disability, and heterosexism have also enriched feminist dialogue. Yet these developments highlight a paradox in feminist theory and practice, which Deborah Rhode describes: "By definition, feminism claims to speak from the experience of women, yet that experience counsels attention to its own diversity, and to the role of contextual variations and multiple identities in mediating gender differences."[8] Many issues — such as the "reasonable-woman" standard for sexual harassment — spark lively disagreement among feminist legal advocates.[9]

Many of the issues that women are raising, like those of violence or sexual harassment, are extremely threatening and bring conflict into the open. Gilligan suggests that in the face of such conflict, men disconnect from women's concerns and women dissociate parts of their selves; both responses might be understood as forms of denial.[10] This description resonates with lawyers' observations that both men and women may be problematic jurors in cases involving battered women who have been charged with homicide or assault of an intimate partner. Male jurors are more likely to minimize the violence or blame the woman; women jurors are more likely to say "I wouldn't let that happen to me."[11]

The general lack of credibility accorded to women is another serious problem. Judges may let women's voices into the courtroom, but state task forces on gender bias, and a wide range of scholarly literature, confirm that women's voices, whether as litigant or expert, are not accorded much weight even when they are admitted.[12] We can also identify many subtle ways of what Gilligan calls "shutting women up" after they have gained access to the institutions where they had historically not been welcome: "reimposing the values of the traditional disciplines,"[13] writing graffiti on the walls of the bathroom, telling women that they will be ostracized if they take women's studies courses or identify themselves as feminists, or including misogynistic comments in course evaluations. And if women's voices *are* really heard, there is always backlash, for the best way to undermine the message is to kill the messenger.[14] Think, for example, of the scrutiny to which Anita Hill has been subjected, ranging from David Brock's scurrilous attack to countless explorations of her personal life.[15]

Nevertheless, I share Carol Gilligan's hope, for women do speak up and resist. Gilligan refers to "political resistance," particularly on the part of adolescent girls with whom she has worked; she perceives "girls continuing to speak what they were feeling and thinking and to talk about what they were seeing and hearing when it went against the grain of what was socially constructed or generally accepted as true."[16] I see this in my own daughter, Anna, and in Shannon Faulkner's courageous fight to enter the Citadel.[17] This sort of resistance is what made Anita Hill speak up and what will give other girls and women the courage to speak up.

Lawyers and Lawyering

The process of feminist lawmaking necessarily involves an investigation of how feminist arguments are developed and constructed by lawyers as well as how they are constructed by courts. Substantive legal doctrines have been developed by men; they were created with the concerns and experiences of men in mind, and reflect their perspectives on the world. Moreover, legal doctrines and legal reasoning have been shaped by perspectives that largely reflect the viewpoints and experiences of the dominant, white, middle-class male. Feminist legal theory has been primarily concerned with the gendered frameworks of legal doctrines and legal reasoning, and with the male standards implicit in the norms that are central to legal reasoning. Feminist legal theory has also been concerned with the epistemological standpoint from which law operates—as Catharine MacKinnon describes, its claim of "point-of-viewlessness."[18]

Bias in the law has a substantial impact on the way many lawyers have understood, and been able to present, arguments based on women's experiences in the legal arena. Although intimate violence is a widespread problem that affects almost every aspect of legal practice, most lawyers are unfamiliar with its dynamics. They have not been adequately trained to consider this issue, or to deal with clients who may have been abused. Many women who have been battered are reluctant to talk about their experiences, particularly to lawyers, and many lawyers do not know how to pick up signals concerning possible battering. The historic predominance of men in the legal profession, along with the male "tilt" in the categories of law, makes such communication even more difficult, but women lawyers may face similar problems. Moreover, lawyers may have been personally involved in violence and have ethical conflicts in representation.[19]

As a result, in almost every field, cases continue to proliferate in which battering may be an issue but is not made visible in either the factual development or the legal argumentation in the case—because the client did not tell the lawyer, because the lawyer did not ask, or because the lawyer was not aware of how abuse might affect the particular legal issue that needed resolution. Lawyers who are sensitive to issues of abuse or experienced with representing women who have been abused frequently discover that some case on which they are working, where there was prior counsel, involves issues of abuse that had not been raised. Often, it is too late to raise them.

For these reasons, it is crucial to educate lawyers and law students about domestic violence. Courses or clinical programs are now being offered in many law schools, and volunteer advocacy groups, law school casebooks, and course materials are being developed. Continuing Legal Education training programs are available for lawyers in practice. The American Bar Association Commission on Domestic Violence has published a book for lawyers in general practice entitled *The Impact of Domestic Violence on Your Legal Practice,* which has been widely distributed to lawyers across the United States, and treatises on domestic violence are being published.[20] Protocols concerning battering should be made even more available to all practicing lawyers, to assist them in being attentive to whether a case involves issues of abuse.

Even if most lawyers were sensitive to these issues, however, there would still be the matter of how they present them to courts. Like any other aspect of legal representation, interpreting what facts are significant, developing creative legal theories and legal argumentation, and carefully choosing the words to convey the impact of abuse on the particular situation are always a matter of judgment and discretion. Biases, myths, misconceptions, and personal experience can have a subtle but powerful impact on a lawyer's judgment. Normative views of intimate violence, personal experience, and gender bias are likely to influence a lawyer's ability to hear the story of a woman who is battered, and to affect whether a lawyer perceives a woman client who is battered as pathological or reasonable. These views and experiences, then, inevitably influence the factual and legal argumentation presented in the case.

The Process of Proof

It is now widely recognized that "women's evidence is often still suspect in the law." Consequently, as Kim Scheppele has observed, law reform and the passage of helpful laws do not inevitably provide victories for women, for application of these laws will still rest on interpretation of the laws of evidence. In the area of domestic violence, overt sexism may be limited, but more persistent aspects of sexism "have been merely pushed underground." Scheppele has examined how sexism operates in the interpretation, construction, and production of "facts." [21] Feminist evidence scholars, who are sensitive to issues of sexism generally and to issues of woman abuse particularly, have begun to challenge assumptions about what evidence "counts." [22]

Scheppele focuses on dimensions of evidentiary "truth" that work to the severe disadvantage of women who have experienced "sexualized violence." Those women who delay in telling their stories of abuse at the hands of men, or who appear to change their stories over time, are likely to be disbelieved and discredited as liars; the fact of delay or change is considered evidence that the story cannot possibly be true. But as Scheppele describes, "abused women frequently have exactly this response: they repress what happened; they cannot speak; they hesitate, waver and procrastinate; they hope the abuse will go away; they cover up for their abusers; they try harder to be 'good girls' and they take the blame for the abuse upon themselves. Such actions produce delayed or altered stories over time, which are then disbelieved for the very reason that they have been revised." [23]

Scheppele suggests that underlying this notion is the premise that "truth is singular, immediately apparent and permanent." But women who have been subjected to abuse are frequently silent—they do not discuss the events with anyone they know, and they are often unwilling to talk to police or other officials. If they do talk about what they have experienced, they frequently underestimate the harm or present versions of what happened that will try to normalize the harm—versions that will describe the abuse in such a way that they do not have to confront the consequences of what they have experienced. In psychological terms, they frequently manifest signs of post-traumatic stress disorder: "Survivors of extraordinary brutality often literally cannot say what they have seen or put into words the terror that they have felt. Picking through the shards of a former life, survivors can no longer put the pieces into relation with each other to tell a coherent and compelling narrative about how things disintegrated. As therapists who have worked with traumatized patients have noted, 'the survivor's initial account of the event may be repetitious, stereo-typed and emotionless. . . . It does not develop or progress in time, and it does not reveal the storyteller's feelings or interpretations of events.' As women's safety in the world has been shattered, so too has their sense of narrative co-herence."[24]

But as women speak out, they frequently revise their stories. Psychologist Judith Herman, who has written on the impact of violence, describes this process of revision as a sign of recovery from abuse. Scheppele observes that these shifting stories may also be responses to mainstream cultural narratives that perceive violence as "normatively unexpected" rather than the reverse. Women then have to explain why the violence happened to them—for, according to common assumptions, "if a man is violent, then he must have had a reason."[25]

This problem of unreliability can be addressed in the law in several ways. First, evidence showing a pattern of conduct, or several women's stories that support each other or corroborating physical evidence that supports the woman's story, may shift the circumstances. Credibility of revised stories can also be reinforced through the use of expert testimony.

But other aspects of lawmaking, truth finding, and the process of proof are, as Scheppele puts it, socially situated practices: "Working out how information is constituted as fact or . . . how information is 'enfacted' requires both looking at the way conventions of practice are historically, socially and cultur-ally situated in the lives of particular people and asking whose truth is being found when judges and jurors find it. But when we look more closely, we see that the whole metaphor of 'finding' rather than 'constructing' the truth relies on the assumption that truth is 'out there' to be located rather than constituted through the operation of social practices."[26] Narrative strategies and problems of proof in these cases must thus be understood as the result of social and cultural forces that are larger than any particular woman's case.

Using Expert Testimony

Expert testimony has been a primary vehicle for addressing the lack of credibility accorded battered women. The argument has been made that expert testimony is needed in order to overcome the myths and misconceptions concerning battered women, and to explain the larger context within which battering occurs. Important normative assumptions are potentially challenged by the notion of admission of expert testimony on women's experiences. The assumption of universal cognitive competence—the idea that all persons share the same schemas for understanding behavior—is questioned by the notion that multiple perspectives of women have not been incorporated into legal decision making, and that incorporating these experiences requires a self-conscious, deliberate assessment of the schemas and generalizations operating in the individual case. One of the crucial ways lawyers can persuade judges and jurors to adopt a different cognitive model is to introduce information about other perspectives, but this evidence is not automatically admissible unless it is beyond the ken of the average layperson. Thus, in order for judges to admit expert testimony, they must identify a set of generalizations and reject them as misrepresentative. This process requires an examination of information on the historical, social, cultural, and economic experiences of battered women generally, not just the experiences of the particular woman.[27]

Although expert testimony may provide an explanation for the woman's conduct at the time in question, it may do so at a high price, depending on the content of the testimony. As Scheppele suggests, the process of using expert testimony may also be problematic in that it may remove a woman's individuality and substitute a "statistically derived average experience that women typically share for the detailed, potentially idiosyncratic experiences each of us has." Scheppele contends that "as the women's movement succeeds in breaking women free from a single conception of femininity, such statistical averages will become less and less accurate as descriptions of women's particular experiences. The reliance on expert witnesses is immensely useful as a transition device between the world today and a world in which women's stories have more power as a source of fact. In the future, however, reliance on such witnesses may be seen as urging another single oppressive image of how women should react to sexualized violence on women who have diverse experiences and diverse reactions."[28]

Another reason why expert testimony may be problematic is that judges tend to see this testimony through the lens of their own common assumptions. As Regina Graycar observes, judges may try to look through a window to see others, but if the window has reflective glass in it, it is really a mirror: "When judges look at it, they see what they think is human nature, human experience and 'ordinary or reasonable people.' What they are really seeing is the society they know. Expert testimony is analogous, in our metaphor, to asking someone else to go over to the window, look through it (rather be reflected in it) and tell us what is out there."[29] Thus although admission of expert testimony may make it easier in some cases for women to bring their experiences to bear on legal decision making, it will not necessarily permit women's voices to be heard.

Judges, Judging, and Legal Method

Judges translate lawyers' and litigants' arguments and claims. Even if "good rules" are passed by a legislature, judges' interpretations can eviscerate them. Kim Scheppele tells us that in Britain, for example, Parliament passed a statute explicitly intended to allow women to obtain temporary restraining orders (TROs) against their battering husbands, "only to find that the courts interpreted men's common-law rights of property in their homes as narrowing the effective range of cases in which such TRO's were obtainable to only those cases in which the woman alone owned the house." James Ptacek's 1999 study of judicial responses to restraining order litigation in Massachusetts suggests that they are complex. Thus, as Regina Graycar has observed, "we need to pay careful attention to what judges know about the world, how they know the things they do, and how the things they know translate into their activity as judges. . . . From their public positions of authority, judges pronounce upon, and are authorised to pronounce upon, the private (and public) spheres. . . . It is through this public process (judging) that judges are able, almost literally, to 'create' women's lives." However, judges' "creation of women's lives" in law may bear little if any relation to the complex realities of the lives of women.[30]

Graycar has written about the degree to which gendered judgments are built into the legal system. The "institution" of law remains, and its "institutional design" is a way of allocating authority across different sets of actors while ensuring that the "legal texts always operate from a particular strategy of framing facts." She suggests that we must closely analyze what judges know, how they know it, how this shapes the construction of reality in judgments, how judges "orient their narratives," and how all this is affected by gender.[31] Judges' "personal" experiences become the empirical framework for their attitudes and legal decisions—judges can equate "knowledge" of women, gained through "private" experience, with "truth." Judges may use judicial notice to incorporate into their judgments commonsense ideas about the world or common assumptions of widely held misconceptions, or they may incorporate such assumptions and myths into their decision making. In New York, the State Commission on Judicial Conduct recommended censure for a former town justice who told a man charged with assaulting his girl-friend that "women can be problems."[32] Marilyn MacCrimmon has suggested that "only by changing the deeper structures of social knowledge will it be possible to incorporate women's experiences into legal reasoning."[33]

For these and other reasons discussed in this book, the transformative possibilities of feminist lawmaking may be limited. Canadian feminist legal scholar Elizabeth Sheehy has examined analogous limitations in litigation in the Canadian Supreme Court under the equality provisions of the Canadian Charter of Rights and Freedoms. Her thoughts are instructive. First, she suggests that structural barriers impede women's claims under the Charter: "The reliance placed on generalizations by legal method permits judges to abstract legal issues from their social, political and historical contexts. Although Charter litigation clearly invites judicial consideration of context and impact of legislative policy, much of the discourse remains abstract and devoid of context. This feature of Charter litigation means that clients, lawyers and judges may fail to see women's claims as raising 'legal' issues which fit into the recognized paradigms." Second, she observes that most judges have only a limited range within which to perceive feminist issues: "If feminist arguments are successful in that they invoke a judicial response, or indeed, win the case, these arguments are often understood only in their simplest or most conservative forms. The more radical feminist arguments are unfamiliar, not within the traditional legal paradigm, and profoundly disruptive of established hierarchies." Finally, because equality jurisprudence is shaped by male experience, "the relative rarity of women's claims means that even if women's organizations achieve intervener status and present briefs in women's litigation, the jurisprudence of equality will be shaped by men's lives and concerns."[34]

Thus, lawyering, evidence rules, and judging result in a process that narrows the possibilities for women's stories to be heard in court, and that subverts the translation of these stories into law. In the next two chapters, I examine this process in action, in case studies of battered women who kill and battered women who are mothers.

8

Battered Women Who Kill

Thousands of battered women daily face the danger of death because the state fails to protect them and because they lack adequate social resources. Sometimes they kill their batterers in order to save their own lives. Cases of battered women who kill their assailants have captured international attention and have generated a virtual cottage industry of judicial opinions, legislative reform, and legal scholarship over the past twenty years. As evidenced by the enormous public and legal attention this issue has attracted, it raises fundamental questions for society at large: questions about women and violence, about state responsibility, and about the meaning of equality. Cases of battered women who kill strike a national chord of anxiety about violent women, the "abuse excuse," and "feminazi" vigilantism.[1]

Legal reform for battered women who kill has been one of the most significant areas of feminist lawmaking on domestic violence. In courtrooms around the United States, lawyers have challenged assumptions about battered women in general, and battered women who kill their assailants in particular. Lawyers have raised issues concerning gender bias in criminal defenses that have begun to make it possible for battered women to obtain what I have called "equal rights to trial." Nevertheless, backlash continues to plague this work.

For many years, I have been involved with this issue as lawyer, teacher, and scholar.[2] In all the settings in which I have done work on this issue—arguing in court, training defense lawyers to handle these cases, educating judges to hear them, teaching law students, giving presentations to law teachers or other professionals, or talking with the media—one theme has been consistent: an extraordinary degree of public misunderstanding exists concerning battered women who kill their assailants. Claims made by battered women to explain their actions as shaped by their experiences of abuse are commonly perceived as "special pleading." There is deep societal resistance to perceiving the circumstances of battered women, and particularly the circumstances of battered women who kill their assailants, as a problem of gender equality.

This resistance is evident not only among the public and in media commentary, but also in legal representation, judicial treatment, and scholarly analysis. Many lawyers who handle these challenging cases fail to place them within an equal-rights framework and are not sufficiently thoughtful in grappling with the legal issues these cases present. Problems of legal representation are manifested in the large number of post-conviction "ineffective assistance of counsel" claims asserted by battered women defendants, by the even larger number of potential claims that might be asserted, and in the many clemency petitions for battered women being filed around the country. Many judges, too, have failed to understand the framework of equality in their application of the law to cases of battered women who kill.

The Problem of Equal Rights to Trial

The insight that first generated legal work on this issue was that, for a variety of reasons, women who were battered and faced criminal charges for homicide or assault of their assailant were likely to be denied equal rights to trial — that is, equal rights to present the circumstances of their acts within the framework of the criminal law. The equal-rights problem in this context flows from an equal-rights problem in criminal law generally: what Stephen Schulhofer has described as the fact that "the criminal justice system is dominated (incontrovertibly so) by a preoccupation with men and male perspectives."[3]

The equal-rights problem for battered women who kill has many sources: widespread views of women who act violently, particularly against intimates, as "monsters";[4] commonly held misconceptions about battered women (that they "ask for" or provoke the violence, for example); gender bias in the concept of reasonableness; societal misperceptions about self-defense and application of the legal standards of imminent danger and proportionality; and deeply held cultural attitudes that pathologize women generally and battered women particularly. Moreover, the law has traditionally viewed husband-killing as a special crime that strikes at the root of all civil government, threatening basic conceptions of traditional society. Long ago, William Blackstone observed that a woman who killed her husband was committing "treason":

"If the baron kills his feme it is the same as if he had killed a stranger, or any other person; but if the feme kills her baron, it is regarded by the laws as a much more atrocious crime, as she not only breaks through the restraints of humanity and conjugal affection, but throws off all subjection to the authority of her husband. And therefore, the law denominates her crime a species of treason, and condemns her to the same punishment as if she had killed the king. And for every species of treason . . . the sentence of women was to be drawn and burnt alive."[5] Based on the confluence of these factors, the equal-rights argument holds that battered women who kill are more likely to be viewed as crazy than reasonable; thus they are likely to face substantial hurdles in asserting self-defense and to be limited in the range of defense options available at trial.

The goal of this work has been to expand defense options in order to equalize women's rights to trial and afford women equal opportunity to present an effective defense. It has not rested on the claim that all battered women are entitled to self-defense, or that there should be a special defense for battered women, either as self-defense or as a special "battered woman defense." To the contrary, the argument is that battered women, like all criminal defendants, have to be included within the traditional framework of the criminal law in order to guarantee their equal rights to trial.

Those insights have generated much legal scholarship, case law, and statutory reform. Nevertheless, much of this work is premised on a fundamental misunderstanding of the original arguments, and is based on the assumption that pleas of self-defense or a special "battered woman defense" are appropriate in all cases of battered women who kill their assailants. These efforts miss the crucial insight that has shaped this work: that the particular facts and circumstances of each case must be evaluated in light of the general problem of gender bias in order to ensure an individual woman's equal right to trial. This is, as Schulhofer puts it, a "feminism of process and particulars."[6]

With respect to battered women who kill, gender bias pervades the entire criminal process. It permeates perceptions of appropriate self-defense and the legal standard of self-defense, the broader problem of choice of defense, and the need for expert testimony on battering, all of which are interrelated. Lawyers' failure to appreciate the problem of gender bias in the law of self-defense and in judicial application of the law of self-defense can lead to problematic judgments concerning the choice of defense in any particular case, as well as all decisions that flow from this (such as expert testimony that might be proffered in support of that defense), since the defense necessarily shapes the content of all testimony at trial.

Insights concerning the experiences of battered women drawn from legal scholarship, litigation, and law reform efforts deepen our understanding of the problem. We now recognize that male physical violence is part of a larger framework of power and coercive control over women, which includes restriction of fundamental rights of freedom, choice, and autonomy. We know that women's assertion of independence, most dramatically in the act of separation, exacerbates the lethality of male violence, and that women who leave their abusers are at greater risk of being seriously injured or killed. We know that services for battered women make a difference, for states where there are relatively fewer resources devoted to battered women have higher rates of homicides committed by battered women.[7] We now recognize the lethal limitations of legal remedies—whether orders of protection, mandatory arrest policies, or anti-stalking laws—intended to provide safety to battered women. We also know that battering affects women's criminal conduct in a wide variety of circumstances, for many women who are in jail on charges that are seemingly unrelated to battering—such as drug offenses or offenses against children—have been battered.[8] Scholars have amply documented that situations involving battered women who kill fall within traditional frameworks of defenses or excusable action, but are nonetheless viewed as different or exceptional by judges who apply the law to these cases,[9] and that battered women of color face particular hurdles in this regard. We know that the denial of equal rights to trial has constitutional consequences.[10] Social and cultural experience continues to confirm that women who act violently toward men, even in self-defense—whether in the movies (*Thelma and Louise*) or in life (Lorena Bobbitt)—are viewed with particular horror.[11]

Despite this overwhelming record, there has been little change in attitudes among legal scholars, lawyers, judges, the media, and the public at large. Legal arguments in battered women's cases are routinely viewed as claims for special and undeservedly lenient treatment for battered women. Indeed, some well-intentioned lawyers, legislators, legal scholars, and judges have made legal arguments, developed legislation, and written articles and judicial opinions that assert "battered women's" or "battered woman syndrome" defenses or claims, whether as the basis for claims of self-defense, for admissibility of expert testimony, or for a special cause of action in tort.[12] This dilemma is a familiar one when gender discrimination claims are made, because the tension between equal treatment and special treatment is inherent to the problem of equality generally, and it is particularly endemic in claims of gender equality.[13] But in the context of criminal cases involving battered women as defendants, the mischaracterization of claims of equal treatment as pleas for special treatment is especially problematic. Battered women's actions in these cases are widely perceived to be outside the traditional justification framework of the criminal law. As a result, the problem of gender bias is not only neither addressed nor remedied; it is exacerbated.

The Legal Framework

Homicide is generally divided into first- and second-degree murder, manslaughter, and justifiable or excusable homicide. If a homicide is justifiable or excusable, it is because special circumstances exist that the law recognizes as justifying or excusing the defendant's acts from criminal liability.[14] Proof that a killing occurred in a sudden, provoked "heat of passion" — upon provocation that would cause a "reasonable man to lose his self-control" — is considered in most jurisdictions to indicate manslaughter.[15] Manslaughter is an "intermediate" crime between murder and justifiable homicide; it means that the homicidal act is not "justifiable" but, because of the circumstances of the individual, is "understandable" or "excusable," and therefore deserving of some mitigation in punishment. Alternatively, where a defendant's belief in the need to use force to defend herself is "reasonable," and she is not the initial aggressor, self-defense is a "complete" defense and results in acquittal. Where a defendant's belief is found to be honest but "unreasonable," some jurisdictions recognize "imperfect" self-defense, permitting a reduction from murder to manslaughter.[16]

Although the law of self-defense is purportedly universally applicable, it is widely recognized that social concepts of justification have been shaped by male experience. Familiar images of self-defense are a soldier; a man protecting his home, his family, or the chastity of his wife; or a man fighting off an assailant. Yet the circumstances in which women kill in self-defense are usually related to physical or sexual abuse by an intimate, not to the conventional barroom brawl or fistfight with a stranger that shapes male experience with self-defense. Society, through its prosecutors, juries, and judges, has more readily excused a man for killing his wife's lover than a woman for killing a rapist. The acts of men and women are subject to a different set of

legal expectations and standards. The man's act, while not always legally con-
doned, is viewed sympathetically. He is not forgiven, but his motivation is
understood by those sitting in judgment. The law, however, has never protected a wife who killed her husband after finding him with another woman.
A woman's husband simply does not belong to her in the same way that she
belongs to him.[17]

The man who kills his wife after finding her with another man is the paradigmatic example of provocation; his conduct is widely perceived to deserve
more lenient treatment than other kinds of killings under the law. In a Maryland case involving a man who shot and killed his wife four hours after
coming home and finding her in bed with another man, the judge sentenced
the man to only eighteen months in a work release program, stating that he
could imagine nothing that would provoke "an uncontrollable rage greater
than this: for someone who is happily married to be betrayed in your personal life, when you're out working to support the spouse. . . . I seriously
wonder how many men married five, four years . . . would have the strength to
walk away without inflicting some corporal punishment."[18] Although many
homicides of women committed by men are now recognized as occurring in
a context of domestic violence, men's killings of their wives are, as Donna
Coker has put it, "seldom recognized as belonging to the universe of 'domestic violence' killings." Conversely, women who have killed their husbands in
response to battering have raised considerable controversy and are perceived
to deserve harsher treatment under the law.[19]

Consequently, it is now generally acknowledged that women defendants
face substantial hurdles in pleading self-defense. Battered women defendants
experience serious problems in meeting the judicial application of the standard of reasonableness and elements of the law of self-defense: the requirement of temporal proximity of the danger perceived by the defendant; the
requirement of equal proportionality of force used by the defendant to that
used against her by the batterer; and the duty to retreat.

Alternatives to self-defense are the insanity defense and the range of partial
responsibility or impaired mental state defenses, which vary among jurisdictions. If a defendant pleads insanity, she claims that, owing to her mental condition at the time of the act, she is not guilty because she either did not know
what she was doing or did not know that it was wrong.[20] The insanity defense
is usually a "complete" defense, in the sense that the defendant is not legally
responsible for the act committed. However, a finding of not guilty by reason

of insanity most often results in institutionalization for an indefinite period of time.[21] Some, but not all, jurisdictions recognize partial responsibility or impaired mental state defenses, such as heat-of-passion and intoxication, where a successful defense will mitigate the act and reduce a charge from murder to manslaughter.[22]

The Goals of Equal Rights to Trial

When the theoretical framework of gender bias in the law of self-defense was developed more than twenty years ago, relatively little was known about the problem of domestic violence. The public and the judiciary had little consciousness even of the existence of battered women who killed their assailants, much less of the nature of the battering these women had experienced. The equal rights framework developed from the experiences of battered women, whose stories, though hardly new, had rarely been told or heard. Lawyers and social scientists who were sensitive to the subtleties of gender bias listened to the experiences of women who had been battered and who killed their assailants.[23] The theory was based on the particular experiences of women who were battered, the social context of battering, and the broader problems of gender subordination within which the particular problem of battering had to be understood.

It is now well established that homicide or assault cases involving battered women who kill their assailants pose serious problems to traditional self-defense work. Work on self-defense for battered women who kill has been premised on the notion that self-defense requirements of reasonableness, imminent danger, and equal force are sex biased: a woman who kills her husband is viewed as inherently unreasonable because she is violating the norm of appropriate behavior for women. A battered woman who kills her batterer has to overcome misconceptions about battered women. She must explain why she stayed in the relationship and did not leave her home; why she did not call the police or get other assistance before acting; and why she believed that the occasion on which she responded to the danger she faced was more serious than other times when she had been beaten, had not acted, and had survived.

Early work on equal rights to trial focused first on choice of defense, for the threshold issue for defense lawyers who represent battered women who kill is to interpret the facts and the law in order to choose a defense. The argument was that lawyers were more likely to rely on partial responsibility and insanity defenses for battered women rather than on self-defense, because lawyers would be more likely to see battered women as irrational. The assumption was that battered women who kill are likely to be seen as either bad or mad or both, but in any case as inappropriate claimants of self-defense, and the judge and jury may share these stereotypes.[24]

As discussed in Chapter 5, the crux of self-defense is the concept of reasonableness. In order for a defense lawyer to believe that a battered woman has a credible claim of self-defense, the lawyer will first have to overcome sex-based stereotypes of reasonableness, understand enough about the experiences of battered women to be able to consider whether the woman's actions are reasonable, and, in a manner sensitive to the problems of gender-bias, be able to listen to the woman's experiences. Early work on women's self-defense claimed that in many cases of women charged with homicide, particularly battered women, self-defense was likely to be overlooked by defense counsel, but might be appropriate and should be considered. The goal was to ensure that the full range of defenses were available and explored for battered women defendants, just as they should be available for all other criminal defendants.

The next step was to make sure that battered women's experiences were heard—first by defense lawyers in the process of representation and choice of defense, and then in the courtroom—regardless of what defense was chosen. Admission of evidence on battering was considered crucial, first from the woman and others who might have observed or known about the violence, and then from experts who might be able to explain those experiences and assist fact finders to overcome misconceptions that might impede their determination. Evidence concerning the history and experience of abuse was not only relevant, but essential to determining guilt. The goal was not to have every battered woman on trial plead self-defense, but to improve the rationality of the fact-finding process. Paradoxically, this argument for the relevance of the social context of battering has become confused with the notion of a separate defense of battering.

The equality framework provides a way of analyzing cases of battered women who kill from a perspective of gender bias, but subsequent case law, legal reform efforts, and legal scholarship suggest a failure to understand the nuances of this approach. First, the framework of gender bias is either ignored or misunderstood as a claim for a particular defense or result, rather than as a mode of case analysis that must be carefully applied in accordance with the facts of each individual case. Second, cases of battered women are viewed in a rigid all-or-nothing way; for example, arguments are made that battered women are or are not, as a class, entitled to claim self-defense as a justification; are or are not entitled to assert an excuse; or should or should not all be able to claim "battered woman syndrome" or a "battered woman" defense. Either all battered women are entitled to self-defense or none are; the common theme is that "they" are all the same.

Defining the Battered Woman

As discussed in Chapter 4, the phrase "battered woman" is interpreted by judges, legislators, and scholars in a rigid and dichotomized fashion. This has particularly serious ramifications for cases of battered women who kill. First, the term "battered woman" implies that there is one model, which excludes women with diverse experiences who do not fit a particular mold.[25] Second, it increasingly connotes victimization, perhaps because of its association with the concept of "battered woman syndrome." This ignores the reality that many women who are battered are also survivors, active help-seekers who find little help and protection from the state, with extraordinary abilities to strategize in order to keep themselves and their families safe under terrible circumstances. Third, case law and statutes in some jurisdictions limit who can be defined as a "battered woman," so that many women who are battered are not recognized by the law.[26] For example, some battered women who kill have been denied the opportunity to seek jury instructions at trial, or to present the issue of self-defense to the jury, because the judge has decided that they were not "real" battered women.[27]

The victimization-agency dichotomy contributes significantly to the confusion about appropriate legal defense strategies for women. A battered woman supposedly cannot be victimized if she has acted in any way that suggests agency or if she is a survivor; in contrast, if she is a victim, she cannot be considered reasonable. Judges and scholars reflect this dichotomized approach in analyses that make broad claims about the criminal liability of battered women. But women who are battered, and particularly battered women who kill, are simultaneously victims and agents: they are abused but they also act to protect themselves. Indeed, as discussed in Chapter 5, it is the very complexity of their situations that makes these cases so difficult to perceive and to adjudicate.

Holly Maguigan's empirical analysis of judicial treatment of cases of battered women who kill demonstrates the problems with this dichotomized thinking, and underscores the tenacity of the widespread misperception that battered women who kill their batterers are per se inappropriate claimants of self-defense. Her review of appellate opinions in cases of battered women who kill suggests that this misperception flows from two flawed assumptions about these cases.[28] First is the assumption that all these women kill sleeping or otherwise nonconfrontational men and then claim "domestic violence made them do it," although at least 75 percent of these cases involved situations where battered women killed during an ongoing attack or under an imminent threat.[29] Second is the assumption that the existing law of self-defense cannot accommodate cases of battered women who kill their batterers, or any other cases where the fact finder must understand the context of the killing in order to apply the law rationally. Maguigan concludes that the problem facing battered women defendants is not the law of self-defense as it currently exists, but rather the disparate application of that law to battered women at trial. She finds that trial judges in these cases misapplied the law of self-defense — primarily by making rulings that kept evidence of the social context of battering from the jury and by failing to instruct the jury, either adequately or at all, on the law of self-defense — and were frequently reversed on appeal. Judges seemed to make these errors because of their stereotypical views of battered women either as vigilantes ("bad") or as otherwise incapable of acting reasonably ("mad").[30]

Reasonableness and Choice of Defense

In considering whether a battered woman charged with homicide has a credible claim of self-defense, defense lawyers who must assist battered women to choose a defense, and judges who rule on these cases, confront the threshold issue of reasonableness. If the lawyer determines that the woman's actions were not reasonable, self-defense cannot be asserted. Consequently, the issue of reasonableness has a critical impact on legal representation and choice of defense.

Serious problems in legal representation shape the analysis and presentation of these cases. Because many defense lawyers who represent battered women do not understand the problems of domestic violence, lack experience in representing women who have been battered, and therefore cannot understand how the law applies to battered women who kill, a lawyer's determination of a battered woman's reasonableness can be problematic. Stereo-typical thinking about available defenses may also impede lawyers from ask-ing questions or from processing the information they receive in a way that permits them to consider the range of defenses that may be appropriate to the case.[31] Because women who have killed their partners frequently suffer mem-ory lapses and confusion following the incident, the defense lawyer may have difficulty in obtaining adequate information to develop an effective defense from the defendant alone.[32] As a result, the lawyer may perceive the woman as "difficult" or may ask questions in a way that evokes her mistrust because the lawyer seems not to believe or understand her battering experience, or seems to blame her for it. In some cases, defense lawyers avoid the issue of domestic violence completely by failing to offer evidence of battering,[33] indicating their lack of knowledge of, or their discomfort with, the threatening subject.

Thoughtfully determining the choice of defense for battered women defen-dants requires lawyers to understand the framework of inequality that shapes these cases. Because the law has been developed with a male norm in mind, and because stereotypes about women, and about battered women in par-ticular, persist in the minds of judges, juries, and lawyers themselves, lawyers need to be critical about their own assumptions, to seek assistance from ex-perts in the field, and to be able to recognize and point out gender bias in the law where it occurs.[34] They must use the resources available to them to make judges and juries aware of the myths and misconceptions about battering that may impede fair trials.

The determination of reasonableness is the area in which judges' resistance to considering the social context of battering has been most visible. In cases of battered women who have killed, the resistance has been especially pro-found. It is simply impossible for many judges—not to mention lawyers, legal scholars, and the public at large—to imagine that women are acting reason-ably when they kill their intimate partners. These cases evoke more discom-fort than cases where men are accused of killing their partners, such as the O. J. Simpson case.

One of the most significant procedural manifestations of this discomfort concerns the much-debated question whether reasonableness for purposes of self-defense must be "objective" or "subjective." In most jurisdictions the standard of self-defense involves some consideration of both the individual's own perspective—a subjective component—and the reasonableness of that perspective—an objective component.[35] But legal scholars and judges have openly manifested their discomfort with the notion that battered women can claim that their actions are objectively reasonable; indeed, trial judges have prevented battered women from going to the jury with self-defense claims on the theory that they meet only the "subjective" prong of the self-defense standard.[36] Yet in fact, evidence of battering is relevant under both an objective and a subjective standard of self-defense. Under either approach the jury must find that the actor acted reasonably.

Battered Woman Syndrome

The use of the term "battered woman syndrome" has intensified the general confusion about domestic violence and battered women, and has increased the likelihood that the law will be misapplied to battered women when they seek protection in the courts or appear as defendants.[37] Battering relationships reflect certain characteristics that arise from the common cultural and historical roots of male violence against women, as well as from the subordination of women in intimate relationships and in the world. Indiscriminate use of the term "battered woman syndrome" tends to shift the blame for intimate violence away from the perpetrator and onto the woman. Widespread use of this term, even in common parlance, tends to reinforce traditional attitudes about women as provokers of their abuse. Because the term is frequently used as shorthand for "evidence of a battering relationship" by judges, legislators, and legal scholars, it is not clear in any particular context what it refers to. Today it is used in courtrooms to describe everything from a woman's prior responses to violence, and the context in which those responses occurred, to the dynamics of the abusive relationship.[38] Some experts have claimed battered woman syndrome as a subcategory of post-traumatic stress disorder.[39]

The use of expert testimony on battered woman syndrome highlights this confusion. It can be admitted in court to demonstrate the reasonableness of women's acts, in support of claims of self-defense, and also to attest to their "irrationality" in support of insanity defenses.[40] It has been used by courts for many different purposes: to explain why a woman stayed in an abusive relationship, to rebut common myths about battered women, to describe battered women's responses to violence in a general way, and to explain why a particular battered woman responded in the way that she did.[41] However, the term and its interpretive framework have been widely criticized. As discussed in Chapter 5, the experiences of battered women are highly diverse and complex, and all battered women defendants do not fit into the same legal mold.[42] Significantly, other interpretive frameworks to describe battering that have been proposed, such as "coercive control," do not focus exclusively on the woman who has been battered, but on the batterer or the relationship.[43]

Many lawyers who represent battered women and know little about battering use the term "battered woman syndrome" as shorthand because it is what they have heard. Frequently what they really mean is "evidence of battering." Reliance on "battered woman syndrome" as an explanatory framework in case analysis is problematic. Not only may it be inaccurate in describing the experiences of many women who are battered, but it will inevitably shape and limit lawyers' views of the available choice of defenses. And because "battered woman syndrome" sounds like a form of mental disease or defect, lawyers relying on this framework are more likely to view the case through the lens of an impaired mental state.

"Battered Woman" or "Battered Woman Syndrome" Defense

Some lawyers, legislators, judges, and legal scholars have suggested that there is a special battered woman or "battered woman syndrome" defense.[44] Feminist legal advocates, however, have never argued for a special defense: there is not a separate defense, and there should not be one. Evidence of battering experiences and a history of battering, whether explained as "battered woman syndrome" or battering generally, may fall within a wide range of available defenses. Because problems of gender bias shape the application of all defenses and excuses, the history of battering may, in different ways, be relevant to all.

Judicial opinions in a number of self-defense cases involving battered women correctly observe that there is no separate "battered woman syndrome" defense.[45] Yet evidence of battering is crucial in dispelling jurors' preconceptions about battered women, and in helping jurors to understand how a woman's experience of being battered influences her understanding of the level of danger she is in and her reaction to the perceived danger.[46] Evidence of battering in a self-defense case is not relevant to justify the killing, but it provides the jury with the appropriate context in which to decide whether a woman's apprehension of imminent danger of death or great bodily harm was reasonable.

Although some trial and appellate courts articulate the relevance of evidence of battering correctly, many judges continue to be confused.[47] Some courts employ a "hybrid" defense.[48] Other courts express confusion about defense strategy or "specialized" application of traditional self-defense law to battered women, indicating that, in practice, there might as well be a "battered woman syndrome" defense.

The Special Problem of Expert Testimony on Battering

To date, the primary legal issue concerning battered women who kill is the admissibility of expert testimony on battering or battered woman syndrome. Legal victories have been won in the general area of what has become known as women's self-defense work and on the particular issue of the admissibility of expert testimony on battered woman syndrome.

Several cases that have admitted this testimony, such as the 1984 decision of the New Jersey Supreme Court in *State v. Kelly,*[49] have done so because the court has accepted the feminist theoretical premises of women's self-defense work. Feminist lawyers argued that there was a need to recognize women's different experiences and the different circumstances in which women kill, and that those different experiences and circumstances need to be explained in the trial process. In theory, expert testimony on battering is the logical extension of this idea, but in fact, the expert testimony cases pose troubling questions about the degree to which these goals have been realized.

First, cases involving expert testimony on battered woman syndrome resound with the very stereotypes of female incapacity that women's self-defense work has sought to overcome. Second, on the level of theory, the cases have revived problematic doctrinal oppositions. Third, on the level of practice, appellate cases on the issue suggest that expert testimony is not being admitted where it is most needed — where the woman's experiences and the circumstances of the homicide are indeed most "different."[50]

The question of the admissibility of expert testimony on battered woman syndrome has been the primary legal issue that appellate courts have addressed in the area of women's self-defense work. There are several reasons for this. First, most women's self-defense cases have involved battered women. The Women's Self-Defense Law Project, which began legal work in this field, had stressed the particular utility of expert testimony in this context, depending on the facts of the case.[51] Many lawyers defending women have sought to introduce expert testimony on "battered woman syndrome" at trial.[52] Although trial judges appear to have admitted this testimony in the majority of cases, where courts have excluded it and the women have been convicted, the question of the admissibility of expert testimony has frequently become the major issue on appeal. As a consequence, the question of expert testimony has received a great deal of attention from courts and commentators. Most appellate courts have ruled that this testimony is admissible, and legal commentators have almost unanimously supported admissibility. Significantly, the majority of appellate courts that have ruled on the trial court's exclusion of expert testimony have determined that expert testimony on battered woman syndrome is relevant to a claim of self-defense. Even where it is found relevant, however, the trial court must find that it has met the general standard for admissibility of expert testimony. In several cases, this requirement has proven to be a substantial hurdle. Moreover, even if the trial court admits the expert testimony proffered by the defense, the prosecution may be permitted to have an expert testify to counter the assertion that the woman is battered or has suffered from battered woman syndrome.[53]

Expert testimony on battering has had a substantial impact on the criminal process. It has been admitted in homicide trials of battered women around the country, not only in those involving claims of self-defense. Defense lawyers have also proffered it at other stages of the criminal process, such as the grand jury, on motions to dismiss, and at sentencing.[54] These cases have demonstrated judicial recognition of the depth and severity of the problems of sex stereotyping in the trial process for battered women claiming self-defense.[55] These cases acknowledge the role that expert testimony can play in a range of contexts.[56] And where expert testimony on battering has been held inadmissible, courts have largely ruled simply that there was an insufficient basis on which to find it admissible on the facts presented.[57]

From the beginning, literature on women's self-defense work has emphasized that expert testimony should not be used in isolation; it should be integrated with overall defense strategy, tied to the particular facts of the case, and focused on the particular defense problems in the case. Commentators have cautioned that emphasizing expert testimony on battering as the sole or even primary vehicle for remedying sex bias in the trial process is problematic for several reasons. First, it was feared that lawyers might not use the testimony carefully and tie it to the particular facts of the woman's case and that the defense strategy might focus on evidence of battering rather than on the reasonableness of the woman's act.[58] Furthermore, presenting the substance of the expert testimony on battering risked that it would be submitted or heard in a way that would unwittingly reinforce sex stereotypes. The New Jersey Supreme Court's opinion in *State v. Kelly* highlights both the importance and the risks of expert testimony.

The New Jersey Supreme Court held in *State v. Kelly* that expert testimony concerning battered woman syndrome was admissible. The court ruled that the testimony was relevant under New Jersey's standard of self-defense, and met the standards of New Jersey's rules for the admissibility of expert testimony.[59] In *Kelly*, the defendant was charged with second-degree murder of her husband. Gladys Kelly had been battered by her husband throughout their seven-year marriage. The beatings had begun on the day after her marriage, when she was beaten in public. On the day of the homicide, Mr. Kelly had been drinking and started beating her in public. During the physical struggle that ensued, she wounded him with a pair of scissors. She claimed that he was biting and clubbing her, and that she responded in self-defense.[60]

At trial, defense counsel attempted to introduce the expert testimony of a clinical psychologist to explain why Gladys Kelly, as a battered woman, had a reasonable belief that she was in imminent danger of death or serious bodily harm and needed to act in self-defense.[61] The trial judge conducted a lengthy examination of the expert but held that the testimony was not relevant under New Jersey's standard of self-defense and did not reach the issue of scientific reliability.[62] On appeal, the state's Appellate Division affirmed the trial court's ruling on relevance and ruled that admission of the testimony was cumulative and unnecessary in light of the defendant's testimony of prior abuse.[63] I submitted an amicus curiae brief on behalf of the New Jersey Coalition on Battered Women to the New Jersey Supreme Court in support of admissibility, and was granted leave to argue. In addition, the American Psychological Association filed a brief in support of admissibility, which focused on the issue of scientific reliability.[64] In the Supreme Court, defendant and *amici* argued that the testimony was relevant and that it met New Jersey's standards for admissibility of expert testimony.

The testimony presented at trial focused on the battered woman syndrome. The expert emphasized the traditional components of the syndrome, as did the briefs on appeal, including the amicus briefs. The expert testimony and the briefs and arguments presented to the Supreme Court claimed that the testimony was important in order to assist the jury in understanding crucial components of reasonableness: the reasonableness of Gladys Kelly's perception of the danger, and the imminence of that danger. Yet the court appears to both accept and minimize that broader view, and in this sense, the opinion focuses only on part of the problem.

The court's analysis of relevance highlights the dilemmas of using expert testimony on battered woman syndrome. First, the court exhaustively and sensitively documented the severity of the problem of woman abuse and the pervasiveness of stereotypes and myths concerning battered women, using the battered woman syndrome as the vehicle for this discussion. The court described the battered woman syndrome as "a series of common characteristics that appear in women who are abused physically and psychologically over an extended period of time by the dominant male figure in their lives,"[65] and analyzed Lenore Walker's research, which breaks down the cycle of violence into three stages (a tension-building stage, an acute battering stage, and a loving respite stage). It discussed both the "psychological impacts of battery" and the external social and economic factors that make it difficult for women to extricate themselves from the battering relationship: lack of money and support systems, primary responsibility for child care, and the well-grounded fear that if the woman leaves the man will follow her and subject her to an even more brutal attack. Nonetheless, the court also recited the "symptoms" of the syndrome and the common personality traits attributed to the battered woman, by noting the following: "low self-esteem, traditional beliefs about the home, the family, and the female sex role, tremendous feelings of guilt that their marriages are failing and the tendency to accept responsibility for the batterer's actions."[66]

Second, the court's understanding of the relevance and importance of the expert testimony was expansive. The court suggested that admission of the testimony was important because it would bolster Gladys Kelly's credibility in the eyes of the jury by demonstrating that her experiences, which the jury would find difficult to comprehend, were in fact common to women in abusive situations. The court ruled that in light of its interpretation of New Jersey's standard of self-defense, the expert testimony would be central to the *honesty* of Gladys Kelly's belief that she was in imminent danger of deadly harm, and it would aid the jury in determining whether a reasonable person could have believed that there was imminent danger to her life. The court characterized this as relevant under the "objective" standard of self-defense.[67]

Third, the court held that the testimony was relevant because the expert could have responded to myths and misconceptions about battered women, particularly that the battered woman was free to leave, with information concerning battered women's inability to leave, "learned helplessness," and the lack of alternatives. The court noted:

> The crucial issue of fact on which this expert's testimony would bear is why, given such allegedly severe and constant beatings, combined with threats to kill, defendant had not long ago left decedent. . . . The expert could clear up these myths, by explaining that one of the common characteristics of a battered wife is her inability to leave despite such constant beatings; her "learned helplessness"; her lack of anywhere to go; her feeling that if she tried to leave, she would be subject to even more merciless treatment; her belief in the omnipotence of her battering husband; and sometimes her hope that her husband will change his ways.[68]

Significantly, the court's analysis of relevance appears to focus on the woman's inability to leave, as opposed to the reasonableness of her act. Indeed, the court contrasts the crucial nature of the expert testimony in rebutting myths concerning why the battered woman does not leave with the relevance of the expert's testimony to the jury's determination of the reasonableness of her act:

> The difficulty with the expert's testimony is that it sounds as if an expert is giving knowledge to a jury about something the jury knows as well as anyone else, namely, the reasonableness of a person's fear of imminent serious danger. That is not at all, however, what this testimony is directly aimed at. It is aimed at an area where the purported common knowledge of the jury may be very much mistaken, an area where jurors' logic, drawn from their own experience, may lead to a wholly incorrect conclusion, an area where expert knowledge would enable the jurors to disregard their prior conclusions as being common myths rather than common knowledge. After hearing the expert, instead of saying Gladys Kelly could not have been beaten up so badly for if she had, she certainly would have left, the jury could conclude that her failure to leave was very much part and parcel of her life as a battered wife. The jury could conclude that instead of casting doubt on the accuracy of her testimony about the severity and frequency of prior beatings, her failure to leave actually reinforced her credibility.[69]

This focus is underscored in the portion of the opinion in which the court defines the scope of the expert's testimony for retrial. The court again emphasizes that "the area of *expert* knowledge relates . . . to the reasons for defendant's failure to leave her husband."[70] The court goes on to observe:

Either the jury accepts or rejects that explanation and, based on that, credits defendant's stories about the beatings she suffered. No expert is needed, however, once the jury has made up its mind on those issues, to tell the jury the logical conclusion, namely, that a person who has in fact been severely and continuously beaten might very well reasonably fear that the imminent beatings she was about to suffer could be either life-threatening or pose a risk of serious injury. What the expert could state was that defendant had the battered-woman's syndrome, could explain that syndrome in detail, relating its characteristics to defendant, but only to enable the jury better to determine the honesty and reasonableness of defendant's belief. Depending on its content, the expert's testimony might also enable the jury to find that the battered wife, because of the prior beatings, numerous beatings, as often as once a week, for seven years, from the day they were married to the day he died, is particularly able to predict accurately the likely extent of violence in any attack on her. That conclusion could significantly affect the jury's evaluation of the reasonableness of defendant's fear for her life.[71]

Kelly, then, exemplifies the contradictory themes that have emerged in the development of the issue of expert testimony. The Supreme Court's opinion reveals both the severity and tenacity of the problem of sex bias in the law of self-defense. The court acknowledges the importance of expert testimony to explain not merely the woman's "subjective" honesty, but also the "objective" reasonableness of her response. At the same time, the court seems to perceive the testimony as primarily relevant to the issue of why Gladys Kelly did not leave, rather than to the reasonableness of her action.

The language of the court's opinion in the previous quotations is perplexing. The court seems to say that admissibility of expert testimony on battering is important precisely because jurors' commonsense experience with domestic relationships will give them the illusion of knowledge; they will not be aware of how their views have been shaped by stereotypes and tainted by bias. Yet the court's primary example is focused only on why the battered woman didn't leave. Indeed, the opinion seems to suggest that if the testimony were focused on the issue of "reasonableness" of the woman's fear (and therefore the reasonableness of her *act* of self-defense as opposed to her failure to leave), the jury's perception that the expert was "giving knowledge to a jury about something the jury knows as well as anyone else, namely the reasonableness of a person's fear of imminent serious danger," would be right.

Certainly the court is correct in observing that the question of why the battered woman did not leave (so as to avoid the possibility of death) is a threshold issue in the jury's mind: the fact that she didn't leave the relationship raises the question of whether she was really battered (if she was, why did she stay?) as well as the question of whether, by staying, she had "assumed the risk" of death. Yet these questions present only the first issue for the jury. The second issue—and the more pressing one in many cases—is the reasonableness of the battered woman's belief that she was in particular jeopardy at the time that she responded in self-defense. A battered woman who has been the victim of abuse for many years and has survived it must credibly explain why it was necessary to act on that particular occasion. Expert testimony, admitted for the purpose of explaining why the battered woman did not leave, does not help the jury answer the question whether she was reasonable in acting violently in order to save her life. It thus does not address the basic defense problem that the battered woman faces. Indeed, if the testimony is limited, or perceived as limited, to the issue of why the woman does not leave, it highlights a contradiction implicit in the message of battered woman syndrome: If the battered woman was so helpless and passive, how could she kill the batterer?

In fairness to the New Jersey Supreme Court, the *Kelly* opinion does mention that "the expert's testimony might also enable the jury to find that the battered wife, because of the prior beatings . . . is particularly able to predict accurately the likely extent of violence in any attack on her" and "that conclusion could significantly affect the jury's evaluation of the reasonableness of defendant's fear for her life." Yet the court seems to minimize the importance of this broader and more central understanding of relevance by its statement that the expert testimony is not relevant to the jury's determination of the reasonableness of a person's fear of imminent severe danger because this is "something the jury knows as well as anyone else."

In fact, the reasonableness of the woman's fear and the reasonableness of her act are *not* issues that the jury knows as well as anyone else. The jury needs expert testimony on reasonableness precisely because the jury may not understand that the battered woman's prediction of the likely extent and imminence of violence is particularly acute and accurate.

One possible explanation for the court's limited view is that the members of the court found it easier to focus on those aspects of the testimony that characterized the woman as passive and helpless (that is, her inability to leave), rather than active and violent but reasonable. This highlights the dilemma of battered woman syndrome: explanation of the battered woman's actions from a solely victimized perspective cannot fully explain why she reasonably believed it was necessary to act.

Although *Kelly* is an extraordinary opinion, it reflects larger problems. In general, courts appear to be willing to recognize the importance of expert testimony when the rationale for admission is women's individual and collective psychological "weakness." The "battered women's perspective" that courts are hearing and to which they are responding is that of damaged women, not of women who perceive themselves to be, and may in fact be, acting competently, assertively, and rationally in light of the alternatives.

The Dilemmas of Expert Testimony for Feminist Legal Theory

The issue of admissibility of expert testimony on battering, as in *Kelly,* illuminates some of the tensions and contradictions implicit in legal work on women's self-defense since *State v. Wanrow,* tensions and contradictions that continue. Courts that have admitted expert testimony have accepted that the law of self-defense incorporates basic assumptions of sex bias, and they have adopted explicitly feminist perceptions of a distinct and shared women's experience.[72] They have ruled on the basis of a heightened consciousness of women's self-defense and an understanding of the pervasiveness and severity of domestic violence.[73] They have acknowledged that there is sex bias in the concept of reasonableness, that myths and misconceptions concerning battered women are widely shared and interfere with juror determinations, and that full and fair consideration of self-defense is impaired by juror bias.[74] Thus, on one level, these cases constitute a genuine advance for feminist legal work. At the same time, they expose contradictions that need to be confronted.

The arguments first raised in *Wanrow* and accepted by the plurality opinion of the Washington Supreme Court rest on several assumptions that have become basic: first, that women act in self-defense under different circumstances and in different ways than men; second, that the law of self-defense incorporates sex bias; and third, that sex-based stereotypes of women generally, and battered or raped women specifically, interfere with jurors' determinations of women's claims of self-defense.[75] *Wanrow* and the substantial work on women's self-defense that flowed from it resulted from efforts to have the reasonableness standard of self-defense expand to include women's different experience and adjust to include sex bias in the law.

On the level of practice, *Wanrow* and subsequent women's self-defense work sought to expand the legal options available to women defending against charges of homicide or assault for killing men who battered or raped them. Through explanations of the circumstances in which women acted to save their own lives, women's acts that had previously been viewed as outside the purview of self-defense but appropriate for insanity, heat-of-passion, or manslaughter defenses, could now be viewed as legitimately within the province of self-defense. But this work was intended to extend even further: to enable individual women to have a wider range of defense options, and for lawyers to have the opportunity to evaluate and present women's diverse situations and circumstances to courts without stereotype and sex bias.

On the level of theory, *Wanrow* posed a radical challenge to a number of dichotomies in legal thought: the dichotomy of differences and sameness in equality theory; the dichotomy of excuse and justification in criminal law jurisprudence; and the dichotomies of individual and group determination and subjective and objective standards generally. Examining the theoretical dilemmas that this work poses raises hard questions about whether *Wanrow's* goals have been furthered.

Differences and Sameness

Wanrow raised the issue of the differences between men and women in the circumstances in which they killed in self-defense, the different means by which they killed, and the different factual contexts, as well as the history and experience of sex discrimination.[76] Women's self-defense work since *Wanrow* has emphasized those differences in the particular context of battered women. *Wanrow* attempted to use acknowledgment of these different circumstances and experiences as the basis for application of the same standard of self-defense. The court's opinion emphasized that failure to accommodate the law to these differences had consequences under the equal protection clause of the Fourteenth Amendment. Otherwise, women could be denied equal rights to trial.

At the time *Wanrow* was litigated, only a few feminist litigators and legal scholars questioned the appropriateness of a formal equality model of analysis — an analysis that emphasized the sameness or similarity of men and women, as opposed to women's differences from men. Those who worked in the field were cautious about acknowledging difference in any sphere, either "real" or "socially constructed," or about arguing for a need for different legal treatment, anticipating that such acknowledgment would subject women to the "patriarchal protectionism" that constituted lesser and unequal treatment. Since then, feminist thinkers and litigators have challenged models of formal equality as based on a male standard and not accommodating women's experiences and perspectives.[77] This debate has centered on legal treatment of pregnancy, particularly state laws that single out pregnancy and maternity for special and more favorable treatment. Proponents of these laws have asserted the need for the law to take into account women's physical differences and socially constructed discrimination.[78] Yet, for some, the fear persists that legalizing "difference" necessarily implies unequal treatment.[79]

In *Wanrow*, this concern over whether acknowledging difference necessarily implies inferiority is heightened by the Washington Supreme Court's use of the word "handicaps" to describe the effect of sex discrimination.[80] Sex discrimination is disabling to women as a class and to individual women. Nonetheless, the court's use of this word was troubling. It played on the stereotype of victimized and mistreated women that has historically limited women's claims for equal treatment, and suggested that the court's responsiveness to Yvonne Wanrow's claim was shaped by patriarchal solicitude.

The expert testimony cases are the natural result of the "differences" approach: the reason for using expert testimony is to explain the content of battered women's *different* experiences and perceptions so that juries can fairly apply the *same* legal standards to them. But the questions that the expert testimony cases pose are these: If battered women's experiences are explained as different, can they ever be genuinely incorporated into the traditional standard and understood as equally reasonable? Are these different experiences inevitably perceived as inferior, as "handicaps"? If so, is it necessary to alter the traditional standard?

These tensions are heightened because the substance of the testimony in these cases is on battered woman syndrome. Theoretically, the phrase "battered woman syndrome" is a vehicle to set apart and describe battered women's "different" but common experiences. Like the word "handicaps" in *Wanrow*, however, "battered woman syndrome" carries with it stereotypes of individual incapacity and inferiority, which lawyers and judges may respond to precisely because they correspond to stereotypes of women that lawyers and judges already internalize. Although it was developed to merely *describe* the common psychological experiences and characteristics that battered women share and is undoubtedly an accurate description of these characteristics, the phrase can be misused and misheard to enshrine the old stereotypes of women—as passive, sick, powerless, and victimized—in a new form. It contributes to the historic theme of the criminal law's treatment of women: women who are criminals are crazy, helpless, or both.[81] Thus the description of battered women's "different" experiences, although purely categorical in intent, carries with it the familiar baggage of female incapacity.

Excuse and Justification

Wanrow and subsequent women's self-defense work has been premised on the view that the traditional boundaries and definitions of self-defense, as a form of justification, were sex biased and shaped by male experience. Assertion of self-defense was therefore not considered an available legal option, and women were more often shunted into some incapacity defense: insanity, heat of passion, or extreme emotional disturbance. Although the line between justification and excuse is often not entirely clear, they have different emphases. Self-defense as justification focuses on the act of defending one's self; it rests on a determination that the act was right because of its circumstances. In contrast, a finding of excuse, like insanity or heat of passion, focuses on the actor; it is a finding that the act, though wrong, should be tolerated because of the actor's particular characteristics or state of mind.[82] Traditionally, because women's acts of violence could not be viewed as reasonable, the inquiry shifted to excuse; women were viewed as incapable. Women's self-defense work has attempted to redraw the lines between justification and excuse, to challenge the stereotypes that might prevent women's acts from being seen as justified.[83] The original goal of admission of expert testimony, too, is to challenge these stereotypes and make it possible for the jury to identify with and understand the circumstances of the act and thereby to see the act as reasonable.

Battered woman syndrome is dangerous because it revives concepts of excuse. Even the New Jersey Supreme Court's thoughtful and comprehensive analysis in *Kelly* has elements of classic excuse description; it focuses on the woman's defects, the woman as subject to the "syndrome." It implies that she is limited because of *her* weakness and *her* problems,[84] and does not appear to affirm the circumstances of her act. The opinion seems to suggest that admission of expert testimony is important primarily because the battered woman "suffers" from the syndrome and therefore should not be expected to leave her home, not because it is relevant to the reasonableness of her act; the court is willing to extend its "protection" and admit the testimony because the battered woman is perceived as weak. So while the purpose of expert testimony on battered woman syndrome is to explain the reasonableness of the woman's action, the psychological aspect of the description sounds like incapacity and excuse.

By emphasizing a strain of excuse, battered woman syndrome tends to rigidify other dichotomies, which are roughly correlated with excuse and justification.[85] Excuse suggests that the act is personal to the defendant, a private act, in contrast with the public and common sense of rightness that justification reflects.[86] Excuse suggests a sense of the subject, while justification implies a more objective statement.[87] Redrawing the boundaries of justification and excuse means recasting the boundaries of the private-public and subjective-objective oppositions, making women's experiences generally, and battered women's experiences and perceptions specifically, more public and legitimate, and also more objective.

The battered woman syndrome perspective is potentially counterproductive because it explains why the woman did not leave but not why she acted; it is in tension with the notion of reasonableness necessary to self-defense since it emphasizes the woman's defects and incapacity. It also does not adequately describe the complex experiences of battered women. The effect is that women who depart from this stereotype, because of their own life situations or because the facts of their cases do not fit this perspective, are not likely to be able to take advantage of judicial solicitude. This has already presented serious defense problems in many cases. The stereotype of the reasonable battered woman who suffers from battered woman syndrome creates a new and equally rigid classification, which has the potential to exclude battered women whose circumstances depart from the model and force them once again into pleas of insanity or manslaughter. It thus reinforces the traditional boundaries of justification and excuse rather than redrawing them.

From the standpoint of the jury's determination of whether the woman acted reasonably in self-defense, the explanation of battered woman syndrome is only partial. Giving commonality to an individual woman's experience can make it seem less aberrational and more reasonable. Yet to the degree that the explanation is perceived to focus on her suffering from a "syndrome," the testimony seems to be inconsistent with the notion of reasonableness, and the substance of the testimony appears to focus on incapacity.

Battered woman syndrome has sounded to many lawyers and judges like either a separate defense or a defense akin to impaired mental state.[88] Some courts have assumed that expert testimony on battered woman syndrome was being proffered as relevant to an impaired mental state defense.[89] This is not merely the problem of the term itself—which intends to be simply descriptive—but the problem of the stereotypes it triggers for lawyers and judges. As courts are still more likely to hear and respond to a perception of women as damaged rather than as reasonable, the presentation of testimony on battered woman syndrome plays into the patriarchal attitudes that courts have exhibited toward women and women defendants.

Individuals and Groups

Wanrow highlighted the importance of the individual's perspective as shaped by her experience as a woman. The court recognized the importance of Yvonne Wanrow's own perspective as the standard of self-defense, but at the same time recognized that this perspective had a distinct and collective component to it. The court in *Wanrow* found that a central aspect of the individual woman's perception was "those perceptions which were the product of our nation's long and unfortunate history of sex-discrimination."[90] The individual woman's experience thus was shaped by the history of sex discrimination: the court saw it as a *particular* experience (that is, separate from that of men) and a *common* experience (one that women share). Thus women have a common experience that is nonetheless "different."

Wanrow challenged the dichotomy between individual and group perspective. Indeed, it stressed the necessary interrelationship between the individual and social perspective. *Wanrow's* suggestion that an individual woman's distinct experience is a crucial aspect of her perspective set the foundation for the admission of testimony concerning the content of that woman's experience.[91]

In the area of expert testimony, courts have recognized that the experiences of battered women are distinct and shared, that these experiences are outside the common experience of jurors, and that it is necessary for the jury to learn about these experiences in order to evaluate whether the woman was acting in self-defense.[92] This view is based on a recognition that the common ways battered women have acted in self-defense (such as not being able to leave, and attacking sleeping assailants) will not be otherwise understandable to jurors.

Many courts have accepted the need for expert testimony. But judicial acceptance also emphasizes the profound gap between the experiences of battered women and those of the rest of society; it reaffirms the notion of a woman's viewpoint *and* separate experience. It suggests that psychological and social factors are interrelated and that individual experience is necessarily shaped by group identity. It also suggests, though, that women's own descriptions of their experiences lack credibility because these experiences differ from the male norm, and because women generally are not considered believable.

Courts are effectively recognizing that an expert, a professional, someone not a battered woman, is needed to translate the experiences of large numbers of women in this society to the rest of society's representatives. One might argue that expert testimony may be necessary only for a transitional period, until women's voices are strong enough to be heard on their own. But the use of experts in feminist litigation poses new risks. Courts may find experts so useful in cases involving women that they regard expert testimony not as a complement to women's own voices, but as a substitute for them.

On a theoretical level, judicial acceptance of expert testimony affirmatively recognizes the substantive experience and content of sex discrimination and validates a "woman-centered" perspective. This collapses the dichotomy between individual and group experience: an experience is not just the individual's, but that of battered women generally. At the same time, judicial acceptance of expert testimony is disturbing, for it suggests that only experts can bridge the gap between individual and collective experience — and the experts who testify are generally psychologists; they are not battered women's advocates or shelter workers. Yet acceptance of expert testimony has the potential to counsel jurors that an individual woman's experience has a social validity and commonality and might be reasonable.

Subjective and Objective

The development of women's self-defense work from *Wanrow* to *Kelly* charts the change in our perspectives on the content of the standard of self-defense. Traditionally, courts and commentators have distinguished "subjective" from "objective" standards of self-defense. The objective standard — the traditional "reasonable-man standard"— looked at reasonableness from the perspective of the hypothetical reasonable man, while the subjective standard regarded reasonableness from the individual's own perspective. It has been recognized that these characterizations of subjective and objective are poles on a continuum, because under either approach the jury must find that the actor acted reasonably.

The objective reasonable-man standard of self-defense has been criticized from many perspectives: for failing to take account of complex social reality, for embodying a rigid view of individual responsibility, and for producing sex bias. Objective standards in general have been criticized by feminist legal theorists who have argued that these standards inherently embody male values. Our understanding of what is "objective" has been based largely on male experience, and stereotypes of men as objective and analytical have been contrasted with stereotypes of women as subjective and emotional.

Wanrow arose in the context of a subjective individualized standard of self-defense, and its arguments about the need for an individualized perspective responded to the traditional "reasonable-man" formulation.[93] *Wanrow,* and the women's self-defense work that has grown out of it, did not rest on the traditional subjective formulation, however.[94] The content of the individualized perspective that *Wanrow* illuminated was not simply psychological but clearly social: the woman's individual perspective shaped by her experience as a woman within the collective and historical experience of sex discrimination.[95] At the time, it seemed difficult enough to convince a jury that the woman might be reasonable even when applying a standard emphasizing the woman's own perspective. It was even more difficult to imagine arguing that the woman's experience was objectively reasonable.

More recent expert testimony cases suggest that perhaps the *Wanrow* approach was too cautious. Expert testimony on battered woman syndrome necessarily challenges the dichotomy of subjective versus objective. The individual woman seeks expert testimony about the characteristics of the larger group of which she is a member to show that she acted reasonably both as an individual and as a member of that group. The very notion of expert testimony about the common character of battered women contains a subjective (individualized) component and an objective (group) component. The substance of the testimony describes experience that in some sense can be considered as objective. Courts have held that this testimony is relevant in jurisdictions with both objective and subjective standards; indeed, in 1996 the

California Supreme Court explicitly ruled that this evidence was "generally relevant to the reasonableness, as well as the subjective existence, of defendant's belief in the need to defend." [96]

Kelly demonstrated this development. The very issue in *Kelly* was whether the expert testimony was relevant under New Jersey's standard of self-defense.[97] The trial court interpreted it as a traditional objective standard; counsel argued that under either standard the testimony was relevant. The court held that the testimony was relevant to the objective reasonableness of the defendant's belief as to whether she "reasonably believe[d] deadly force to be necessary to prevent death or serious bodily harm." [98] This recognition of a woman's and a battered woman's experiences and perceptions as objectively reasonable is vitally important. The court thereby accorded a woman's experience a group-based "public" dimension rather than merely an individual, "private" subjective one. At the same time, perhaps it is not surprising that the content of what is deemed "objective" is an image of a victimized, passive battered women. Perhaps, in fact, this is the reason the court sees it as objective and acceptable.

I close this discussion of the problem of expert testimony with a 1998 opinion written by Judge Claire L'Heureux Dubé of the Canadian Supreme Court, one of the most thoughtful jurists who has addressed the issue of expert testimony on battering. This concurring opinion, *R. v. Malott*, highlights this tension of victimization and agency in the concept of reasonableness, and clarifies the complexity of this issue of "objectiveness." In her opinion in this battered woman's self-defense case, Judge L'Heureux Dubé discusses an important prior decision of the Canadian Supreme Court, *R. v. Lavallee*, which recognized the importance of admission of expert testimony. In *Malott* she explores the ramifications of *Lavallee* for feminist lawmaking on battering generally. This opinion, from which I quote extensively, addresses many of the problems I have identified.

> First, the significance of this Court's decision in *Lavallee* . . . reaches beyond its particular impact on the law of self-defence. A crucial implication of the admissibility of expert evidence in *Lavallee* is the legal recognition that historically both the law and society may have treated women in general, and battered women in particular, unfairly. *Lavallee* accepted that the myths and stereotypes which are the products and the tools of this unfair treatment interfere with the capacity of judges and juries to justly determine a battered women's

claim of self-defence, and can only be dispelled by expert evidence designed to overcome the stereotypical thinking. The expert evidence is admissible, and necessary, in order to understand the reasonableness of a battered women's perceptions, which in *Lavallee* were the accused's perceptions that she had to act with deadly force in order to preserve herself from death or grievous bodily harm. Accordingly, the utility of such evidence in criminal cases is not limited to instances where a battered woman is pleading self-defence, but is potentially relevant to other situations where the reasonableness of a battered woman's actions or perceptions is at issue (e.g. provocation, duress or necessity).

. . . Concerns have been expressed that the treatment of expert evidence on battered woman syndrome, which is itself admissible in order to combat the myths and stereotypes which society has about battered women, has led to a new stereotype of the "battered woman." . . .

It is possible that those women who are unable to fit themselves within the stereotype of a victimized, passive, helpless, dependent, battered woman will not have their claims to self-defence fairly decided. For instance, women who have demonstrated too much strength or initiative, women of colour, women who are professionals, or women who might have fought back against their abusers on previous occasions, should not be penalized for failing to accord with the stereotypical image of the archetypal battered women. . . . Needless to say, women with these characteristics are still entitled to have their claims of self-defence fairly adjudicated, and they are also still entitled to have their experiences as battered women inform the analysis. Professor Grant . . . warns against allowing the law to develop such that a woman accused of killing her abuser must either have been "reasonable 'like a man' or reasonable 'like a battered women.'" I agree that this must be avoided. The "reasonable women" must not be forgotten in the analysis, and deserves to be as much a part of the objective standard of the reasonable person as does the "reasonable man."

How should the courts combat the "syndromization" . . . of battered women who act in self-defence? The legal inquiry into the moral culpability of a woman who is, for instance, claiming self-defence must focus on the *reasonableness* of her actions in the context of her personal experiences, and her experiences as a woman, not on her status as a battered woman and her entitlement to claim that she is suffering from "battered woman syndrome." . . . By emphasizing a woman's "learned helplessness," her dependence, her victimization, and her low self-esteem, in order to establish that she suffers from "battered woman syndrome" the legal debate shifts from the objective rationality of her actions to preserve her own life to those personal inadequacies which apparently explain her failure to flee from her abuser. Such an emphasis comports too well with society's stereotypes about women. Therefore, it should be scrupulously avoided because it only serves to undermine the important advancements achieved by the decision in *Lavallee*.

There are other elements of a woman's social context which help to explain her inability to leave her abuser, and which do not focus on those characteristics most consistent with traditional stereotypes. As Wilson J. herself recognized in *Lavallee*, . . . "environmental factors may also impair the woman's ability to leave—lack of job skills, the presence of children to care for, fear of retaliation by the man, etc. may each have a role to play in some cases." To this list of factors I would add a woman's need to protect her children from abuse, a fear of losing custody of her children, pressures to keep the family together, weaknesses of social and financial support for battered women, and no guarantee that the violence would cease simply because she left. These considerations necessarily inform the reasonableness of a woman's beliefs or perceptions of, for instance, her lack of an alternative to the use of deadly force to preserve herself from death or grievous bodily harm.

How should these principles be given practical effect in the context of a jury trial of a woman accused of murdering her abuser? To fully accord with the spirit of *Lavallee*, where the reasonableness of a battered woman's belief is at issue in a criminal case, a judge and jury should be made to appreciate that a battered woman's experiences are both individualized, based on her own history and relationships, as well as shared with other women, within the context of a society and a legal system which has historically undervalued women's experiences. A judge and jury should be told that a battered woman's experience are generally outside the common understanding of the average judge and juror, and that they should seek to understand the evidence being presented to them in order to overcome the myths and stereotypes which we all share. Finally, all of this should be presented in such a way as to focus on the reasonableness of the woman's actions, without relying on old or new stereotypes about battered women.[99]

In this opinion, Judge L'Heureux Dubé ties together the need for expert testimony to address reasonableness, the interplay between the individual and the social, the hurdles of "syndromization." She highlights the possibilities and dilemmas of expert testimony on battering, details the obstacles to fair consideration, and illuminates the profound challenge that feminist lawmaking poses to judges. Her insightful and important decision shows both how far feminist lawmaking on battering has come and how far it has yet to go.

The Impact of "Special" Legislation

State legislation has been proposed and enacted which seeks to remedy perceived inequities in the treatment of battered women at trial by addressing the "special" problems of battered women who kill. Statutes that focus exclusively on battered women, largely centering around admissibility of expert testimony, are problematic for several reasons. First, they tend to single out problems of battered women as though they are "special" and should not be understood within the general framework of the criminal law. For example, a statute that makes evidence of battered woman syndrome admissible suggests that this evidence would not otherwise be admissible. Second, it is questionable whether wholesale legislative reforms are the best solution to the problem of unequal treatment of battered woman defendants, since many problems result from unequal application of the law. Third, experience demonstrates that the language used in these statutes may be too limiting and will restrict their utility.

Two examples are a Maryland statute that permits evidence of abuse of the defendant and expert testimony on "battered spouse syndrome," and two Ohio statutes that authorize expert testimony on "battered-woman syndrome" in self-defense and insanity defenses.[100] The Ohio statutes permit the introduction of expert testimony only to support either the imminence element of a self-defense claim or "to establish the requisite impairment of the Defendant's reason necessary for a finding that the Defendant is not guilty by reason of insanity."[101] Both the Ohio statutes and the Maryland statute assume that this evidence would not be otherwise admissible. This assumption can create the impression that a separate defense for battered women has been codified.[102]

The need for special legislation concerning battering may also be questioned on other grounds. Depending on the particular state, it may be the legal standard of self-defense or the law governing the admissibility of evidence of battering that is problematic and needs reform, or it may be simply that judges apply these laws in a gender-biased fashion.[103] In many states, special legislation has been rushed through as a "quick fix" to the problem of domestic violence, without careful analysis of the particular state's criminal-law statutory scheme and of case law on procedural issues, such as burden of proof on self-defense.[104]

If special legislation to admit expert testimony is developed, it is important that the statutory language be as inclusive as possible to admit evidence of battering generally. One example is a Texas statute, which states that in all prosecutions for murder, the defendant shall be permitted to offer "relevant evidence that the defendant had been the victim of acts of family violence committed by the deceased and relevant expert testimony regarding the condition of [her] mind . . . [including] relevant facts and circumstances relating to family violence that are the basis of experts' opinions." Similarly, in Louisiana, the relevant statute does not refer at all to "battered woman syndrome" but provides simply that "an expert's opinion as to the effects of the prior assaultive acts on the accused's state of mind is admissible." A Massachusetts statute provides for admissibility of evidence "that the defendant is or has been the victim of acts of physical, sexual or psychological harm or abuse" in a wide range of circumstances, including self-defense, defense of another, duress or coercion, or "accidental harm."[105]

Post-Conviction Problems

In sum, misconceptions about battered women who kill have led to considerable confusion in judicial opinions, legal scholarship, and in more "public" sources of information, such as the media. Issues of admissibility of evidence and expert testimony on battering are confused with "special" defenses for battered women; the term "battered woman syndrome" becomes the shorthand for both. Not surprisingly, it appears that homicide cases involving battered women have a substantially higher appellate reversal rate than other comparable cases.[106] Two final areas of law reform for battered women who kill underscore these problems: ineffective assistance of counsel cases, and the host of clemency cases that have surfaced around the country.

Over the past several years, battered women defendants have initiated post-conviction efforts to claim ineffective assistance of counsel against lawyers who represented them at trial. These cases are notoriously difficult to win, for the standard for ineffectiveness set by the Supreme Court requires egregious error resulting in prejudice to the defendant; at trial the defendant has the burden of proof to show such error, and anything that may be characterized as a tactical decision by the trial attorney is nonreviewable.[107]

Of the many claims of ineffective assistance of counsel that have been brought by battered women who have been convicted at trial, a majority tend to fall into the category of claimed attorney error that courts rarely review, particularly if they are based on an attorney's failure to interview possible defense witnesses, or to otherwise investigate sources of information which could possibly be helpful to the defense.[108] Among cases involving battered women defendants where ineffective assistance of counsel claims have been successful, the most common ground appears to be faulty advice, either in the plea-bargaining process or regarding whether the defendant should testify. Courts have also found ineffective assistance based on the attorney's failure to adduce evidence or examine witnesses at trial.[109] Generally, the attorney's failure in either of these areas has resulted in no evidence of battering being offered at trial from such sources as medical reports, lay witnesses, family members, or the defendant's own testimony, or in no expert testimony on battering being offered.

From the number of claims of ineffective assistance of counsel based on faulty advice regarding plea bargains or the defendant testifying, and on attorney failure to present evidence and testimony that could have assisted the jury to understand and eradicate the very same misconceptions apparently held by counsel, it is apparent that attorneys are susceptible to misconceptions about battered women. Cases involving claims of ineffective assistance based on counsel's failure to offer jury instructions on battering suggest that many attorneys lack knowledge about the particular complexities of representing battered women.[110] Nevertheless, because many of the judges who rule on ineffective assistance of counsel claims also lack knowledge about domestic violence, and have not been sensitive to the complex issues of choice of defense and admission of evidence, they may not be particularly thoughtful or rigorous in evaluating these claims.

Clemency efforts for battered women in many states suggest a widespread recognition of the problems battered women charged with homicide have faced at trial.[111] One of the major arguments advanced by proponents of clemency for battered women has been that clemency is necessary and will continue to be necessary so long as individual battered women are denied their rights to present an adequate defense at trial and until society responds adequately to the problem of woman abuse.[112] The "clemency movement" first gained national recognition in October 1990, when Richard Celeste, then governor of Ohio, issued a mass clemency, just before leaving office, of twenty-five battered women who had been convicted of killing or assaulting their batterers. Shortly after this highly publicized act, Governor William Schaefer of Maryland granted clemency to eight battered women incarcerated in that state for killing their batterers. Governors in several other states, including Jim Edgar of Illinois, Lawton Chiles of Florida, and Pete Wilson of California, have granted clemency to battered women convicted of killing or assaulting their batterers. In 1998, Colorado Governor Roy Romer granted clemency to four battered women, and six women were granted clemency in Florida. International human rights appeals for clemency for battered women outside the United States have also begun.[113]

Of the nearly forty thousand women in prison in the United States, roughly two thousand are incarcerated for killing a husband, ex-husband, or boyfriend—a number that constitutes around one-third of all women in prison for homicide.[114] Studies have concluded that at least 45 percent and perhaps as many as 97 percent of incarcerated women who killed a partner were abused by the person they killed.[115] We do not know exactly how many of these women may not even have gone to trial, consenting to plea-bargain arrangements on the advice of attorneys who were unaware that their clients were battered, or who were ignorant of the possible legal significance of evidence of battering.[116] Many of those women who did go to trial may have received unfair trials, either because of attorney ineffectiveness or judicial error in applying the law where evidence of battering was present. Because clemency petitions can be based on many different grounds, including attorney error or ineffectiveness, or judicial error that was not appealed or affirmed on appeal, we can only speculate about the number of cases in which clemency might be sought. Nonetheless, the number of cases of women in prison for killing their batterers in which clemency has been sought, and the number in which clemency might be sought, suggest that attorney and judicial conduct has had a substantial impact on women's lives and on the criminal justice system.

Resistance to Equality

The premise of the work seeking to ensure battered women equal rights to trial has been the radical idea that battered women's experiences had to be articulated, genuinely heard, and taken into account in reshaping the law. Recognizing the social context—women's experiences of battering and society's response to battering—was crucial, because without understanding the social context and the social circumstances of battering, the facts of a particular case could not be understood. As in all legal cases, the critical struggle is who gets to define the facts. Without first listening to women's experiences, and without understanding the social framework and experience of battering, it was simply not possible for lawyers to fairly represent battered women in these circumstances. Truly listening to women who have been hurt and traumatized, who may not have words to express their pain, who may not trust that anyone will listen, who may be viewed as "difficult" because they are angry, or whose gender, racial, cultural, or class experiences may be different from the lawyer's, judge's, or juror's, is not easy. But really hearing the women's experiences in these cases is not only transformative; it can mean the difference between life and death. For battered women who kill, these experiences, whether told to defense lawyers, in court, on clemency petitions, or in other contexts, are, as Jody Armour puts it, "their social reality, constitute their social identity, and vindicate their social existence." The stakes attached to the telling of this narrative are high; this "explains much of the stubborn resistance to this work."[117]

Resistance to equality takes many forms. First, there is the resistance of lawyers who may find it hard to listen to the voices and experiences of battered women, even when they can be surfaced and articulated, and who then must thoughtfully consider the implications of these stories for the defenses that may be available within an equal rights framework. Resistance to hearing these experiences as complex and nuanced is explicit in the crude characterization of "abuse excuse." Judges' resistance may lead them to engage in a process of gender construction in which women's experiences are considered, "but in the form of sexist stereotypes (of women as "bad" or "mad") which reinforce the oppression and control of women in general."[118] Finally, because this work argues for affirmative recognition of the significance of social context, and of the necessary interrelationship between individual action, social context, and social responsibility, it challenges fundamental assumptions about "free will" in the criminal law, and triggers considerable resistance for some criminal law scholars. All these aspects of resistance are forms of resistance to equality. The legal problems of battered women who kill demonstrate the devastating impact of social failure to link violence to equality.

9

Motherhood and Battering

The attitudes that society has toward battered women in general are made even more complex when they are mothers. It is difficult for most people to understand why an adult would "choose" to put up with abuse from another adult. But in the public mind, the stakes change dramatically when an abused woman has children. Mothers carry enormous ideological weight in our culture. Because we consider that a mother's fundamental duty is to protect her children, maternal behavior that exposes children to harm is viewed as unthinkable, unnatural, and incomprehensible. Battered women who are mothers are reviled.

Feminist theorists have begun to address the particular problems associated with women as mothers. As Martha Fineman has observed: "Mother is a universally possessed symbol (although its meaning may vary across and within cultures). We all have a mother—some of us are mothers. As a lived experience, Mother is virtually universally shared in our culture and, therefore, more intimately and intensely personalized than many other symbols. Mother, however, is an ambiguous symbol—one about which there is contest. For that reason, the importance of Mother as a symbol is greatly enhanced on both an individual and a societal level. In its various configurations, Mother is a significant factor in defining our understanding of our own familial, sexual, and social circumstances. In this way, it is also significant in our construction of universal meanings—defining the general qualities of life for us."[1] Motherhood is an enormously complex subject, and a crucial one for feminist legal theorists and practitioners. Much important theoretical work has begun to explore the diverse contexts in which women mother—as single mothers, teen mothers, lesbian mothers, mothers in heterosexual relationships with "boyfriends," and mothers with HIV—and the roles of race, class, poverty, age, and disability in shaping motherhood.

Motherhood is critical to women's subordination. It is what Fineman has called a "colonized concept—an event physically practiced and experienced by women, but occupied and defined, given content and value, by the core concepts of patriarchal ideology." Women's status as childbearers determines their identity; women bear the primary responsibility for childbearing—work that is revered in flowery language but degraded in fact. Being a mother is also considered women's primary social role; all women are mothers or potential mothers, and there is enormous pressure on women to become mothers. Social and legal construction of motherhood is important, because as Fineman suggests, "motherhood is central to the social and legal definition of woman. A woman who does not have children will still, in the context of law and legal institutions, be treated as though she is (or may become) a mother. Social construction and legal ramifications tend to operate independently of individual circumstances."[2]

The social meaning of motherhood does not capture women's far more complex experiences of mothering in life. Dorothy Roberts explains: "Adrienne Rich distinguished between motherhood, the experience—the relationship between a woman and her children—and motherhood as enforced identity and political institution. Some women may experience motherhood as debilitating and intrusive. Even though some feminist theory calls motherhood oppressive, many women experience fulfillment and happiness in mothering. Motherhood contains this fascinating paradox: Although it is devalued, exhausted, confining and a principal way that women are shackled to an inferior status, motherhood is for many women life's greatest joy."[3]

In this chapter I examine the particular experiences of battered women who are mothers as a second case study of feminist lawmaking on battering.

Battered Motherhood

Public attitudes toward battered women who are mothers are shaped first by the operation of the traditional myths and misconceptions that shape views of battered women generally. As it is, battered women are pathologized, and are viewed either as helpless victims or as independent agents. When motherhood is added to the mix, still another set of factors comes into play: the general cultural attitudes that shape our views that mothers are all responsible, that mother-love is sacred, and that mothers are people who would and should sacrifice anything for their children. Powerful cultural revulsion is directed against women who do not conform to these stereotypes—Susan Smith, who drowned her children; "crack" mothers who have addicted their children; mothers who do not want their newborns to be tested for HIV; or women who leave their children unprotected and vulnerable.

The severe problems faced by battered women who are mothers may begin with pregnancy, for the correlation between pregnancy and battering is astonishingly high. Forty percent of assaults by male partners begin during a woman's first pregnancy, and battered women are three times as likely as nonbattered women to be injured during pregnancy.[4] Approximately 23 percent of obstetric patients are in abusive relationships. Women who are battered during pregnancy suffer two times the number of miscarriages as those who are not domestic violence victims.[5] For those whose babies survive, violence threatens the babies' health and safety. Not only are these babies born into abusive homes, but some have been born with ruptured abdominal organs or broken bones resulting from blows or kicks to the mother's abdomen.[6]

Given the societal importance placed on childbearing and motherhood, the very notion that a woman would be subject to battery during her pregnancy is shocking. In the media, this type of battering is rarely exposed except in cases involving famous people; for example, athlete Lamar Thomas' "personal problem" of being charged with battery on his then-pregnant fiancée.[7] Yet despite the lack of press coverage, police files are littered with instances of pregnancy battering. A few examples over the course of one year reveal the pervasiveness of this crime. In St. Petersburg, Florida, Eldon John Beall violated his domestic battery probation by hitting his girlfriend on Valentine's Day, 1997—the day after she discovered she was pregnant. On March 8, 1997, in New Orleans, George Martin was booked for second-degree battery after dragging his girlfriend, who was five months pregnant, into his apartment and causing injuries to her lower abdominal area. In Chicago on May 15, 1997, José Sanchez hit his pregnant wife in the stomach with a wrench and was charged with aggravated battery. In Orlando on May 22, 1997, a pregnant woman miscarried after being kicked in the stomach. On May 25, 1997, an Orlando man was charged with aggravated battery for shoving his pregnant girlfriend when she argued with him about striking her other four children with a leather strap. In New Orleans on May 31, 1997, a twenty-nine-year-old man was booked for battery following a domestic violence dispute with his pregnant girlfriend. On July 10, 1997, a man was charged with domestic battery in Orlando after hitting his pregnant wife. José Fernandez was wanted in Ft. Lauderdale as of July 16, 1997, for domestic battery on a pregnant woman and violation of probation of charges of battery on a pregnant woman. In Aurora, Illinois, on July 23, 1997, a twenty-two-year-old man was being held for beating his wife, who was thirty-one weeks pregnant; although he knew that she had a high-risk pregnancy, he repeatedly kicked her in the abdomen. In Palm Bay, Florida, on August 1, 1997, a thirty-four-year-old man was arrested and charged with battery on a pregnant woman. On August 2, 1997, in Jacksonville, Florida, a thirty-nine-year-old man was arrested for beating his pregnant girlfriend.[8] The list goes on.

A medical anthropologist studying pregnancy and drug use determined that violence was the central theme in the lives of women interviewed for the study. Of the 84 women who had been battered (out of a total of 120 in the study), 38 of them (45 percent) reported being battered during their current or most recent pregnancy. The comments these women made during their interviews are chilling. Darlene, a twenty-two-year-old African American woman who was four months pregnant when interviewed, talked about the father of her baby and her uncertainty: "When he gets mad at me, he'll threaten to hit me. When I'm pregnant it's like, 'I'll hit you in your stomach.' " Eliza, a twenty-nine-year-old African American woman, described how she miscarried twins following abuse by their father: "He told me he'd kill me and these babies too. Well, the babies was dead. They was gone and dead and gone. I mean, he put his knee all the way into my stomach. Hey, there's no way they could have survived." Another woman recounted how her husband caused her to miscarry by hitting her across the back with a hammer and fracturing the baby's skull.[9]

Why do men batter their pregnant partners? Dorothy Roberts explains that battering is often particularly directed at a woman's identity as a mother. Violence, therefore, begins or intensifies when a woman becomes pregnant. Some theorize that the violence ensues because of the man's sense of competition with the child for the mother's attention. Roberts contends, however, that battering pregnant women and new mothers is "part of men's continued quest to enforce the woman's compliance with her role as mother." She cites situations in which men batter their pregnant partners to coerce them to carry the pregnancy to term, or to attempt to enforce women's maternal role. Battering during pregnancy is linked to women's inferior status in the family and her resistance to that inferiority.[10] Not surprisingly, men who batter their pregnant partners also abuse and batter their children.

Studies have suggested a high correlation between male battering of women and child abuse; indeed, some researchers argue that domestic violence may be "the single most important context for child abuse."[11] Children of battered women are not only likely to suffer because they experience their father hurting their mother; they are also likely to suffer serious injury themselves at the hand of their father. Statistical evidence also suggests that men who batter their wives are more likely than other men to batter their children.[12] Motherhood, then, compounds the harm that battered women face, for where a child is beaten by a father or even simply exposed to violence, the mother is likely to be held primarily or even exclusively responsible for any harm that the child suffers.[13] These tensions are dramatized by highly publicized cases, by legislative reform efforts to hold battered mothers responsible, and by problems that battered women may face with child custody.

Our culture constructs two kinds of mothers—"good" mothers who are self-sacrificing and "bad" mothers who do not conform to that stereotype. Mothering is perceived as a single entity, outside any social context and without any understanding of social, economic, or psychological constraints. Because women are viewed as exclusively responsible for children, the problems that children face in the particular family, as well as in the society at large, are held to be the fault of the mother; hence women are held to be responsible for the oft-asserted societal decline in "family values."

There are many different grounds for accusations of bad mothering—working outside the home, being sexually active, having a homosexual relationship, using drugs—but a whole category of bad mothering is reserved for women who appear to be placing their own needs or interests ahead of their responsibility to the children. Classic cases of "bad mothers" are mothers who are charged with abuse or neglect or other such grounds for the termination of parental rights. Such cases frequently involve women whose mothering is constrained by poverty, teen-age pregnancy, or drug or alcohol abuse, and battering is almost always in the background.

For many cases that come to court, however, judicial judgments of "bad" mothering occur even though the facts concerning family violence are fragmented or invisible. Bernadine Dohrn, a lawyer who represents poor mothers and children, notes: "Where child abuse or neglect is adjudicated, for example, domestic violence against the mother may not be apparent. At the same time . . . the adjudication of child abuse or neglect takes place in a troubling vacuum which rejects consideration of context: a mother's need to survive and to protect her children, their economic dependency, or their fear of physical violence. This snapshot, legal isolation from social context, institutional neglect, and complex relationships of power, therefore relies exclusively on maternal accountability and blame. Fathers, step-fathers and "boyfriends," as well as larger social institutions, are absent during the legal and moral adjudication of mothers."[14] A woman with children who talks about her experience of domestic violence in any context that can bring the legal or child-protective process to bear on her life may fear, with good reason, that she will be blamed; the mother, not the father who commits the violence, is likely to be held responsible for child abuse or neglect either because of her presumed failure to protect her child or because of her silence. These attitudes dramatically affect battered women who are mothers in a range of circumstances where children are sexually abused, seriously hurt, or killed by battering fathers. Battered women face serious consequences for their behavior; they may be charged with criminal conduct for failure to protect, held liable for abuse and neglect, have their parental rights terminated, or face criminal responsibility for endangering the welfare of a child, for assault and battery, or for homicide. Women who do seek divorce may very well be viewed as "unfit" to have custody of the children. The concern of most abused women for the safety and well-being of their children and their active steps to protect them are ignored or diminished. These cases present complex factual circumstances over which public opinion is often deeply divided, even among battered women's advocates.

Hedda Nussbaum is perhaps the archetypal symbol of the battered mother in recent times. She was severely beaten over many years by her partner, Joel Steinberg, who killed their daughter, Lisa Steinberg. Commentary concerning Hedda Nussbaum seemed to suggest that her failure to act to protect Lisa was more shocking than Steinberg's violent acts. The case of Susan Smith, the South Carolina woman who killed her two sons, is seen as much more disturbing; her acts threaten our deeply entrenched views of appropriate maternal conduct. Comparing public responses to her behavior with those to the behavior of, say, O. J. Simpson, is illuminating. Male violence in the family, even when it is extreme and lethal, seems like a natural extension of male patriarchal authority in general; women's failure to mother makes them monsters.[15]

Hard as it is for society to imagine that a woman who is battered is "reasonable," it is even more difficult to imagine that a women who is battered could be a good mother. Our conception is that a "good mother" is entirely self-sacrificing, that mothers should transcend their experiences and act on behalf of children regardless of their own lives. Since as a society we expect more of women who are mothers, women who are battered require us to revise our expectations.

Hedda Nussbaum's situation attracted national attention perhaps because "we are fascinated by that which we recognize."[16] During Joel Steinberg's trial for Lisa's murder, considerable controversy arose among feminists concerning whether Hedda Nussbaum should share responsibility for Lisa's death. In particular, feminist writer Susan Brownmiller charged that despite Hedda Nussbaum's experiences as a severely battered woman, she should not have been treated as a victim and absolved of all liability. Instead, she should have been prosecuted along with Steinberg, for she was also responsible for the death. Views absolving Nussbaum were "simplistic and alarming," Brownmiller maintained. She wrote in the *New York Times:* "Systematic battering combined with misguided, though culturally inculcated, notions of love is not a sufficient excuse to exonerate Hedda Nussbaum from her share of culpability in Lisa Steinberg's death. . . . When decent, honorable women insist that a piece of Hedda Nussbaum resides in us all, they give the Joel Steinbergs of this world far too much credit and far too much power. More insidiously, they perpetuate the specious notion that women are doomed to be victims of the abnormal psychology of love at all cost."[17]

The dilemma that women who are battered face is precisely being forced to choose between their battering partners and their children. Brownmiller's contempt for women who face that circumstance is shared by society, even though it is hypocritical in light of the role "romance" plays in shaping women's self-definitions, identities, and conceptions of their futures. In an essay written about the Susan Smith case in 1995, Barbara Ehrenreich saw the dilemma of the "zero-sum choice between romantic love and mother love" for Susan Smith, and women in general, in this way:

But there is a theme implicit in the Smith story that ought to be familiar to every woman with a functioning heart, and that theme is love. Not the good kind of love, obviously, the kind that results in homemade cookies and all-night vigils with feverish children, but the ungovernable, romantic kind of love that the songs tell us about, as in "addicted to love" and "I would do anything to hold on to you." Whether Smith intended to kill herself or just wanted to win back her lover by getting rid of the kids, we will never know for sure. Either way, she was an extremist in the cause of love, and her sons, horribly enough, were human sacrifices to it. "Good" women put the children first. They forgo disruptive romantic entanglements, if necessary, they endure loveless marriages until the children grow up. This is what Susan Smith would have done if she had any capacity for conventional feminine virtue; stuck by her philandering husband and of course refrained from fooling around herself.

But Susan Smith was not programmed to be "good." Everything in her own story taught her to put the pull of sexual, romantic love above the needs of little children. When she was six, her father killed himself in response to the heartbreak of divorce. Susan had been his favorite, but this didn't make her important enough for him to stick around.

It was her mother, though, who most clearly prefigured Susan's crime. In the wake of Susan's own suicide attempt at age 13, psychiatrists recommended that she be hospitalized for depression. Her mother and stepfather refused, and if we find it "unthinkable" that a mother could kill her own children, it is not a whole lot less unthinkable that a mother could reject a chance to help a child bent on killing herself.

Two years later, Susan got another vivid lesson in the priority of adult desires over children's needs. Her stepfather, a pillar of the community, started sexually molesting her. Susan reported the abuse, but she and her mother decided to drop the charges. Message to Susan from Mom: I'm willing to sacrifice you—your physical integrity, your self-esteem, if necessary even your life—in order to hold on to this man.

The creepy details are peculiar to Smith's case, but the message to girls is similarly demeaning. Love (of men) is the supreme adventure! The peak experience! The only possible redemption for a worthless little creature like you! And, needless to say, the love celebrated in songs and soap operas and romance novels is not the love for sticky-faced toddlers.

So we have, in the Susan Smith case, the female dilemma at its starkest: Not the pallid "family-vs.-career" predicament, but a zero-sum choice between romantic love and mother love, with guaranteed misery no matter which you chose. . . . One socially redeeming lesson we can derive from the Susan Smith case, then, is that girls need the possibility of some great adventures other than romantic love. Yes, love is a joy and a shining moment of transcendence in our life. But it is not the only one. If I controlled the nation's playlists, there'd be a lot fewer songs about "giving all for love," and plenty of danceable tunes about running for Congress or getting through community college as a single mother.[18]

Social workers, child protective workers, and many judges openly express attitudes that blame women for the dilemma of being caught between their partners and their children. Mothers who are "too dependent on men" or fail to put their children's interests first are routinely condemned. But in these cases, battered women's active efforts to extricate themselves or attend to their children's needs frequently remain invisible, ignored by those who render judgments about their behavior.

In *Commonwealth v. Cardwell*, for example, the court affirmed the conviction of a battered mother for endangering the welfare of her daughter because she failed to leave home after she learned that her daughter was being sexually abused by the batterer. The court interprets the facts in this way: "In the case sub judice, approximately ten months elapsed from the date appellant Julia Cardwell learned that her daughter Alicia was being sexually abused by Clyde Cardwell to the date Alicia ran away from home to escape the intolerable situation. In those ten months, Julia's only actions directed at protecting her daughter consisted of: writing two letters to Clyde that did little more than express her knowledge of and anger at his abuse of Alicia; applying for Alicia to transfer schools; and moving some of her and Alicia's clothing to Julia's mother's house. We note that the remedy of moving to Julia's mother's house was tragically frustrated by the destruction by fire of that house in May 1984, but the fact remains that Julia took no further steps to relieve her daughter's desperate situation in the four months that ensued from May 1984 until Alicia ran away from home in September 1984."[19]

In another case involving termination of parental rights, the court expressed a similar attitude. The judge stated that "the children were removed from their home in 1986 because of respondent's inability or unwillingness to protect them from their father's acts of domestic violence, physical abuse and suspected sexual abuse. Rather than cooperate with petitioner, learn to act as a protective parent and avoid contact with individuals who were reasonably likely to place the children at risk, respondent repeatedly 'made up'

with the father and secretly permitted him and a succession of other para-
mours to reside with her and be present with the children during periods of
visitation. Clearly faced with a choice between her various romantic interests,
respondent consistently elected in favor of the latter." [20]

Failure to Protect Children

The Steinberg case is one illustration of the link between woman abuse and
child abuse that is now being brought to public attention.[21] These situations
raise critical questions as to whether the abused woman has any legal responsibility and should therefore face criminal or civil charges of failure to protect, child abuse, or child neglect. Many battered women's advocates were
outraged by Brownmiller's condemnation of Hedda Nussbaum. Organizing
letter-writing campaigns and public statements in response, battered women's
groups suggested that Brownmiller was falling into the historic role of "blaming the victim." [22]

In this circumstance, "victim" seems to be an accurate characterization of
the battered woman's experience and situation; she is trapped by a man who
is abusing both her and her children. Nevertheless, because of her role as a
mother, characterizing the battered woman as a victim becomes problematic.
Society expects mothers to transcend their victimization and to act on behalf
of their children, regardless of their own situation. This societal expectation
is fortified by a host of legislation that penalizes battered women, both criminally and civilly, for the "failure" to protect their children from abuse. In fact,
a battered woman may be held liable for her batterer's abuse of children on
a number of statutory grounds: child endangerment, injury to child, neglect,
abuse, and even battery to an unborn child.[23]

Battered mothers whose children are abused by their batterers have been
prosecuted for manslaughter, child abuse, or child neglect based on the theory
that they failed to protect their children from the batterer. This effort to criminalize parental inaction, particularly the inaction of mothers, blurs the distinctions between child abuse, child neglect, and other crimes against children. In fact, several states expressly criminalize omissions by parents as well
as commissions; in addition, several states expressly define the crime of failure
to protect. In Mississippi, for example, a person is guilty of felonious abuse
or battery of a child if that person "omits the performance of any duty." In

Hawaii, a person is guilty of endangering the welfare of a minor "by violating or interfering with any legal duty of care or protection owed to such minor."[24]

Surveys of reported cases reveal the pattern of prosecutions against battered women where their batterer is also the abuser of the child.[25] In many states, in fact, the mens rea ("state of mind") element of a crime involving children is "knowledge" or "criminal negligence."[26] These statutes permit prosecutions against battered women who are *not* the actual abusers of their children. The critical inquiry for courts becomes what kind of affirmative act must a non-abusive parent undertake to protect children from an abusive parent, boyfriend, guardian, or other person. In 1997 the Arizona Supreme Court held that evidence of battered women's syndrome does not negate the mother's requisite mens rea for purposes of criminal conviction.[27] In a similar vein, Kentucky's Supreme Court held that there is an affirmative duty to prevent physical injury to children.[28] Despite the relative ease in proving abuse, negligence, or endangerment under the current statutes, few states provide battered women with an affirmative defense to a charge relating to crimes against their children.[29]

Many cases that involve battered women with children who are abused are just being uncovered; numerous reported cases involving abuse or neglect do not mention the fact that the mother had been battered.[30] The reasons for this omission are the same ones we have seen in other contexts: the woman may not have felt comfortable enough to talk about it; the lawyer who heard the information may have trivialized it, may not have known what to do with the information, or may have failed to understand the impact the information had on the charges the woman was facing. Mothering is such a powerful cultural phenomenon that the pressure to be a "good mother" (or to not admit to any behavior that would suggest "bad" mothering) is enormous. Mothers inevitably internalize these dichotomous stereotypes. Lawyers who have represented "bad mothers" in a range of contexts frequently report that the women they represent continue to insist, in the face of terrible circumstances and tragedies (including the deaths of their own children), that they have been "good mothers."

Judges and juries may not be told that a woman is battered, or may not consider that fact to be relevant in deciding whether to find her culpable for failure to protect. But having been battered can actually work against women. A judge can decide that a woman's experience of battering shows her awareness of the dangerousness of her husband.[31] These dilemmas are common in situations involving abuse, neglect, or termination of parental rights. A 1989 Illinois case held that continuing physical abuse of one parent by another, where the child is not physically abused, will cause emotional damage to a child and thus constitutes child neglect and "an environment injurious to the minor's welfare." Recent New York cases have also held that children's witnessing domestic violence constitutes a basis for neglect. A 1992 New York case, *In the Matter of Glenn G,* involved a battered woman who discovered that her husband was sexually abusing their children.[32] The father was charged with possession of lewd photographs and sexual contact; the mother was charged with sexual abuse and neglect. After an extensive hearing, and the testimony of an expert who testified about the mother's experience with battering, the judge determined that the mother was "afflicted" with battered woman syndrome so that she was not liable for abuse, but held that she was still liable for neglect because neglect was a strict-liability offense. Yet analysis of the facts of this case suggests that this mother was anything but passive; she made extraordinary, though ultimately unsuccessful, efforts to contact helping institutions and to get the police to intervene, and she had left the state. The characterization of her as "afflicted" with "battered woman syndrome" does not capture her experience. It ignores her repeatedly thwarted efforts, her acts of "resistant self-direction." *Glenn G.* highlights the problem of viewing mothering in an individual context when social oppression is obscured.

In contrast, *In the Interest of Betty J. W.,* a West Virginia case concerning a battered mother that involved termination of parental rights, demonstrates acknowledgment of this social responsibility. The court held that termination of parental rights was not appropriate unless services were offered to the battered mother to address the problems she was facing. The appellate opinion does not refer to explicit testimony on battering, at least by an expert. Yet the appellate court reversed the trial court and granted an improvement period (a period of time by which she must improve her parenting or have her parental rights terminated) because of the woman's experience of being battered. In another termination case, *In re Farley,* the appellate court upheld the lower court's termination of parental rights to a battered woman without opinion. A dissenting judge wrote an opinion protesting the failure of the trial judge and the other appellate judges to consider the woman's experience of being battered and to grant her an improvement period.[33]

A series of cases involving criminal liability of battered women for harm to children illustrates patterns of ineffective lawyering and problematic judicial consideration of battering that are similar to the patterns seen in cases of battered women who have killed assailants. In each of the cases, battered women sought to present testimony at trial concerning their experiences of battering and the way these experiences constrained their actions, resulting in their failure to protect their children from harm. Nonetheless, they were convicted at trial. They appealed their convictions, but in only one of these cases did the appellate court recognize the relevance of and need for testimony on battering and reverse the conviction on that ground.

In *Arizona v. Mott*, Shelly Kay Mott was charged with child abuse and first-degree murder for the death of her two-and-a-half-year-old daughter, Sheena.[34] Mott lived with her boyfriend, Vincent Near, and had left her two young children with him on the night of the incident. She returned to find Near standing over Sheena, fanning her head with a towel. He told Shelly that she had fallen off the toilet and hit her head. An acquaintance who was a former paramedic happened to stop at the house, and after looking at Sheena told Near to take her to the hospital. Near refused. The next morning Mott found Sheena dead. According to the Arizona Supreme Court opinion, the following events took place at trial:

> Defendant disclosed as a defense that she "lacked the capacity to act due to the Battered Woman Syndrome." Defendant then filed a motion to admit the testimony of Dr. Cheryl Karp to prove that defendant was unable to form the requisite intent to have acted knowingly or intentionally. The trial court initially ordered that Dr. Karp could testify regarding her opinions of defendant's "emotional make-up and capabilities." Upon hearing Dr. Karp testify at trial, however, the trial court found that the testimony regarding the battered-woman syndrome was an attempt to determine a diminished capacity defense. The court ruled the testimony was inadmissible.
>
> Defendant offered the expert testimony of Dr. Karp to challenge the element of knowledge or intent on the child abuse counts. Defendant made an offer of proof before trial to the trial court regarding Dr. Karp's testimony. Additionally the trial court allowed the doctor to testify at the mitigation hearing after the trial to make a further record of the proffered testimony.
>
> Dr. Karp had concluded that defendant was a battered woman and that being a battered woman was relevant to her ability to protect her children. According to the doctor, a battered woman forms a "traumatic bond" to her batterer. She does not feel that she can escape her environment; she is hopeless and depressed. Furthermore, the battered woman cannot sense dangers or protect

others from danger. She is inclined to believe what the batterer tells her and will lie to protect him. Dr. Karp concluded that defendant's history of being abused, in conjunction with her limited intelligence, prohibited her from being able to decide to take Sheena to the hospital. Prior to trial, defendant's counsel offered the evidence to "explain to the jury why [defendant] lacked the capacity to defy [her partner]."

As a threshold issue, the state claims that defendant has waived any claim of error because she withdrew the battered-woman syndrome defense. Though defendant withdrew the syndrome as a defense, she continued to argue that evidence of the syndrome and her own history of being abused were relevant evidence of her decisionmaking process and her inability to form the requisite mental state for the charged offenses. Consequently we find that defendant has not waived her claim that the trial court erred by precluding the proffered testimony.

Defendant's purpose in offering Dr. Karp's testimony was to demonstrate that defendant was not capable of forming the requisite mental state of knowledge or intent. Thus the evidence of defendant's history of being battered and of her limited intellectual ability was not offered as a defense to excuse her crimes but rather as evidence to negate the mens rea element of the crime. Courts have referred to the use of expert psychiatric evidence to negate mens rea as a "diminished capacity" or "diminished responsibility" defense.[35]

Mott presents familiar themes. First, according to the Arizona Supreme Court's opinion, the trial lawyer had apparently proffered the testimony as relevant to a "battered-woman syndrome defense." Second, the lawyer appears to have failed to explain why the purpose of this testimony is not a claim of impaired mental state equivalent to diminished capacity. The trial judge (and the Supreme Court majority) understand this testimony as diminished capacity and hold that it is inadmissible under prevailing Arizona law.

A vigorous dissent contests the majority's interpretation of the defendant's offer of proof and the prevailing law. The dissenting judge argues that "defense counsel assured the trial judge that Dr. Karp would not be asked to testify about Defendant's state of mind at the time of the offense but only about the effect such a history might have on Defendant's decisionmaking, rationalization, comprehension and the like"; this "offer complied with the rule we have set down for such evidence in cases in which prosecution witnesses are allowed to testify about the behavioral patterns of victims of incest or child molestation."[36] Judge Feldman, the dissenting judge, comments:

The trial judge nevertheless precluded Dr. Karp's testimony; in fact he even re-fused to even allow defense counsel to make a more specific offer of proof. It was not until defense counsel raised the issue again just before closing argu-ments that he was allowed to put the following in the record:

Dr. Karp would have testified to Defendant's history, history of suffering physical abuse as a child at the hands of her parents, sexual abuse, rape, mo-lestation at the hands of her brother, her friend's father and other individuals while she was a child and then her continued physical abuse by boyfriends, by her husband and by Mr. Near, and that abuse made her—how she fit the category of being a battered woman, along with all the expert testimonies of what a battered woman means, how that would relate to her decisionmaking as an adult.

As her later testimony at Defendant's mitigation hearing illustrated, Dr. Karp would have provided the jurors with information from which they might con-clude that fear, low intelligence and psychological trauma resulting from a life-time of abuse affected Defendant's ability to make "the kind of decision it would take in order to take her child to the hospital." [37]

According to Judge Feldman, the majority are wrong because they confuse the use of psychiatric testimony to negate mens rea with diminished capacity. To Judge Feldman, the trial court's preclusion of the defendant's expert testi-mony deprived "Defendant of the ability to test the mens rea element of the state's case in the adversarial process . . . and violate[d] Defendant's right to due process of law." Significantly, Judge Feldman, too, sees the Defendant's proffer as testimony concerning "mental impairment" and "mental disorder"; his disagreement with the majority is that it should not be precluded under Arizona law.[38]

In *State v. Wyatt*, Julie Wyatt was charged with child abuse resulting in bodily injury, child neglect resulting in bodily injury, first-degree murder of a child caused by failure or refusal to provide medical care, malicious assault, and first-degree murder.[39] She was convicted on all but the last count. Julie lived with Kevin Browning and his two sons—Derek, age two-and-a-half, and Derek's four-year-old brother. The opinion of the Supreme Court of West Vir-ginia described the facts as follows:

Evidence at trial indicated that Derek had been beaten over a period of days before his collapse. Ms. Wyatt alleged that Derek's father, Kevin Browning, in-flicted those beatings. The evidence further indicated that Derek's body was covered with bruises, especially his feet, which were totally black. Derek also had a bald spot on the back of his head, which Ms. Wyatt explained was the result of Kevin Browning repetitively pushing Derek backwards, causing him to hit his head on the floor. Ms. Wyatt further alleged that she failed to seek help for Derek because her relationship with Kevin Browning, who was absent at the time of the child's collapse, had been violently abusive over a period of time. Ms. Wyatt testified that, at the time immediately prior to the child's collapse, she was afraid to seek medical attention for the child, and thus report the extensive abuse inflicted on the child by Kevin Browning, for fear he would return and further abuse her. However, upon the child's collapse, Ms. Wyatt immediately ran for help.

In light of Ms. Wyatt's assertions that she feared for her safety by reason of her abusive relationship with Kevin Browning, the defense attempted to pursue a battered woman syndrome theory of defense. In support of this theory, defense counsel offered the testimony of an expert witness, a psychologist, Dr. Lois Veronen. The State objected to the use of the theory and also objected to the expert's testimony on the grounds that it did not satisfy the criteria for scientific expert testimony. After *in camera* testimony [testimony "in chambers" before the judge alone] by the expert, the trial court refused to allow her to testify regarding battered women's syndrome, but ruled that the expert would be permitted to testify regarding the appellant's mental state at the time of the alleged offense. Trial counsel ultimately declined to call the expert to testify before the jury.[40]

The court reversed Julie Wyatt's conviction on the ground that the instruction to the jury on failure to provide medical care had failed to specify that the accused had to intend the death of the child. But the court also discussed the issue of expert testimony on battering:

As noted above, the principal defense offered by the appellant was that her condition as a battered woman interfered with her freedom of action in the care of the deceased child and left her afraid to report and otherwise deal with the condition of the child prior to the time the child collapsed. Appellant argues that the trial court erred in refusing to permit an expert on "battered women" to testify concerning what has come to be known as the battered women's syndrome and appellant's state of mind or mental condition arising from her alleged status as a battered woman.

Apparently, this issue first arose in pre-trial proceedings related to defense expenses. At that time, the trial judge said that he did not "really think there is such a thing" as battered women's syndrome. Nevertheless, defense counsel obtained the services of a Dr. Lois Veronen, a psychologist, who, after interviewing Ms. Wyatt, prepared to testify at trial. During the trial, the prosecution requested an *in camera* hearing to determine the admissibility of Dr. Veronen's testimony. Near the end of the State's case, the doctor gave her testimony *in camera*. The trial court initially ruled that Dr. Veronen's testimony would be excluded. The court commented first, that he did not believe that the use of the battered women's syndrome had been expanded beyond use in a claim of self-defense, and second, it was not clear that the appellant had suffered abuse at the hands of the child's father. Defense counsel then asked if the court would reconsider its ruling if there was testimony that Kevin Browning, Derek's father, abused the appellant. The court indicated that if such testimony were presented, it would reconsider allowing the doctor to testify regarding the appellant's frame of mind. Near the end of appellant's case, counsel asked the court whether Dr. Veronen would be permitted to testify. The court ruled that the doctor would be permitted to testify only to appellant's state of mind and that she would be permitted to testify about the battered woman's syndrome as such. Because of some difficulty in the transcription of the record, it cannot be discerned whether counsel objected to the court's ruling at that time. In any event, the defense opted not to call Dr. Veronen, even on the issues for which the trial court indicated it would admit her testimony.

At the *in camera* hearing, Dr. Veronen testifies as follows: "Julie Wyatt is suffering from post-traumatic stress disorder; more specifically, the battered woman's syndrome, which contains some additional elements that are not necessarily stated in the post-traumatic stress disorder diagnosis. And that is the identification of the mental disorder. . . ."

Her perception was not that this child was in danger or that this child was being intentionally harmed in a grave manner. Her perception that she adopted was that of Kevin Browning's. . . . she did not perceive the child in grave danger. She did not recognize the severe condition . . .

She did not recognize her—her obligation because she did not recognize it as a severe condition.

Further, Ms. Wyatt's counsel questioned Dr. Veronen as follows: "Do you believe that . . . the condition that you have diagnosed would have caused her to be unable, if the law placed upon her a duty to interfere or a duty to report, unable to conform her conduct to the requirement on the law?"

"Yes . . .

". . . But because of this disorder perpetrated and caused by violence, she was not able to conform to the point—her perception was altered to the point that she did not act." [41]

The court concluded that the trial judge did not commit reversible error in limiting Dr. Veronen's testimony to psychological testimony relating to Ms. Wyatt's state of mind and prohibiting her testimony on battered women's syndrome. It noted: "[A]lthough we are baffled by the failure of defense counsel to utilize the opportunity presented by the trial court to offer the permitted testimony, we believe any retrial of this case will present ample opportunity for the court and counsel to revisit the issues presented by Dr. Veronen's testimony."[42]

In *Wyatt,* as in *Mott,* we again see familiar themes. The trial lawyer did not appear to have perceived the importance of the testimony and characterizes the testimony on abuse as "battered women's syndrome." The testimony is proffered to explain why Julie Wyatt might not have felt able to seek medical help. Yet the court also sees it in the context of an impaired mental state.

Commonwealth v. Lazarovich involves a similar set of facts.[43] Janice Lazarovich was convicted by a jury of having committed mayhem and assault and battery on her two-year-old daughter, Laura. The state's theory at trial was that the defendant either abused the child herself or engaged in a joint venture with her husband, Roger, to abuse the child. Dr. Charles Ewing testified at trial that Janice Lazarovich suffered from "battered woman syndrome," and the trial judge instructed the jury that it could consider the testimony about battered woman syndrome when determining whether the defendant shared her husband's intent for purposes of establishing whether a joint venture existed between them to commit mayhem upon the child. The defendant argued that the judge erred in failing to instruct the jury that they could also consider the battered woman syndrome testimony to determine whether the defendant had the specific intent to commit the mayhem herself without the assistance of her husband.

The defendant claimed that she was tending to her two other young children when she heard a loud noise coming from the bathroom in the trailer where the family lived; she found Laura lying unconscious on the floor next to her "potty" seat. Lazarovich and her husband ultimately took the child to the hospital, where doctors diagnosed Laura as having been abused, with several fractures, brain injuries, dehydration, permanent loss of vision, and delayed development. At trial, the defendant testified about the physical and psychological abuse that her husband had inflicted on both her and the child: he had hit her and forced her to have sex with him, hit her on the head with a tire iron, tried to choke her with a telephone cord, trapped her in the closet, and beaten Laura. She claimed that she had waited a day to take her daughter to the hospital because she was afraid of leaving the other two children with her husband, and that, except for a number of spankings, she had never struck Laura.

Dr. Ewing testified that the battered woman syndrome was "characterized by the physical and psychological abuse of a woman by her partner." He described the three cycles of abuse, that women who are abused "respond with depression, with feelings of learned helplessness, feelings of being psychologically trapped in the relationship. That of course, explains why many battered women stay in these relationships, despite the fact that they are being abused." Dr. Ewing explained how abused women lose their self-esteem, and how most women who suffer from the syndrome are too ashamed to seek help." He testified that the defendant's response "was also typical of that of women suffering from this syndrome. She became depressed, fearful, suffering from learned helplessness, felt there was no way out, contemplated suicide, but couldn't see that as a way out because she feared what would happen if she left her kids—the situation that it would leave her children in. She felt trapped in the relationship." [44]

At trial, defense counsel argued that this testimony was relevant on the issue of intent, both as to whether the defendant had acted and as to whether she had acted in a joint venture with her husband. Although the judge initially agreed—over the objection of the prosecutor, who argued that because she claimed she had never hit the child it was relevant only on the joint venture theory—he said during the conference on jury instructions that he was going to instruct the jury that they could consider battered woman syndrome only on the joint venture theory. Defense counsel did not object. The judge then charged the jury, without objection by defense counsel, that they could consider the battered woman syndrome if it is "of assistance to you in deciding why the defendant did not leave the husband in this case. If that is a factor in your deliberations, you may consider it on that aspect of the case. And secondly, you may consider [it] on the aspect as to whether or not the defendant here was a joint venturer or had a joint enterprise in sharing her husband's criminal specific intent and his maliciousness." [45]

The Massachusetts Supreme Court ruled that the jury instruction was not reversible error:

Even if we assume, for purposes of deciding this case, that the battered woman syndrome constitutes the type of mental impairment which juries may consider when determining whether a defendant formed the required specific intent, there was no substantial likelihood of a miscarriage of justice in the circumstances of this case. The defendant could have chosen to argue alternative defenses. She could have argued both that she did not hit Laura and that, if she did hit the child, she was incapable of forming the specific intent to injure her. The defendant chose, however, to pursue a different trial strategy. She chose to maintain that she did not strike Laura and that it was her husband who injured the child. The fact that the defendant might have suffered from the battered woman syndrome, and that the syndrome might have impaired the defendant's ability to form the required specific intent, cannot be claimed to create a substantial risk of a miscarriage of justice where it is not relevant to the defendant's chosen trial strategy.[46]

Moreover, the court observed that "since the defendant's trial strategy in the case at bar was to convince the jury that her husband was solely responsible for the child's injuries and no objection was made to the charge given, she cannot convincingly claim a miscarriage of justice arising from the judge's failure to instruct the jury that the battered woman syndrome should be taken into consideration when determining whether the defendant had the specific intent to injure the child."[47]

In *Barrett v. Indiana*, Alice Barrett was convicted of neglect of a dependent following the death of her four-year-old child at the hands of Barrett's live-in boyfriend.[48] At trial, Barrett had sought to present testimony concerning battered woman syndrome, and the trial court judge precluded her from presenting that evidence. Barrett had argued that the testimony of a social worker, Gail Beaton, was necessary to show that she did not knowingly or intentionally neglect her child. She claimed that she was denied the right to present a defense because she was prevented from responding to the prosecutor's question during both opening and closing arguments regarding why she stayed with Sherwood, her boyfriend. The judge agreed with Barrett, holding that the testimony was both relevant and admissible and that she was denied the opportunity to present evidence essential to her defense under the Sixth Amendment.

These cases illustrate the importance of admission of evidence on battering in cases involving abuse, neglect, termination of parental rights, and criminal liability. They also suggest that lawyers who are representing these women do not comprehend the significance and content of this testimony. The result is that both lawyers and judges are likely to see the tragic circumstances of these cases in terms that suggest that the women are crazy, and that "battered woman syndrome" testimony is thus a form of impaired mental state, or diminished capacity, defense.

These cases also raise questions concerning the appropriate boundaries of individual responsibility and social oppression. If mothers who are battered abuse their children or participate in child abuse, they must be held responsible in some way. Advocates in New York have been struggling with these issues in attempting to reform the statute at issue in *Glenn G.* Advocates in other states have faced similar issues. Should proof of battering constitute a rebuttable presumption of no liability? Should it constitute an affirmative defense that could be offered by the battered woman to explain her conduct? Should evidence of a history of battering be admissible on the merits of the charge of abuse or neglect, or only at sentencing? What should the standard of defense be? Is a battered woman's "expectation, apprehension, or fear of a substantial bodily harm" too high a standard?

Custody

Dimensions of victimization and agency emerge in another context involving battered women and their children: child custody. Custody has always been an important issue for battered women because, above all, they fear losing their children to the batterer. In recent years it has become even more urgent, because many men fight the issuance of restraining orders by initiating divorce and custody proceedings against battered women.[49] Battered women now have even more reason to take this threat seriously: although many states now require judges to make findings of fact concerning domestic violence in determining custody, a mother with "battered woman syndrome" will not appear to be "fit" and therefore appropriate to obtain custody.

Custody is perhaps the most charged legal issue concerning battered women as mothers. Even when both mothers and fathers work full time, in most marriages women are the primary caregivers.[50] It is widely recognized that husbands threaten to seek custody as a ploy in post-separation negotiations, usually to seek financial gain, and that wives will sacrifice financial support to which they may otherwise be entitled in order to avoid even the possibility of losing their children. A parallel dynamic in the context of battering has also been recognized. Rather than face custody suits, women accept mutual orders of protection, which are inappropriate if the woman has not been violent and which hinder the effectiveness of the protective order. As Martha Mahoney has observed, "In both instances, women lose protection they need and to which they are legally entitled, because they fear the treatment that they are likely to receive in court."[51]

Battered women's fears of losing custody are realistic. Women who depart from traditional stereotypes of good mothers, which include women who are sexually active, lesbian, or battered, are penalized in custody decisions.[52] Many divorcing women report that they have experienced violence. As Mahoney puts it, "Violent men will likely seek new means of control when old ones fail. Batterers use the legal system as a new area of combat when they seek to keep their wives from leaving":

Men who pursue custody have a better than even chance of gaining custody. Even violent men are frequently successful in custody suits. In one study, fifty-nine percent of the judicially successful fathers had physically abused their wives; thirty-six per cent had kidnapped their children. A recent article estimated that at least one half of all contested custody cases involved families with a history of some sort of domestic violence; in approximately forty percent of those cases, fathers were awarded the children irrespective of their history of violence. Another study reported many awards of custody to battering fathers, including one case in which the judge made his decision after walking past the shelter to which the mother and children had fled. The judge found the shelter to be an inappropriate living arrangement and concluded the father provided the better home.[53]

Major changes in custody litigation over the past several decades have also contributed to the problems that battered women face: "With the advent of no-fault divorce, violence against women is less likely to be raised. It may be dangerous for women to raise the issue of domestic violence, since it invokes the stereotypes that judges or social workers may hold. It may not even be helpful: in the absence of physical harm to a child, violence against the mother might not be seen as relevant to the welfare of the children. Women therefore must decide whether to describe the violence against them—and risk judicial stereotyping—or keep silent, and allow the violence of their spouse to be judicially invisible."[54]

Mahoney also describes how the simultaneous development of several liberal legal reforms—efforts to make motherhood less central to women's identity, and the development of no-fault divorce—has exacerbated these problems: "The evolution of a dysfunctional portrait of battered women therefore occurred simultaneously both with the changes wrought by no-fault and the move to joint custody. . . . Indeed by making violence against women less visible at divorce, no-fault divorce laws may have indirectly contributed to cultural stereotypes of battered women by removing public blame of the perpetrator of the violence. Once the man as bad actor disappears, it is easy to shift the focus to the woman. Rather than asserting his harm to her from the beginning, the woman must raise battering as an issue defensively, while she is being clinically evaluated, with greater attendant risk of stereotyping."[55] No-fault standards also put more power in the hands of social workers; judges follow their recommendations in evaluations 90 percent of the time.[56] Yet reliance on these professionals creates problems for battered women. It may be dangerous for them to trust counselors who may later be called on to testify regarding their parenting qualities. Therapists can prove susceptible to the charm of batterers. A woman's unwillingness to compromise can also be a problem and be held against her by a therapist.

In the context of battering, a double standard exists as to fitness of fathers or mothers. If a father seeks custody at all, a judge will often take the attempt at custody as prima facie evidence of paternal fitness. In these cases, violence against the women is held not to be of importance.[57] In some extreme cases, even the murder of the mother by the father has been held to be irrelevant for purposes of determining parental fitness.[58]

Although battering fathers are usually not penalized because of their attacks, battered mothers often are. The standard stereotype of battered women as helpless victims works against women in the context of a custody proceeding.[59] This stereotype blames women for not leaving, instead of men for perpetuating the abuse; it also characterizes "batteredness" as deviant, abnormal, and different from what "normal" women experience. Some states have now passed legislation that permits or requires domestic violence to be taken into consideration by judges in awarding custody.[60] Even if the court considers violence as a factor in custody decisions, however, women who have been battered may be seen as, or required to appear as, weak, helpless, and economically dependent.

Clearly, the "dysfunctional portrait of battered women,"[61] which has emerged in cases involving battered women on trial for the killing of their assailant, has created a legal stereotype. When a battered woman decides to identify her abuse in the context of a custody suit, courtroom professionals, many of them trained in family systems theory, may shunt her into a stereotypical category that characterizes her as weak, passive, victimized, and therefore unable to care properly for her children.

Battered women (and women in general), then, are put in a double bind. A woman who is strong, capable, and assertive is bucking the common stereotype of the battered woman. For example, women have lost custody of their children because of their "propensity for violence" — behavior that in actuality was an aggressive show of self-defense, such as when a mother allegedly fired a rifle at her ex-husband when he came to visit the child.[62] Because a mother's act of self-defense is more likely to be understood as violent than a father's battering, such mothers are unlikely to be awarded custody.[63]

Martha Mahoney notes that the hazards of stereotypes such as "learned helplessness" in the custody area are obvious:

> In self-defense claims, we have pressed upon judges and juries a portrait of induced dysfunctionality. In custody cases, we must prove functionality — or at least recovery. The concept of "learned helplessness" is a factor that may influence negative custody decisions. The needs of battered women in custody cases seem almost directly inverse to self-defense cases: women must prove our subjective reasonableness for self-defense claims, our objective rationality and competence as parents; learned helplessness may "explain" why a woman "stayed" in the self-defense context, but may be interpreted as making her a poor model in childbearing and possibly a poor caregiver as well when custody is in question. The cases may not always be tried before the same judges, but they work within the same legal system and popular culture. To the extent that court psychological literature has been focused on "battered women" rather than the violent power and control moves against these women, it perpetuates stereotypes that damage us in our other encounters with the legal system.[64]

Stories abound of women who lose custody because of their battering experiences. Christine Littleton relates that one woman who had obtained a temporary restraining order against her husband was attacked by him in her bedroom. She fled the attack, but the husband got custody because he claimed, and the judge believed, that she had abandoned her children by running from him.[65] Other researchers tell of a case in which a woman ran away from home because her husband was chasing her with a shotgun. She had de-cided to leave the children in the house as she fled into the woods because her husband had never harmed them before, and because she was in immi-nent danger of losing her life. The judge granted custody to the batterer, who asserted that he was angry at the woman for leaving her children behind.[66]

The move toward consideration of violence in custody determination has been an important development. For example, a 1996 decision of the Massa-chusetts Supreme Judicial Court, *In re Vaughan,* held that a trial court's de-termination of physical and legal custody without making findings of fact on domestic violence issues constituted reversible error.[67] A four-hundred-page trial record detailed a long history of battering in the relationship between Leslie and Ross, who lived with Leslie's two children from a previous mar-riage, Laura and John, and their child, Vaughan. The trial judge found that Ross would "fly into rages" and strike out at Leslie, once causing her to lose consciousness and requiring her to be sent to the hospital in an ambulance. According to testimony at trial, Ross inflicted injuries on Leslie on numerous other occasions, and Laura and John witnessed a number of these incidents and were terrified of Ross and his rages. The testimony and findings of fact reflected that Ross was also physically and verbally abusive toward them, and the police were regularly called. Ross sought psychiatric help; lithium was pre-scribed, and there was testimony that when Ross discontinued taking it on his own, his mood worsened. There was testimony that Leslie took the chil-dren out of the house on several occasions, that Ross had taken Vaughan out of the house in the course of arguments, and that Ross had used the threat of taking Vaughan from his mother as a way of keeping her in the relationship. Vaughan was present at many of the episodes of abuse; there was also testi-mony that Ross was physically abusive to Vaughan, and that Ross had acted in a sexually inappropriate manner to Laura when she was a teenager.

Tension and violence finally led Leslie to seek an order of protection, re-quiring Ross to vacate the couple's home, to surrender custody of Vaughan to Leslie, and to remain away from Leslie and their home. The next day, Ross initiated an action for custody. The parties entered into an agreement for joint legal custody, and they agreed to have a clinical psychologist whom they had previously seen together with Vaughan to make an evaluation concerning cus-tody. The psychologist recommended joint custody, but that the boy's pri-mary home during the week should be with his father, with weekends to be spent with his mother. The trial court agreed with these recommendations, gave Ross primary custody, and set up a schedule for weekend, midweek, and holiday visitation by Leslie.

The trial judge found that the father should have primary physical custody because he had done the shopping and cooking for the household for five years before the breakup of the relationship, while the mother had supported the family by working as a real estate agent during the day and a cocktail waitress at night. According to the Supreme Judicial Court, Ross "was greatly occupied with his son's activities, followed his son's progress in school, visited his teachers, attended his sporting events and joined him in target shooting and other activities. Indeed the evidence suggests that Ross was, if anything, overly involved with his son. He embarrassed his son at times by participating in games with him or cheering with excessive enthusiasm at his team sports, and the two would shower together and give each other massages. Ross has been very generous to Vaughan — the mother complains — overly generous — buying him motorbikes and electronic equipment." [68]

The Appeals Court reversed the decision of the trial court on the ground that the trial judge had failed to make findings regarding the evidence that Ross had physically abused the mother throughout the relationship and regarding the effect of this abuse on the child. The Appeals Court relied on findings in the Gender Bias Study of the Court System of Massachusetts that "the legislature and/or appellate courts should make it clear that abuse of any family member affects other family members and must be considered in determining the best interests of the child in connection with any order concerning custody." [69]

Judge Charles Fried, writing for the Supreme Judicial Court, wrote as follows:

> We endorse the Appeals Court's commitment to the propositions that physical force within the family is both intolerable and too readily tolerated, and that a child who has been the victim . . . of such abuse suffers a distinctly grievous kind of harm. It might be helpful to emphasize how fundamental these propositions are. Quite simply, abuse by a family member inflicted on those who are weaker and less able to defend themselves — almost invariably a child or a woman — is a violation of the most basic human right, the most basic condition of civilized society: the right to live in physical security, free from the fear that brute force will determine the conditions of one's daily life. What our study and the growing movement against family violence add to this fundamental insight is that, for those who are its victims, force within the family and

in intimate relationships is not less but more of a threat to his basic condition of civilized security, for it destroys the security that all should enjoy in the
very place and context which is supposed to be the refuge against the harsh-
ness encountered in a world of strangers. . . . The Gender Bias Study concludes
that our courts have too often failed to appreciate the fundamental wrong and
the depth of the injury inflicted by family violence. In subtle and overt ways
the decisions of courts fail to take these factors into account and have treated
them with insufficient seriousness in making dispositions, particularly in cases
involving custody of children and the realignment of family relationships in
divorce and related proceedings. The Appeals Court found just such failures of
attention and emphasis in the Probate Court's treatment of this case.[70]

Significantly, there had been expert testimony on battering before the trial
court. Judge Fried describes this testimony in the following way:

The mother's expert, Dr. Peter G. Jaffe, who is a specialist in matters relating
to family violence and battered women's syndrome, casts all the incidents unfavorable to Leslie as manifestations of that syndrome. Leslie had been abused
as a child and in the two marriages that preceded her relationship with Ross.
The judge summarized Dr. Jaffe's judgments in his findings of fact, including
Dr. Jaffe's statement that children who grow up in abusive households tend to
repeat that pattern in their own relationships: "Dr. Jaffe feels that children who
are witnesses to violence are also victims of violence. He expressed a concern
that if [Vaughan] remained in his father's physical custody, it would reinforce
the acceptability of the father's behavior to [Vaughan] which has the potential
to make [Vaughan] a batterer himself in the future. The judge did not, however, make any findings of fact based on Dr. Jaffe's testimony and did not say
whether he considered Dr. Jaffe's testimony credible.
    Rather, the judge seemed moved to give particular weight to the guardian ad
litem, Dr. Abbruzzese and less weight to the analysis and conclusions of Leslie's
expert, Dr. Jaffe. . . . There is no doubt that Dr. Abbruzzese was particularly
moved by the love and attachment the father has for Vaughan, the attachment
Vaughan seemed to have for his father, and by Vaughan's wish to spend more
time with him and perhaps to have his primary base at his father's house. Certainly, some of this affection came across as concern for his father's welfare,
and as Dr. Jaffe pointed out, may for that reason be deemed an inappropriate
role reversal and one that is encountered in families with a history of violence.[71]

The court concluded that the trial court had "failed to make detailed and
comprehensive findings of fact on the issues of domestic violence and its effect

upon the child as well as upon the father's parenting ability." The court held that these findings are important as a matter of policy, because "domestic violence is an issue too fundamental and frequently recurring to be dealt with only by implication. Requiring the courts to make explicit findings about the effect of the violence on the child and the appropriateness of the custody award in light of that effect will serve to keep these matters well in the foreground of the judges' thinking." [72] The court also relied on Massachusetts statutory law that requires detailed findings where there is an outstanding order of protection.

Vaughan is an important case that highlights the way feminist lawmaking has shaped judicial thinking. However, it also illustrates the factors keeping battered women's experiences from being acknowledged and given the weight they deserve. The Probate Court judge heard the testimony of two sets of experts and was clearly moved more by the testimony that emphasized the father's caring and nurturance of the son. The mother's expert appeared to have not only explained the mother's actions, but also interpreted the father's relationship with the son as problematic. Indeed, Ross's behavior toward Vaughn could be interpreted as an extension of his behavior toward Vaughan's mother, and further evidence of his need for power and control over his son. Yet the trial judge was so influenced by testimony that suggested Ross's attention to and bonding with Vaughan (because caretaking that we tend to take for granted when it comes from mothers looks heroic when it comes from fathers) that the father's violence with the mother, and the impact of this violence on the son (not to mention Ross's sexual abusiveness with his step-daughter) were considered unimportant.

The opinion of the Massachusetts Supreme Judicial Court is careful to separate out the strands of these issues. The opinion suggests that the Probate judge did not give proper weight to the testimony of the mother's expert. Certainly the court's emphasis on detailed findings of fact is important. Yet what is the trial judge who sees the couple in this way likely to do on remand, even with the appellate command of detailed findings? The Supreme Court tells the trial court: "We do not by this decision require the judge to hear further testimony if he does not consider that necessary, but at least he must hear both parties and make explicit findings on the matters set out above." The Court adds a footnote: "As almost three years have gone by since the Probate Court issued its judgment and Vaughan is now almost fourteen years of age, it may be appropriate for the judge to interview the child again as to his preference and for the judge to evaluate the success of the stipulated custody arrangement the parties have been living under in the interim."[73] As long as the trial judge makes detailed findings on remand, his decision on custody is immune from review.

The Supreme Judicial Court has made an important first step in requiring trial judges to take the issue of violence seriously and in opening up the process so that testimony on battered women's experiences, particularly expert testimony, is likely to be heard at trial in custody cases. If the trial judges know that they have to make detailed findings, they are more likely to admit evidence on battering, and lawyers for battered women are likely to conclude that they need to submit expert testimony. Yet there is still substantial judicial discretion permitted in the way these experiences are characterized by experts (whether as "battered woman syndrome" or something else), in the content of the testimony, and in the way facts on violence and parenting are presented by lawyers and experts and interpreted by judges. The only way to limit that exercise of judicial discretion is through the imposition of a statutory rebuttable presumption against custody to the batterer. Significantly, after *Vaughan,* Massachusetts did pass a statute that did precisely that.[74] But even those few states that have passed these stronger statutes still confront problems with judicial interpretation.[75]

In many cases, of course, expert testimony on battering is entirely excluded. In *Pratt v. Wood,* the New York Appellate Division reversed a Family Court judge's decision refusing to allow an expert on domestic violence to testify.[76] Maternal grandparents were seeking to obtain custody of their grandchild from the natural father, who had battered the mother. The mother had pleaded guilty to manslaughter in the death of an older child and was in prison. Kelli Wood, the mother, had testified that the father had abused her five times a week over a five-year period, and that the father also assaulted the child two or three times a week, although she said that she had never told anyone about these incidents and had not sought medical treatment. The grandparents then sought the testimony of Colleen McGrath, "an expert in the field of domestic violence, for the purpose of eliciting evidence regarding battered wife syndrome." The trial judge held that the testimony should be excluded since "it would simply serve to bolster Wood's testimony."[77]

The Appellate Division reversed the trial court's finding with the following language: "In our view, Family Court erred in excluding McGrath's testimony as it has come to be recognized that expert testimony in the field of domestic violence is admissible since the psychological and behavioral characteristics typically shared by victims of abuse in a familial setting are not generally known by the average person. Family Court's ruling was particularly prejudicial to petitioners since it found Wood's testimony to be incredible because she never went to a hospital or sought treatment. In fact, Wood's failure to tell anyone about the abuse or to seek help is a characteristic typically shared by victims of domestic violence. Thus, had Family Court admitted McGrath's testimony, it is conceivable that its resolution of Wood's credibility might have been different." [78]

The Connecticut Supreme Court has also affirmed the importance of expert testimony on battering in custody cases. In *Knock v. Knock*, the court held that an expert witness, Evan Stark, a sociologist and expert on "the subject of battered woman's syndrome," "aided in establishing that the defendant displayed battered woman's syndrome and that the plaintiff had been abusive toward the defendant." The court cited various national studies on violence and custody, particularly the recommendations of the National Council on Juvenile and Family Court Judges that "when the issue of family violence is found to exist in the context of a dissolution of marriage, domestic relations case of any kind, or in a juvenile court case . . . the violent conduct should be weighed and considered in making custody and visitation orders." [79] Admitting evidence and weighing and considering battering are the first steps, but there is no assurance that the evidence will really be heard. Without clear statutory guidance that battering renders a parent unfit for custody, admission of evidence and consideration of battering will be ineffective.

Battered Mothers and Feminist Lawmaking

On the macro level, these cases involving battered mothers present the formidable problem of how to take the social constraints and experience of motherhood into account in determining individual responsibility. Doing so is particularly difficult in light of gender bias and lack of social and economic resources to assist women, particularly mothers.

What are the appropriate boundaries of responsibility for a mother who is battered? We are just beginning to explore the implications of motherhood for feminist legal theory and practice generally. [80] Many battered women report that they were able to mobilize and change their lives only when their children began to be abused. [81] Responsibility for children does heighten the need for safety, but we cannot place that responsibility exclusively on the mother, lest it deter women from seeking help. Battered women's advocates have observed that many battered mothers maintain their silence in the face of healthcare providers, child protection teams, or juvenile court proceedings because their lives and the lives of their children are threatened if they speak up. Mothers who are abused face enormous pressures to protect themselves and their children, and to maintain their families even under terrible and constrained circumstances. It is difficult to determine the contours of maternal responsibility in a culture that blames mothers for all problems relating to children, gives mothers so little material and social support, and absolves fathers of all responsibility. Unless we place problems of motherhood and battering within a framework of gender socialization and subordination, we cannot fully and fairly assess the contours of responsibility.

The circumstances of battered mothers dramatize the challenge of feminist lawmaking: the need for legal advocates to describe and make visible all the dimensions of battered women's experience as mothers within a broader gender framework. They also highlight the enormous obstacles to both accurate description and significant change. The task of incorporation of accurate description of the experiences of battered women as mothers into legal frameworks is considerable. Resisting the impulse to distance ourselves from battering, recognizing the continuum of intimate relationships, and acknowledging the "good" and "bad" mother in all of us constitute a start.

Part

IV

Aspirations, Limits, and Possibilities

10

Engaging with the State

Legislative work has been a major aspect of feminist legal reform efforts respecting domestic violence. State domestic violence coalitions have formed, lobbied for, and helped to pass state legislation on issues ranging from mandatory arrest and child custody to insurance. On the federal level, a coalition of women's and civil rights organizations spearheaded the passage of the Violence Against Women Act of 1994 (VAWA) and have continued to develop and lobby for Congressional efforts on a variety of issues. In vision and purpose, much of this legislation has been groundbreaking.

Innovative legal reform efforts focused on intimate violence, such as state mandatory arrest policies and VAWA, underscore the complex issues that emerge when feminists "engage with the state" on issues of violence.[1] Feminist efforts to use state or federal governmental mechanisms for law reform on intimate violence present both theoretical and practical contradictions.[2] In this chapter I explore these contradictions through the lenses of mandatory arrest legislation and VAWA.

The development of mandatory arrest legislation, which made domestic violence a crime, came after years of debate within the battered women's movement concerning the degree to which criminalization of battering was an appropriate response in light of historic feminist ambivalence about state power. Despite extensive efforts to train police, police continue to resist arresting battering men, and they frequently arrest both battering men and the women they batter. Many women who are battered are reluctant to charge their batterers with a crime, and many prosecutor's offices have developed controversial "no-drop" policies, which can force women to face criminal charges if they refuse to testify against their assailant.

The civil rights remedy of VAWA is also controversial, because it explic-

itly links violence with gender and because it is premised on federalizing offenses of intimate violence, which have historically been in the province of
the state. Here, too, enforcement is plagued by longstanding tensions: the historic public-private dichotomy, which labels intimate violence as a "private"
matter that should not be litigated in the federal courts; and resistance to the
connection between violence and gender.

With both mandatory arrest legislation and VAWA, familiar tensions are
replicated—public and private, victimization and agency—which reemerge
in the process of enforcement and raise questions concerning the potential
utility and effectiveness of these statutes. Moreover, because of the dialectical
dimensions of lawmaking, each of these issues reveals dilemmas in law reform
strategies and provides useful insights for further work.

The Role of the State

Recent public and legal attention to domestic violence grew from the work of
an activist battered women's movement in the United States, which began in
the late 1960s. The role of the state was one of the most vexing issues that this
movement faced.[3] The battered women's movement was an outsider movement, a grassroots movement that developed from the civil rights and feminist movements of the 1960s.[4] Many feminists saw battering as the product of
patriarchy, as male control over women. Many in this movement were skep-
tical of an affirmative role for the state; they saw the state as maintaining, en-
forcing, and legitimizing male violence against women, not remedying it; they
rejected the idea that battered women activists ought to trust the state, expect much from the state, or engage with the state in any way.[5] The movement
developed shelters, safe houses, and alternative institutions. Groups rejected
governmental funding for battered women's services and programs. The legal
remedies supported by the movement also reflected a fundamental ambivalence about engagement with the state: many feminist activists initially rejected criminalization as an appropriate remedy or strategy to redress domestic violence because battered women "did not necessarily want their partners
jailed, they wanted the violence condemned and stopped."[6]

Yet, as the movement developed, engagement with the state became inevitable. Susan Schechter, an activist in and historian of the movement, has
detailed the contradictions of state involvement in the movement. Schechter
describes the resistance of some grassroots organizations in the battered

women's movement to accept funding from the Law Enforcement Assistance Agency in the late 1970s on the ground that acceptance of governmental aid would result in the relinquishment of control and principles. She observes that funding from the government operated as a mixed blessing for the shelter movement: although it helped to legitimize the movement, it also served to undermine shelters' philosophy and organizational structure, requiring the employment of credentialed staff and transforming grassroots shelters into social service agencies serving clients instead of empowering battered women.[7] She also discusses how governmental support of the battered women's movement redefined feminist political analysis of violence. Government-produced pamphlets and educational material on "spouse abuse" and other generic categorizations of domestic violence obscured the feminist grassroots history and politics of the movement.[8]

Over the past twenty-five years, this critical view of engagement with the state has changed. First, on the theoretical front, the notion of the state has been modified. Catharine MacKinnon's early notion of the state as "male in the feminist sense," and a tool for further subordination of women, coincided with and reflected the activist and anti-statist stance of the movement.[9] Feminists have continued to explore the way the gendered nature of the state is masked by the purportedly gender-neutral rhetoric of liberty, equality, and citizen's rights.[10] More recently, these accounts of the state have been criticized by feminists influenced by postmodern approaches, particularly Michel Foucault.[11] For Foucault, power is discursively constituted, is both diffuse and dynamic, and can be challenged anywhere and everywhere. Power is viewed as residing not only in government and governmental institutions, but in many more sites within the culture.[12] Each of these perspectives is important and deepens our analysis—for it is true both that there is a "male" tilt to the state and that power is not exclusively lodged in the state. Although the state may not be the only "power" player, it is an important one.

From a historical perspective, there also has been change on the issue of state engagement. Advocates are actively involved in legislative reform efforts, and the issue of intimate violence is now on the legislative agenda of every state and the federal government. As this issue has moved from one raised on the margins to one that has been appropriated by government, feminist liberatory discourse challenging patriarchy and female dependency, which shaped this work, has been replaced by discourse emphasizing crime control.[13] Many battered women's activists have moved from a view that rejected state engagement to one that supports state and federal legislative reform as well as both the pro-criminalization stance of VAWA and mandatory arrest.[14] This, in turn, has led to considerable debate within the battered women's movement and among legal advocates, particularly among communities of color, who do not see the state as benevolent.[15] But the impact of state and federal involvement continues to be complex, as money provided by states and by VAWA grants now supports many battered women's organizations, educational projects, and legal programs across the United States.[16]

Mandatory Arrest and No-Drop Policies

A "mandatory arrest" law requires police to arrest a suspect if there is probable cause to believe that domestic violence has occurred, removes the decision to press charges from the victim, and generally limits or eliminates police discretion. A "no-drop policy" denies the victim of domestic violence the option of withdrawing a complaint at her discretion once formal charges have been filed, and limits prosecutors' discretion to drop a case based only on the fact that the victim is unwilling to cooperate or participate. Both these policies have garnered a great deal of public attention.[17] Historically, criminalizing domestic violence has been a strategy dogged by controversy. Because the state has been deficient in protecting women from abuse in the past, feminists have been wary of using state mechanisms to intervene on behalf of battered women. Although studies in the 1980s claiming that arrest and prosecution were the most effective legal remedies led to implementing criminalization on the state level, and although VAWA reflects a strong pro-criminalization position, many feminist advocates continue to be critical.[18]

The historic rationales for criminalization generally, and mandatory arrest in particular, are deterrence and the importance of encouraging a more public response to domestic violence: a clear statement that assault in intimate relationships will be treated the same as assault by strangers. Deterrence itself is a matter of controversy. Furthermore, reconciling the necessity for greater public concern about domestic violence with the necessity to preserve a woman's autonomy from excessive state intervention presents considerable difficulty.

Feminist advocates are deeply divided as to whether mandatory arrest, mandatory prosecution, and no-drop prosecution are a better policy choice than the courts' current practice of dismissing cases when the battered woman refuses to participate. For a host of reasons, women who are battered routinely refuse to prosecute complaints after they have been filed. They may be afraid of retribution, guilt-ridden about prosecuting a loved one, torn between conflicting emotions, afraid of losing economic support or taking a father away from children, or weakened by violence.

It is widely recognized that mandatory arrest and no-drop rules are, at best, imperfect solutions to domestic violence because of the extreme risk to women's autonomy. Studies regarding the effectiveness of mandatory prosecution are inconclusive; both those in favor of and those opposed to it can cite studies to bolster their respective positions.[19]

Four major areas of arguments favor mandatory prosecution and no-drop. First, proponents of these measures argue that they best effectuate the state and prosecutors' roles regarding domestic violence, compensate for problems associated with victims of domestic violence, wrest control away from batterers, and send a strong message regarding the "public" wrong of domestic violence.[20] Those who support mandatory prosecution and no-drop view them as furthering the proper roles of the state and prosecutor in domestic violence cases. A prosecutor's "client" is the state, not the victim. Moreover, it is the role of the prosecutor to represent the people of the state; the decision whether to prosecute a crime should not rest with victims but with the state. Because domestic violence affects society as a whole, and not just the victim of abuse, it concerns public safety and the protection of children. Thus, the state cannot ignore human tragedies caused by domestic violence, just as it cannot ignore tragedies caused by other crimes.[21] Supporters of mandatory arrest and no-drop maintain that these policies place the state in a better position to combat domestic violence.

Second, proponents maintain that this approach protects victims because it removes the pressure exerted by a batterer to drop the case; it relieves the victims of making this decision and puts it on the shoulders of the state, where it belongs. Because victims may be unable to trust that criminal intervention can assist in the shared goal of ending the violence, this approach shows victims that criminal intervention works. Even though forcing a victim to participate in a trial violates her autonomy, those who support mandatory prosecution and no-drop argue that this loss of autonomy cannot be equated with the loss of autonomy and harm that results from battering and violence.

A third argument advanced to support mandatory prosecution and no-drop is the effect they have on the batterer. These policies tell the batterer that violent conduct and abuse are criminal and unacceptable, and that incarceration is an appropriate sanction. Shifting the decision to prosecute from the victim to the state disempowers batterers and prevents them from further manipulating justice and endangering their victims' lives. In short, mandatory prosecution and no-drop take control of the justice system out of the hands of batterers.

Building on this control issue is a fourth, broader reason favoring mandatory prosecution and no-drop: they send a message that domestic violence shall not be treated as a less serious crime than violence between strangers, and thus they transform the private nature of domestic violence into a public matter. Otherwise, by refusing to intervene under a rationale that domestic violence is a private family matter, the state not only condones battering, but in fact promotes it. Once the presence of mandatory prosecution policies are common knowledge, proponents maintain, battered women will be more likely to cooperate and batterers will be less likely to intimidate women throughout the prosecution process.

Critics argue that a number of overarching problems with mandatory prosecution and no-drop policies must be realistically considered.[22] Criticisms of these policies fall into four major categories: they are paternalistic and essentialize women's experiences by presuming that society knows what is right for all women; they re-victimize women by subjecting them to further coercion at the hands of the state; they increase the risk of retaliation against the victim by the batterer; and, finally, they disempower women by taking their autonomy away from them.

According to these arguments, a battered woman needs the opportunity to make a choice for herself regarding violence in her life. Deciding whether to prosecute an intimate may well be the first opportunity that a battered woman has to take an affirmative step in a generally powerless relationship. Mandatory prosecution and no-drop thus disempower battered women by robbing them of their decision to prosecute. Not only are battered women powerless in their ability to control their relationship, but they become powerless to prevent the government from interfering in their lives. All of this hurts battered women by reinforcing the notion that they are incapable of making rational decisions, and by increasing the chance that they will be blamed for being reluctant to take action about their battering.

Critics maintain that additional state interference into a battered woman's life can hardly be described as liberating. If arrests lead to automatic prosecution, women will be less likely to call police for help. Indeed, these policies may reinforce battered women's distrust of police and the justice system. In addition, the effect of forcing prosecution may well be that the battered woman becomes aligned with her batterer in order to protect him, thereby further entrenching her in the abusive relationship. At the extreme, these policies even lead to jailing and punishing battered victims who refuse to cooperate— an ironic result indeed for policies that purport to protect battered women.[23]

In theory, the ideal model for state intervention proposed by battered women's advocates has been a "coordinated community response." But as Donna Coker explains, the ideal is rarely met by the reality:

> In a coordinated response, criminal sanctions are accompanied by strong supports for battered women. Prosecutors craft their strategies so as to maximize victim safety; police provide victims with information about rights as well as referrals to services including shelters; courts routinely order victim compensation; and detectives and prosecutors follow up with victims to monitor threats or intimidation tactics of the batterer. In addition, the justice system works closely with service providers to assist women in safety planning and advocacy with other systems, such as public assistance, child protective services, and employers, and also to encourage support from victims' family and friends. The reality in many jurisdictions, however, is very different. Without these supports, legal intervention may not create the kind of change in either the victim's or the batterer's milieu necessary to provide real safety or to enhance the victim's autonomy. The emphasis on legal intervention has served to develop prosecution and civil protection order proceedings without commensurate development of services and resources for women.[24]

For these reasons, feminist advocates have recently argued more vigorously against criminalization. Linda Mills, for example, has suggested that a more flexible and individualized approach to domestic violence is necessary. She argues that criminal justice intervention requires a severance of relationship that is too rigid for many women, who say they want the relationship to continue but the battering to stop. Mills notes that each woman's situation and experience of abuse demands some type of tailored response, so lawyers need to be flexible enough to exercise judgment and apply "intuition and insight" in representing and strategizing with the woman, rather than to follow a rigid formula.[25]

Sally Merry's study of the courts in Hawaii, discussed in Chapter 3, supports the notion that criminalization may be theoretically transformative but limited and unrealistic in practice. The problems posed by mandatory prosecution and no-drop policies highlight the degree to which formal legal remedies and particular legal strategies may not take account of the complexity of the relationship and the social and economic realities of battered women's lives. The criminalization model underscores the dilemma that Merry observed: the promise of an "autonomous liberal legal self," which does not encompass the human and material experiences of women who are battered or take into account the gendered realities of their lives.[26]

The Civil Rights Remedy of VAWA

The Violence Against Women Act is the first federal legislation to address the problem of violence against women. It resulted from the work of an extraordinary coalition of women and civil rights groups over several years.[27] It is a comprehensive legislative effort to address the problem of violence against women through a variety of different mechanisms, including funding for women's shelters, a national domestic abuse hotline, rape education and prevention programs, and training for federal and state judges.[28] It includes new remedies for battered immigrant women and a number of other reforms, including criminal enforcement of interstate orders of protection and the development of an innovative civil rights remedy for gender violence.[29] The passage of the civil rights provision is significant, although the provision has been plagued by controversy concerning whether federal jurisdiction is appropriate for "domestic" matters, and the particular meaning of the phrase "motivated by gender," and the United States Supreme Court is presently determining its constitutionality. These areas of controversy reflect the continuing power of privacy discourse.

The redefinition of violence against women as violating a federally protected civil right, which affords women a right to be free from gender-motivated violence, has considerable theoretical potential in shaping public consciousness and transforming our concept of violence. For the first time, there is a law that explicitly links violence with equality. The legislative history of the Act documents in great detail the impact that gender violence has on the economy, commerce, travel, and women's freedom to work, travel, live freely, and make choices about their own lives. It equates and connects the national with the individual, the public with the private.

The civil rights remedy of VAWA must be placed within the broader context of issues of gender discrimination. The Act was intended to remove the "veil of relationship" from the treatment of violence, and it rested on extensive findings that link violence and equality. The drafters of the Act sought to extend the impact of gender discrimination laws to reach violence. Senator Joseph Biden, its principal sponsor, put it this way: "In this country, we already prohibit much subtler forms of discrimination against women—discrimination that prevents promotion or a pay raise. If we do that, as we should, why do we leave unattended the far more violent discrimination of gender-based attacks?"[30] The core of the Act is embodied in the notion that it is a civil right to be free from violence, and that all persons within the United States have a right to be free from crimes of violence motivated by gender.[31] As has been the case in the articulation of many other rights that women have identified and fought for, the core concept of the right is profound. The legislative history of the Act states that women are targeted for violence because of their gender. The Act itself protects women from violence that is "motivated by gender." For this reason, VAWA could be a potential vehicle of empowerment. At the same time, both the statutory language and the legislative history of the Act reflect profound contradictions.

The Act must be understood as part of a continuum of reform of laws relating to gender violence over the past twenty-five years. The law of rape, for example, has undergone a wide range of reforms: the abolition of requirements that a complainant's story be corroborated, of cautionary instructions (telling the jury that rape was a charge easily made and difficult to disprove), and of the rule that the complainant must have resisted the rape "to the utmost."[32] Rape "shield" legislation, which excludes evidence of a woman's prior sexual conduct, has been enacted in many states,[33] and the formal and informal barriers to women's ability to obtain justice in the courts have been widely recognized. But even when we change the laws, social attitudes lag behind and limit their effective implementation. Despite the change in the corroboration requirement and in the cautionary instruction, for example, commentators on the Mike Tyson rape case still ask, "Why did she go to the hotel room? If she did, she was asking for it." Jurors in "stranger" rape trials still want to know what the woman was wearing. So while new laws can be vehicles for changing social attitudes, the persistence of these very social attitudes can impair the meaningful implementation of legal reforms. Dramatic changes in domestic violence legislation have been accompanied by the familiar lag in social attitudes that shapes implementation of rape reforms.

The premise of VAWA is that gender-based violence has a systematic impact on women's equality and that a federal civil rights remedy is necessary because the state courts had failed to treat women victims fairly. Substantial testimony at the congressional hearings on VAWA demonstrated that gender violence helps to keep women powerless and subordinate, and affects not just women who have been targets of that violence, but women as a class. Gender violence tells women to keep silent, to stay home and out of the streets, and to stay out of public arenas. It reinforces the notion of domination and privilege that is fundamental to patriarchy. Nonetheless, in the context of domestic violence, this link between violence and gender equality may be difficult for society and courts to comprehend.

Indeed, it is arguable that while the impact of gender-based violence as an issue of equality may be difficult for society and courts to comprehend generally, it may be easier for society and courts to comprehend in the area of rape or sexual assault than in domestic violence. The role that rape, particularly stranger rape, plays in keeping women cowed and powerless, has elicited broader social understanding than has "relationship" violence. Because it is acknowledged that all women can be the targets of stranger rape, it is easier for the public to see how the fear of rape shapes women's actions than to see how the generally unacknowledged assertion of power or control or violence within an intimate relationship shapes the fabric of women's lives. Rape and domestic violence must be understood as functioning on a continuum of gender terrorism. In order for judges to understand and interpret the meaning of the phrase "motivated by gender" in a manner consistent with this radical vision, an extraordinary amount of public and judicial education is required. Judges will have to interpret the meaning of "gender motivation" in light of the "totality of the circumstances." [34] But what will the "totality of the circumstances" be? What circumstances will be taken into account in determining whether violence is motivated by gender, and more particularly whether domestic violence is motivated by gender?

An analogous problem of interpretation exists under the Hate Crimes Statistics Act, which provides for the collection of data for "hate crimes" committed not on the basis of gender, but only on the basis of race, religion, sexual orientation, or ethnicity. [35] This is an important federal issue; in 1997 the Justice Department convened a national meeting on hate crime legislation, and hate crime legislation is pending in Congress. [36] What circumstances indicate the existence of a "hate crime"? The following sections of the FBI guidelines that have been applied under the Hate Crimes Statistics Act in situations involving racial, ethnic, and religious animosity highlight this problem of interpretation. As you read these examples, try to translate them into the context of violence against women:

a. The offender and the victim were of different racial, religious, ethnic/national origin, or sexual orientation groups. For example, the victim was Black and the offenders were White.
b. Bias-related oral comments, written statements, or gestures made by the offender which indicates his/her bias. . . .
c. Bias-related drawings, markings, symbols or graffiti were left at the crime scene. For example, a swastika was painted on the door of a synagogue.
d. Certain objects, items or things which indicate bias were used ([such as] the offenders wore white sheets with hoods covering their faces) or left behind by the offender(s) (. . . a burning cross was left in front of the victim's residence).
e. The victim is a member of a racial, religious, ethnic/national origin, or sexual orientation group which is overwhelmingly outnumbered by members of another group in the neighborhood where the victim lives and the incident took place. . . .
f. The victim was visiting a neighborhood where previous hate crimes had been committed against other members of his/her racial, religious, ethnic/national origin, or sexual orientation group and where tensions remain high against his/her group.
g. Several incidents occurred in the same locality, at or about the same time, and the victims were all of the same racial, religious, ethnic/national origin, or sexual orientation group.
h. A substantial portion of the community where the crime occurred perceives that the incident was motivated by bias.
i. The victim was engaged in activities promoting his/her racial, religious, ethnic/national origin, or sexual orientation group. For example, the victim is a member of the NAACP, participated in gay rights demonstrations, etc.
j. The incident coincided with a holiday relating to, or a date of particular significance to, a racial, religious, or ethnic/national origin group ([such as] Martin Luther King Day, Rosh Hashanah, etc.).
k. The offender was previously involved in a similar hate crime or is a member of a hate group.
l. There were indications that a hate group was involved. For example, a hate group claimed responsibility for the crime or was active in the neighborhood.

m. A historically established animosity exists between the victim group and offender group.[37]

These guidelines provide a set of indicators or circumstances that, in the
racial context, are generally understood to suggest bias. It is difficult, however,
to find parallels for interpreting gender violence under VAWA, even under
Hate Crimes Prevention Act proposed in 1999, which would expand the definition of a hate crime to include gender.[38] Consider the problem of the context
of domestic violence, which, to begin with, is commonly viewed not as a "hate
crime," but, if anything, as a "love crime."[39] Some of the legislative history
of the Act, particularly statements by Senator Biden, suggests that "ordinary"
domestic violence would not qualify as an act of violence "motivated by gender" under VAWA's civil rights provision.[40] So how do judges interpret verbal
abuse, physical abuse, or stalking in the context of domestic violence? The
same social attitudes that we have seen emerge and shape the law in other domestic violence contexts—that it is a "private," personal, or family issue—are
likely to prevent intimate violence from being understood or interpreted as
an issue of gender. Consequently, the view that intimate violence is an "individual family problem," a matter of privacy, is likely to limit the implementation of the Act.

Cases in which a woman is beaten and gender epithets or verbal abuse are
actually articulated are analogous to a traditional hate crime. But how often
does a man say, "I'm beating you because you're a woman!" The deeply gendered nature of domestic violence—the way the assertion of power and control, verbal abuse, and physical abuse are part of a continuum—is something
that is easy for judges to deny without substantial education, particularly in
light of the new move toward seeing intimate violence in the context of gender
neutrality. Yet if Senator Biden's view prevails, VAWA's civil rights provision
will be rendered meaningless. Thus, our task must be to do the hard work of
public and judicial education that makes the broader link to gender equality.

Congressional identification of a harm of gender violence in VAWA is important theoretically, but will the promise of this legislation be fulfilled? When
the state does adopt a framework of gender equality for law reform respecting intimate violence, will it make a difference? Examination of early judicial
interpretation of the civil rights remedy of VAWA provides an opportunity to
consider this question. Even when a gender framework for intimate violence
is explicit in legislation, as in VAWA's civil rights remedy, engaging with the

state is tricky. The "male" tilt to state power means that there will be resistance to the notion that intimate violence is an aspect of gender inequality.

Because VAWA has been in effect for only a few years, it is too early to draw any definitive conclusions. At the moment, its future is uncertain, since the Supreme Court is determining the constitutionality of the civil rights remedy.[41] Nonetheless, a brief survey of VAWA cases on the civil rights remedy that have reached the federal courts suggests that the controversies that have dogged its legislative progress are likely to continue even if its constitutionality is upheld. First, the civil rights remedy provision appears to be the least utilized of the various VAWA provisions for issues of domestic violence.[42] Not surprisingly, VAWA provisions regarding interstate enforcement of orders of protection and interstate domestic violence have been most heavily litigated.[43] Cases involving the civil rights remedy have almost exclusively involved situations of sexual assault and rape, not domestic violence.

Second, in 1997 the civil rights remedy of VAWA was held unconstitutional by an *en banc* decision of the Fourth Circuit in *Brzonkala v. Virginia Polytechnic*.[44] In this case, which involves a campus gang rape, the Fourth Circuit ruled that the civil rights remedy was unconstitutional on the ground that Congress had overreached its power under the Commerce Clause and under the Fourteenth Amendment. The Women's Freedom Network, a right-wing group, filed an amicus curiae brief in the Fourth Circuit arguing that VAWA is not based on sufficient evidence that sexual and domestic violence are gender based, and that violence against women is a problem for local police and does not require federal intervention. The brief also claimed that it is only "date rape" that feminists believe is not treated seriously by local courts and thus provides a basis for federal jurisdiction; in actuality, it is the fear of stranger rape that keeps women from working late at night or venturing out by themselves in certain areas, and thus provides the economic basis for the federal law.[45]

Third, because many VAWA civil rights remedy cases have been mired in threshold constitutional challenges, there have been only a few cases that have interpreted gender motivation on the merits. The legislative history of the civil rights remedy suggests that gender motivation must be assessed in light of the "totality of the circumstances." However, the few cases that have been decided suggest the difficulty that many judges have in seeing domestic violence within a framework of equality.

There have been only a handful of published opinions involving allegations of domestic violence under VAWA.[46] In one, *Dolin v. West,* the District Court dismissed the case on summary judgment, concluding that the plaintiff's allegations of physical abuse were insufficient to prove that her ex-husband's physical abuse amounted to felonious conduct and was motivated by gender.[47] Only two have thus far addressed the sufficiency of plaintiffs' claims.[48] In *Kuhn v. Kuhn,* the plaintiff alleged that during their marriage, her ex-husband had restrained and battered her, attempted to strangle her, raped her, and threatened to murder her.[49] In *Ziegler v. Ziegler,* the plaintiff alleged that during their ten-year marriage, her ex-husband voiced gender-specific epithets, acted in ways to perpetuate the stereotype of the submissive female, severely attacked her physically (especially during pregnancy), raped her, and became violent without provocation (in particular when the plaintiff asserted her independence).[50] Although the allegations in the two cases were similar, the outcomes of the cases differed. In *Kuhn,* the court found evidence of gender animus in the plaintiff's allegation of marital rape, and defined sexual assault as a crime motivated by gender animosity, but held that the plaintiff's other allegations of battering did not meet the requirement of "gender animus."[51] In *Ziegler,* the District Court found gender animus based on the totality of the plaintiff's allegations.[52]

Cases brought under the VAWA civil rights remedy for sexual assault or rape and for "inappropriate sexual behavior" have fared somewhat differently. As in *Kuhn,* district courts appear to have been able to equate heterosexual rape and sexual assault with gender-motivated crimes.[53] Thus, although the data is preliminary because of the small number of cases, cases in which there are clear allegations of rape may fare better under VAWA than cases involving clear allegations of domestic violence.[54]

Yet the VAWA cases on domestic violence do show some hopeful signs. Fourth Circuit Judge Diana Motz's opinion in the first Fourth Circuit decision in *Brzonkala,* which has since been reversed by the *en banc* panel, is one.[55] The plaintiff, Christy Brzonkala, alleged a gang rape committed by two fellow college students. In concluding that there was a legally sufficient claim under VAWA, Judge Motz emphasized not just the physical fact of the rape, but a number of gender-based epithets. Brzonkala alleged that when Morrison, one of the rapists, had finished raping her for the second time, he told her, "You better not have any fucking diseases." She also claimed that Morrison had announced in the college dining room, "I like to get girls drunk and fuck the shit out of them." Judge Motz concluded: "As the district court noted, Morrison's statement reflects that he has a history of taking pleasure from having intercourse with women without their sober consent. And that this statement indicated disrespect for women in general and connects this gender disrespect to sexual intercourse." Judge Motz also noted that Brzonkala was "brutally raped . . . three times within minutes after first meeting [her assailants]," and that "the severe and unprovoked nature of the crime triggered by no other motive, is an indication that the crime was motivated by gender bias." [56] In her dissenting opinion in the *en banc* Circuit Court decision, she goes even further: "Brzonkala has alleged virtually all of the earmarks of a violent, felonious 'hate crime'; an unprovoked, severe attack, triggered by no motive other than gender-based animus and accompanied by language clearly reflecting such animus." [57] Judge Motz's link between an attitude of disrespect and verbal abuse with other aspects of battering is pathbreaking. But Judge Motz's decision was vacated *en banc* by the historically conservative Fourth Circuit,[58] and the Supreme Court has granted review.

In *Ziegler,* District Judge William Nielsen also recognized the continuum upon which intimate violence occurs.[59] He ruled that gender motivation must be determined "from the totality of the circumstances," rather than discerning gender animus from discrete instances. "Totality of the circumstances" in this case included rape and other sexual violence, gender-specific epithets directed at the plaintiff, acts perpetuating the stereotype of the submissive female such as control of the family's finances and plaintiff's personal documents, and severe and excessive unprovoked violent attacks, particularly when the plaintiff asserted her independence. Judge Nielsen deemed these allegations to be more than conclusory in nature. Looking at them together, he held, "could reasonably result in an inference of gender-motivated violence." [60] This is a promising reading of the gender animus requirement of the civil rights provision of VAWA.[61]

With passage of VAWA, we have opened the door to this process of change. Nevertheless, the same social attitudes that have limited the effectiveness of reforms in the area of rape and domestic violence are likely to limit VAWA. As Reva Siegel suggests, even legal status reforms that appear to be dramatically revising the law inevitably contain the seeds of limiting privacy discourses, which reflect social ambivalence and are likely to reemerge in legal interpretation.[62] If the Supreme Court favorably resolves the threshold and more general, seemingly "neutral" question of the constitutionality of the Act under the Commerce Clause and Fourteenth Amendment, much of this resistance will ultimately focus on legal interpretation of gender animus, particularly issues of domestic violence. The civil rights remedy of VAWA has the potential to transform social understanding of the critical connection between violence and equality. But only if the Supreme Court upholds this provision can we realize the potential of VAWA and effectuate its radical vision.

The State, Law Reform, and Gender Equality

What are the implications of developments respecting mandatory arrest and VAWA for both theory and practice? First, we must understand the roles of the state, other institutions, law, and culture in encouraging, legitimizing, and perpetuating violence. Government is an important source of power but not the exclusive source of power. Recognition of the range of institutions that are complicitous in violence is an important dimension of a more nuanced approach to the role of the state concerning intimate violence.

Second, we need to critically examine the murky middle ground between total rejection and total endorsement of working with the state. As Claire Reinelt has argued, "the state itself is a contradictory and uneven set of structures and processes that are the product of particular struggles. The state is neither a neutral arbiter of gender nor simply a reproducer of existing gender inequalities. It is a site of active contestation over the construction of gender inequalities and power. Legislative decisions and institutional practices are made in historically specific social, political, and economic contexts that shape, by either perpetuating or altering, particular social formulations of gender."[63] Both mandatory arrest and VAWA are examples of shifts in ascription of state responsibility, on both the state and federal levels. The move toward mandatory arrest, criminal prosecution, and prosecutorial "no-drop" policies has been widespread, yet for many battered women criminal prosecution is deeply problematic. Many activists and legal reformers continue to raise questions concerning criminalization, reflecting tensions around issues involving women's autonomy, poor women, and women of color, and problems of "dual arrests," where both women and men are arrested. Criminalization may be an appropriate strategy in some contexts, but it is only one of many strategies that we ought to be considering.

Far more important and more challenging is the need for provision of state and state-supported resources to deal with the real problems that battered women face—child care, shelters, welfare, work, and workplace violence—

and thus make it possible for women to have the economic and social independence that is a prerequisite to women's freedom from abuse. Indeed, the coalition of activist groups that organized VAWA have recognized this in the organizing work they have done for VAWA '99; the proposed VAWA '99 now pending in Congress focuses on the interrelationship among violence, employment, insurance, and economic and social service resources, placing domestic violence within a broader framework of gender discrimination.[64] For example, a provision of VAWA '99, the Domestic Violence and Sexual Assault Victims' Housing Act, amends the McKinney Homeless Assistance Act to provide available funding for housing services for domestic violence victims, including rental assistance; The Workplace Violence Against Women Prevention Tax Credit Act implements tax credits to businesses providing workplace safety programs to combat violence against women.[65] These provisions are an important antidote to the criminalization emphasis in the 1994 VAWA, and represent a different form of state involvement and assistance.

This leads to the third and most significant facet of state involvement in domestic violence issues, the need for an explicit framework of gender equality for state and federal law reform efforts respecting intimate violence. The civil rights remedy of VAWA, which explicitly identifies "gender-motivated" violence as a harm and requires proof of "gender animus," is an example of this important approach. The identification of intimate violence, sexual abuse, and rape as gendered, as affecting women's freedom, citizenship, and autonomy, and as fundamental to women's equality, revives the core precept of the battered women's movement that generated the past twenty-five years of important legal work on battering.

Sadly, this context of gender equality has been lost in both public and legal discourse concerning domestic violence. Our highest governmental officials, like President Clinton and Attorney-General Janet Reno, talk about domestic violence and legitimate it as an important topic of public discourse, but this discourse does not link violence to larger issues of gender. In 1995 I was at the White House for the program establishing October as Domestic Violence Awareness Month, at the same time that welfare "reform" legislation was being debated in Congress. The White House domestic violence program emphasized criminalization reforms, but failed even to mention a link between violence and welfare.[66] Indeed, the fact that President Clinton could eliminate welfare payments to battered women while simultaneously proclaiming an end to domestic violence reflects the contradictions of feminist engagement with the state. But the good news is that, in response, advocates on domestic violence and welfare have now forged connections that have had significant legislative consequences, and have made some difference in the lives of battered women on welfare.[67]

The identification of a concept of gender violence, as in VAWA, is a critical theoretical move; the work of building connections between welfare and violence documents the crucial relationship between gender equality and the economic impact of violence on women's lives. However, the work that needs to be done to build more explicit connections between violence and gender equality is just beginning. If feminists are to engage with the state, it must be to ensure that the interrelationships among violence and gender, work and violence, economic resources, homelessness, and the material constraints of gender are central to both theory and practice in domestic violence legal reform efforts.

In conclusion, in legal work on domestic violence we have moved beyond simple rejection of the state or a simple assumption that the state can solve the problem. So should we move beyond uncritical engagement with the state, particularly in the criminal context, and toward more critical theoretical and practical analysis. An explicit framework of gender equality, which makes the link between battering and power and control, battering and attitudes of disrespect, battering and verbal abuse, battering and economic coercion, battering and the workplace, battering and housing, battering and welfare, and battering and childcare, is necessary to the possibility of meaningful reform. At the same time, as early case law on VAWA suggests, a gender equality framework is not sufficient to ensure that the state will be genuinely accountable to battered women. The contradictions of engaging with the state on domestic violence continue.

11

Lawmaking as Education

Lawmaking can be a form of public education that shapes public perceptions and social attitudes; education can open new ways of seeing the world that can spark and shape new ways of thinking about law. If feminist lawmaking has made a difference in the lives of battered women, it is not only because of the particular legal reforms that have been implemented and the legal strategies that have been developed, but because of the public education campaigns that have been galvanized by the struggles for legal reform. Conversely, the process of public education generally, and legal education in particular, has generated new laws and new legal reforms. The next two chapters explore this interrelationship between lawmaking and education.

In this chapter I examine the educational role of lawmaking through a close look at the O. J. Simpson criminal and civil trials and their impact on public education concerning domestic violence. Because of intense media saturation, the Simpson trials provided a major opportunity for national education on the issue of domestic violence over the past thirty years. These trials offer useful lessons concerning the limitations of high-profile cases in accomplishing education on important social issues.

The Simpson Case: Three Stories

In June 1994, when Nicole Brown Simpson was found murdered and O. J. went on his freeway run, I was in Phoenix, Arizona, speaking about violence against women at a conference of academics in the fields of law and social sciences. My colleagues and I thought that the facts which had begun to unfold about the history of the Simpsons' relationship were a "textbook case," familiar to anyone who had done work with battered women and battering

men. We were simultaneously excited by the opportunity for national public education about the severity of the problem of battering and fearful that
the issue of domestic violence would get lost in the other facets of the case
that were already emerging: the cult of O. J. Simpson's celebrity, the role of
racism, and the media circus that the freeway run presaged. To many of us,
the prospect that the issue of domestic violence would explode in the media
and then be subtly subverted in the legal process seemed even worse than
silence. It was frightening to consider how much this opportunity for public education would depend on a series of events and factors over which we
and other advocates had almost no control. As events unfolded, many of us
realized how right we were to have been afraid.

In January 1995, in the middle of the trial, I participated in a meeting of
scholars and activists convened by the Ford Foundation to discuss domestic violence and focus on directions and possibilities for reform. Threaded
through the discussion was the impact the Simpson trial was having on our
work. Many people in service organizations reported that the case had produced an increase in calls for help from battered women, and that the early
media attention had led to some increased public and legislative attention. At
the same time, we lamented that the issue of domestic violence had now been
submerged in the trial, that the fact that the case fit the familiar scenario of
woman abuse, separation, and homicide was apparently being ignored, and
that the media blitz on the substantive problem of domestic violence (as opposed to the daily details of the trial) had stopped. We worried about the
impact that an acquittal would have on the lives of many battered women and
on public consciousness about domestic violence.

By October 1995, the criminal trial had ended. Although Nicole Simpson's
chilling call to 911 and the "telephone counseling" that the court had sanctioned had been heard by the jury, the full history of abuse, and the role that
her separation from Simpson might have played in exacerbating his violence
and providing a motive for the homicide, had not been heard. As the Simpson
jury went into deliberation, I joined other battered women's advocates at the
White House for the Domestic Violence Awareness Month program. Sitting
in the East Room next to a senatorial legislative aide, who told me about the
positive changes in congressional attitudes toward domestic violence, I cautioned (not knowing that the jury had already reached a verdict of not guilty)
that we should wait to see what the Simpson jury did.

I begin with these stories because they highlight an important lesson illuminated by the Simpson trials: major legal cases, particularly those that go to trial, play only a limited role in public education on serious social issues like domestic violence. Like any major public case, the Simpson case had the potential to educate the public about such issues in the context of a particular set of facts and circumstances. But a legal case, particularly a public trial (even when spotlighted by the saturation of media coverage that the Simpson case received), cannot be relied upon to do the serious job of public education. The social issues that underlie the case may not be adequately presented in the trial process; they are only part of the picture that is presented at trial and ultimately may be subverted. This is precisely what happened in the Simpson case.

The Context of Domestic Violence

The first set of press stories about the Simpson case focused on the issue of domestic violence. Newspaper accounts emphasized that O. J. had beaten Nicole in 1989, that she had called the police (and that the call had been taped), and that O. J. had received only a modest sanction, counseling by phone, and no criminal penalty. The media reported that there were other beatings, that Nicole and O. J. had separated months before, that he had been angry at the separation, and that he had tried to break down her door. There were reports that Nicole had expressed fear for her life to a number of people, that she had called a local battered women's shelter for help just days before she was murdered, and that she had left a photograph and note in a safe deposit box expressing her fear that O. J. would kill her, to be opened after her death. The press reported that on the day of the homicide Nicole and O. J. had been together at a school recital, and that the children had gone home with Nicole and then out to dinner with her family and friends, a dinner to which O. J. was not invited. To experts knowledgeable about battering, about the issue of maintenance of power and control that underlies battering, and about the degree to which battered women's assertion of separation and independence heightens the likelihood of the batterer's lethal violence, the homicide was tragically explicable.

From the beginning, the story that unfolded of the history of Nicole and O. J. Simpson's relationship manifested a common pattern within battering relationships, including the fact that when O. J.'s battering was ultimately reported to the police, no serious sanction was imposed by either the judicial system or his employers. Indeed, the facts presented a powerful motive for the homicide: the history of abuse, the separation, the rumors that Nicole had developed another relationship, that O. J.'s girlfriend had broken up with him that day, and the circumstances of their being together at the recital that day with the children. Battered women recognized the facts of the Simpson case in their own experiences, particularly the 911 call; battering men recognized themselves in O. J.'s rambling suicide letter.[1]

For the jury in the criminal trial to have been able to consider, much less accept, this history of domestic violence as the context of the crime, and to identify O. J.'s rage and jealousy as the motive for the homicide, the jury would have needed to understand the crucial link between domestic violence and homicide. They would have to have been presented with the full history of abuse within Nicole and O. J.'s relationship so as to grapple with the facts of the violence. Most important, they would have to have been sufficiently educated about domestic violence in order to be able to genuinely hear this evidence without distancing it as the "private" province of "other" people's experiences. To acknowledge this pattern of domestic violence as the motive, they also would have had to cast aside the public glorification of O. J., the racism and incompetence of the Los Angeles Police Department, and a number of other factors, none of which may have been possible for them to do in this trial.

Tragically, the history of domestic violence that might have explained O. J.'s motive to kill Nicole was not fully presented to the jury even though domestic violence evidence was allowed by Judge Ito on some counts. The evidence that Judge Ito ruled admissible included the following:

- A 1982 incident in which O. J. allegedly smashed photos of Nicole's family, threw her against a wall, and threw her and her clothes out of the house.
- A 1985 call to a private security officer in which a crying, puffy-faced Nicole alleged that O. J. had bashed her car with a baseball bat.
- A 1987 incident in Victoria Beach in which O. J. allegedly struck Nicole and threw her to the ground.
- The 1989 incident that resulted in O. J.'s conviction for spousal abuse after he pleaded no contest, and letters from Simpson apologizing for his behavior.
- Another 1989 incident in which O. J. allegedly slapped Nicole and pushed her from a slow-moving car.
- Six statements made by O. J. in 1993 and 1994. These include statements from the tape of Nicole's 911 call and one incident in which O. J. showed a friend the

secret back way into his ex-wife's home. "Sometimes she doesn't even know I'm here," Simpson allegedly said.

• Seven allegations of "stalking behavior," including two times that O. J. allegedly followed Nicole to restaurants when she was with another man, as well as one incident in which he claimed to have observed them having sex on a couch in her home.

• A 1994 incident in which O. J. saw Nicole with Ronald Goldman and another man having coffee at Starbucks, at which point he allegedly stopped his car and angrily motioned her to come over. Judge Ito said the episode was relevant because it connected Simpson to Goldman and was "evidence of jealousy and motive."

Evidence that Judge Ito barred included:

• A 1977 incident in which neighbors said they heard O. J. beating Nicole and saw her with black eyes.

• Seven statements made by Nicole, including entries in a diary and a telephone call that she allegedly made to the Sojourn House shelter for battered women five days before she was killed. Among these statements was Nicole's remark to her mother that her ex-husband was following her to the gas station.[2]

Even if a fuller range of evidence had been presented, the jury would have required education about domestic violence in order to evaluate it fairly. Although the prosecution did not introduce any expert testimony about the abuse, the defense clearly anticipated that the prosecution would seek to present testimony about the common characteristics of batterers: Johnnie Cochran announced in his opening statement that the defense would have an expert, Dr. Lenore Walker, testify that O. J. did not fit the common characteristics of batterers (a statement that outraged battered women's advocates around the country because Walker is an expert on battered women, not battering men, and has testified in many cases on behalf of battered women). Although the prosecution apparently submitted a motion to introduce expert testimony on battering on rebuttal,[3] it did not press this motion, and Judge Ito apparently never ruled on it. The defense never called Lenore Walker.

The spate of books on the criminal trial suggest that the prosecution was ambivalent about the importance of domestic violence in the case. The prosecutors do not appear to have understood (or chose to deny) the degree to which the facts suggested that this was a classic case of "femicide" — woman killing in the context of a battering relationship. Defense lawyer Alan Dershowitz certainly understood the case in this way. In his book on the case, Dershowitz says: "As soon as the morning newscaster announced that the bloody body of the woman found in Brentwood was Nicole Brown . . . I told my wife O. J. probably did it. The former husband is generally the perp in a case like this."[4] The police refused to fully investigate the incidents of domestic violence that Nicole Simpson reported because they admired O. J.'s celebrity and were not willing to take responsibility for prosecuting him.[5] Prosecutor Christopher Darden stated in his opening: "She left him. She was no longer in his control. He could not stand to lose her and so he murdered her," but according to Jeffrey Toobin the prosecution's case failed to develop, demonstrate, or explain this theory. To Toobin, Darden's lack of enthusiasm for this theory in his treatment of witnesses effectively "demonstrated the limits of [the prosecution's] domestic violence presentation."[6]

The lead prosecutors have somewhat varying explanations for these limits. In his book on the trial, Christopher Darden reports that he initially ignored the domestic violence aspect of the case. Because he was responsible for coordinating *all* the evidence, he simply did not have enough time to devote to the domestic violence evidence. Although Darden says that he later realized the importance of the domestic violence context of the case, and even personally attempted to convince his lead co-counsel, Marcia Clark, of its importance, it was not until the *defense* filed a motion seeking to preclude evidence of domestic abuse that the prosecution was forced to respond.[7]

In her book on the case, Marcia Clark is quite open in explaining the source of her ambivalence toward the domestic violence aspect of the case. She admits that she avoided it because domestic violence was what she calls her own "demon issue"; she did not want to face her own experience of being raped as a teenager and being stalked by her ex-husband—behavior that at the time she thought was "normal," not criminal. She saw chilling parallels between her own life and Nicole Brown Simpson's life, particularly in each of their efforts to minimize the violence in their lives. Clark says: "The photos of Nicole, her voice on the 911 tape—these produced in me sensations of dread. . . . I'm sure I knew that, when the time came, I'd have to confront my own personal history as well." She confesses: "Deep down, I knew [that the issue of domestic violence] lay at the center of the case, but I was too weak to carry the burden of it." She wanted to emphasize the physical evidence because "the domestic violence aspect of the case . . . left [her] deeply conflicted."[8]

Clark admits that she knew that "this *was* a case of domestic violence that ended in murder," but she "also knew from experience, both personal and professional, that the very mention of the words 'domestic violence' aroused volatile emotions in people. . . . Female jurors often view victims of domestic violence with uncomprehending disdain." Clark herself had "always hated the culture of victimization," and her "approach to domestic violence cases over the years was one of extreme caution"; she had "never gotten up on a pulpit to spout a feminist line."[9] In light of her feelings of identification and avoidance, it is no surprise that the prosecution did not affirmatively furnish the judge and jury with a domestic violence framework to explain O. J.'s behavior and provide a motive for the homicide.

As a result, the jury in the criminal case was not offered an overall interpretation of the case as a femicide. The jurors were not presented with witnesses and facts that they would have needed to hear concerning the history of abuse in order to explain the motive for the homicide; they did not even hear expert testimony that might have assisted them to overcome their inclinations to disregard or minimize the evidence that they did hear. According to some sources, focus groups and telephone polls suggested that black women tended to be more accepting of Simpson's violence and minimized it.[10] We know that some of the jurors had personal experience with domestic violence. One juror was dismissed when she came to court with visible bruises reported to have been inflicted by her boyfriend; another was dismissed when it was discovered that she had filed a restraining order against her husband in 1988, accusing him of forcing her to have sex against her will, and that she had not previously disclosed the incident on voir dire. Statements made by some of the jurors after the verdict indicated that they did not understand why domestic violence was even "relevant" to the case, given that Simpson was charged with homicide, not battering; these comments suggest the depth of the jurors' inclination to minimize the battering evidence and the need for the prosecution affirmatively to present countervailing explanations.

As the criminal trial went on, the issue of domestic violence suggested in the prosecution's opening got lost, subsumed in the prosecution's presentation of physical evidence, in the defense's exploration of the DNA evidence, in the incompetence of the Los Angeles Police Department and Mark Fuhrman's racism, and in the defense's direct appeal to racial solidarity. Given the lack of effort to educate the jury on domestic violence early in the prosecution's case in order to overcome the likely trivialization of the issue, there was

206 Aspirations, Limits, and Possibilities

almost no chance for the jury to understand the true context of the case. Even if there had been a more serious and sustained effort by the prosecution, and even if the jury had been able to overcome substantial resistance to understand the connections and to accept the motive, it would still have had to find no reasonable doubt.

The Verdict in the Criminal Trial

Many battered women, domestic violence advocates, and commentators were frightened and disheartened by the speed with which the criminal jury arrived at a verdict, and by the verdict itself. The trial went on for 372 days, and the jury deliberated less than four hours. During the criminal trial, many battered women reported to advocates that men battered and threatened them with a greater sense of impunity because "O. J. could get away with it," and they read the verdict as further support for the view that men would continue to "get away with it." One battered woman survivor interviewed after the verdict said, "My fear is that this verdict is sending a message that violence is ok." Another said she feared that her husband and other battering men would use the Simpson case as justification to treat women more violently. Jurors' comments suggested that the jury had not taken the issue of domestic violence seriously or even understood its relevance to the charge of homicide. One juror, Brenda Moran, asserted that domestic violence was not an issue in the case and that evidence on domestic violence had been "a waste of time. This was a murder trial, not domestic abuse."[11] Moreover, the fact that the acquittal was celebrated, although O. J. had been convicted of abuse, was troubling. For although Simpson was acquitted of murder, it is indisputable that he was a batterer who was not held duly accountable for his use of violence and threats early on — by a judge who allowed counseling by phone, by police who applied a double standard, and by employers like Hertz and NBC who ignored Simpson's arrest for a violent crime.

The trial may also have reinforced false and misleading stereotypes, because domestic violence is unquestionably a considerable risk factor for homicide, and a batterer's public persona or his loving relationship with children is not inconsistent with his propensity to abuse or commit domestic homicide. Nonetheless, the case did not involve only the issue of domestic violence, and it was not a social referendum on the significance of the problem. Many other issues were involved, most significantly the degree to which racism and incompetence within the Los Angeles Police Department had irreparably tainted the prosecution's case and had served to raise reasonable doubt for the jury.[12]

The Civil Trial and Verdict

The civil trial and the jury verdict that found O. J. Simpson liable for damages provide a sharp contrast to the criminal proceedings. Not only is the burden of proof in a civil case— preponderance of the evidence—lower than the burden of proof in a criminal case—guilt beyond a reasonable doubt—but the proof presented in the civil case differed significantly from that in the criminal case. Most important, the trial judge in the civil case ruled that he would allow testimony about domestic violence and would limit Simpson's ability to claim a racist frame-up.[13] First, O. J. himself testified, and his denial of the fact that he had ever hit Nicole raised serious questions as to his credibility. Second, more evidence was admitted concerning domestic violence: Nicole's call to the battered women's shelter days before her death, the testimony of eyewitnesses who bolstered plaintiffs' theory regarding domestic violence and recounted their observations of past fights between O. J. and Nicole, and the recording by a police officer of Nicole saying that O. J. got an "animal look" during a 1993 fight.[14] Finally, more physical evidence linking O. J. to the crime—such as admission of his failure of the lie detector test, and thirty photographs of him wearing the Bruno Magli shoes linking him to the footprints at Nicole's house[15]—was admitted at the civil trial. Other witnesses also chipped away at O. J.'s credibility; evidence was admitted that he had received the voice-mail message that afternoon from Paula Barbieri in which she broke up with him, a fact that he had previously denied.[16] Finally, Mark Fuhrman did not testify.

There were other significant differences as well. The racial and gender composition of the jury contrasted starkly with the composition of the jury in the criminal trial. The criminal trial had one white, nine blacks, and one Hispanic/Latino—two men and ten women. The civil jury was composed of nine whites, one Asian, one Hispanic, one Asian/black—six men and six women. At the civil trial, Simpson's denial that he had ever hit Nicole received considerable public attention. In an interview, he specifically claimed that Nicole had "fabricated tales of physical abuse." Commentators judged his assertions sharply; one observed that he was digging himself into an untenable position, as there was "too much evidence indicating that he was a spousal batterer."[17]

Finally, in the civil case, the jury deliberated for six days, and had as a backdrop the benefit of sustained public analysis of the criminal verdict.

The Simpson trials challenge us as a society to address seriously the problem of domestic violence, and there is much work to do. The initial media blitz on domestic violence was useful, and some amount of public education was accomplished. It is heartening now to see posters addressing domestic violence in buses and subways, and to hear public service announcements on television (one such announcement, aired in New York, shows a couple ignoring sounds of abuse in the apartment upstairs while the headline reads, "It *is* your problem!"). National public education programs such as "There's No Excuse for Domestic Violence," developed by the Family Violence Prevention Fund in San Francisco, include public service announcements on television, on the radio, and in print designed to increase public awareness of battering. The Simpson case has also focused attention on the link between domestic violence and the glorification of male athletes and other sports figures, which is now more openly discussed in newspapers and magazines such as *Sports Illustrated*.[18]

Trials as Education

Education to change public perceptions of domestic violence is a long haul, for violence is deeply threatening to our concepts of the family as "a haven in a heartless world." The Simpson trials suggest the complexity of trial presentation of issues of domestic violence. In the criminal trial, a female prosecutor and female jurors were deeply resistant to acknowledging the domestic violence aspects of the case.[19] Given the pervasiveness of domestic violence in the United States, it would not be surprising if members of the largely female criminal jury in the Simpson trial were, like Marcia Clark herself, afraid to acknowledge their own demons of domestic violence and were even unconsciously denying the role that domestic violence and broader issues of male power and control played in Nicole Simpson's death, for fear of confronting these issues in their own lives.

Yet, lawmaking *can* lead to education, and education can generate further lawmaking. One important consequence of the Simpson cases has been the recognition that femicide is a serious national problem. Domestic Violence Fatality Review Commissions, which examine homicides caused by domestic violence, have been established in many states.[20] A number of innovative law reform proposals have been made concerning prosecutions for femicide. For example, in a series of articles, Myrna Raeder has suggested that our criminal laws and evidence rules contain gender-biased views of women's lives and femicide, which clearly devalue and blame women.[21] She recommends a number of reforms to correct the "historic effects of gender imbalance," such as enacting a domestic violence statute requiring a first-degree murder conviction if there is proof of a pattern of domestic violence; admitting all evidence of prior domestic violence in a prosecution's case-in-chief; and enacting a new hearsay exception for statements of a domestic violence homicide victim if she has suffered at least three instances of violence at the hands of the defendant.[22] Raeder and other commentators have recommended exceptions to the general evidentiary rule that prohibits propensity evidence for specific acts of domestic violence or abuse.[23] Admitting this type of evidence, she asserts, will allow a jury to consider violent acts as evidence that the defendant had a propensity to abuse his spouse.[24]

In California and elsewhere, the Simpson trials prompted the passage of new legislation and a number of proposals for reform. In 1996 a new hearsay rule was signed into law in California which allows statements that are recorded, written, or made to police by victims of domestic violence describing their injuries or threats of injury to be admitted into evidence, if the victim is unavailable as a trial witness. Two days after the verdict in the criminal case, California's Governor, Pete Wilson, signed a new law requiring either a guilty plea or a jury trial for first-time abusers to ensure that charges of abuse are not dropped and that first-time abusers will have a criminal record. The City of Buffalo, New York, has instituted a plan in which local women in fear of abuse can be given a portable 911 transmitter to place in a purse or attach to a bracelet. Maryland law now requires police officers responding to domestic abuse calls to inform victims and their children of the availability of relief by restraining orders, shelters, and anti-stalking laws, and to give them telephone numbers they can call for help and for information.[25]

Reform proposals in the wake of the Simpson trial include exceptions to the hearsay rule and laws that would deny child custody to a parent found guilty or liable for a spouse's death.[26] These proposals can now be evaluated, debated, and perhaps even adopted by state legislatures. They are a positive legacy of this troubling case.

The public education on domestic violence that we need as a society cannot happen in the "quick fix" of any trial; the trial process is too chaotic and unpredictable, and it depends too much on personality, wealth, and the vagaries of media attention. Court TV is not the only site of education about lawmaking; it must take place in every elementary school and high school, every court, welfare office, hospital, and law school around the country in order to address the everyday deaths of so many women, in the United States and around the world.

12

Education as Lawmaking

The critical work of feminist lawmaking on domestic violence can be accomplished only if there are lawyers who are sensitive to these issues of gender and violence, lawyers who are committed to representing battered women and understanding the problems of domestic violence, and lawyers who are not so personally involved with or conflicted about violence that they are hindered from effective representation. The O. J. Simpson case and many other cases discussed in this book underscore the urgency of the need for competent and thoughtful lawyers for women who are abused. Until recently, lawyers who faced issues of domestic violence in the wide range of settings in which these issues arise—in criminal matters, torts, insurance, civil rights, or family law—would not have been exposed to these issues in law school, for issues of violence against women have historically been omitted from the law school curriculum. Over the past several years, this has begun to change. Many law schools now offer courses and clinical programs on these issues, and student advocacy organizations are involved in working with battered women's groups and legal organizations.

Yet legal education on domestic violence is important beyond the instrumental purpose of preparing law students to handle these issues. Violence against women—woman abuse—is a crucial subject for legal education. It is an important lens for understanding our experiences of family and intimate relations generally and for examining the role of law and social change. Legal education concerning domestic violence also provides significant opportunities for exploring the interrelationship between theory and practice, and for building bridges between scholarship and activism.

In the spring of 1991, I began teaching a course at Harvard Law School while I was visiting there for the year, which I named "Battered Women and the Law." It was not my first time teaching these issues, as I had taught courses called either "Women and the Law" or "Gender Discrimination" at Brooklyn Law School since 1974, and at Harvard Law School since 1989. These courses included sections on domestic violence and battered women who kill, as well as on rape and sexual harassment, but they did not focus exclusively on domestic violence.

The concept of the course emerged from two interrelated aspects of my work: involvement in legal advocacy on a wide range of issues regarding violence against women, and a focus on the importance of linking theory and practice generally. I had recently completed a report for the Ford Foundation assessing legal reform efforts for battered women,[1] and in the process of researching it and interviewing activists around the country, I had found considerable dissociation between the activist and scholarly communities in the battered women's movement. Activists and advocates too frequently had no idea of the enormous wealth of theoretical and empirical work that had been done on battering and thus were unable to use it; conversely, many academics were out of touch with the breadth of activist experiences that needed to be documented and integrated into their work.[2] The "Battered Women and the Law" course was a way to bring the two worlds together—not just theory and practice, but scholarship and activism.

The Course: Battered Women and the Law

Like many other law schools, Harvard had an active group of students who were dedicated to doing legal work on battered women. The group founded a Battered Women's Advocacy Project, which was training students to assist and advocate for battered women.[3] Several students who were active in the project had taken my class on gender discrimination, and they enthusiastically supported the development of the new course.

In "Battered Women and the Law," I wanted the class to focus explicitly on the link between theory and practice because I believed that activist and scholarly work in this field needed to be more practically integrated. Discussions with Harvard Law School faculty and students led to the decision to incorporate a special clinical component for a limited number of students. This course would help develop a model of elective courses for upper-class students that would integrate classroom and clinical dimensions.[4] I also saw this explicit link between theory and practice in the class and in the special clinical component as critical because of the serious lack of legal representation for battered women that I had identified in the Ford Foundation report. Both the classroom dimension of the course and the clinical experience was a way to encourage students to perform legal advocacy for battered women. My hope was that this training would help meet immediate legal service needs as well as lead to students' long-term professional interest in this work.

The course had three parts: a classroom component; a requirement that all students produce a substantial research paper; and the special clinical component for some of the students. The syllabus and reading materials emphasized the interrelationship between feminist theory, academic research, writing on violence against women (particularly in the social sciences), activist writing, and the experiences of women who had been abused. These materials were integrated with cases and law review articles. The class began with a theoretical overview of themes in legal work on battered women, with sections on the historical and social context of battering that examined conflicting definitions and interpretations of the problem; historical, social, and cross-cultural perspectives; lesbian and gay battering; and battered women as mothers, including issues of child welfare, child abuse, and child custody. It then turned to social and legal reform efforts to assist battered women, including the concept and experience of shelters, civil restraining orders, arrest, domestic violence and torts, and a section that I called "alternative procedural frameworks," including civil rights, mediation, and international human rights. We then explored issues involving battered women's advocates, legal representation, and programs for batterers. We examined problems faced by battered women who killed their assailants, focusing on choice of defense, expert testimony on battering, and judicial and jury education. We ended with a section on rethinking theory and practice that focused on the theoretical contributions and dilemmas of different jurisprudential perspectives, such as feminist legal theory, law and society, critical legal studies and critical race theory, and a section on the implications of our work for public policy and practice.

Forty students enrolled in the class: thirty-eight women and two men, including several students of color. Seventeen students elected to take the clinical component. Every student was required to write a substantial and original research paper of publishable quality and three "reflection pieces." The class met for two hours a week, and I taught an additional class hour each week for students who were taking the clinical component.[5]

Clinical placements of the students who were taking the clinic also served as a means to connect scholarship and activism. Sarah Buel, a former student of mine and a recent Harvard Law School graduate who had co-founded the Battered Women's Advocacy Project, was the clinical supervisor, and we planned the students' clinical placements together.[6] Because there was a wide range of legal work and activism on the issue of domestic violence in Massachusetts, we developed a diverse group of placements: working with the Harvard Battered Women's Advocacy Project to help battered women who needed restraining orders; with the Harvard Legal Aid Bureau and Legal Services Center on family law cases that involved battering; with the Massachusetts Gender Bias Commission of the Supreme Judicial Court, Massachusetts Law Reform Institute, and other law reform organizations; with Massachusetts battered women's advocacy groups on clemency appeals for battered women in prison; and with prosecutors' offices and private practitioners who did family law. The variety of placements allowed students in the clinical class to learn from each other about activist work in different areas, and to see the common themes that emerged in all the different settings.

The third component of the class, which was essential to linking theory with practice and scholarship with activism, was the requirement of a research paper. I wanted their papers to be original, scholarly, and useful to both activists and scholars in the field; as part of the link to activist work, the papers should be responsive to the needs of battered women's advocates around the country. Because Sarah and I had been involved in work on battered women for many years, both of us were connected with a larger national network of academics and activists. I canvassed this larger community, contacting lawyers and advocates around the country to get ideas on legal and empirical research and law reform projects that would be useful to them. These ideas were then presented to the students as a substantial list of possible research topics distributed to them early in the semester. All the students chose their paper topics from this list.

Another purpose of the scholarship component was to develop a sense of scholarly community among the students themselves and to encourage them to think of themselves as part of a larger community of scholars and activists in the battered women's movement. I wanted them to view themselves as serious contributors to the generation of important and useful scholarship on violence against women. I scheduled regular meetings with all the students in the class to talk about their papers, and Sarah worked with many of them as well. Because I knew that many of their research projects were related and overlapping, and because I was constantly asking one of them to share materials or contacts with another, I decided to make the collaborative aspect of the course's research component more explicit: halfway through the semester I devoted the first half of one class to a discussion of the students' ongoing research projects. Students made a brief presentation on the subject matter of their paper, noting where they were in their research and what areas they still needed help on. The students were excited to hear about the range and importance of the projects on which their colleagues were working. Coming together in this way enabled students to brainstorm with each other on overlapping topics or issues. Their presentations formalized and legitimized the research agenda for the course and encouraged them to take themselves seriously as a collaborative scholarly think tank or, as one student humorously suggested, a "scholarly SWAT team" on violence against women.

The research projects connected the students to the larger network of lawyers, advocates, and scholars working in the battered women's movement. The paper topics involved empirical investigation, emphasizing interviews and consultation with activists and practitioners. This class collaboration, and the interaction with people actively involved in the work, transformed the students' research paper requirement from what could have been (and is frequently) a solitary, individualistic project into one that connected them with colleagues and others in an activist community. They became enthusiastic about their own scholarship and the contribution they could make to the knowledge base on violence against women; accordingly, they produced impressive work.

The two-hour weekly class became the centerpiece where everything in the course coalesced. Class meetings were always charged with energy. Discussion involved critical analysis of the problems battered women face, and of the theoretical, practical, and strategic dilemmas posed by legal and social responses to battering. Major themes of the class were connections between legal and activist responses to battering, and how law could be used as a tool for social change.

The students in the class were deeply interested in the subject. Because of the high level of student interest in issues concerning violence against women in undergraduate colleges, and the fine work of the Harvard Battered Women's Advocacy Project in generating student interest in these issues at Harvard Law School, many in the class had already done work relating to battered women before they came to the course. On the first day of class, I asked the students to talk about themselves and their backgrounds, and give their reasons for taking the course. It was clear that the level of prior work and both professional and personal involvement in the issue was high. The fact that many students in the class had prior work experiences with issues of battering also meant that they saw themselves in multiple roles, not just as law students but as activists, advocates, and lawyers. They wanted the class to connect theory and practice, to link their theoretical interests and their activist experience and aspirations.

Students' experiences with the topic provided a wealth of background knowledge that enhanced classroom discussion. In many ways, their prior experiences complemented the purpose of the clinical component of the class, for they added the dimension of activism to classroom theory. In addition, the class regularly attracted visitors. Several lawyers, law professors, scholars, and activists who worked on issues of domestic violence in the Boston area came to class to learn and to share their insights. They added another layer of richness and excitement to class discussions.

I structured the class to maximize the students' active involvement. I saw my task as directing and facilitating dialogue within the class, encouraging students to reject simplistic formulations and to challenge each other's thinking. Each week I began class with a brief introduction, connecting the subject of that week's discussion to past and future topics, briefly synthesizing the reading materials, identifying major themes and tensions, and focusing the discussion; then I opened the class up to discussion. In addition, I had panels of two or three students make a short presentation to the class. The panels were selected on the basis of their participants' connection to the readings for the day. For example, those students who were either writing their paper on child custody, or who had experience in working on legal issues involving custody, were chosen to make the presentation for the class on custody. In this way, the students with the most experience or knowledge of the area were asked to reflect on the topic in advance and then to share their knowledge and experiences with the class. This arrangement worked particularly well and allowed the students to learn from each other. In general, I encouraged the students to draw on their own experiences—whether in practice or other settings—in formulating their ideas, and to disagree with each other and me, honestly and supportively.

On a more personal level, the course was one of the most stimulating teaching experiences I have had because it had the feel of a genuinely collaborative intellectual project. I was directing and working with a group of smart, committed, energetic, and wonderfully open students on a topic in which I am deeply involved, and we were learning together. Each of us in the class, including me, was thinking and writing on issues that he or she cared deeply about, and there was a powerful sense of intellectual engagement, lively dialogue, and an openness to challenge each other's ideas and approaches. Teaching the class enriched my own thinking and scholarship and strengthened my commitment to develop more educational opportunities that contain similar qualities of engagement and dialogue.

The semester was extraordinarily intense and emotional for another reason. Midway through the semester, in early April, my close friend and colleague Mary Joe Frug, a professor at New England School of Law in Boston, was brutally murdered on a street corner near her house in Cambridge, in a still unsolved act of violence. Mary Joe's teaching and writing had been devoted to issues of women's rights and feminist theory; she wrote one of the earliest articles on the interrelationship between women's rights in the home and in the workplace, and her article on gender bias in a contracts casebook had been a model of scholarship on gender bias in the law school curriculum.[7] Her course materials for "Women and the Law," which I had used and which were posthumously published as a casebook, contained a brilliant chapter on domestic violence, reflecting her deep concern with the issue.[8] Mary Joe and I had worked on many projects together, and we had traveled to Poland together the previous year on a delegation of progressive law teachers. The day of her murder we had spent the morning together. She was excited about my course, and students at New England Law School had asked her to teach a course on domestic violence. She said she wanted to talk with me about the class, and we planned to get together to discuss it the following week, excited at the prospect of sharing a new intellectual and political project. Instead, I spent that day at her memorial service.

Students' Voices

For my students, the course demonstrated the power of combining scholarship and activism and the possibility of transforming legal education from a frequently passive and intimidating experience into an active, motivating experience. The issue of woman abuse presents a vital topic through which this connection can be made. In their "reflection pieces," many students expressed how the course had transformed their law school experience into something that, as one said, they had "never dreamed it could be."

The purpose of the three reflection pieces, which I asked students to write during the course of the semester, was to assist them in reflecting on the educational process of the class and the issues we were exploring. Because the course involved issues that were so intellectually and emotionally volatile, I hoped the reflection pieces would be a way for me to know what the students were getting out of the class, to understand how they were reacting to class dynamics, and to stay in touch with the way the class was affecting them. The reflection pieces could take any form the students wanted: poems, stories, narratives of their own experiences, or comments on the readings or clinical work they were doing.

The students used their reflection pieces to comment on a range of topics, including the course's effect on their perceptions of battered women, the power of envisioning solutions to problems as the next step beyond critique of the current remedies available to battered women, and their difficulties with coming to terms with their role as lawyers. Here I present some excerpts, quoted with permission from the students, to show how the integration of theory and practice affected their experience of the course, and how this integration gave them a sense of community, legitimized their commitment to work on violence against women, and shaped their view of themselves as lawyers.[9] These excerpts express one of the most powerful aspects of teaching on violence against women: the connection between the students' intellectual and personal lives. Because Mary Joe's murder related to the themes of the course and heightened this link between the intellectual and the personal both for me and for many students, this section ends by describing the class's experience in discussing her death. The students' words express both their horror and sadness, and their determination to commemorate her life by committing themselves to working for change.

For the students who were taking the additional clinical component, the integration between theory and practice was particularly intense. One observed:

> I'm truly impressed with how much serious work this class full of students has been able to do in three months. In part, this is because you've helped each of us to find a focus that we can become invested in. In part it's because of the personal connections that you and Sarah have to the advocates in this move-

ment and your sense of it as a movement, as something whole that we can each fit into.

My own experience of the result has been that I've been welcomed into a network of scholars and activists and I've quickly been relied upon to fulfill as much of a role as I choose. The immediate sense is that I'm not an outsider. . . . I've quickly been inducted as a full participant into an advocacy movement in which I have an immediate place to make a real contribution.

The creation of a community within the classroom, and the welcome the students felt in entering an existing community as full-fledged members, clarified their abilities as lawyers and activists committed to this work. Another student commented:

How do I sum up the experience of the class? Exhausting and defeating but also invigorating. I felt reinvigorated and inspired by what I learned and the endless possibilities of effecting change. In class, we often spoke about empowering battered women in the decisions they face. Similarly, I think it is necessary to recognize that lawyers, and especially women lawyers, also need to feel empowered to do work with battered women. The work itself is very hard and can be defeating. Having the class, which acted as a sort of support group, and sharing the stories that we all had with each other was crucial. I felt so much more empowered (overcoming my pessimistic tendencies) and indeed hopeful, that there was a group of women out there who were ready and willing to tackle the work.

For many students, feeling part of an intellectual community was a new experience: "I've been able to feel for the first time in my life that I'm part of a community of people who share my concerns and hopes for change." One wrote: "I have been dealing with a lot of personal pain and struggling with a lot of conflicting feelings about my working in the area of violence prevention. And yet these feelings have been somewhat offset by the incredible sense of community out there for people working in these areas, a community that I have grown to feel a part of."

The creation of an intellectual community was particularly important because it was unusual in their law school experience:

Mostly the class made me hopeful — to some people the class might be depressing, but mostly it's depressing when you feel helpless and as if there is nothing that is being done. I felt that when I first came to law school, as did many others.

My feeling was allayed somewhat through my joining the Legal Aid Bureau—but as you pointed out at the BWAP dinner—clinics such as the Bureau are often marginalized and it's as if you're living outside law school.

Being in your class made me feel far less marginalized and to some extent legitimized my clinical experience.

The class provided support for students' aspiration that law could be a practical vehicle for social change: "The class has been a source of inspiration that law can be a useful and workable tool for helping those who desperately need help and are denied access to resources. Beyond the land of corporations and taxes, it is inspiring to see formal recognition by the law school of the importance of using law to deal with issues. I feel great optimism in that I can be a part of a solution, a sense of commitment that says that change is possible and that lawyering can be socially useful." It also expanded the students' view of themselves as lawyers: "The Battered Women and the Law class moved away from the ubiquitous model of legal education that objectifies the subject and engages students in detached and unreflective discussion. The process of persuasion and advocacy that the class offered provided a model of changing positions and breaking down denial of women abuse. It required us to adjust our model of lawyer as detached professional to that of legal advocate."

The students' work affected their immediate representation of clients: "In an area of law which is constantly changing, and which has changed so dramatically over the last 20 years, the synergy of theory and practice is immediate and powerful. . . . Much of the brainstorming in which we engaged as a class was directly useful in my clinical experience . . . my responses to judges were more intelligent and thoughtful than they would have been had I done the clinical without the classroom experience. Conversely the clinical brought the theoretical to life and threw in the variable of human inconsistency."

The integration of theory and practice played a large role in the success of the class, but the real power of the course was its subject matter. The topic of woman abuse was immediately compelling because it touched on issues that are central to our deepest experiences of family life and aspirations for human intimacy. In light of the statistical pervasiveness of domestic violence, it should come as no surprise that many students reported their own experiences with violent family members or intimates. However, students did not need personal experience to identify with the subject matter. The pervasiveness of woman abuse in the United States and the widespread social denial of its existence make it immediate and palpable, an issue that cuts across class, race, and ethnicity. One student expressed her exhilaration at being able to discuss it in a classroom setting: "The class was magical in that I felt that every week, we dealt with real issues, not just hypotheticals—the readings made me think about being a future lawyer, as a woman in a largely patriarchal society." Another wrote: "It is a rare course that affects me so deeply and personally that I think about it, talk about it or work on it every single day, but this was one of those courses. . . . I also found that anger and sadness about society could be channeled into productive energy. . . . I have seen what can be accomplished with a few people working on a smaller-scale project, and how each of these small projects can add up to dramatic change." Yet another student noted that her work with battered women was part of a process of healing, and that "the ability to be able to act like a lawyer and to develop ways of helping women in their personal lives feels like a privilege."

Developing and teaching "Battered Women and the Law" was an extraordinary experience and a privilege for me, as well. Mary Joe's murder in the middle of the semester heightened the intensity of this experience. Her death was a terrible and painful loss, but I was grateful to have the class to share the sadness, mourn, and commemorate her spirit.

Many of the students knew Mary Joe or had heard her speak, and others were familiar with her work; several knew we were friends. Because the students were also grieving over Mary Joe's death, many attended her memorial service and many came to see me individually. The day after the memorial service we were scheduled to have class. I was in great pain, not only from experiencing the loss of a close friend, but also because the stress of the past few days had caused intense back pain, and I was barely able to walk. I thought about canceling the class but decided that it was important for all of us to be able to use the class to share our grief.

I opened the class with my feelings and told the students about the last time I had seen Mary Joe, when we had planned to discuss the "Battered Women and the Law" class so that she could develop a similar course at New England Law School. Then I asked the students if they wanted to speak. The class sat for a long time in silence. From the look on the students' faces, the silence was due to their own overwhelming sense of not knowing where to begin, not wanting to cry, and grasping at how to express their feelings. Finally, one student talked about her experience of meeting Mary Joe. Slowly, others started to add their experiences, either from their acquaintance with her or their reactions to her work. Gradually, the tears started to flow. Students expressed their fear, their anger, and their feelings of hopelessness, and they were able to link these feelings to the subject of the class.

The ultimate tribute to the class was that their feelings gave way to motivation to work for change on issues of violence against women:

> I really appreciated your providing the opportunity for us to listen and talk with each other about Mary Joe Frug's death. The sense of community has never been stronger. I only wish that Mary Joe could have been in the class or at the memorial service to share in the spirit she created. In addition to carrying on her feminist scholarship, I also wish to keep alive Mary Joe as a symbol of the kind of community that takes the time to listen and understand its members. If, for example, more people would try to understand the plight of battered women instead of blaming them for staying in a violent relationship, we could do so much more to protect them against violence and create safe options.

Another student wrote:

> Mary Joe's tragic death in its shocking brutality and unexpectedness has caused me not only inexpressible feelings of sadness and grief, as it has so many other people, but it has also given me a new lens with which to understand my own relationship to people and my involvement in the legal profession. In particular, it has made me stop and reevaluate what I have been learning from you and my fellow students in your Battered Women class this semester.
>
> Commitment makes life worth living, yet ironically it can destroy that very life. Commitment and care are two elements sorely missing from the legal environment, as exemplified in its purest form by disturbing discussions I have listened to in my Legal Profession class. Your class had a feel of care and commitment. Yet, what was even more impressive to me, was that students were willing to question and examine the very issues about which they cared so deeply. Ideological closemindedness was strikingly absent in all of our discussions. This, from my experience, is highly unusual especially among folks who have a great emotional investment in the issue. Perhaps, it is the ugly reality and unique experiences of every battered woman which made closemindedness impossible. I also think it's a matter of the intellectual approach which you encouraged. I hope to take and apply that approach in everything I pursue.
>
> For me, one of the most fun aspects of learning is seeing connections between different ideas; how they color, expand and change the meaning of each other. But for me, the ultimate connection, though not fun, was between the

emotional feelings evoked by Mary Joe's death and the substance and structure of your class. It made me appreciate the power of class interactions and the material itself. Every one of the students in your class could make a difference through what they learned and that is not some slight truism to be scoffed at. I felt it in a way unique and different from all my other Harvard experiences.

As a result of the class discussion, some members of the class organized a "speak-out" about Mary Joe's death and violence against women a few days later. All members of the law school community were invited to come and share their thoughts and grief. Many came, and the event gave the students a sense that they could build on their collective work on violence against women to reach out to others and take action together.

Integrating Domestic Violence into the Law School Curriculum

"Battered Women and the Law" was not the first law school course on domestic violence (although it was one of the first), but the interest and enthusiasm it generated reflects an enormous wave of student interest in legal work on domestic violence. Since teaching the course at Harvard, I have taught it several times at Brooklyn Law School as a seminar, and at Florida State University Law School as an intensive, week-long "mini-course," and these experiences have been equally gratifying. Everywhere I travel, every law school that I go to, students want to do this work. Many law schools now have courses or clinical programs that focus on problems of battered women, and a great number have student-run advocacy programs that address these issues. While battering is an issue that has particularly grabbed the attention of many law students around the country, it should be understood as part of a larger wave of interest in public-interest legal work.

There is now a significant literature that documents the serious problem of gender bias in the law school curriculum,[10] and specific courses that focus on issues of gender and violence against women are widely recognized as crucial to contemporary legal education. Yet there is still a need for "mainstream" courses, including first-year courses, to expand to include issues of violence against women. These issues must also be integrated within a wide range of courses in the law school curriculum. Programs on domestic violence and legal education that have been held at the Annual Meeting of the Association of American Law Schools (AALS) and at other professional development conferences have discussed the breadth of potential curricular options. In 1997 the American Bar Association (ABA) Commission on Domestic Violence published a report, *When Will They Ever Learn? Educating to End Domestic Violence,* which surveys the range of programs in law schools around the country and underscores the importance of these programs. The ABA Commission has also sponsored a series of regional conferences around the country to encourage curricular development in law schools concerning violence against women.[11]

There is hardly a first-year law school course into which issues of violence against women could not be integrated: civil procedure, torts, property, contracts, criminal law, and constitutional law are obvious candidates. In civil procedure, for example, the issue of the effectiveness of injunctive relief available for battered women, such as restraining orders, poses important questions, as does the "domestic relations" exception to federal subject-matter jurisdiction and the Violence Against Women Act. In torts courses, there are important issues relating to state responsibility, negligence, failure to provide police protection and enforce orders of protection, and battered women and self-defense. Each of these courses could include materials that raise issues of domestic violence. I have taught classes of my own or for colleagues at other institutions in all these subjects, and other law teachers in this field are doing so as well. At AALS Annual Meeting programs or ABA Commission meetings, numerous law teachers have described similar efforts in first-year courses. Several years ago, first-year faculty at Northeastern Law School developed a "bridge" segment on domestic violence that links a number of first-year courses together.

In addition, segments on violence against women fit easily into courses on family law, evidence, civil rights, racial discrimination, health law, alternative dispute resolution, remedies, law and poverty, international human rights, advanced courses in criminal justice, and more "obvious" courses such as gender discrimination or feminist theory. For example, while I was at Harvard I was invited by colleagues to teach classes on domestic violence in courses on criminal law, human rights and foreign policy, and mediation, and in a course called "Advanced Criminal Justice: Law Enforcement."

Domestic violence is also a natural topic for the development of clinical courses. The clinical component of the "Battered Women and the Law" course was just a beginning. Many other law schools around the country, including Georgetown, Boalt, American University, NYU, Northeastern, the University of Maryland, University of Denver, Pace, and CUNY have now developed full in-house clinical programs where students represent battered women in a variety of settings.[12]

The time has come to move this work into the mainstream of the law school curriculum and to send the message that domestic violence is a crucial part of legal education. Over the past several years, I have been working with an informal network of law school teachers around the country to create more opportunities to integrate this work into the curriculum. A growing number of law schools now have some kind of special curricular offering in the area of domestic violence. Some compilations of course materials are available, and Clare Dalton, professor of law and director of the Domestic Violence Institute at Northeastern University Law School, and I are in the process of writing a law school casebook on battered women and the law.[13] It is vital that we educate the broader legal education community on the reasons why domestic violence is a critical aspect of the law school curriculum, and develop teaching materials that could be used in a range of courses.

Integrating domestic violence into the law school curriculum has the potential to foster greater opportunities for legal representation for battered women, which could save the lives of many battered women. My report for the Ford Foundation highlighted the serious lack of legal representation available for battered women.[14] Despite statutory remedies, such as restraining orders, that have been developed to assist battered women, no states provide for free legal representation. Classroom and clinical courses that address legal issues affecting battered women can increase access to legal representation not only because they provide direct service, but also because they introduce law students to these issues. Many younger lawyers who now do legal assistance for battered women, whether by working with shelters or as part of pro bono projects with law firms, were, as law students, involved in battered women's projects, courses, or clinics.

A postscript to my "Battered Women and the Law" course is that many of the students in this course, and in the subsequent courses I have taught, have made important contributions to feminist lawmaking for battered women. Several students' papers were published in law reviews, and several have continued to write on these issues.[15] One example of student work that has had national impact is a manual that three students produced as a guide for national advocacy efforts on clemency petitions. This manual has been widely distributed by the National Clearinghouse for the Defense of Battered Women to advocates around the country, and has been used by clemency projects in many states.[16] Other student papers were widely distributed to advocates and scholars working in the field. In addition, several students have devoted their legal practice to representing battered women, several do pro bono work, several are now involved with the work of the ABA Commission on Domestic Violence, and several are now teaching the very same course or related courses at law schools across the country, reaching a new generation of law students. Expanding legal educational opportunities for students in this field is the best way to ensure that there will be more sensitive, thoughtful, and effective lawyers to assist battered women in the future, and that feminist lawmaking will continue to grow and be enriched by new perspectives.

Toward a Different Vision of Legal Education

The "Battered Women and the Law" course is one example of the links that can be developed between theory and practice and between scholarship and activism. It highlights the need for more self-conscious affirmative efforts within legal education to view law schools as potential laboratories for social change. American legal education has the potential to be transformative and to provide experiences for students that make the intellectual, human, and political connections that empower and create change. Law schools should be the sites for the building of bridges between theory and practice, between scholarship and activism. They should be laboratories for experimentation in public policy and for work on social change. While many law schools have public interest programs or public service programs that do some of this work, and while many law teachers have committed themselves to these goals in their own institutions, few schools have maximized their potential to do this work.

Law schools can and should be think tanks for the development of new and innovative social policies; they can and should be the places where we bring activists and scholars together to brainstorm on social problems. We should be moving our law schools to make institutional commitments beyond individual courses and programs: law schools should create interdisciplinary institutes to develop legislation, litigation strategy, and social policy. For example, a law school could institutionalize the contributions that a course like "Battered Women and the Law" can make to social policy by creating centers for research and advocacy. These centers, like the Domestic Violence Institute at Northeastern University Law School, could bring scholars and activists from different fields together to brainstorm on policy and strategy regarding domestic violence. Given the present state of social crisis in the United States concerning so many public issues, law schools should give a high priority to developing innovative social policy. Legal education has an important role to play in lawmaking generally, and a particularly crucial role to play in the evolution of feminist lawmaking on domestic violence.

13

Feminist Lawmaking, Violence, and Equality

In this book, I have chronicled the development of the process of feminist law-making on intimate violence since the 1960s. Generated by visions of women's equality, full citizenship and participation, autonomy, freedom from abuse, and liberty, this legal struggle has sought to transform the law of intimate violence. Activists and lawyers have used women's diverse experiences of violence, of physical abuse, of coercion and control, of economic threats, and of threats of harm to children and family members as the starting point for the development of legal doctrine and legal theory in courtrooms, legislatures, and classrooms.

The process of feminist lawmaking began with this vision. Lawyers and activists took it as their starting point for the assertion of legal claims. Thirty years later, there have been tremendous accomplishments: public recognition of the seriousness of the problem and legal recognition of many of the harms that generated this work. *Planned Parenthood v. Casey,* lower-court cases that have been discussed in this book, and many other cases that are decided every day in courts but never reported, have recognized the harms of intimate violence in a way that did not seem possible thirty years ago. Public education on these issues has been significantly advanced through legal decision making, through the media, and through courses in grade schools, colleges and universities, law schools, and medical schools, and in popular culture. Assertion of legal claims concerning battering has advanced "political conversation" concerning women's rights and gender equality. Legal claims concerning battering have exposed new harms, expanded public understanding by labeling what was previously private as public, and made important statements concerning women's autonomy.

Yet, in the dialectical process of lawmaking, these cases have only highlighted political contradictions and emphasized the deeply political nature of these claims. As feminist lawmaking has developed and more directly confronted issues of gender equality, intimate violence has in many ways become more decontextualized. In the very assertion of claims to equal treatment, tensions of victimization and agency and privacy consistently re-emerge in the form of resistance to equality. There has been tremendous subversion of the fundamental vision of equality that generated this work.

This process of subversion happens in many ways. In order for feminist lawmaking to be successful, lawyers who handle these claims, and judges who rule on them, must be genuinely able to hear them. Yet for lawyers, the process of hearing experiences that may be threatening or unfamiliar, of really listening to those experiences and "taking them in" in order to reshape factual examination or theory of the case, is complex and difficult. Lawyers who do not know about the complexity of intimate violence, or who bring to the process of representation biases and misconceptions concerning battered women, are not going to be able to listen. They will dismiss the woman's story as trivial or see the woman as "difficult." Lawyers like Marcia Clark, who have their own demons of violence in their past, may not be able to make important decisions about choice of defense, or the need to pursue certain areas of investigation, because of biases that they have about intimate violence. Judges, too, need to recognize myths and misconceptions concerning battered women; judges who have a history of or experience with violence have their own biases and limitations in ruling on legal claims. For this reason, legal education plays a crucial role in shaping the attitudes of future lawyers and judges who will be handling these cases, and in directing the future of feminist lawmaking.

The case studies of battered women who kill and battered women who are mothers highlight generic dimensions of this process of subversion. For battered women generally, but particularly battered women in these situations, it is difficult for both lawyers and judges to see them as "reasonable." Because the experience of battering may be so foreign to many legal decision makers, the fact of being battered alone may make a women unreasonable in the eyes of her lawyer or the judge ruling on the case. Yet for a woman to kill her male partner brings back the historic view of "treason." A comparison of her situation in killing her partner ("representative of the state" in the household) with that of a man who kills the woman he has beaten (who is viewed as having no independent legal identity), underscores the underlying views of appropriate female conduct that shape these perceptions. Battered women who are mothers are equally maligned, and their circumstances are viewed with horror; they could not have acted "reasonably" if they did not, first and foremost, intervene to protect their child. In both examples we see similar patterns of legal subversion, tendencies toward pathologizing battered women rather than viewing them as reasonable, uses of expert testimony on "battered woman syndrome" that individualize the harm rather than explaining a broader systemic pattern of gender socialization and "coercive control." At the same time, there is a tendency to isolate the particular legal circumstance, the fact of the homicide or the relationship between the mother and her child, within a framework that renders invisible the interrelated webs of inequality: the woman's role within the family, her responsibility for children, her economic circumstances.

In the area of innovative law reform, we see similar problems. Current controversies concerning criminal prosecution and mandatory arrest reveal how the criminal justice system removes the woman from this larger context of gender. The legal discourse of "crime control" minimizes the liberatory discourse of inequality. Intimate violence becomes just one other "crime" problem that is unmoored from its social, historical, and cultural context. At the same time, the promise of the civil rights remedy of the Violence against Women Act — to put violence within a framework of equality and gender subordination — is contested and resisted by advocates and judges. The threshold issue of the constitutionality of VAWA, and the issue of the sufficiency of claims of domestic violence to constitute gender-motivated violence under VAWA, reflect similar resistance to the "public" nature of the problem, to the link between violence and liberty, violence and autonomy, violence and women's full participation and citizenship. The proposed VAWA II begins to address these issues, for the first time linking women's violence to employment, homelessness, and the host of larger gender issues.

Intimate violence has now been recognized as a "public" harm, but it is significant that this recognition is, in a sense, conditioned on a view that intimate violence is an individual problem, not a systemic or social one. Of course, in some sense it is always both an individual and a social problem. Intimate violence is shaped by a larger culture of social violence, and is affected by a range of psychosocial factors. It arises in individual circumstances that belie the broader context. But just as feminist reformers in the past viewed male violence as linked to alcohol, our culture wants a quick-fix explanation and denies the link to gender.

What would it take to make things different, to make domestic violence subject to social sanction, to shift the burden of social response from acceptance—even that painful and resigned acceptance that still functions as complicity—into affirmative public rejection? Could feminist lawmaking that describes battered women's experiences with greater accuracy and complexity make a difference and be more effective in making change? Will feminist legal advocacy that more carefully explains women's acts of resistance to violence, and seeks to shift cultural and legal discourse from exclusive focus on the woman's exit to the woman's "resistant self-direction," help? Problems of distancing and denial of domestic violence, reinforced by traditional concepts of privacy and resistance to gender equality, stand in the way of social change.

A conservative interpretation of the reasons for social passivity toward domestic violence is that it is widely viewed as both inevitable and intractable. Intimate violence is at once too personal—because it has the potential to affect all intimate relationships—and too deeply political—because gender roles are so deeply ingrained in our social structure. In 1995 the National Organization for Women held a demonstration in Washington, D.C., protesting violence against women.[1] The demonstration's slogan, "The Power to STOP VIOLENCE Against Women Begins with Me," highlights this contradiction between the private and public dimensions of violence, and the dilemma it poses for those who wish to accomplish social change. On the one hand, this slogan is a useful ideological step, for it places the responsibility on individuals to act to stop violence in their own daily lives. On the other hand, it takes the pressure off government to declare domestic violence a public problem, reinforces the historic link between domestic violence and privacy, and affirms individual solutions, individualism generally, and, perhaps inadvertently, individual self-blaming at the expense of collective action. Individuals do have the power to stop violence in individual circumstances, and to actively participate in social condonation, but government has the power and responsibility to transform social norms, provide resources, and ensure safety. So while the slogan stresses the necessity for personal responsibility, it also seems to endorse the privatization "solutions" for social problems that have characterized the 1990s.

We deny that battering and woman abuse is the inevitable product of a culture that raises young girls to "stand by their man" no matter what, to put men first, and to make the "magic of love" the most important thing. Given a culture that still emphasizes marriage as far more important for women than for men, that places primary responsibility on women to keep the family together, that blames mothers for any problem in the family, it is a miracle that women ever leave abusive and controlling relationships when the risk to their lives and their children's lives may be so great. And when women stay in abusive relationships, as our culture has told them to do, we render invisible their heroic efforts to keep themselves and their children alive. Until we acknowledge and seek to change this broader cultural complicity, and frame legal and social remedies for abuse within the problem of gender socialization and appropriate gender roles, little will change.

The thirty-year history of feminist lawmaking on battering reveals both the affirmative vision of equality, liberty, and freedom that has shaped legal strategy and decision making, and the inevitable limitations of legal reform that does not take gender into account. Until we see violence squarely linked to gender, and situate the problem of abuse within broader problems of gender subordination, thus reaffirming this historic link between violence and equality and making the promise of equality real, we will not and cannot move forward.

Notes

Chapter 1: Introduction

1. I use several terms interchangeably in this book: "intimate violence," "violence against women," "domestic violence," "gender violence," and "woman abuse." As I describe more fully in Chapters 3 and 4, each phrase conveys a different meaning, but I mean to be inclusive when using these terms. Despite my misgivings about the phrase "battered woman," which I discuss in Chapter 4, I use it in this book because it is the most familiar and widely known term.
2. *Planned Parenthood v. Casey,* 505 U.S. 833, 891–92 (1992).
3. Wendy Webster Williams, "Fixing Locke: Liberal Orthodoxies and the Feminist Challenge to Intimate Violence" (manuscript on file with author, 1998).
4. bell hooks, "Theory as Liberatory Practice," 4 *Yale Journal of Law and Feminism* 1 (1991).

Chapter 2: The Battered Women's Movement and the Problem of Domestic Violence

1. Patricia Tjaden and Nancy Thoennes, "Prevalence, Incidence, and Consequence of Violence Against Women: Findings from the National Violence Against Women Survey," National Institute of Justice (1998); Jan M. Chaiken, "Violence by Intimates: Analysis of Data on Crimes by Current or Former Spouses, Boyfriends and Girlfriends," U.S. Department of Justice, Bureau of Justice Statistics (1998).
2. Evan Stark, "Mandatory Arrest of Batterers: A Reply to Its Critics," in *Do Arrests and Restraining Orders Work?* 115, 121 (Eve S. Buzawa and Carl G. Buzawa, eds., 1996).
3. Donna Coker, "Enhancing Autonomy for Battered Women: Lessons from Navajo Peacemaking," 47 *UCLA Law Review* 1, 39–41 (1999).
4. Reva B. Siegel, " 'The Rule of Love': Wife Beating as Prerogative and Privacy," 105 *Yale Law Journal* 2117 (1996).
5. See generally *Sanctions and Sanctuary: Cultural Perspectives on the Beating of Wives* (Dorothy Ayers Counts, Judith K. Brown, and Jacquelyn C. Campbell, eds., 1992).
6. R. Emerson Dobash and Russell P. Dobash, *Violence Against Wives: A Case Against the Patriarchy* 34–36 (1979).

7. Terry Davidson, *Conjugal Crime: Understanding and Changing the Wifebeating Pattern* 99 (1978).

8. Elizabeth Pleck, *Domestic Tyranny: The Making of Social Policy Against Family Violence from Colonial Times to Present* 17, 21, 23 (1987).

9. *Bradley v. State*, 1 Miss. (1 Walker) 156, 158 (Miss. 1824).

10. *Poor v. Poor*, 8 N.H. 307, 310–13 (1836).

11. Pleck, *Domestic Tyranny*, 91, 98–101.

12. Linda Gordon, *Heroes of Their Own Lives: The Politics and History of Family Violence* 254 (1988).

13. Siegel, "The Rule of Love," 2128.

14. Gordon, *Heroes of Their Own Lives*, 253–54.

15. Siegel, "The Rule of Love," 2129–30, 2140–41.

16. Id. at 2151, 2153.

17. Id. at 2168–69.

18. Gordon, *Heroes of Their Own Lives*, 256–57.

19. Id. at 258.

20. Id. at 260.

21. Id. at 271.

22. Pleck, *Domestic Tyranny*, 182.

23. Id. at 183.

24. Id. at 189.

25. Susan Schecter, *Women and Male Violence: The Visions and Struggles of the Battered Women's Movement* 314, 316, 317, 318, 319 (1982).

26. For psychological perspectives, see David Adams, "Treatment Models of Men Who Batter: A Postfeminist Analysis," in *Feminist Perspectives on Wife Abuse* 178–88 (Kersti Yllö and Michele Bograd, eds., 1988); John E. Snell, Richard J. Rosenwald, and Ames Robey, "The Wifebeater's Wife," 111 *Archives of General Psychiatry*, August 1964.

27. See generally Lenore E. Walker, *The Battered Woman* (1979); see also Lenore E. Walker, *Terrifying Love*, 35–37 (1989). Even the symptoms that have been grouped under the heading of battered woman's syndrome are themselves diverse and do not all occur in any one woman: "major depressive, sexual, and dissociative disorders; cognitive changes in how one views oneself and understands the world . . . the 'Stockholm syndrome' or 'traumatic bonding'" (*Terrifying Love*, 36). Walker identified the typical cycle of violence in the violent relationship, consisting of a tension-building period, a violent episode, and a "honeymoon" period. The cycle of violence, according to Walker, gives an appearance of randomness to the abuse, contributing to the development of "learned helplessness"—a theory that explains how people lose the ability to predict whether their natural responses will protect them after they experience inescapable pain in what appear to be random and variable situations. People who suffer from learned helplessness restrict the number of responses they make to those with the highest probability of success. When a battered woman who has developed learned helplessness perceives she is in danger, she is likely to use the most predictable method of protecting herself. Sometimes

that means deadly force. Walker's work has been criticized by other psychologists who have worked with battered women. See Mary Ann Dutton, "Understanding Women's Responses to Domestic Violence: A Redefinition of Battered Woman Syndrome," 21 *Hofstra Law Review* 1191 (1993); Evan Stark, "Re-presenting Woman Battering: From Battered Woman Syndrome to Coercive Control," 58 *Albany Law Review* 973 (1995).

28. Dutton, "Understanding Women's Responses," 1195. Dutton notes: "Typically, the testimony offered in forensic cases is not limited to the psychological reactions or sequelae of domestic violence victims, and this has led to confusion about what is encompassed by the term 'battered woman syndrome.'" Expert witness testimony may also be offered to explain the nature of domestic violence in general, to explain what may appear to be puzzling behavior on the part of the victim, or to explain a background or behavior that may be interpreted as suggesting that the victim is not the "typical" battered woman or that she herself is the abuser. Dutton argues that "descriptive references should be made to 'expert testimony concerning battered women's experiences,' instead of the term 'battered woman syndrome.'" Id. at 1201. See also Walker, *Terrifying Love,* 48; Stark, "Re-presenting Woman Battering," 974.

29. Typical sociological studies, which examine the social structures leading to wife abuse, are David Finkelhor, Richard J. Gelles, Gerald T. Hotaling, and Murray A. Straus, *The Dark Side of Families: Current Family Violence Research* (1983); Diana E. H. Russell, *Rape in Marriage* 96 (1990); *The Social Causes of Husband-Wife Violence* (Murray Straus and Gerald T. Hotaling, eds., 1980); Murray Straus et al., *Behind Closed Doors: Violence in the American Family* (1980).

30. Wini Breines and Linda Gordon, "The New Scholarship on Family Violence," 8 *Signs* 490, 492 (1983).

31. Martin Schwartz and Walter S. DeKeseredy, "The Return of the 'Battered Husband Syndrome' Through the Typification of Women as Violent," 20 *Crime, Law and Social Change* 249–65 (1993).

32. Russell P. Dobash, R. Emerson Dobash, Margo Wilson, and Martin Daly, "The Myth of Sexual Symmetry in Marital Violence," 39 *Social Problems* 71–90 (February 1992).

33. Id. at 95–96.

34. Evan Stark, "Heroes and Victims: Constructing Family Violence," 19 *Socialist Review* 137, 139 (January–March 1989).

35. Claire Renzetti, "On Dancing with a Bear: Reflections on Some of the Current Debates among Domestic Violence Theorists," 9 *Violence and Victims* 195, 197–98 (1994); see Dobash et al., "Sexual Symmetry."

36. Renzetti, "On Dancing with a Bear," 197–98. See, for example, Judith Sherven and James Sniechowski, "Women Are Responsible Too," *Los Angeles Times,* B7 (June 21, 1994).

37. Evan Stark and Anne Flitcraft, "Social Knowledge, Social Policy, and the Abuse of Women," in *The Dark Side of Families: Current Family Violence Research,* 330–49, 332 (David Finkelhor, ed., 1983).

38. Pleck, *Domestic Tyranny,* 183. See also Kathleen J. Tierney, "The Battered Woman

Movement and the Creation of the Wife Beating Problem," 29 *Social Problems* 207 (1982); Liane V. Davis, "Battered Women: The Transformation of a Social Problem," 32 *Social Work* 306 (July–August 1987).

39. Rhonda Copelon, "Introduction: Bringing Beijing Home," 21 *Brooklyn Journal of International Law* 599, 602 (1996). See also Brief Amici Curiae on Behalf of International Law Scholars and Human Rights Experts in Support of Petitioner, *Brzonkala v. Morrison*, filed by Rhonda Copelon and Cathy Albisa, International Women's Human Rights Clinic, CUNY Law School, and Peter Weiss and Jenny Green, Center for Constitutional Rights, U.S. Supreme Court, November 1999. This brief is an effort to "bring Beijing home." It seeks to link international human rights materials on gender violence to the constitutionality of the civil rights remedy of VAWA.

Chapter 3: Dimensions of Feminist Lawmaking on Battering

1. 559 P.2d 548 (Wash. 1977). Nancy Stearns and I were co-counsel in *Wanrow* on appeal.
2. 559 P.2d at 548.
3. 559 P.2d at 555–57.
4. 559 P.2d 558–59.
5. 559 P.2d at 557 (citing *State v. Dunning*, 506 P.2d 321, 322 [Wash. Ct. App. 1973]).
6. 559 P.2d at 559 (citation omitted).
7. National attention on women "fighting back" first focused on the cases of Inez Garcia and Joan Little, who had both killed assailants following sexual assault. *People v. Garcia*, Cr. No. 4259 (Super. Ct. Cal. 1977); *State v. Little*, 74 Cr. No. 4176 (Super. Ct. N.C. 1975).
8. In this book I use the term "women's self-defense work" to describe legal work on issues of sex bias in the law of self-defense and criminal defenses generally. The term was first used as the name of a project jointly sponsored by the Center for Constitutional Rights and the National Jury Project, the Women's Self-Defense Law Project, which assisted lawyers with problems of sex discrimination in homicide and assault cases involving women, primarily battered women who had defended themselves against physical or sexual assault from 1978 to 1980. The work of the Women's Self-Defense Law Project is compiled in the book *Women's Self-Defense Cases: Theory and Practice* (Elizabeth Bochnak, ed., 1981).
9. Robert M. Cover, "Nomos and Narrative," 97 *Harvard Law Review* 4, 15 (1983).
10. Karl Klare, "Law Making as Praxis," 40 *Telos* 124 n.5 (1979). Klare explains the dialectical theory of consciousness as the basis for a "constitutive" theory of law. He uses praxis in the broadest sense—"any social world producing activity." Id. at 124 n.5. See also Richard Bernstein, *Praxis and Action*, 42–43 (1971), using praxis to describe "a unity of theory and action."
11. Bernstein, *Praxis and Action*, 20–21.
12. The notion of a dialectical process is a critical aspect of feminist theory. The term *dialectical* and the concept of dialectic are frequently used by feminist theorists in a wide range of contexts. See, e.g., Simone de Beauvoir, *The Second Sex*, xvi–xxi (1952)

(discussing the dialectical relationship between one and other, master and slave); Kathy Ferguson, *The Feminist Case Against Bureaucracy* 197 (1984) (writing that "a community that recognizes the dialectical need for connectedness within freedom and for diversity within solidarity would strive to nurture the capacity for reflexive redefinition of self"); Carol Gilligan, *In a Different Voice,* 174 (1982) (discussing "the dialectic of human development"); Alison M. Jaggar, *Feminist Politics and Human Nature* 12 (1983) (discussing "the on-going and dialectical process of feminist theorizing"); *New French Feminisms: An Anthology,* xi–xii (Elaine Marks and Isabelle de Courtivron, eds., 1981) (writing that recent French feminists "take from . . . dialectics those modes of thinking that allow them to make the most connections between the oppression of women and other aspects of their culture"); Carrie Menkel-Meadow, in Ellen D. Dubois, Mary C. Dunlap, Carol J. Gilligan, Catharine A. MacKinnon, and Carrie J. Menkel-Meadow, "Feminist Discourse, Moral Values and the Law—A Conversation" 34 *Buffalo Law Review* 11, 86 (1985) (discussing the process of development within the women's movement as "part of a much larger dialectical process where we begin with a reform, be it liberal, radical, or in some cases even conservative, and some of us unite behind it while others do not").

13. Catharine MacKinnon maintains that "consciousness-raising is the major technique of analysis, structure of organization, method of practice, and theory of social change of the women's movement." MacKinnon, "Feminism, Marxism, Method and the State: An Agenda for Theory," 7 *Signs: Journal of Women, Culture and Society* 519 (1982). Sylvia Law also emphasizes the critical role that consciousness-raising has played in the rise of feminism and still can play in social problem solving generally. She observes that "feminist consciousness-raising is a process of self-reflection and action that values women's personal experience and understands that experience as political." Sylvia Law, Book Review, 95 *Yale Law Journal* 1769, 1784 (1986) (footnote omitted). Consciousness-raising also reflects a political understanding about the interrelatedness of women's subordination in the private sphere (the family) and the public sphere (the market). For feminist works on consciousness-raising, see Joan Cassell, *A Group Called Women: Sisterhood and Symbolism in the Feminist Movement* 15–20 (1977); Sara M. Evans, *Personal Politics: The Roots of Women's Liberation in the Civil Rights Movement and the New Left* 214–32 (1979).

14. Ferguson, *The Feminist Case,* 198, 157 (emphasis omitted).

15. Edward V. Sparer, "Fundamental Human Rights, Legal Entitlements and the Social Struggle: A Friendly Critique of the Critical Legal Studies Movement," 36 *Stanford Law Review* 555 (1984).

16. Duncan Kennedy, "Critical Labor Theory: A Comment," 4 *Industrial Relations Law Journal* 503, 506.

17. Kathryn Abrams, "The Constitution of Women," 48 *Alabama Law Review* 861, 862 (1997).

18. Nancy C. McGlen and Karen O'Connor have identified three stages of women's rights activity in the United States: (1) the early women's rights movement (1848–1875), (2) the Suffrage movement (1890–1925), and (3) the current women's rights movement (1966–present). McGlen and O'Connor, *The Struggle for Equality in the*

Nineteenth and Twentieth Centuries 2 (1983). See generally Eleanor Flexner, *Century of Struggle* (1968).

19. Frances Olsen, "Statutory Rape: A Feminist Critique of Rights Analysis," 63 *Texas Law Review* 387, 392 (1984).

20. See *Hoyt v. Florida,* 368 U.S. 57 (1961); *Goesaert v. Cleary,* 335 U.S. 464 (1948); *Muller v. Oregon,* 208 U.S. 412 (1908); *Bradwell v. State,* 83 U.S. (16 Wall.) 130 (1872) (Bradley, J., concurring).

21. Catharine A. MacKinnon, "Excerpts from MacKinnon/Schlafly Debate," 1 *Law and Inequality: Journal of Theory and Practice* 341, 342 (1983). MacKinnon notes, in analyzing the radical potential of feminism: "Liberalism has been subversive for us in that it signals that we have the audacity to compare ourselves with men, to measure ourselves by male standards, on male terms. We *do* seek access to the male world. We *do* criticize our exclusion from male pursuits. But liberalism limits us in a way feminism does not. We also *criticize* male pursuits, from women's point of view, from the standpoint of our social experiences as women." Id. at 342–43.

22. Frances Olsen has suggested: "The claim that women have rights may be seen, however, simply as a way of asserting that women should be allowed to do something; rights are merely the generic vehicle for making such claims. From this perspective, one's inner experience of a right is nothing more than the claim that one should be allowed to do a particular thing." Olsen, "Statutory Rape," 391 n.12. In contrast, Linda Gordon phrased the issue in conversation with me as women's *entitlement* to relief from the state. The choice of words reflects a difference in perspective on whether rights claims have more potential for activation than pacification. I agree that the inner experience of a right has the self-defining aspects that Olsen suggests, but I believe that this inner experience has a collective dimension as well. Rights claims tie the individual experiences of a woman to the larger experience of women as a class.

23. See, e.g., *Roe v. Wade,* 410 U.S. 113 (1973) (holding that state criminal abortion laws that prohibit certain classes of abortions without accounting for stage of pregnancy and other interests violates the Fourteenth Amendment); *Reed v. Reed,* 404 U.S. 71 (1971) (holding that a provision of the Idaho probate code that gives preference to men over women for appointment as administrators of a decedent's estate violates the Fourteenth Amendment).

24. Wendy Williams framed the issue of self and moral equation for me. Kathy Ferguson underscores the importance for women of asserting rights as a means of "active participation in public life." Ferguson, *The Feminist Case,* 174. Ellen DuBois also emphasizes that "women act in history." DuBois, in "Feminist Discourse," 70.

25. Mary Dunlap observed: "As one reads, or as one perceives, feminist involvement in law as an agenda, it is plain that such an agenda encompasses every realm of our lives, every aspect of who we are, who we are becoming, and what our experiences are." "Feminist Discourse," 14. Carrie Menkel-Meadow explores this issue as an aspect of a woman's lawyering process. See Menkel-Meadow, "Portia in a Different Voice: Speculations on a Woman's Lawyering Process," 1 *Berkeley Women's Law Journal* 39, 55–60 (1985). Menkel-Meadow agrees with Catharine MacKinnon that the

methodology of consciousness-raising "creates knowledge from shared, collective experience" and suggests that this may affect the way that women practice law. She observes that "virtually every report of women lawyers discusses the impact of personal lives on professional lives and vice versa, where one finds almost no such reports on the descriptions and ethnographies of male lawyers." Finally, she concludes that the concern for the relation between one's work and personal life is consistent with Carol Gilligan's ethic of care and relationship. Id. at 55, 57.

26. Karen O'Connor, *Women's Organizations' Use of the Courts* 100 (1980). An early example is the amicus brief submitted by the National Abortion Rights Action League (NARAL) and sixteen other groups in *Thornburgh v. American College of Obstetricians and Gynecologists,* 476 U.S. 747 (1986). The idea for the brief came from "the thousands of letters written by women and men from all over the country in response to NARAL's call for letters under the 'Silent No More' Campaign." Lynn M. Paltrow, "Amicus Brief: Richard Thornburgh v. American College of Obstetricians and Gynecologists," 9 *Women's Rights Law Reporter* 3 (1986). The brief "reflects the goals of the reproductive rights movement by including the voices of women and men talking not just about abortion but also the conditions of their lives." Id. See also Ruth B. Cowan, "Women's Rights Through Litigation: An Examination of the American Civil Liberties Union Women's Rights Project, 1971–1976," 8 *Columbia Human Rights Law Review,* 373 (1976) (discussing an amicus curiae brief filed by the Center for Constitutional Rights in *Weinberger v. Wiesenfeld,* 420 U.S. 636 [1975]).

27. Rosalind P. Petchesky, *Abortion and Woman's Choice: The State, Sexuality and Reproductive Freedom* 7 (1984) (footnote omitted). Does rights formulation make it hard for us to think beyond the language of rights and get to the task of social reconstruction? For one answer, see Olsen, "Statutory Rape," 429 n.199 ("rights . . . are devices used by feminists to deny what we really want while getting what we want indirectly").

28. Elizabeth M. Schneider, "The Dialectic of Rights and Politics: Perspectives from the Women's Movement," 61 *New York University Law Review* 589, 644–48 (1986).

29. Linda Gordon, "Women's Agency, Social Control, and the Construction of 'Rights' by Battered Women," in *Negotiating at the Margins* 126 (Sue Fisher and Kathy Davis, eds., 1993). See also Linda Gordon, *Heroes of Their Own Lives: The Politics and History of Family Violence* (1988).

30. Gordon, "Women's Agency," 127.

31. Id. at 129, 131.

32. Id. at 131; Gordon, *Heroes,* 256–57.

33. Laurie Woods, "Litigation on Behalf of Battered Women," 5 *Women's Rights Law Reporter* 7 (1978).

34. The Violence Against Women Act of 1994 (VAWA) is the first comprehensive federal statute to deal with domestic violence and violence against women. It includes a criminal statute and sanctions for interstate domestic violence, violations of orders of protection, and repeat violators. See 18 U.S.C. §§2247, 2261, and 2262. It also authorizes a cause of action for a crime of violence motivated by gender and provides for compensatory and punitive damages as well as injunctive and declaratory re-

lief; 42 U.S.C. §13981. The Violence Against Women Act provides funding for shelters and advocate organizations; education for judges, police officers, and advocates; and funding for research on violence against women. See 8 U.S.C. § 1154, 42 U.S.C. §§10418, 13701, 13991, 13992, and 14036. The Violence Against Women Office in the Department of Justice maintains a web site that provides much information on domestic violence and has links to many organizations throughout the United States: http://www.usdoj.vawo.

35. An expansion of the 1994 Violence Against Women Act, dubbed VAWA '99, has been introduced in Congress. H.R. 357, 106th Congress (1999). The new legislation addresses the problems of battered women at work. For example, VAWA '99 contains provisions that prohibit employment discrimination and allow for payment of unemployment compensation to domestic violence survivors, encourage employers to establish programs to assist survivors, and encourage employers to provide time off for survivors to attend court hearings. The need for such legislation is widely recognized by advocates. See, e.g., Jody Raphael, "Domestic Violence and Welfare Receipt: The Unexplored Barrier to Employment," 3 *Georgetown Journal on Fighting Poverty* 29 (1995); Ellen J. Morrison, "Insurance Discrimination Against Battered Women: Proposed Legislative Protections," 72 *Indiana Law Journal* 259 (1996).

36. Martha Mahoney, "Legal Images of Battered Women: Redefining the Issue of Separation," 90 *Michigan Law Review* 1, 2 (1990). See also Carol Smart, *Law, Crime and Sexuality: Essays in Feminism* (1995).

37. See, e.g., Liz Kelly, "How Women Define Their Experiences of Violence," in *Feminist Perspectives on Wife Abuse,* 130 (Kersti Yllö and Michele Bograd, eds., 1988); Christine Littleton, "Women's Experience and the Problem of Transition: Perspectives on Male Battering of Women," 1989 *University of Chicago Legal Forum* 23, 27 n.18; Laurie Woods, "Litigation on Behalf of Battered Women," 5 *Women's Rights Law Reporter* 7, 8 (1978). Woods has suggested: "The naming of the problem [of men beating women] . . . reflects one's view of the causes of the problem, and it restricts one's perception of the nature of the problem. None of the terms currently used to name the problem are satisfactory. The violence is not confined to acts by husbands against wives. Women who are not married may also be subjected to violence by the men in their lives so terms like wife-abuse and wife-assault are under-inclusive. The terms woman-abuse, woman-assault and woman-battering all focus on the woman and ignore the man, who is, after all, the problem." Id. at 8. Littleton has observed: "Both the traditional and the quasi-egalitarian labels seem to me to miss the point. First, wives are battered as members of the class of women; wife battering is therefore gender related in a way that is different from occasional violence against men. Second . . . treating battering as 'the problem' of the person who is battered (whether she is called woman, wife or spouse) obscures the responsibility of the batterer. Why isn't battery considered 'the problem' of violent husbands?" Littleton, "Women's Experience and the Problem of Transition," 27 n.18.

38. Siobhan Lloyd, "A Political Breaking of Silence," 6 *Feminism and Psychology,* no. 2, 281–285 (1996). Lloyd observes that "silence ensure[s] the maintenance of male

power in the private domain of the family and in the public arenas in which men
continue to dominate the lives and experiences of women and children." Id. at 281.

39. For "coercive control," see Evan Stark, "Re-Presenting Woman Battering: From Battered Woman Syndrome to Coercive Control," 58 *Albany Law Review* 973, 975–976
(1995); for "separation assault," see Mahoney, "Legal Images of Battered Women,"
6; for "loss of self," see Charles Ewing, *Battered Women Who Kill: Psychological Self-
Defense as Legal Justification* 62–66 (1987); for "stalking," see Susan E. Bernstein,
"Living under Siege: Do Stalking Laws Protect Domestic Violence Victims?" 15 *Cardozo Law Review* 525 (1993); Brenda A. Sanford, "Stalking Is Now Illegal: Will A
Paper Law Make a Difference?" 10 *Thomas M. Cooley Law Review* 409 (1993).

40. Stark, "Re-Presenting Woman Battering," 975–76. Stark says that a description of
battering as "coercive control" was first presented in Susan Schechter, *Guidelines for
Mental Health Practitioners in Domestic Violence Cases* 4 (1987).

41. Mahoney, "Legal Images of Battered Women," 6, 65–66.

42. Id. at 6–7.

43. Ewing, *Battered Women Who Kill,* 62.

44. "Stalking and Domestic Violence: The Third Annual Report to Congress under
the Violence Against Women Act," U.S. Department of Justice, Violence Against
Women Office (1998), http://www.ojp.usdoj.gov/vawo/statistics.htm (January 25,
2000). For an analysis of state stalking statutes, see Jennifer L. Bradfield, "Anti-
Stalking Laws: Do They Adequately Protect Stalking Victims?" 21 *Harvard Women's
Law Journal* 229 (1998). One example is California's stalking law, which reaches a
person who "willfully, maliciously, and repeatedly follows or harasses another person and who makes a credible threat with the intent to place the person in reasonable fear for their safety, or the safety of their immediate family." Cal. Penal Code
§646.9(a) (West 2000). A person who violates this law shall be punished by imprisonment for up to one year, or a fine of up to $1,000, or both. Id. Additionally,
any person who is found guilty of stalking while there is a temporary restraining
order in place shall be imprisoned for two, three, or four years. Cal. Penal Code
§646.9(b). The court "shall also consider issuing an order restraining the defendant
from any contact with the victim, that may be valid for up to 10 years." Cal. Penal
Code § 646.9(k).

45. Isabel Marcus, "Reframing Domestic Violence: Terrorism in the Home," in *The Public Nature of Private Violence* 11 (Martha Albertson Fineman and Roxanne Mykitiuk,
eds., 1994) (redefining "domestic violence" as "terrorism within the home" to emphasize the social consequences of battering and its resemblance to political terrorism); Rhonda Copelon, "Recognizing the Egregious in the Everyday: Domestic Violence as Torture," 25 *Columbia Human Rights Law Review* 291, 295 (1994) (arguing
that domestic violence should be considered violative of international human rights
standards condemning torture); Joyce E. McConnell, "Beyond Metaphor: Battered
Women, Involuntary Servitude and the Thirteenth Amendment," 4 *Yale Journal of
Law and Feminism* 207 (1992) (identifying domestic violence as involuntary servitude); Jane Maslow Cohen, "Regimes of Private Tyranny," 57 *University of Pitts-*

burgh Law Review 757 (1996) (placing intimate violence within framework of political tyranny).

46. Reva B. Siegel, "'The Rule of Love': Wife Beating as Prerogative and Privacy," 105 *Yale Law Journal* 2117, 2205–6 (1996).

47. For the public frameworks, see *State v. Stewart*, 763 P.2d 572, 584 (Kan. 1988) (Herd, J., dissenting) (arguing that the majority should have accepted a battered woman's claim of self-defense, comparing her situation to that of a hostage, in which case the court would accept the same argument); McConnell, "Beyond Metaphor," 207 (arguing that extreme domestic violence should be considered involuntary servitude prohibited by the Thirteenth Amendment); Martha Chamallas, "Hostile Domestic Environments," 57 *University of Pittsburgh Law Review* 809 (1996) (placing intimate violence within the framework of a hostile workplace environment); Dorothy Q. Thomas and Michele E. Beasley, "Domestic Violence as a Human Rights Issue," 58 *Albany Law Review* 1119, 1120 (1995) (arguing that international law should recognize domestic violence as a human rights issue because it violates basic human rights principles of the inherent dignity and equal worth of all human beings, the right to freedom from fear and want, and the equal rights of men and women).

48. Violence Against Women Act of 1994, 42 U.S.C. § 13981 (1994).

49. Sally Engle Merry, "Resistance and the Cultural Power of Law," 29 *Law and Society Review* 11, 14 (1995). Merry describes this process in the following way: "Courts, for example, provide performances in which problems are named and solutions determined. These performances include conversations in which the terms of the argument are established and penalties determined. The ability to structure this talk and to determine the relevant discourse within which an issue is framed—in other words in which the reigning account of recent events is established—is an important facet of the power exercised by law, as carefully described by studies of legal discourse. Legitimacy takes on critical importance since the culturally productive role of law occurs only if the texts, the performances, and the impositions of violence authorized by law are seen as legitimate." Id.

50. Sally Engle Merry, "Wife Battering and the Ambiguities of Rights," in *Identities, Politics, and Rights* 271, 273 (Austin Sarat and Thomas R. Kearns, eds., 1995).

51. Id. at 274–75.

52. Id. at 292, 275.

53. Merry, "Resistance," 19.

54. Merry, "Wife Battering," 300.

55. Id.

56. Id. at 301–2.

57. Id.

58. Id at 300; Merry, "Resistance," 19.

59. Merry, "Resistance," 20.

60. See generally Copelon, "Recognizing the Egregious in the Everyday"; Patrick A. Seith, "Escaping Domestic Violence: Asylum as a Means of Protection for Battered Women," 97 *Columbia Law Review* 1804, 1811 (1997); Berta Esperanza Hernandez-Truyol, "Women's Rights as Human Rights—Rules, Realities and the Role of Cul-

ture: A Formula for Reform," 21 *Brooklyn Journal of International Law* 605 (1996); Dorothy O. Thomas and Michele E. Beasley, "Domestic Violence as a Human Rights Issue," 58 *Albany Law Review* 1119 (1995); Joan Fitzpatrick, "The Use of International Human Rights Norms to Combat Violence Against Women," in *Human Rights of Women: National and International Perspectives* 326–339 (Rebecca J. Cook, ed., 1994).

61. "U.N. Special Session to Reassess Advancement of Women," March 12, 1998, Inter Press Service.

62. "Gov'ts Indifferent to Domestic Violence, U.N. Says," April 19, 1999, Inter Press Service; Hilary Charlesworth, "The Mid-Life Crisis of the Universal Declaration of Human Rights," 55 *Washington and Lee Law Review* 781, 794 (1998).

63. See Aihwa Ong, "Strategic Sisterhood or Sisters in Solidarity? Questions of Communitarianism and Citizenship in Asia," 4 *Indiana Journal of Global Legal Studies* 107 (1996).

64. *International Union, UAW v. Johnson Controls, Inc.*, 499 U.S. 187 (1991).

65. Douglas Jehl, "Arab Honor's Price: A Woman's Blood," *New York Times*, A1 (June 20, 1999).

66. "She Strays, He Shoots, Judge Winks," *New York Times*, A22 (October 22, 1994).

Chapter 4: Defining, Identifying, and Strategizing

1. Martha Minow helped me formulate this characterization of the tension between particularity and generality in feminist theory.

2. See generally Elizabeth V. Spelman, *Inessential Woman: Problems of Exclusion in Feminist Thought* (1988); Angela P. Harris, "Race and Essentialism in Feminist Legal Theory," 42 *Stanford Law Review* 581 (1990).

3. See, e.g., Katherine T. Bartlett, "Feminist Legal Methods," 103 *Harvard Law Review* 829 (1990); Martha Minow and Elizabeth V. Spelman, "In Context," 63 *Southern California Law Review* 1597 (1990).

4. See Susan Schechter, *Woman and Male Violence: The Visions and Struggles of the Battered Women's Movement* 252 (1982); Martha Mahoney has also described this resistance in "Legal Images of Battered Women: Redefining the Issue of Separation," 90 *Michigan Law Review* 1, 8, 25 (1991).

5. Mahoney, "Legal Images," at 25. Christine Littleton, in "Women's Experience and the Problem of Transition: Perspectives on Male Battering of Women," 1898 *University of Chicago Legal Forum* (1989), used the phrase "male battering of women."

6. See, e.g., Ann Jones and Susan Schechter, *When Love Goes Wrong* (1992); Edward W. Gondolf and Ellen R. Fisher, *Battered Women as Survivors: An Alternative to Treating Helplessness* (1988); Lee Ann Hoff, *Battered Women as Survivors* (1990)

7. See, e.g., Spelman, *Inessential Woman*, ix; Kimberlé Crenshaw, "Mapping the Margins: Intersectionality, Identity Politics, and Violence Against Women of Color," 43 *Stanford Law Review* 1241 (1991); Christine E. Rasche, "Minority Women and Domestic Violence: The Unique Dilemmas of Battered Women of Color," 4 *Journal of Contemporary Criminal Justice* 150 (1986); Beth Richie, "Battered Black Women: A Challenge for the Black Community," 16 *Black Scholar* 40 (1985); Angela P. Har-

ris, "Race and Essentialism in Feminist Legal Theory," 42 *Stanford Law Review* 581 (1990).

8. See Linda J. Nicholson and Nancy Fraser, "Social Criticism Without Philosophy: An Encounter Between Feminism and Postmodernism," in *Feminism/Postmodernism,* 19–38 (Linda J. Nicholson, ed., 1990); Jane Flax, "Postmodernism and Gender Relations in Feminist Theory," in *Feminism/Postmodernism,* 39, 41; Denise Riley, *"Am I That Name?" Feminism and the Category of "Women" in History* (1988); Judith Butler, *Bodies That Matter* (1994); Joan Wallach Scott, *Only Paradoxes to Offer* (1996).

9. See Crenshaw, "Mapping The Margins," 1258–59. However, Crenshaw points out the lack of reliable statistical evidence about the incidence of battering across race and class lines, thereby challenging the assumption that battering is not predominantly a problem of the poor and people of color: "No reliable statistics bear out [the] claim . . . that it is equally a problem across races and classes. . . . Statistics that do address the issues suggest that there is a greater frequency of violence among the working class and poor which, in turn, translates to overall rates that are higher for minorities who are disproportionately poor." Id. at 1259 n.60. Crenshaw's argument is provocative because of its focus not on the issue of battering as existing across classes and races, but rather on why feminist scholars feel compelled to assert this claim, why it is so crucial in the discourse surrounding battering to assert continually that battering happens to people "like us." She concludes that such tactics, although obviously useful in raising the consciousness of the white community, reinforce the "otherness" of women of color. Id. at 1260. The bottom line is that a significant gap exists in the disclosure and literature about battering in communities of color.

10. A dearth of information exists concerning battering and women of color, and diverse experiences of battered women generally, but activists and scholars are beginning to point out this deficiency and to raise issues specific to the intersection of these concerns. See Beth Richie, *Compelled to Crime: The Gender Entrapment of Battered Black Women* (1996); Jo-Ellen Asbury, "African-American Women in Violent Relationships: An Exploration of Cultural Differences," in *Violence in the Black Family,* 89 (Robert L. Hampton, ed., 1987); Soraya M. Coley and Joyce O. Beckett, "Black Battered Women: A Review of Empirical Literature," 66 *Journal of Counseling and Development* 266 (1988); Crenshaw, "Mapping the Margins"; Rasche, "Minority Women and Domestic Violence." For African American women and domestic violence, see also Zanita E. Fenton, "Domestic Violence in Black and White: Racialized Gender Stereotypes in Gender Violence," 8 *Columbia Journal of Gender and Law* 1 (1998); Linda L. Ammons, "Mules, Madonnas, Babies, Bathwater, Racial Imagery and Stereotypes: The African-American Woman and the Battered Woman's Syndrome," 1995 *Wisconsin Law Review* 1003. Angela Ginorio and Jane Reno have observed that the "absence of information about Latina women reflects the triple burden of discrimination under which we function in this society." Angela Ginorio and Jane Reno, *Violence in the Lives of Latina Women: Working Together to Prevent Sexual and Domestic Abuse* 1 (1985); see also Jenny Rivera, "Domestic Violence Against Latinas by Latino Males: An Analysis of Race, National Origin, and Gender Differ-

entials," 14 *Boston College Third World Law Journal* 231 (1994). Nilda Rimonte has emphasized the relationship within the Asian community between the resistance to reporting domestic violence and commonly held attitudes toward family honor. See Crenshaw, "Mapping the Margins," 1299 n.52 (citing Nilda Rimonte, *Domestic Violence Against Pacific-Asians: Making Waves* 328 [1989]); Nilda Rimonte, "A Question of Culture: Cultural Approval of Violence Against Women in the Pacific-Asian Community and the Cultural Defense," 43 *Stanford Law Review* 1311 (1991); see also Karin Wang, Comment, "Battered Asian American Women: Community Responses from the Battered Women's Movement and the Asian Community," 3 *Asian Law Journal* 151 (1996). For Jewish women, see Beverly Horsburgh, "Lifting the Veil of Secrecy: Domestic Violence in the Jewish Community," 18 *Harvard Women's Law Journal* 171 (1995). For Native American Women, see Donna Coker, "Enhancing Autonomy for Battered Women: Lessons from Navajo Peacemaking," 47 *UCLA Law Review*1 (1999); Virginia H. Murray, "A Comparative Survey of the Historic Civil, Common, and American Indian Tribal Law Responses to Domestic Violence," 23 *Oklahoma City Law Review* 433 (1998); Gloria Valencia-Weber and Christine P. Zuni, "Domestic Violence and Tribal Protection of Indigenous Women in the United States," 69 *St. John's Law Review* 69 (1995). Coley and Beckett report that a search of the psychological and sociological abstracts from 1967 to 1987 garnered only four citations that mentioned black battered women. Soraya M. Coley and Joyce O. Beckett, "Black Battered Women: Practice Issues, Social Casework," 69 *Journal of Contemporary Social Work* 483 (1988). This article begins with a discussion of how the particular circumstances of the black community may make the information and services about battering modeled on white women's experiences inappropriate. Black women may analyze their experience of physical abuse differently, using a racial perspective that attempts to understand the battering of the "displaced aggression of the black male." Id. at 486. Richie's research finds a similar analysis predominant among a group of battered minority women she observed. Richie, "Black Battered Women," 42. Although this outlook challenges the traditional framework of gender subordination, it is critical that it be understood, because the battered women's movement as it has been constructed may not speak to their experiences at all.

11. Crenshaw, "Mapping the Margins," 1245–46. Crenshaw and others have observed how women of color in violent relationships are doubly affected by the subordination of both their race and gender. Id. at 1245–49; see also Sharon Allard, "Rethinking Battered Women Syndrome," 1 *UCLA Women's Law Journal* 191, 196–200 (1991).

12. Crenshaw, "Mapping the Margins," 1256–57; Richie, "Black Battered Women," 40–41.

13. Richie, "Black Battered Women," 43; Harris, "Race and Essentialism," 601 (footnote omitted); Rasche, "Minority Women and Domestic Violence," 160 (quoting Martha Garcia, "Double Jeopardy: Battered Women of Color," 11 *Wives Tales: A Newsletter about Ending Violence Against Women in the Home* 1, 1–2 [1985]).

14. See Rimonte, "A Question of Culture," 1313–15, 1317–19.

15. See Ginorio and Reno, *Violence in the Lives of Latina Women,* 198–99.

16. Quotations are from Crenshaw, "Mapping the Margins," 1247 n.21, 1248 n.28. The

Marriage Fraud Amendments of the 1986 Immigration Act reinforced the structural dependence of the immigrant wife by requiring that she wait two years before being granted permanent residency, and that both spouses file jointly. See Immigration Marriage Fraud Amendments of 1986, Pub. L. No. 99–639, 216, 100 Stat. 3537, 3538 (1986). The Immigration Act of 1990 set up an exception to the joint filing requirement: an alien spouse could petition for the removal of conditional residency without help from her U.S. citizen spouse, if she could prove that marriage had been entered into in "good faith" and she had been "battered or subject to extreme cruelty." Pub. L. No. 101–649, 104 Stat. 4978 (1990). See Linda Kelly, "Stories from the Front: Seeking Refuge for Battered Immigrants in the Violence Against Women Act," 92 *Northwestern University Law Review* 665 (1998). Under the Violence Against Women Act of 1994, a battered woman can self-petition for immigration status, which applies to undocumented women. 8 U.S.C. 1154(a)(1)(A)(iii)(I). A battered woman who is undocumented and subject to deportation can apply for "cancellation of removal": she can ask that she not be deported because she is battered and removal would be "extreme hardship." Violent Crime Control and Law Enforcement Act, Pub. L. No. 103–322, 108 Stat. 1796 (1994); 8 U.S.C. 1254(a)(3). Most recently, however, the Anti-Terrorism and Effective Death Penalty Act of 1996 eliminated suspension of deportation for undocumented immigrants, making battered spouses ineligible for VAWA suspension of deportation proceedings. Pub. L. No. 104–132, 110 Stat. 1259 (1996). The "cancellation of removal" provision of the Illegal Immigration Reform and Responsibility Act of 1996 cancels removal of undocumented women with the same requirements as under VAWA's suspension of deportation proceeding: if granted, the woman can adjust her status to lawful permanent residency. However, this provision is limited to only four thousand aliens in any fiscal year. Pub. L. No. 104–208, 1996 H.R. 3610, Slip Copy (1996); IIRRA-Pub. L. No. 104–208, 1996 H.R. 3610, Slip Copy (1996). See Note, "Trapped in Domestic Violence: The Impact of United States Immigration Laws on Battered Immigrant Women," 6 *Boston Public Interest Law Journal* 589 (1997).

17. Deborah Anker, Lauren Gilbert, and Nancy Kelly, "Women Whose Governments Are Unable or Unwilling to Provide Reasonable Protection from Domestic Violence May Qualify as Refugees under United States Asylum Law," 11 *Georgetown Immigration Law Journal* 709 (1997).

18. Gayatri Chakavorty Spivak, "'Strategic Essentialism,' Subaltern Studies: Deconstructing Historiography," in *Selected Subaltern Studies*, 3, 13–15 (Ranajit Guha and Gayatri Spivak, eds., 1988).

19. Linda Gordon, "Women's Agency, Social Control, and the Construction of 'Rights' by Battered Women," in *Negotiating at the Margins*, 126 (Sue Fisher and Kathy Davis, eds., 1993).

20. See, e.g., Michele Bograd, "Feminist Perspectives on Wife Abuse: An Introduction," in *Feminist Perspectives on Wife Abuse*, 12 (Kersti Yllö and Michele Bograd, eds., 1988) (defining "wife abuse" as the use of physical force by a cohabiting partner); Daniel G. Saunders, "Wife Abuse, Husband Abuse or Mutual Combat? A Feminist Perspective on the Empirical Findings," in *Feminist Perspectives*, 94 (defining the

term "battered woman" to include women who are subjected to all forms of physical force by their intimate partners who intend to hurt them, and documenting the range of severity from slaps to beating to use of weapons); Angela Browne, *When Battered Women Kill* 13 (1987) (distinguishing and defining the terms "battering," "violence," "abuse," and "assault").

21. Some feminists define violence committed by a husband against his wife through the examination of the power structure within their relationship. Because society believes men to be the "power carriers" of the couple, "wife abuse" was accepted as a means of subordination. See Bograd, "Feminist Perspectives on Wife Abuse," in *Feminist Perspectives,* 14. Feminists have also argued that "wife abuse" is related to the belief that women are legally bound to their husbands. Id. at 14–15; see also U.S. Commission on Civil Rights, "Under the Rule of Thumb: Battered Women and the Administration of Justice," 1–3 (1982) (linking the origin of wife abuse to advent of marriage, whereby women became property of, and were subjugated to, husbands).

22. Lenore Walker has emphasized the repetition of violence in the relationship by classifying a woman as a "battered woman" only if the couple has gone through the "battering cycle" at least twice. See Mahoney, "Legal Images," 28–29 (citing Lenore Walker, *The Battered Woman,* xv [1979]).

23. See generally Schechter, *Woman and Male Violence,* 29–52. See also R. Emerson Dobash and Russell P. Dobash, "Research as Social Action: The Struggle for Battered Women," in *Feminist Perspectives,* 58–59; bell hooks, *Talking Back: Thinking Feminist, Thinking Black* 87–88 (1989); David Adams, "Treatment Models of Men Who Batter: A Postfeminist Analysis," in *Feminist Perspectives,* 191; Liz Kelly, "How Women Define Their Experiences," in *Feminist Perspectives,* 114–15; Susan Schechter, "Building Bridges Between Activists, Professionals, and Researchers," in *Feminist Perspectives,* 310; Kersti Yllö, "Political and Methodological Debates in Wife Abuse Research," in *Feminist Perspectives,* 28.

24. Kelly, "How Women Define Their Experiences," 120, 127.

25. See David Finkelhor and Kersti Yllö, *License to Rape: Sexual Abuse of Wives* 22–24 (1987); Diana E. H. Russell, *Rape in Marriage* 90–91 (1990); Elizabeth A. Stanko, *Intimate Intrusions: Women's Experience of Male Violence* 51 (1985). Diana Russell's study found that physical violence employed by the husbands often ensured future submission by their wives, such that although the act of intercourse would not be called rape by the woman, it was forced intercourse accomplished through the threat of force. One woman described her husband's actions: "He used his arms and body to pin me down so I couldn't move. With all of the violence that had occurred before—him beating me all the time—I was afraid of him when he told me I better not move." Russell, *Rape in Marriage,* 94. The topologies Russell provides are useful because, instead of setting up artificial distinctions between rape and battering, they encompass the continuum of violence, both sexual and physical, that constitutes the different forms of abuse occurring in violent relationships. On emotional abuse see Kevin McGowan, "Taking Bullies at Their Word," *ABA Journal* 34 (December 1999).

26. For discussion of men in battering programs, see Ellen Pence and Melanie Shepard, "Integrating Feminist Theory and Practice: The Challenge of the Battered Women's

Movement," in *Feminist Perspectives,* 282. For an overview of the possibilities and pitfalls of programs that seek to treat men who batter, see Adams, "Treatment Models of Men Who Batter," 177–95.

27. Bograd, "Feminist Perspectives on Wife Abuse," in *Feminist Perspectives,* 14, sets out the traditional view. The heterosexist assumption implicit in the term "battered woman" becomes clear when one considers that the term could apply equally to a woman who is beaten within a heterosexual relationship and to a woman who is beaten in a lesbian relationship.

28. For feminist critiques of various psychological approaches, see Gail A. Goolkasian, U.S. Department of Justice, *Issues and Practices Concerning Domestic Violence: A Guide for Criminal Justice Agencies* 2–13 (1986); Adams, "Treatment Models of Men Who Batter," 194; James Ptacek, "Why Do Men Batter Their Wives?" in *Feminist Perspectives,* 152–53; Schechter, *Woman and Male Violence,* 210; Lenore E. Walker, *The Battered Woman Syndrome* (1984); Bograd, "Feminist Perspectives on Wife Abuse," in *Feminist Perspectives,* 558; Dobash and Dobash, "Research as Social Action," in *Feminist Perspectives,* 65–67; "A Feminist Examination of Family Systems Models of Violence Against Women in the Family," in *Women and Family Therapy* (Marianne Ault-Richie, ed., 1986). For a feminist response to the sociological perspective, see Elizabeth Stanko, "Fear of Crime and the Myth of the Safe Home: A Feminist Critique of Criminology," in *Feminist Perspectives,* 75. Feminists have criticized both these approaches on many different levels. See also Bograd, "Feminist Perspectives on Wife Abuse," in *Feminist Perspectives,* 11–12; Wini Breines and Linda Gordon, "The New Scholarship on Family Violence," 8 *Signs: Journal of Women in Culture and Society* 490, 508–16 (1983); R. Emerson Dobash and Russell P. Dobash, *Violence Against Wives: A Case Against the Patriarchy* (1979). Finally, feminists not only criticize but also suggest reformulations of methods of research. See Bograd, "Feminist Perspectives on Wife Abuse," in *Feminist Perspectives,* 20–25.

29. L. Kevin Hamberger and Theresa Potente, "Counseling Heterosexual Women Arrested for Domestic Violence: Implications for Theory and Practice," 9 *Violence and Victims* 125 (1994).

30. Claire Renzetti, "On Dancing with a Bear: Reflections on Some of the Current Debates among Domestic Violence Theorists," 9 *Violence and Victims* 198 (1994).

31. See Minnesota Coalition for Battered Women, Lesbian Battering Intervention Project, *Confronting Lesbian Battering* 5 (1980); Ruthann Robson, "Lavender Bruises: Intra-Lesbian Violence, Law and Lesbian Legal Theory," 20 *Golden Gate University Law Review* 567, 584 (1990); Phyllis Goldfarb, "Describing Without Circumscribing: Questioning the Construction of Gender in the Discourse of Intimate Violence," 64 *George Washington Law Review* 582 (1996). For discussion of the problem of lesbian violence, see National Coalition Against Domestic Violence Lesbian Task Force, *Naming the Violence; Speaking Out About Lesbian Battering* 10 (Kerry Lobel, ed., 1986); see also Schechter, *Woman and Male Violence,* 47; Nancy Hammond, "Lesbian Victims and the Reluctance to Identify Abuse," in *Naming the Violence,* 190.

32. See Minnesota Coalition for Battered Women, *Confronting Lesbian Battering,* at 45 (suggesting that the silence of lesbians and gay men can be partially attributed to

society's homophobic attitudes). Whereas lesbian women became involved in the battered women's cause to aid heterosexual women, gay men had no similar cause. See Schechter, *Woman and Male Violence,* 56–57.

33. For discussions of same-sex violence, see generally Nancy J. Knauer, "Same-Sex Domestic Violence: Claiming a Domestic Violence Sphere While Risking Negative Stereotypes," 8 *Temple Political and Civil Rights Law Review* 325 (1999); Kathleen Finley Duthu, "Why Doesn't Anyone Talk About Gay and Lesbian Domestic Violence?" 18 *Thomas Jefferson Law Review* 23 (1996); Goldfarb, "Describing Without Circumscribing"; Denise Bricker, "Fatal Defense: An Analysis of Battered Woman's Syndrome, Expert Testimony for Gay Man and Lesbians Who Kill Abusive Partners," 58 *Brooklyn Law Review* 1379 (1993); Claire M. Renzetti, *Violent Betrayal: Partner Abuse in Lesbian Relationships* (1992); *Violence in Gay and Lesbian Domestic Partnerships* (Claire H. Renzetti and Charles Harvey Miley, eds., 1996); Angela West, "Prosecutorial Activism: Confronting Heterosexism in a Lesbian Battering Case," 18 *Harvard Women's Law Journal* 249 (1992); David B. Dupps, "Battered Lesbians: Are They Entitled to a Battered Woman Defense?" 29 *Journal of Family Law* 879 (1991); Minnesota Coalition for Battered Women, *Confronting Lesbian Battering;* David Island and Patrick Letellier, *Men Who Beat the Men Who Love Them: Battered Gay Men and Domestic Violence* (1991); National Coalition Against Domestic Violence Lesbian Task Force, *Naming the Violence;* Mahoney, "Legal Images," 49–53; Robson, "Lavender Bruises," 591; Amy Edgington, "Anyone but Me," *Gay Community News,* 55 (July 16, 1989); Barbara Hart, "Lesbian Battering: An Examination," in *Naming the Violence,* 194.

34. Lesbian Battering Intervention Project, "Incidence of Battering in Lesbian Relationships," 2 (Summer 1991) (citing Jane Garcia, "The Cost of Escaping Domestic Violence," *Los Angeles Times,* E2 [May 6, 1991]).

35. See, e.g., Robson, "Lavender Bruises," 571–72, 585 (citing Catharine A. MacKinnon, *Towards a Feminist Theory of the State* 178 [1989]), both noting and refuting this claim.

36. For a refutation of the claim that the only lesbian couples who had a problem with violence were those locked into strict butch-femme roles, see Mahoney, "Legal Images," 52–53 (citing Ann Strach, Nan Jervey, Susan Jan Hornstein, and Nomi Porat, "Lesbian Abuse: The Process of the Lesbian Abuse Issues Network (LAIN)," in *Naming the Violence,* 88–89. The claim that gender-role transcendence leads to violence is described in Mahoney, "Legal Images," 29 (quoting Walker, *The Battered Woman,* xi).

37. Robson, "Lavender Bruises," 574, 585. The legal system is unresponsive to even fundamental lesbian legal claims such as marriage and child custody. The prevalence of homophobia in society and the courts has deterred many lesbians from seeking legal redress, even in cases involving criminal conduct. In many states, lesbians are unable to pursue types of relief available to heterosexuals, such as restraining orders.

38. For example, Barbara Hart examines the roots of lesbian relational violence. She attributes lesbian battering to the violent, patriarchal culture in which we are all socialized. Although lesbian batterers are not men, they seek the power and control

that patriarchs have historically enjoyed over family life. Hart asserts that battering lesbians use violence and the threat of violence because it is an extremely potent way of controlling the family environment. See Hart, "Lesbian Battering," 173, 174–75; see also Mahoney, "Legal Images," 53–54; Barbara Hart, "A Theoretical Model of Lesbian Battering," in *Confronting Lesbian Battering,* 68.

39. See Minnesota Coalition for Battered Women, *Confronting Lesbian Battering,* 41; see also Mahoney, "Legal Images," 49–53. Mahoney notes that homophobia often deters battered lesbians from invoking the legal system, and that restraining orders are not available against same-sex partners in some states.

40. See generally Hart, "Lesbian Battering," 180–81. Even if both partners abuse each other repeatedly and a pattern evolves, it is not considered battering "unless the effect of the violent conduct is to render the perpetrator more powerful and controlling in relation to the recipient." Id at 183.

41. See Mahoney, "Legal Images," at 351 (citing Nancy Hammond, "Lesbian Victims and the Reluctance to Identify Abuse," in *Naming the Violence,* 190, 195–96); Minnesota Coalition for Battered Women, *Confronting Lesbian Battering,* 3, 10; Janice Irvine, "Lesbian Battering: The Search for Shelter," *Gay Community News,* 25 (January 14, 1984).

42. The quotation is from Suzanne McNamara, "Elderly Abuse," *Chicago Tribune,* 3 (May 19, 1991). See also Seymour Moskowitz, "Saving Granny from the Wolf: Elder Abuse and Neglect—The Legal Framework," 31 *Connecticut Law Review* 77 (1998).

43. Researchers have developed a number of models to explain elder abuse. The "situational model," with its focus on situational stress and structural factors as aggravating forces that increase the likelihood of abuse directed at the person associated with the stress, has many adherents. See generally Linda R. Phillips, "Theoretical Explanations of Elder Abuse: Competing Hypotheses and Unresolved Issues," in *Elder Abuse: Conflict in the Family* 197, 198–202 (Karl A. Pillemer and Rosalie S. Wolf, eds., 1986). Another conceptual model, termed social exchange theory, looks at power imbalances in social exchange that facilitate abusive relationships. Id. at 202–7. Although the critical element in such an examination would seem to be the abused elder, at least one study has shown that the relevant factor was not the dependence of the elder, but rather the dependence of the abuser caregiver. Abuse can be viewed, then, as an expression of "when the abuser feels powerless and impotent and seeks to compensate for the lack of control or power loss with the resources available." Id. at 205. Other researchers have noted the importance of behavior practiced within the particular family and the impact that negative attitudes toward the elderly may exert upon tendencies toward abuse. See Joann Blair, "Honor Thy Father and Thy Mother—But for How Long? Adult Children's Duty to Care For and Protect Elderly Parents," 35 *University of Louisville Journal of Family Law* 765 (1996–97); Robert Polisky, "Criminalizing Physical and Emotional Elder Abuse," 3 *Elder Law Journal* 377 (1995); *Abuse of the Elderly: Issues and Annotated Bibliography* 18–19 (Benjamin Schlesinger and Rachel Schlesinger, eds., 1988).

44. See Audrey S. Garfield, "Elder Abuse and the States' Adult Protective Services Response: Time for a Change in California," 42 *Hastings Law Journal* 859, 861 (1991)

(citing "Elder Abuse: A Decade of Shame and Inaction," 3, Hearing Before the Subcommittee on Health and Long-Term Care of the House Select Committee on Aging, 101st Cong., 2nd Sess. [1990]). As one social worker commented, "Often the abusing child may be the only access that the elderly person has to the outside world." McNamara, "Elderly Abuse," 3.

45. See Terry T. Fulmer and Terrence A. O'Malley, *Inadequate Care of the Elderly: A Health Care Perspective on Abuse and Neglect* 18–19 (1987). Fulmer and O'Malley summarize six studies and how they define abuse. The author of another study examined the interactions between the elderly and the caregiver and concluded that the behavior engaged in by both parties reflected a struggle over control. See Suzanne K. Steinmetz, *Duty-Bound: Elder Abuse and Family Care* 18 (1988).

46. See "Help for the Terrified Elderly," *New York Times,* A18 (April 2, 1991). This editorial discusses how abused and abuser are bonded by money, emotional co-dependency, and guilt.

47. Phillips, "Theoretical Explanations of Elder Abuse," 199; Diane Brady, "A Hidden Terror: Abuse of the Elderly Is Increasing," *Maclean's,* 36 (August 19, 1991).

48. Jordan I. Kosberg, "Preventing Elder Abuse: Identification of High Risk Factor Prior to Placement Decisions," 28 *Gerontologist* 43, 45 (1988) (suggesting that women are more likely to be abused in part because there are more older women than men and because they are less likely to resist); Mary Joy Quinn and Swan K. Tomita, *Elder Abuse and Neglect: Causes, Diagnosis and Intervention Strategies* 28–31 (1986) (citing two studies in which at least 80 percent of elders abused were women). But see also Karl Pillemer and David Finkelhor, "The Prevalence of Elder Abuse: A Random Sample Survey," 28 *Gerontologist* 51, 55 (1988) (finding roughly equal percentages of abuse of elderly men and women).

Chapter 5: Beyond Victimization and Agency

1. This theoretical framework has been called "dominance feminism." Dominance feminism is used to describe that strand of feminist (legal) theory that locates gender oppression in the sexualized domination of women and the eroticization of that dominance through pornography and other aspects of popular culture. Catharine MacKinnon is probably the primary and most visible exponent of this theory, but there are a "range of feminists who have worked theoretically, and often through political practice, to raise consciousness about male sexualization of and aggression against women." Kathryn Abrams, "Songs of Innocence and Experience: Dominance Feminism in the University," 103 *Yale Law Journal* 1533, 1549 (1994) (reviewing Katie Roiphe, *The Morning After: Sex, Fear and Feminism on Campus* [1993]).

2. An extraordinary amount of media attention has focused on the theme of feminism as victimization. See generally "Sexual Correctness: Has It Gone Too Far?" *Newsweek,* 62 (October 25, 1993); Tamar Lewin, "Feminists Wonder If It Was Progress to Become 'Victims,'" *New York Times,* 6 (May 10, 1992). See Katie Roiphe's *The Morning After* and Naomi Wolf's *Fire with Fire: The New Female Power and How It Will Change the 21st Century* (1993).

3. This is largely because the media has lionized Catharine MacKinnon as *the* primary feminist legal thinker and spokesperson. See, e.g., Fred Strebeigh, "Defining Law on the Feminist Frontier," *New York Times,* F28 (October 6, 1991) (interviewing Catharine MacKinnon and tracing the development of her theories on pornography). See also "The First Amendment, Under Fire From the Left: Whose Free Speech? A Discussion by Two Leading Authorities, Moderated by Anthony Lewis," *New York Times,* F40 (March 13, 1994) (featuring Catharine MacKinnon debating Floyd Abrams, a prominent defender of the First Amendment, on the issue of pornography).

4. At his Senate confirmation hearings, Clarence Thomas was accused of sexual harassment by Anita Hill, a former aide. *Hearings on the Confirmation of Clarence Thomas to the Supreme Court of the United States Before the Senate Committee on the Judiciary,* 102d Cong., 1st Sess. (1991). See also Joseph P. Kahn, "Susan Faludi Lashes Back; 'Backlash' Author Is Angry as Ever, but Heartened by a Renewed Fervor for Feminism," *Boston Globe,* 57 (October 13, 1992); Deborah Sontag, "The Changing Face of Harassment," *New York Times,* B3 (November 2, 1992). "Date rape" or "acquaintance rape" has received tremendous national attention because it is increasingly recognized as a common form of rape, and because of many highly publicized cases, such as those involving William Kennedy Smith and Mike Tyson, in which the rape victim and the accused had some prior relationship.

5. Lisa Duggan, Nan Hunter, and Carole S. Vance, "False Promises: Feminist Antipornography Legislation in the United States," in *Women Against Censorship* 130 (Varda Burstyn, ed., 1985). Carlin Meyer uses the term "porn-suppression" feminists. Carlin Meyer, "Sin, Sex and Women's Liberation: Against Suppressing Porn," 72 *Texas Law Review* 1097 (1994).

6. Duggan et al., "False Promises," 130.

7. See, e.g., such material as the "Domestic Violence Cover-Up" (challenging facts on domestic violence); "Stop Beating Me, I've Got to Make a Phone Call" (challenging the National Domestic Violence Hotline); an article by Sally L. Satel, "The Abuse Excuse" (challenging the link between welfare and domestic violence); and "Violence Against Taxpayers" (challenging VAWA); all from the International Women's Forum (IWF) web page (http://www.iwf.org, visited January 11, 2000). The IWF is moving to organize young women on college campuses. Sarah Blustain, Field Notes, "Ladies of the Right," *Lingua Franca* 8–9 (October 1999). The IWF, and other similar organizations such as the Eagle Forum and the Woman's Freedom Network, have filed amicus curiae briefs in the United States Supreme Court in *Brzonkala v. Morrison* supporting the unconstitutionality of the civil rights remedy of the Violence Against Women Act of 1994. *Brzonkala v. Virginia Polytechnic and State University,* 935 F. Supp. 779 (W.D. Va. 1996), *rev'd,* 132 F.3d 949 (4th Cir. 1997), *rev'd en banc,* 169 F.3d 820 (4th Cir. 1999), *cert. granted* 120 S.Ct. 605 (1999) *sub nom. United States v. Morrison, Brzonkala v. Morrison.*

8. Roiphe, *The Morning After,* 51–112, 138–60; Wolf, *Fire With Fire,* 135–42, 191–97 (noting the recent emergence of "victim culture" critics, who have attacked femi-

nists for focusing on women as mere victims). See Margaret Emery, "Feminism under Fire," *Time,* 86 (September 20, 1993); Deirdre English, "Take Back the Fight," *Newsday,* 37 (October 10, 1993); Linda Bird Francke, "Woman the Conqueror," *New York Times,* G9 (November 28, 1993); bell hooks, "Color Roiphe Privileged Says Black Feminist," *Newsday,* 57 (October 27, 1993); Michael Kakutani, "Helpful Hints for an Era of Practical Feminism, *New York Times,* C29 (December 3, 1993); Karen Lehrman, "Fire with Fire," *The New Republic,* 40 (March 14, 1994); "Sexual Correctness, Has It Gone Too Far?" *Newsweek,* 62 (October 25, 1993); Adele M. Stan, "Women Warrior," *New York Times,* A39; Cathy Young, "Women Writers Disagree on Rape, Porn and Victimhood," *San Francisco Examiner,* A21. In spring 1994 a computer search on the topic "victim feminism" turned up more than a thousand articles in national magazines and newspapers; by fall 1999 the number was considerably less.

9. See Roiphe, *The Morning After,* 51–112, 138–60; Wolf, *Fire with Fire,* 135–42, 191–97. I deal with both those books together, although there are differences between them. Katie Roiphe's book is anecdotal, based on her experiences as a Harvard undergraduate and a Princeton graduate student, and is clearly written from the vantage point of an observer of the women's movement. Naomi Wolf writes as a feminist, and sees her book as a manual for feminist work in the 1990s. Both, however, fall into the trap of simplifying themes of victimization and agency in feminism and seeing them as opposites. See Roiphe, *The Morning After,* 29–50; Wolf, *Fire with Fire,* 135–42, 305–21.

10. On women's passivity, see Roiphe, *The Morning After,* 29–50, 85–112; Wolf, *Fire with Fire,* 149, 185. For an illustration of the lack of compassion, see Roiphe, *The Morning After,* 51–112; Wolf, *Fire with Fire,* 135–42, 180–214. For an illustration of the inadequacy of either victimization or agency, see Roiphe, *The Morning After,* 29–50, 85–112; Wolf, *Fire with Fire,* 135–42, 161–79.

11. Martha Minow, "Surviving Victim Talk," 40 *UCLA Law Review* 1411, 1415, 1429–31 (1993).

12. But see Lewin, "Feminists Wonder If It Was Progress," 6 (quoting Professor Martha Mahoney of the University of Miami Law School: "Anita Hill never said she was a victim or that she was terrorized. She spoke as someone who had been trying to do her job and get on with her life. She talked about her struggle and the context of her struggle. But what she was heard as, and judged as, was someone claiming victim status because that's the only way we're heard at all").

13. Martha Mahoney, "Exit: Power and the Idea of Leaving in Love, Work, and the Confirmation Hearings," 65 *Southern California Law Review* 1303 (1992).

14. See Ann Jones, "Is This Power Feminism? The Push to Get Women Hooked on Guns," *Ms.* (May–June 1994) (special-edition cover story); see also Melinda Henneberger, "The Small-Arms Industry Comes on to Women," *New York Times,* D4 (October 24, 1993); Ann Jones, "Living with Guns Living with Fear," *Ms.,* 38 (May–June 1994); Ellen Neuborne, "Cashing In on Fear: The NRA Targets Women," *Ms.,* 46 (May–June 1994).

15. Martha R. Mahoney, "Victimization or Oppression? Women's Lives, Violence and Agency," in *The Public Nature of Private Violence* 59, 64 (Martha Albertson Fineman and Roxanne Mykitiuk, eds., 1994).

16. Martha Fineman emphasized this point in her presentation at the panel "Victim Feminism" at the Law and Society Annual Meeting of 1994. The Feminism and Legal Theory Workshop at Columbia Law School that Fineman organized in June 1994 was entitled "Direction and Distortion: The Centrality of Sexuality in the Shaping of Feminist Legal Theory." One of the themes that emerged at the workshop was the way feminist theoretical focus on sexuality as an issue had given a more personal cast to recent feminist work. See also Katha Pollitt, "Subject to Debate," *Nation*, 224 (February 21, 1994) (treating "victim feminism" as a class phenomenon).

17. Vicki Schultz, "Reconceptualizing Sexual Harassment," 107 *Yale Law Journal* 1683 (1998); Carlin Meyer, "Sexuality and the Workplace" (June 1994) (manuscript presented at the workshop "Direction and Distortion").

18. See, e.g., Edward W. Gondolf and Ellen R. Fisher, *Battered Women as Survivors: An Alternative to Treating Helplessness* (1988); Lee Ann Hoff, *Battered Women as Survivors* (1990); Mahoney, "Victimization or Oppression?" 40, 59.

19. See, e.g., Christine Littleton, "Women's Experience and the Problem of Transition: Perspectives on Male Battering of Women," 1989 *University of Chicago Legal Forum* 37–38 (analyzing the consequences of focusing on the woman's failure to leave rather than the man's violence). See generally Mahoney, "Victimization or Oppression?" 61–65 (stating that the question "Why did the woman fail to leave?" is in fact an assertive statement that the woman did not leave, thereby discounting any actual separations or attempts by the woman to separate from her batterer).

20. See, e.g., *State v. Stewart*, 763 P.2d 572 (Kan. 1988). For further discussion of this case, see Mahoney, "Victimization or Oppression?" 85–87.

21. Mahoney, "Victimization or Oppression?" 65–68.

22. Id. at 64 (citing Angela Browne, *When Battered Women Kill* [1987]); Littleton, "Women's Experience," 52.

23. Id. at 57–59. See also Mahoney, "Exit."

24. There are a variety of reasons for this bias, including: sex-stereotypical attitudes that men are reasonable and women are unreasonable or hysterical or emotional; intuitive, patriarchal attitudes held by judges and jurors that battered women are inherently crazy for taking abuse and staying in relationships; and stereotypes of women as particularly vicious and threatening for killing men with whom they are intimate.

25. See Leslie Bender, "A Lawyer's Primer on Feminist Theory and Tort," 38 *Journal of Legal Education* 3, 20–25 (1988); Lucinda M. Finley, "A Break in the Silence: Including Women's Issues in a Torts Course," 1 *Yale Journal of Law and Feminism*, 41, 57–65 (1989).

26. 478 A.2d 364 (N.J. 1984).

27. For discussion of the range of circumstances in which expert testimony has been admitted, including recantation, see Janet Parrish, "Trend Analysis: Expert Testimony of Battering and Its Effects in Criminal Cases," 11 *Wisconsin's Women's Law Journal* 75, 103–27 (1996).

28. When a battered woman becomes part of the criminal justice system after killing her abusive partner, racial assumptions and prejudices can play a critical role in the jury's acceptance of her self-defense plea. Lenore Walker has noted that the conviction rate of black women who have killed their abusers is double that of white women. See Lenore Walker, *The Battered Woman*, 206 (1979). Sharon Allard argues that the construct of battered woman syndrome may not only exclude the perspective and experiences of black battered women but also erect additional obstacles. See Sharon Allard, "Rethinking Battered Woman Syndrome," 1 *UCLA Women's Law Journal* 191, 204 (1991).

29. Numerous courts adjudicating sexual harassment claims have adopted the reasonable-woman standard, an extension of the reasonable-victim standard, which focuses on the perspectives of the victim rather than that of the alleged perpetrator. See *Ellison v. Brady*, 924 F.2d 872, 880 (9th Cir. 1991); *Yates v. Avco Corp.*, 819 F.2d 630, 637 (6th Cir. 1987); *Robinson v. Jacksonville Shipyards, Inc.*, 760 F. Supp. 1486, 1524 (M.D. Fla. 1991). See also Howard A. Simon, "Ellison v. Brady: A 'Reasonable Woman' Standard for Sexual Harassment," 17 *Employment Relations Law Journal* 71, 78 (1991); Caroline Forell, "Essentialism, Empathy, and the Reasonable Woman," 1994 *University of Illinois Law Review* 769 (1994); Ellen Goodman, "A Reasonable Standard," *Boston Globe*, B3 (October 13, 1991). For differing feminist views on the reasonable-women standard, see Kathryn Abrams, "Gender Discrimination and the Transformation of Workplace Norms," 42 *Vanderbilt Law Review* 1206 (1989) (arguing for the adoption of a standard in sexual harassment cases that "reflects women's perception of sexual harassment"), and Nancy S. Ehrenreich, "Pluralist Myths and Powerless Men: The Ideology of Reasonableness in Sexual Harassment Law," 99 *Yale Law Journal* 1177, 1216–19 (1990) (arguing that the "reasonable-woman" standard is not neutral and cannot by itself constrain choices that judges must make when defining its limits).

30. *Thelma and Louise* depicts two women who resort to violence against men in an effort to escape male violence and the confinement of male society. Its release generated criticism concerning the ways the two women used violence in retaliation, especially as compared with male violence against women. See, e.g., Margaret Carlson, "Is This What Feminism Is All About?" *Time*, 57 (June 24, 1991) (criticizing movies for having women play out a male fantasy and showing that Hollywood is still a man's world); John Leo, "Toxic Feminism on the Big Screen," *U.S. News and World Report*, 20 (June 10, 1991) (criticizing the movie as clearly the most upsetting of a new crop of woman-kills-man movies and comparing the movie's message to fascism); Richard Schickel, "Gender Bender," *Time*, 52 (June 24, 1991) (documenting a raging debate over whether Thelma and Louise celebrates liberated females, male bashers, or outlaws); Laura Shapiro, Andrew Murr, and Karen Springen, "Women Who Kill Too Much: Is *Thelma and Louise* Feminism, or Fascism?" *Newsweek*, 63 (June 17, 1991). Many commentators noted that women identified with the retaliatory response of *Thelma and Louise*, and some commentators were concerned that the movie advocated an "open season on men."

31. By itself, Anita Hill's testimony was credible. Therefore, she was attacked for being

delusional, which was easier than claiming she was an outright liar. See Felicity Barringer, "Psychologists Try to Explain Why Thomas and Hill Offer Opposing Views,"
New York Times, A10 (October 14, 1991). Hill was also portrayed in an unflattering,
"unfeminine" light, designed to show that she was the type of woman who would
not have been bothered by dirty movies and the like. "Statements by Character Witness in Defense of Judge Thomas," *New York Times*, A14 (October 14, 1991). After
the hearings concluded, it became clear that Professor Hill's self-confident and composed demeanor had actually undermined, rather than enhanced, her credibility
among members of the American public. In a telephone poll of 501 adults conducted
on October 13, 1991, 58 percent believed Clarence Thomas more, whereas only 24
percent believed Anita Hill more. See Elizabeth Kolbert, "Most in National Survey
Say Judge Is the More Believable," *New York Times*, A1 (October 15, 1991). Forty-six
percent of those surveyed had an "unfavorable" image of Hill. Fifty-four percent of
the people surveyed thought that Anita Hill's charges were not true on October 13
(after her testimony); before her testimony (Oct. 9), only 47 percent had made their
minds up that her allegations were untrue. Id. See also Maureen Dowd, "Image More
Than Reality Became Issue, Losers Say," *New York Times*, A5 (October 16, 1991).

32. The reactions of the national press to the Thomas confirmation hearings reflected,
and largely reinforced, national stereotypes of female provocativeness and tendency
to hysteria. A surprising, and saddening, number of women publicly asserted their
support for Clarence Thomas in spite of the charges brought by Anita Hill. One
woman asserted, "She's consumed with [having power] over him and getting her
way." An Atlanta man stated, "Every woman who's brought down a major man in
the last five years has made millions of dollars. . . . I look at what Anita Hill is saying,
and I don't believe it." A number of people actually "diagnosed" Professor Hill as "a
victim of erotomania — or the 'Fatal Attraction' syndrome," perhaps in an effort to
distance Hill's experience from the "normal" woman's workplace experience. Joyce
Price, "Thomas Will Not 'Cry Uncle,'" *Washington Times*, A1 (October 13, 1991).

33. Just as in the battered women's cases, there can be no standard "reasonable woman"
or even a standard "reasonable harassed woman." Working-class women interviewed
in Baltimore all found Anita Hill unbelievable because they claimed they would
have stopped the harassment. Many of them had encountered harassment in the
past and said that they put a stop to it themselves. In contrast, lawyers, human
services workers, and politicians believed Anita Hill. See Felicity Barringer, "The
Thomas Confirmation: Hill's Case Is Divisive to Women," *New York Times*, A10
(October 18, 1991).

34. Linda Gordon, "Women's Agency, Social Control, and the Construction of 'Rights'
by Battered Women," in *Negotiating at the Margins* 126 (Sue Fisher and Kathy Davis,
eds., 1993).

35. Kathryn Abrams, "The Constitution of Women," 48 *Alabama Law Review* 861, 884
(1997).

36. Quotations are from Dorothy E. Roberts, "Deviance, Resistance and Love," 1994
Utah Law Review 179, 182–83 (1994); Angela P. Harris, "Race and Essentialism in
Feminist Legal Theory," 42 *Stanford Law Review* 581, 601 (1990). See also Dorothy E.

Roberts, "Motherhood and Crime," 79 *Iowa Law Review* 95 (1993); Dorothy E. Roberts, "Punishing Drug Addicts Who Have Babies: Women of Color, Equality and the Right of Privacy," 104 *Harvard Law Review* 1419 (1991); Mahoney, "Exit," 1304; Martha R. Mahoney, "Legal Images of Battered Women: Redefining the Issue of Separation," 90 *Michigan Law Review* 1 (1991); Mahoney, "Victimization or Oppression?"; Martha R. Mahoney, "Whiteness and Women, in Practice and Theory: A Reply to Catharine MacKinnon," 5 *Yale Journal of Law and Feminism* 217 (1993).

37. Kathryn Abrams, "From Autonomy to Agency: Feminist Perspectives on Self-Direction," 40 *William and Mary Law Review* 805, 834–35 (1999).

38. Id.

Chapter 6: The Violence of Privacy

1. The phrase "veil of relationship" is from Reva Siegel, "'The Rule of Love': Wife Beating as Prerogative and Privacy," 105 *Yale Law Journal* 2117, 2196–2206 (1996).

2. 489 U.S. 189 (1989).

3. Frances Olsen, "The Family and the Market: A Study of Ideology and Legal Reform," 96 *Harvard Law Review* 1497, 1499–1501 (1983).

4. Nadine Taub and Elizabeth M. Schneider, "Perspectives on Women's Subordination and the Role of Law," in *The Politics of Law,* 328, 331–32 (David Kairys, ed., 3rd ed., 1998).

5. Id. at 331–32.

6. Linda Kerber, "Separate Spheres, Female Worlds, Women's Place: The Rhetoric of Women's History," 75 *Journal of American History* 9, 17 (1988); Alan Freeman and Elizabeth Mensch, "The Public-Private Distinction in American Law and Life," 36 *Buffalo Law Review* 237 (1987); Martha Minow, "Adjudicating Differences: Conflicts Among Feminist Lawyers," in *Conflicts in Feminism* 156–60 (Marianne Hirsch and Evelyn Fox Keller, eds., 1990); Symposium, "The Public/Private Distinction," 130 *University of Pennsylvania Law Review* 1289 (1982).

7. Olsen, "The Family and the Market," 1507 n.39, 1537.

8. The dichotomy of women as private and men as public changes when women are childbearers. In *Muller v. Oregon,* 208 U.S. 412, 421 (1908), the Supreme Court emphasized that "as healthy mothers are essential to vigorous offspring, the physical well-being of women becomes an object of public interest and care in order to preserve the strength and vigor of the race." See Chapter 9 of this book for a fuller analysis of pregnancy and battering.

9. Taub and Schneider, "Perspectives on Women's Subordination," 332–33.

10. Catharine M. MacKinnon, *Toward a Feminist Theory of the State* (1989); Rhonda Copelon, "Unpacking Patriarchy: Reproduction, Sexuality, Originalism and Constitutional Change," in *A Less Than Perfect Union: Alternative Perspectives on the U.S. Constitution* 303 (Jules Lobel, ed., 1988); Minow, "Adjudicating Differences."

11. Anita Allen's work has explored the importance of privacy to women. See Anita Allen, *Uneasy Access: Privacy for Women in a Free Society* 70–72 (1988). Allen has subsequently emphasized that these aspects of privacy must be preserved in legal reme-

dies for intimate violence. Anita Allen, "Coercing Privacy," 40 *William and Mary Law Review* 723, 746 (1999).

12. Frank Michelman, "Private, Personal but Not Split: Radin v. Rorty," 63 *Southern California Law Review* 1783, 1794 (1990).

13. Martha Mahoney's article "Legal Images of Battered Women: Redefining the Issue of Separation," 90 *Michigan Law Review* 1 (1991), played a significant role in my development of this section. For an exploration of the phenomenon of denial and the importance of naming violence generally, see Liz Kelly, "How Women Define Their Experiences of Violence," 114–31 in *Feminist Perspectives on Wife Abuse* (Kersti Yllö and Michele Bograd, eds., 1988).

14. For a discussion of jurors' attitudes toward battered women, see Elizabeth Bochnak, Elissa Krauss, Susie McPherson, Susan Sternberg, and Diane Wiley, "Case Preparation and Development," in *Women's Self-Defense Cases: Theory and Practice* (Elizabeth Bochnak, ed., 1981); Karen Jo Koonan and Marilyn Waller, "Jury Selection in a Woman's Self-Defense Case," 18 *CACJ Forum* (May–June 1989); Note, "Juror Misconduct and Juror Composition," 18 *Golden Gate University Law Review* 589, 598 (1988).

15. The Joel Steinberg–Hedda Nussbaum case involved the murder of their daughter, Lisa Steinberg, who was beaten to death by Joel Steinberg. This case focused on examination of Hedda Nussbaum as both a victim of abuse and a bad mother. See Ronald Sullivan, "Defense Tries to Show Nussbaum Liked Pain," *New York Times,* B2 (December 9, 1988). For a discussion of feminist responses to the case, see Chapter 9 of this book.

16. See, e.g., "Report of the New York Task Force on Women in the Courts," 15 *Fordham Urban Law Journal* 11 (1986); "First Year Report of the New Jersey Supreme Court Task Force on Women in the Courts," 9 *Women's Rights Law Reporter* 129 (1986); "Report of the Gender Bias Study of the Court System in Massachusetts," 24 *New England Law Review* 745 (1990).

17. Martha Minow, "Words and the Door to the Land of Change: Law, Language, and Family Violence," 43 *Vanderbilt Law Review* 1665, 1671–72 (1990).

18. Id.

19. *DeShaney v. Winnebago County Department of Social Services,* 489 U.S. 189 (1989). For a thoughtful analysis of *DeShaney,* see Minow, "Words and the Door to the Land of Change," 1666–76. *DeShaney* has made it difficult for victims of woman abuse to bring section 1983 claims against the state for failure to protect them from battering. Courts are rejecting substantive due-process claims, which are typically based on the alleged existence of a "special relationship" between the victims and the state (whether as a result of previous knowledge of the harm they faced at the hands of their abusers or because the state had issued a protective order), as incompatible with *DeShaney.* See, e.g., *Hynson v. City of Chester,* 731 F. Supp. 1236, 1239 (E.D. Pa. 1990); *Dudosh v. City of Allentown,* 722 F. Supp. 1233, 1235 (E.D. Pa. 1989). As a result of the diminishing availability, after *DeShaney,* of section 1983 due-process claims based on the notion of a special relationship, battered women had to develop alternative theories to sue the state for its failure to protect them, such as equal protection, claims that the state had failed adequately to train its agents in domestic

violence situations, or claims based on state tort law. None of these theories have been successful, however. See *Soto v. Flores,* 103 F.3d (1st Cir. 1997); *cert. denied* 522 U.S. 819 (1997).

20. On civil remedies, see Peter Finn, "Statutory Authority in the Use and Enforcement of Civil Protection Orders Against Domestic Abuse," 23 *Family Law Quarterly* 43–44 (1989); on criminal remedies, see Marion Wanless, "Mandatory Arrest: A Step Toward Eradicating Domestic Violence, but Is It Enough?" 1996 *University of Illinois Law Review* 533, 554–557 (1996).

21. For example, Mo. Rev. Stat. §455.205 (Supp. 1997) authorizes a surcharge of five dollars for a marriage license, to go toward domestic violence shelters. Fees have been imposed on marriage licenses to establish, maintain, and fund shelters for battered women or domestic violence programs in several other states. See Ala. Code §§30-6-11 (1999); Conn. Gen. Stat. §§ 7-73 (1999); N.J. Stat. Ann. §§37:1-12.2 (West 1999). Some marriage license statutes have been upheld in the face of constitutional challenges on a range of grounds. See, e.g., *Browning v. Corbett,* 734 P.2d 1030 (Ariz. Ct. App. 1986); *Villars v. Provo,* 440 N.W.2d 160 (Minn. Ct. App. 1989). Others have been struck down as unconstitutional. See, e.g., *Safety Net for Abused Persons v. Seglura,* 692 So.2d 1038 (La. 1997).

22. See Karla Fischer, Neil Vidmar, and Rene Ellis, "The Culture of Battering and the Role of Mediation in Domestic Violence Cases," 46 *Southern Methodist University Law Review* 2117 (1993); Myra Sun and Laurie Woods, *A Mediator's Guide to Domestic Abuse* (1989); Barbara Hart, "Gentle Jeopardy: The Further Endangerment of Battered Women and Children in Custody Mediation," 7 *Mediation Quarterly* 317 (1990); Lisa Lerman, "Mediation of Wife Abuse Cases: The Adverse Impact of Informal Dispute Resolution on Women," 7 *Harvard Women's Law Journal* 57, 88–89 (1984). For a more general analysis of the problems that mediation poses for women, see Trina Grillo, "The Mediation Alternative: Process Dangers for Women," 100 *Yale Law Journal* 1545 (1991). But see Donna Coker, "Enhancing Autonomy for Battered Women: Lessons from Navajo Peacemaking," 47 *UCLA Law Review* 1 (1999), arguing that methods of informal adjudication, such as Navajo peacemaking, should be considered.

23. See Clare Dalton, "Domestic Violence, Domestic Torts and Divorce: Constraints and Possibilities," 31 *New England Law Review* 319 (1997). See also *Giovine v. Giovine,* 663 A.2d 109 (N.J. 1995) (holding that a wife can sue for prolonged acts of battering throughout a marriage, and that damages may take into account both physical and emotional injury).

24. Several states have civil rights statutes that protect citizens from violence motivated by the victim's gender. It is arguable that these statutes may provide civil rights remedies for victims of domestic violence. See Cal. Civ. Code §422.6 (West 1992); Mass. Gen. Laws Ann ch. 265 §37 (West 1990); N.J. Stat. Ann. §§ 10:5-1–10.5-42 (West 1976 & Supp. 1991); Wash. Rev. Code Ann. §9A.36.080 (West 1998). The Violence Against Women Act of 1994 also defines gender bias as a civil rights violation in Title III of the act. For discussion of domestic violence as an international human rights violation, see generally Patricia A. Seith, "Escaping Domestic Vio-

lence: Asylum as a Means of Protection for Battered Women," 97 *Columbia Law Review* 1804, 1811 (1997); Berta Esperanza Hernandez-Truyol, "Women's Rights as Human Rights—Rules, Realities and the Role of Culture: A Formula for Reform," 21 *Brooklyn Journal of International Law* 605 (1996); Dorothy O. Thomas and Michele E. Beasley, "Domestic Violence as a Human Rights Issue," 58 *Albany Law Review* 1119 (1995); Joan Fitzpatrick, "The Use of International Human Rights Norms to Combat Violence Against Women," in *Human Rights of Women: National and International Perspectives* 326–39 (Rebecca J. Cook, ed., 1994). For the articulation of battering as involuntary servitude, see Joyce E. McConnell, "Beyond Metaphor: Battered Women, Involuntary Servitude and the Thirteenth Amendment," 4 *Yale Journal of Law and Feminism* 207 (1992). McConnell notes that "embodied in the definition of battering is the concept that the batterer is acting violently not only out of rage, but also out of the desire to 'coerce [the woman] to do something he wants her to do without any concern for her rights.' Thus, from this definition of battering the concept of coerced services emerges." Id. at 230 (internal citations omitted). More succinctly, "battering is not simply violence, it is violence used as a tool to effect total domination of a woman by a man." Id. at 233.

25. Siegel, "Rule of Love," 2117, 2206–7 (1996).
26. Judith Resnik, "Due Process: A Public Dimension," 39 *University of Florida Law Review* 405, 419 (1987).
27. Nevertheless, the media have focused on cases involving battered women who have killed their assailants, rather than on the "ordinary" cases of battered women who cannot get into shelters, cannot get restraining orders, or may risk losing custody of their children for failing to protect them from the batterer. Emphasis on these situations would direct public attention on the battering man and on the failure of social responsibility. See Molly Chaudhuri and Kathleen Daly, "Do Restraining Orders Help? Battered Women's Experience with Male Violence and Legal Process," in *Domestic Violence: The Changing Criminal Justice Response* (Eve Buzawa, ed., 1992).
28. Id.
29. Most civil restraining order statutes have no provisions for counsel and are designed for *pro se* applicants. Though legal advocates are bridging the representational gap in new and creative ways, battered women are still in desperate need of adequate legal representation because civil restraining order litigation inevitably involves issues of custody, support, and visitation. See Elizabeth M. Schneider, "Legal Reform Efforts to Assist Battered Women: Past, Present, and Future," 1–2, 56–59 (1990) (manuscript on file with author); Kathleen Waits, "Battered Women and Family Lawyers: The Need for an Identification Protocol," 58 *Albany Law Review* 1027 (1995); Linda Mills, "On the Other Side of Silence: Affective Lawyering for Intimate Abuse," 81 *Cornell Law Review* 1225 (1996). For a discussion of the problem of legal representation in restraining order litigation, see Finn and Colson, *Civil Protection Orders* (1990).
30. James Ptacek, *Battered Women in the Courtroom: The Power of Judicial Response* 177–78 (1999). Ptacek's study of battered women and the restraining order process in Massachusetts found that "fully 70 percent of the women in Quincy mentioned advocates . . . as the most helpful aspects of the restraining order process" (177).

Ptacek emphasizes the importance of woman-defined advocacy, which "builds a partnership between advocates and battered women and ultimately has each battered woman defining the advocacy and help she needs" (citing Jill Davies, Eleanor Lyon, and Diane Monti-Catania, *Safety Planning for Battered Women: Complex Lives, Difficult Choices* 2 [1998]).

31. Nancy Fraser, "Struggle over Needs: Outcome of a Socialist-Feminist Critical Theory of Late-Capitalist Political Culture," in *Women, the State, and Welfare* 199, 213–14 (Linda Gordon, ed., 1990).

32. Id. at 214.

33. Id.

34. Id. at 214–25.

Chapter 7: Battered Women, Feminist Lawmaking, and Legal Practice

1. Martha A. Fineman, "Challenging Law, Establishing Difference: The Future of Feminist Legal Scholarship," 42 *Florida Law Review* 25, 37–39 (1990).

2. See Jeannette F. Swent, "Gender Bias at the Heart of Justice: An Empirical Study of State Task Forces," 6 *Southern California Review of Law and Women's Studies* 1 (1996).

3. The narrative turn in feminist legal scholarship, based on the sharing of personal stories, has also brought the range of women's experiences into the open. In order to emphasize the multiplicity of voices, however, it is important that these narratives be complex and ambiguous, rather than posit a particular experience or perspective as unitary or "the truth." See Kathryn Abrams, "Unity, Narrative and Law," 13 *Studies in Law Politics and Society* 3, 21 (1993). It is also important that the narratives link the particular experience with more general implications and that they connect to feminist practice. See Fineman, "Challenging Law, Establishing Difference," 25–26; Jane Murphy, "Lawyering for Social Change: The Power of the Narrative in Domestic Violence Law Reform," 21 *Hofstra Law Review* 1243 (1993).

4. Amicus Brief for the Pennsylvania Coalition Against Domestic Violence et al., in *Planned Parenthood v. Casey*, 505 U.S. 833 (1992). Significantly, despite the importance of the Court's language and holding on the spousal notification provision, *Casey* has only formally maintained the right to reproductive choice; in practice, it has substantially limited access to abortion.

5. Domestic violence groups or organizations have submitted briefs in a range of cases, including *People v. Federal Communications Commission*, 75 F.3d 1350 (9th Cir. 1996); *People v. Humphrey* 921 P.2d.1 (Cal. 1996); *Jaffee v. Redmond*, 518 U.S. 1 (1996); *U.S. v. Brant*, 112 F.3d 510 (4th Cir. 1997); *Johnson v. Rodriguez*, 110 F.3d 299 (5th Cir. 1997); *Saenz v. Roe*, 526 U.S. 489 (1999); *U.S. v. Morrison*, cert. granted 120 S.Ct. 605 (1999); *Weiand v. State* 732 So. 2d 1044 (Fla. 1999).

6. Carol Gilligan, "Getting Civilized," 63 *Fordham Law Review* 17 (1994). Carol Gilligan's work, particularly her book *In a Different Voice*, has had a considerable impact on feminist legal theory. For examples of application of Gilligan's work to law, see Pamela Karlan and Daniel Ortiz, "In a Different Voice: Relational Feminism, Abortion Rights and the Feminist Legal Agenda," 87 *Northwestern University Law*

Review 858 (1993); Deborah L. Rhode, "Missing Questions: Feminist Perspectives on Legal Education," 45 *Stanford Law Review* 1547 (1993); Leslie Bender, "From Gender Difference to Feminist Solidarity: Using Carol Gilligan and an Ethic of Care in Law," 15 *Vermont Law Review* 1 (1990); Carrie Menkel-Meadow, "Portia in a Different Voice: Speculations on a Woman's Lawyering Process," 1 *Berkeley Women's Law Journal* 39 (1985); Suzanna Sherry, "Civic Virtue and the Feminine Voice in Constitutional Adjudication," 72 *Virginia Law Review* 543 (1986). Gilligan's work is now a staple of casebooks on women and the law and feminist legal theory. See Katherine T. Bartlett and Angela P. Harris, *Gender and Law* 708–11, 731–32, 734, 744–48, 759 (2d ed., 1998); Mary Becker, Cynthia Grant Bowman, and Morrison Torrey, *Feminist Jurisprudence: Taking Women Seriously* 59–64 (1994).

7. For example, major casebooks on feminism and law describe many different feminist theories. In *Gender and Law,* there are six different feminist theoretical frameworks: formal equality, substantive equality, non-subordination, women's different voice(s), autonomy, and non-essentialism. In *Feminist Jurisprudence,* the chapter on feminist theory includes discussions of feminist methodology, difference in the 1980s, dominance theory, formal equality, hedonic feminism, pragmatic feminism, socialist feminism, postmodern feminism, essentialism, and heterosexism.

8. Rhode, "Missing Questions," 1554.

9. *Ellison v. Brady,* 924 F.2d 972 (9th Cir. 1991). The reasonable-woman standard is discussed in Chapter 5 of this book.

10. Gilligan, "Getting Civilized," 20.

11. Many feminist attorneys claim that female jurors often judge female victims more harshly than male jurors do. See David Margolick, "Ideal Juror for O. J. Simpson: Football Fan Who Can Listen," *New York Times,* B18 (September 23, 1994) (citing Linda Fairstein, Chief, Sex Crimes Unit, Manhattan District Attorney's office).

12. For a discussion of problems of lack of credibility accorded women, see Lynn Hecht Schafran, *The Three C's of Credibility* (1995). Schafran, Director of the National Judicial Education Program to Promote Equality for Women and Men in the Courts, defines "credibility" as "a word that encompasses many meanings, truthful, believable, trustworthy, intelligent, convincing, reasonable, competent, capable, someone to be taken seriously, someone who matters in the world. 'Credible' is the crucial attribute for a lawyer, litigant, complainant, defendant or witness. Yet for women, achieving credibility in and out of the courtroom is no easy task." Id. See also Kathy Mack, "Continuing Barriers to Women's Credibility: A Feminist Perspective on the Proof Process," 4 *Criminal Law Forum* 327 (1993); Kim Lane Scheppele, "Just the Facts, Ma'am: Sexualized Violence, Evidentiary Habits, and the Revision of Truth," 37 *New York Law School Law Review* 123, 128–33 (1992); "Gender and Justice in the Courts: A Report to the Supreme Court of Georgia by the Commission on Gender Bias in the Judicial System," 8 *Georgia State University Law Review* 539, 703–4 (1992).

13. Gilligan, "Getting Civilized," 28.

14. Susan Faludi, *Backlash* (1991).

15. David Brock, *The Real Anita Hill* (1992).

16. Gilligan, "Getting Civilized," 25.

17. Shannon Faulkner, who fought her way into the Citadel military college in South Carolina, is an example of a young woman who had the courage to speak up. She was articulate, poised, and direct, not afraid to confront the military's powerful status quo and eager to forge a path for other women to follow. Although she left the Citadel for health reasons, "her suit [has] started brush fires across the state." See Catherine S. Manegold, "The Citadel's Lone Wolf," *New York Times Magazine,* 56 (September 11, 1994).

18. Bartlett and Harris, *Gender and Law,* 422, citing Catharine A. Mackinnon, "Feminism, Marxism, Method and the State: Toward Feminist Jurisprudence," 8 *Signs: Journal of Women in Culture and Society* 635, 638 (1983); Regina Graycar, "The Gender of Judgments," in *Public and Private: Feminist Legal Debates* 267 (Margaret Thornton, ed., 1995).

19. Kathleen Waits, "Battered Women and Family Lawyers: The Need for an Identification Protocol," 58 *Albany Law Review* 1027 (1995); Pauline Quirion, "Why Attorneys Should Routinely Screen Clients for Domestic Violence," 42 *Boston Bar Journal* 12 (September–October 1998). See also Ann Shalleck, "Theory and Experience in Constructing the Relationship Between Lawyer and Client: Representing Women Who Have Been Abused," 64 *Tennessee Law Review* 1019 (1997), in which she discusses the complexity of effective legal representation.

20. American Bar Association Commission on Domestic Violence, *The Impact of Domestic Violence on Your Legal Practice: A Lawyer's Handbook* (Deborah H. Goelman, Fredrica L. Lehrman, and Roberta L. Valente, eds., 1996); Leonard Karp and Cheryl L. Karp, *Domestic Torts: Family Violence, Conflict and Sex Abuse* (1998).

21. Scheppele, "Just the Facts, Ma'am," 123–28.

22. Myrna S. Raeder, "The Better Way: The Role of Batterers' Profiles and Expert 'Social Framework' Background in Cases Implicating Domestic Violence," 69 *University of Colorado Law Review* 147 (1997); Myrna S. Raeder, "The Double-Edged Sword: Admissibility of Battered Woman Syndrome By and Against Batterers in Cases Implicating Domestic Violence," 67 *University of Colorado Law Review* 789 (1996); Ann Althouse, "The Lying Woman, the Devious Prostitute and Other Stories from the Evidence Casebook," 88 *Northwestern University Law Review* 914 (1994); Aviva Orenstein, "'My God!': A Feminist Critique of the Excited Utterance Exception to the Hearsay Rule," 85 *California Law Review* 159 (1997).

23. Scheppele, "Just the Facts, Ma'am," 127.

24. Id. at 127, 139 (quoting in part from Judith Lewis Herman, *Trauma and Recovery* 175 [1992]).

25. Id. at 141, 143; Herman, *Trauma and Recovery,* 175.

26. Scheppele, "Just the Facts, Ma'am," 166.

27. Marilyn MacCrimmon, "The Social Construction of Reality and the Rules of Evidence," 25 *University of British Columbia Law Review* 36, 42–43 (1991).

28. Scheppele, "Just the Facts, Ma'am," 171.

29. Graycar, "The Gender of Judgments," 278.

30. Scheppele, "Just the Facts, Ma'am," 172 n.1, citing William Twining and David Miers, *How to Do Things with Rules: A Primer of Interpretation* 356–73 (1991); James Ptacek,

Battered Women in the Courtroom: The Power of Judicial Response (1999); Graycar, "The Gender of Judgments," 267–68.

31. Graycar, "The Gender of Judgments," 269 (quoting from Kim Lane Scheppele, "Facing Facts in Legal Interpretation," in *Law and the Order of Culture* [Robert Post, ed., 1991], 60, 62).

32. This justice, Paul Bender of Marion, Wayne County, had been admonished for similar misconduct in 1992. Today's News, *New York Law Journal* 1 (January 10, 2000).

33. MacCrimmon, "The Social Construction of Reality," 44.

34. Elizabeth A. Sheehy, "Feminist Argumentation Before the Supreme Court of Canada in *R. v. Seaboyer, R. v. Gayme:* The Sound of One Hand Clapping," 18 *Melbourne University Law Review* 450, 460–63 (1991).

Chapter 8: Battered Women Who Kill

1. See, e.g., Alan M. Dershowitz, *The Abuse Excuse and Other Cop-Outs, Sob Stories, and Evasions of Responsibility* (1994). Dershowitz claims that although some battered women are legally justified in killing their abusers, it was these cases that first sparked his fear that the "abuse excuse," a "legal tactic by which criminal defendants claim a history of abuse as an excuse for violent retaliation," is "quickly becoming a license to kill and maim." According to Dershowitz, acceptance of the abuse excuse "is dangerous to the very tenets of democracy, which presuppose personal accountability for choices and actions. It also endangers our collective safety by legitimating a sense of vigilantism that reflects our frustration over the apparent inability of law enforcement to reduce the rampant violence that engulfs us." Id. at 4. See also Kathryn Abrams, "Sex Wars Redux: Agency and Coercion in Feminist Legal Theory," 95 *Columbia Law Review* 304, n.100 (1995) (attributing the popularization of the term "feminazi" to the television and radio commentator Rush Limbaugh); Holly Maguigan, "Battered Women and Self-Defense: Myths and Misconceptions in Current Reform Proposals," 140 *University of Pennsylvania Law Review* 379, 384 (1991) (noting the "dominant portrayal of the typical battered woman homicide defendant as a vigilante").

2. In addition to my work in *State v. Wanrow*, detailed in Chapter 3, I argued the need for admissibility of expert testimony on battering as amicus curiae in *State v. Kelly*, 478 A.2d. 364 (N.J. 1984). More recently, I have testified as an expert in a habeas corpus proceeding raising claims of ineffective assistance of counsel in a homicide case involving a woman defendant with a history of battering. *Foreshaw v. Commissioner of Correction*, 708 A.2d 600 (Conn. App. 1998). In addition, I have consulted with many lawyers on such cases in the United States and in other countries.

3. Stephen J. Schulhofer, "The Feminist Challenge in Criminal Law," 143 *University of Pennsylvania Law Review* 2151, 2153 (1995).

4. See, e.g., Elisabeth Ayyildiz, "When Battered Woman's Syndrome Does Not Go Far Enough: The Battered Woman as Vigilante," 4 *American University Journal of Gender and Law* 141, 146 (1995): "[The battered woman] is both a law-abiding hero and a law-breaking villain. . . . She has, often for many years, abided by the law,

taking abuse without retaliation. She has often turned to the justice system for help, generally to no avail. Yet when she finally strikes and defends herself, it is she who becomes the villain, the pariah disrupting home and hearth. She is the murderous monster." The particular horror with which women who dare to behave as law-breaking agents, rather than passive victims of crime, are viewed is seen in early criminological research on women. Deborah W. Denno, "Gender, Crime, and the Criminal Law Defenses," 85 *Journal of Criminal Law and Criminology* 80, 86, n.79 (1994).

5. 1 William Blackstone, *Commentaries,* 418, n.103 (1897).
6. Schulhofer, "The Feminist Challenge," 2207.
7. Angela Browne and Kirk R. Williams, "Exploring the Effect of Resource Availability and the Likelihood of Female-Perpetrated Homicides," 23 *Law and Society Review* 75 (1989).
8. It has been estimated that 80–85 percent of incarcerated women are incarcerated as a result of their affiliation with an abusive partner. National Clearinghouse for the Defense of Battered Women, *Statistics Packet,* Philadelphia (3d ed. 1995). Almost 50 percent of women in prison reported a history of physical or sexual abuse. Id. See also Russ Immarigeon, "Few Diversion Programs Are Offered Female Offenders," 11 *National Prison Project Journal* 10 (1987). Sources cite a range of statistics concerning the number of women in prison who were abused before imprisonment. Department of Justice statistics show that almost six out of ten women in state prisons have been abused in the past. Lawrence A. Greenfeld and Tracy L. Snell, "Women Offenders," Department of Justice, Bureau of Justice Statistics (1999). Other researchers have estimated that as many as 85 percent of incarcerated women have been battered. Karl Rasmussen, Executive Director of the Women's Prison Association in New York, has stated that 85 percent of the women he has seen would not have gone to prison in the first place if it were not for their involvement with abusive male criminals. National Clearinghouse for the Defense of Battered Women, *Statistics Packet.*
9. Maguigan, "Battered Women and Self-Defense," 391–97.
10. See Erich D. Anderson and Anne Read-Anderson, "Constitutional Dimensions of the Battered Woman Syndrome," 53 *Ohio State Law Journal* 363 (1992). Although the authors focus on the implications of exclusion of expert witness testimony on "battered woman syndrome" under the Sixth Amendment, their argument and observations are consistent in other respects with the equality framework defined by the early work on women's self-defense.
11. See Susan N. Herman, "Thelma and Louise and Bonnie and Jean: Images of Women as Criminals," 2 *Southern California Review of Law and Women's Studies* 53 (1992); Elizabeth V. Spelman and Martha Minow, "Outlaw Women: An Essay on Thelma and Louise," 26 *New England Law Review* 1281 (1992). In 1993 Lorena Bobbitt charged that she suffered emotional, physical, and sexual abuse from her husband and cut off his penis, which was surgically reattached the same day. Her husband was charged with and acquitted of marital sexual assault for raping her before she mutilated him. Ms. Bobbitt was acquitted of malicious wounding by reason of temporary insanity and committed to a mental hospital, from which she was released after five

weeks. "Lorena Bobbitt Is Released, Ordered to Get Counseling," *Arizona Republic* 1 (March 1, 1994).

12. For claims of self-defense, see, e.g., *State v. Scott*, 1989 WL 90613 (Del. Super. Ct. 1989); *Larson v. State*, 766 P.2d 261 n.4 (Nev. 1988); *State v. Vigil*, 794 P.2d 728, 729 (N.M. 1990); *Commonwealth v. Miller*, 634 A.2d 614, 619 (Pa. Super. Ct. 1993); *Commonwealth v. Ely*, 578 A.2d 540, 541 (Pa. Super. Ct. 1990); *Commonwealth v. Tyson*, 526 A.2d 395, 397 (Pa. Super. Ct. 1987); see also Anne M. Coughlin, "Excusing Women," 82 *California Law Review* 6 (1994) (arguing that the "defense of battered woman syndrome" does more harm than good for women); but see Maguigan, "Battered Women and Self-Defense," 382 (noting fundamental misunderstandings and incorrect assumptions about the law of self-defense with regard to battered women defendants). For a special cause of action in tort, see *Cusseaux v. Pickett*, 652 A.2d 789 (N.J. Super. Ct. Law Div. 1994); see also Thom Weidlich, " 'Battered Woman' Tort Gains," *National Law Journal*, A6 (August 28, 1995) (reporting on *Giovine v. Giovine*, A-2134-94T5 (N.J. Sup. Ct. 1995), noting that *Giovine* marks only the third court, and the highest, in the country to recognize a tort specific to battered women); but see *Laughlin v. Breaux*, 515 So. 2d 480 (La. Ct. App. 1987) (declining to recognize such a tort).

13. Feminists and other modern and postmodern theorists have long recognized the conflict between the need to identify "differences" that define a political group, for purposes of developing unity within the group and identifying unequal treatment of individual group members within the dominant culture, and traditional liberal conceptions of equality, which call for universal norms that can be applied to all individuals and groups, regardless of particular social, historical, cultural, gender-based, or other experiences, needs, or values. See, e.g., Iris M. Young, *Justice and the Politics of Difference* 168–72 (1990); Martha Minow, *Making All the Difference: Inclusion, Exclusion, and American Law* (1990); Linda J. Nicholson and Nancy Fraser, "Social Criticism Without Philosophy: An Encounter Between Feminism and Postmodernism," in *Feminism/Postmodernism* 19–38 (Linda J. Nicholson, ed., 1990); Margaret Jane Radin, "Affirmative Action Rhetoric," 9 *Social Philosophy and Policy* 130, 147 (1991).

14. 2 Wayne R. LaFave and Austin W. Scott, Jr., *Substantive Criminal Law*, chap. 7 (1986). The classifications described in this text are general. Some jurisdictions do not divide murder into degrees; others divide it into three degrees. Some jurisdictions also divide manslaughter into degrees, or into "voluntary" and "involuntary."

15. 2 LaFave and Scott, *Substantive Criminal Law*, 252. Most jurisdictions require the emotion causing the "passion" that makes manslaughter "understandable" to be anger (thus requiring that there not have been a "cooling off" period sufficient to make the provocation unreasonable), although a few include fear or "terror." Id. at 255. Most jurisdictions consider provocation to be grounds for manslaughter. Id. at 271–72; 1 LaFave and Scott, *Substantive Criminal Law*, 650.

16. 2 LaFave and Scott, *Substantive Criminal Law*, 251, 256, 271; 1 LaFave and Scott, *Substantive Criminal Law*, 663.

17. See 2 LaFave and Scott, *Substantive Criminal Law*, 258–59 (noting that "it is the law

practically everywhere" that a husband's discovery of his wife in the act of adultery is sufficient provocation under the law of manslaughter, and at one time was sufficient for a justification defense as well).

18. See "She Strays, He Shoots, Judge Winks," *New York Times*, A22 (October 22, 1994). For a thoughtful discussion of this case in light of shifting social norms, see Dan M. Kahan and Martha C. Nussbaum, "Two Conceptions of Emotion in Criminal Law," 96 *Columbia Law Review* 269, 346, nn.350–56 (1996).

19. Donna Coker, "Heat of Passion and Wife Killing: Men Who Batter/Men Who Kill," 2 *Southern California Review of Law and Women's Studies* 71, 73 (1992).

20. Generally, partial responsibility defenses include intoxication, infancy, automatism, and heat-of-passion manslaughter. 1 LaFave and Scott, *Substantive Criminal Law,* 427, 522–23. On the legal impact of insanity, see id., 427–28.

21. Id., 483.

22. Id., 522–23, 528. An important distinction between insanity and partial responsibility defenses is that, traditionally, psychological expert testimony was relevant only to an insanity defense. A few jurisdictions that recognize partial responsibility defenses have allowed the admission of psychological evidence without the usual requirements, which apply in insanity defense cases that make use of such testimony, of notice to the prosecution and adverse examination by the prosecution's experts. This has posed particular problems for battered women. For analysis of the problem of adverse examination for battered women's cases, see Janet Parrish, "Trend Analysis: Expert Testimony on Battering and Its Effect in Criminal Cases," 11 *Wisconsin Women's Law Journal* 75, 86, 131–32 (1996).

23. For example, the Women's Self-Defense Law Project, founded jointly by the Center for Constitutional Rights and the National Jury Project in 1978, conducted training sessions for lawyers and consulted on and monitored more than one hundred cases. For a more detailed description of the project's work, see Elizabeth Bochnak, "Introduction," in *Women's Self-Defense Cases: Theory and Practice,* xv–xviii (Elizabeth Bochnak, ed., 1981). The National Clearinghouse for Defense of Battered Women in Philadelphia, headed by Sue Osthoff, is a legal resource center that consults on cases where battered women are charged with homicide and assault, has a brief bank, works with experts, and is a repository of statistical and strategic information. See Sue Osthoff, Preface, in Parrish, "Trend Analysis."

24. See Regina Schuller, Vicki Smith, and James Olsen, "Jurors' Decisions in Trials of Battered Women Who Kill: The Role of Prior Beliefs and Expert Testimony," 24 *Journal of Applied Social Psychology* 316 (1994). See also Neil Vidmar and Regina A. Schuller, "Is the Jury Competent? Juries and Expert Evidence: Social Framework Testimony," 52 *Law and Contemporary Problems* 133 (1989); Charles Patrick Ewing, *Battered Women Who Kill: Psychological Self-Defense as Legal Justification* (1987); Alana Bowman, "A Matter of Justice: Overcoming Juror Bias in Prosecutions of Batterers Through Expert Witness Testimony of the Common Experiences of Battered Women," 2 *Southern California Review of Law and Women's Studies* 219 (1992).

25. Some courts have been sensitive to the problem of stereotyping of battered women. For example, in *McMaugh v. State,* 612 A.2d 725 (R.I. 1992), the Rhode Island Su-

preme Court reversed the trial court's denial of a state habeas corpus for a battered woman who had been convicted of first-degree murder and conspiracy. The court's decision was made on several grounds, including the fact that the trial judge had refused to believe that the woman, who appeared assertive at trial, was battered and had been coerced by her husband into adopting a defense strategy that made her responsible. The court observed: "It is well established that battered women have several common personality traits. These traits include low self-esteem, traditional beliefs about the home, the family, and the female sex role, tremendous feelings of guilt that their marriages are failing, and the tendency to accept responsibility for the batterer's actions. The presence of these characteristics leads to the stereotype of the battered woman as fragile, haggard, fearful, passive, lacking job skills, and economically dependent on her batterer. Nevertheless, the existence of this list of traits does not mean that all battered women look and act the same. Although some battered women may have some or all of these characteristics, it is entirely possible for a battered woman not to evidence any of these characteristics." *McMaugh,* 731 (citing *State v. Kelly,* 372).

26. See, e.g., *Banks v. State,* 608 A.2d 1249 (Md. Ct. Spec. App. 1992); *State v. Donner,* 645 N.E.2d 165 (Ohio Ct. App. 1994).

27. See also Anderson and Read-Anderson, "Constitutional Dimensions," 376; Maguigan, "Battered Woman and Self-Defense," 381. A California case that drew some media attention illustrates the tendency to see battered women as helpless victims, and the difficulty of reconciling the image of a physically or emotionally strong woman with that of the helpless victim. One news story noted that the defendant was "a bodybuilder, wrestler, and occasional boxer" and that the killing was "either the act of a habitually violent and enraged woman or the justifiable response of a brutally battered wife." Greg Moran, "Jury Hears Scenarios of Violent Last Hours of a Stormy Marriage," *San Diego Union-Tribune,* B2 (February 27, 1996); see also *McMaugh v. State,* 725 (noting the problem of stereotyping battered women).

28. Maguigan, "Battered Women and Self-Defense," 381, 396. In support of her conclusions, Maguigan mentioned that the women in her study had a 40 percent reversal rate on their convictions, a figure significantly higher than the national average for homicide appeals, which is 8.5 percent, according to the National Center for State Courts. Id. at 432–33 (citing Joy A. Chapper and Roger A. Hanson, *National Center for State Courts, Understanding Reversible Error in Criminal Appeals: Final Report* 38 [1990]). In a more recent study, the reversal rate of convictions was 32 percent. Parrish, "Trend Analysis," 86–87, 132–39.

29. Maguigan, "Battered Women and Self-Defense," 397. In 5 percent of the cases, there was insufficient discussion of the facts to determine whether a confrontation was occurring at the time of the killing or not.

30. Id. at 432, 434–47.

31. See, e.g., *Brooks v. State,* 630 So. 2d 160, 162 (Ala. Crim. App. 1993) (the defense attorney failed to object to the court's instruction on whether battering was sufficient provocation for reduction of murder to manslaughter, and thus failed to preserve the issue for appeal); *Neelley v. State,* 642 So. 2d 494 (Ala. Crim. App. 1993), *cert. de-*

nied, 514 U.S. 1005 (1995) (the defense counsel's failure to present expert testimony on domestic violence and publicity contract with a defendant in a high-profile case was ruled not to constitute ineffective assistance of counsel); *People v. Day,* 2 Cal. Rptr.2d 916 (Cal. Ct. App. 1992) (the defendant was held to be prejudiced at trial by defense counsel's failure to present evidence of battering); *People v. Rollock,* 177 A.D.2d 722 (N.Y. App. Div. 1991) (the defense lawyer claimed that he didn't know that the defendant was a battered woman, so his failure to introduce expert testimony on battering was held not to constitute ineffective assistance of counsel); *State v. Donner,* 165 (the defense attorney told the battered woman defendant that she "had no defense").

32. See, e.g., *State v. Koss,* 551 N.E.2d 970, 971 (Ohio 1990); *State v. Felton,* 329 N.W.2d 161, 164–65 (Wis. 1983); see also *Women's Self-Defense Cases,* 53; Kim Lane Scheppele, "Just the Facts, Ma'am: Sexualized Violence, Evidentiary Habits, and the Revision of Truth," 37 *New York Law School Law Review* 123, 126–28 (1992). Memory loss, or inability to adequately express the experience of having been battered, can be one result of trauma that women experience in a battering relationship or one of the many survival tactics with which women may respond to abuse. This phenomenon, like other aspects of battering, has been characterized by an expert in the field as arising "as much from the deprivation of liberty implied by coercion and control as it does from violence-induced trauma." Evan Stark, "Re-Presenting Woman Battering: From Battered Woman Syndrome to Coercive Control," 58 *Albany Law Review* 986 (1995).

33. See *People v. Day,* 916; *Commonwealth v. Miller,* 614; *State v. Donner,* 165.

34. I focus on the self-defense context in this chapter, but where a battered woman claims duress, she may face similar problems to those encountered in self-defense.

35. See Maguigan, "Battered Women and Self-Defense," 391.

36. *People v. Humphrey,* 921 P.2d 1 (Cal. 1996). George Fletcher argues that only an objective standard should govern the determination of self-defense, and that there is a clear difference between the woman's "reasonable belief" and "interaction in the real world." Fletcher, "Theory of Justification and Excuse," 553. *Commonwealth v. Miller,* 614, is an example of the complex impact that gendered assumptions about reasonableness continue to have on the cases of battered women who kill.

37. See, e.g., Renee Callahan, "Will the 'Real' Battered Woman Please Stand Up? In Search of a Realistic Legal Definition of Battered Woman Syndrome," 3 *American University Journal of Gender and Law* 117 (1994); Mary Ann Dutton, "Understanding Women's Responses to Domestic Violence: A Redefinition of Battered Woman's Syndrome," 21 *Hofstra Law Review* 1193 (1993); Elizabeth Sheehy, Julie Stubbs, and Julia Tolmie, "Defending Battered Women on Trial: Battered Woman Syndrome and Its Limitations," 16 *Criminal Law Journal* 369 (1992).

38. Lenore E. Walker, *Terrifying Love* 1196 (1989).

39. Id. at 48; Dutton, "Understanding Women's Responses," 1198; Stark, "Re-Presenting Woman Battering," 974.

40. See, e.g., Ohio Rev. Code Ann. §2901.06 (1993) (expert testimony on "battered woman syndrome" admissible in self-defense); Ohio Rev. Code Ann. §2945.39.2

(1993) (making expert testimony on "battered woman syndrome" admissible in insanity defenses). See also *Anderson v. Goeke*, 44 F.3d 675 (8th Cir. 1995).

41. See, e.g., *State v. Kelly*, 375–77 (on why a woman stayed in an abusive relationship). On why a battered woman responded in the way that she did, see, e.g., *People v. Minnis*, 455 N.E.2d 209, 217–18 (Ill. App. Ct. 1983).

42. For examples and discussions of the diverse experiences of battered women, see Beth Richie, *Compelled to Crime: The Gender Entrapment of Battered Black Women* (1996); *Naming the Violence: Speaking Out about Lesbian Battering* (Kerry Lobel, ed., 1986); Sharon A. Allard, "Rethinking Battered Woman Syndrome: A Black Feminist Perspective," 1 *UCLA Women's Law Journal* 191 (1991); Linda L. Ammons, "Mules, Madonnas, Babies, Bathwater, Racial Imagery and Stereotypes: The African-American Woman and the Battered Woman Syndrome," 5 *Wisconsin Law Review* 1003 (1995); Kimberlé Crenshaw, "Mapping the Margins: Intersectionality, Identity Politics, and Violence Against Women of Color," 43 *Stanford Law Review* 1244 (1991); Dutton, "Understanding Women's Responses," 1194; Beverly Horsburgh, "Domestic Violence in the Jewish Community," 18 *Harvard Women's Law Journal* 171 (1995); Martha Mahoney, "Legal Images of Battered Women: Redefining the Issue of Separation," 90 *Michigan Law Review* (1991); Nilda Rimonte, "A Question of Culture: Cultural Approval of Violence Against Women in the Pacific-Asian Community and the Cultural Defense," 43 *Stanford Law Review* (1991); Jenny Rivera, "Domestic Violence Against Latinas by Latino Males: An Analysis of Race, National Origin, and Gender Differentials," 14 *Boston College Third World Law Journal* 231 (1994); Julie Stubbs and Julia Tolmie, "Race, Gender and the Battered Woman Syndrome: An Australian Case Study," 8 *Canadian Journal of Women and the Law* 122 (1995).

43. See Dutton, "Understanding Women's Responses," 1193; Stark, "Re-Presenting Woman Battering," 1000. Stark notes: "At best, [battered woman syndrome and post traumatic stress disorder] remain psychiatric designations which possess the attendant risks of misuse and stigma and which diminish, but do not eliminate, the burden of insanity attached to battered women in the past."

44. For lawyers, see, e.g., *State v. Scott; Larson v. State*, 261 n.4; see also Maguigan, "Battered Women and Self-Defense," 426–27, n.169. For legislators, see Sue Osthoff, "Defending Battered Women" (fact sheet written in response to proposed state legislation, available from the National Clearinghouse for the Defense of Battered Women [on file with author]). For judges, see, e.g., *Moran v. Ohio*, 469 U.S. 948 (1984) (Brennan, J., dissenting); *State v. Vigil*, 728, 729; *Commonwealth v. Tyson*, 395; see also *Cusseaux v. Pickett*, 789 (a tort case in which "battered woman syndrome" was recognized as a separate harm) and the discussion of *Cusseaux* in Martha Chamallas, "Hostile Domestic Environments," 57 *University of Pittsburgh Law Review* 816–17 (1996). Finally, for legal scholars, see Coughlin, "Excusing Woman," 4–5; Claire O. Finkelstein, "Self-Defense as a Rational Excuse," 57 *University of Pittsburgh Law Review* 621, 631 (1996); Mira Mihajlovich, "Does Plight Make Right: The Battered Woman Syndrome, Expert Testimony and the Law of Self-Defense," 62 *Indiana Law Journal* 1253, 1280 (1987); Elizabeth Vaughan and Maureen L. Moore, "The Battered Spouse Defense in Kentucky," 10 *Northern Kentucky Law Review* 399 (1983).

45. See, e.g., *State v. Coleman*, 870 P.2d 695, 697 (Kan. Ct. App. 1994); *State v. Koss*, 970, 974; *Commonwealth v. Miller*, 619; see also *Women's Self-Defense Cases*, 43; Maguigan, "Battered Women and Self-Defense," 421–24. In Pennsylvania and other states, courts have expressed varying views on the admissibility of evidence of battering in both self-defense and duress cases. See *Commonwealth v. Miller*, 614 (rejecting a "battered woman syndrome theory of self-defense"); *Commonwealth v. Ely*, 541 (discussing implications of "battered woman syndrome theory of self-defense" for duress). This inconsistency is due in part to differing views among judges about whether and how "battered woman syndrome" evidence is relevant to defenses of self-defense or duress, and in part to some judges' fear that admission of this evidence indicates an entirely separate defense available only to battered women. See, e.g., Scott Graham, "Justices Weigh Battered Woman's Self-Defense Claim; Court Sounds Troubled by Limit on Expert Testimony," *American Lawyer*, 1 (June 7, 1996); *Commonwealth v. Miller*, 619; *Commonwealth v. Ely*, 541; *Witt v. State*, 892 P.2d 132, 135 (Wyo. 1995).
46. See, e.g., *State v. Kelly*, 364, 368; see also Ewing, *Battered Women Who Kill*.
47. In *Anderson v. Goeke*, 675, the Eighth Circuit denied post-conviction relief to a battered woman, where the trial judge had allowed reference to battered woman syndrome during voir dire and trial "only as evidence of diminished mental capacity" even though the Missouri statute on "Battered Spouse Law" provided that "evidence that the actor was suffering from the battered spouse syndrome shall be admissible upon the issue of whether the actor lawfully acted in self-defense or defense of another," Mo. Rev. Stat. §563.033(1) (1996), 44 F.3d at 680.
48. In *Banks v. State*, 1252, defense at trial was "an amalgam of self-defense, hot-blooded response to provocation, and battered spouse syndrome."
49. 478 A.2d 364 (N.J. 1984). I was co-counsel to amicus curiae American Civil Liberties Union of New Jersey and New Jersey Coalition for Battered Women (with Stephen Latimer) in *State v. Kelly*. We filed an amicus brief in the New Jersey Supreme Court. Subsequently, I was granted leave to participate in the oral argument of the case. For a discussion of the oral argument in *Kelly* see "Workshop: Lesbians, Gays and Feminists at the Bar: Translating Personal Experience into Effective Legal Argument," 10 *Women's Rights Law Reporter* 107, 137–38 (1988).
50. For a discussion of the contradictions presented by cases involving expert testimony on battered women, see Chapter 5 of this book.
51. Early work on women's self-defense stressed the positive role that expert testimony might play at trial but cautioned that it should not be reflexively proffered. See, e.g., Susie MacPherson, Cookie Ridolfi, Susan Sternberg, and Diane Wiley, "Expert Testimony," in *Women's Self-Defense Cases*, 88–90. This work emphasized that the need for experts ought to be evaluated based on the facts in each particular case, and that "the task of the expert is to provide the jury with information that complements the defendant's testimony and makes her particular experience plausible to them." Id. at 89.
52. Apart from the appellate cases that have reviewed exclusions of expert testimony from trial court, or appellate cases reviewing some other trial issue that mention

whether expert testimony was proffered, there is no authoritative record of lawyers' efforts to introduce expert testimony on battered woman syndrome. My own experience in consulting with lawyers and discussing these issues with the media leads me to believe that there are now several hundred cases around the country in which this testimony has been proffered. Janet Parrish's survey and analysis, published in 1995, is the most recent picture of battered women's criminal cases. Parrish, "Trend Analysis."

53. This is a serious problem in many cases involving battered women. For example, in Gladys Kelly's remand trial, the defense called Dr. Lenore Walker, and the prosecution put on an expert witness who testified that Gladys Kelly did not have battered woman syndrome. Gladys Kelly was convicted at her second trial. Her trial attorney, Charles Lorber, believes that the prosecution's rebuttal use of expert testimony created serious obstacles to acquittal. Telephone conversation with Charles Lorber (November 14, 1985).

54. See discussion of case referred to as *State v. Green* (expert testimony presented in grand jury) in Julie Blackman, "Innovative Involvements for an Expert Witness: Ideas Toward the Representation of Battered Women Who Kill," 9 *Women's Rights Law Reporter* 227 (1986); *People v. Livingston* (expert testimony admitted at sentencing hearing) in Blackman, "Innovative Involvements," 234; *People v. Salerno* and *Commonwealth v. Devore* (expert testimony admitted at a sentencing hearing) in Blackman, "Innovative Involvements," 238. See also *Neelley v. State*, 494 So.2d 669 (Ala. Crim. App. 1985) (expert testimony presented at a motion for retrial); *Wisecup v. State*, 278 S.E.2d 682 (Ga. Ct. App. 1981) (expert testimony presented in a brief of amicus curiae on appeal); *Fennell v. Goolsby*, 630 F.Supp. 451 (E.D. Pa. 1985) (expert testimony presented on a petition for writ of habeas corpus); *People v. Powell*, 83 A.D.2d 719 (N.Y. App. Div. 1981) (expert testimony presented on a post-trial motion to set aside the verdict on the grounds of newly discovered evidence of expert testimony).

55. See, e.g., *Thomas v. Arn*, 728 F.2d 813, 815 (6th Cir. 1984) (Jones, C.J., concurring), *aff'd*, 474 U.S. 140 (1985); *State v. Hundley*, 693 P.2d 475, 479 (Kan. 1985); *State v. Anaya*, 438 A.2d 892, 894 (Me. 1981); *State v. Branchall*, 684 P.2d 1163, 1169 (N.M. Ct. App. 1984); *State v. Allery*, 682 P.2d 312, 316 (Wash. 1984).

56. See, e.g., *Smith v. State*, 277 S.E.2d 678, 683 (Ga. 1981); *People v. Torres*, 488 N.Y.S.2d 358, 362 (N.Y. Sup. Ct. 1985); *State v. Leidholm*, 334 N.W.2d 811, 820 (N.D. 1983).

57. See, e.g., *Ibn-Tamas v. United States*, 455 A.2d 893, 894 (App. D.C. 1983); *State v. Burton*, 464 So. 2d 421 (La. Ct. App. 1985); *State v. Martin*, 666 S.W.2d 895, 899 (Mo. Ct. App. 1984); *Mullis v. State*, 282 S.E.2d 334, 337 (Ga. 1981).

58. See discussion of the Carol Gardner case in *Women's Self-Defense Cases*, 179–202. In this case "post-trial interviews revealed that over-reliance on the theme of battering prevented the defense team and the jurors from focusing on the legal elements of self-defense." Id. at xvii.

59. In *State v. Kelly*, the New Jersey Supreme Court ordered the case remanded for a new trial to determine whether the proffered expert testimony would satisfy New Jersey's standard of acceptability for scientific evidence. 478 A.2d at 381. One judge

dissented from the remand on the issue of scientific acceptability, finding that defendant Kelly had sufficiently demonstrated both scientific acceptance and reliability. 478 A.2d at 385 (Handler, J., concurring in part and dissenting in part).

60. 478 A.2d at 368–69.

61. 478 A.2d at 372–73, 375.

62. 478 A.2d at 368. The trial court ruled that New Jersey's standard of self-defense as set forth in *State v. Bess*, 247 A.2d 669 (N.J. 1968), did not permit admission of evidence concerning the defendant's state of mind. The trial court stated: "I will assume arguendo that [the expert] is eminently qualified as a psychologist, that the state of research and art of her profession is such that there, and I could find that there is a battered wife syndrome, that this defendant falls well within the purview of the guidelines of that battered wife syndrome, that syndrome has been plausibly and reasonably determined by reasonable scientific efforts on her part, notwithstanding that she herself has had, she being this witness has had what we might call in a quantitative sense a limited number of subject women that those tests are plausible, findings are plausible. . . . That she would be appropriate to give testimony to a lay jury as to the consequences of the syndrome, but that's not the bottom line. The bottom line is, to put it vulgarly, so what? Because, under our law what can it go to and that's what I want to ask you. What would that evidence go to? It does not go to self-defense." Trial Transcript at 2T, 126, *State v. Kelly*.

63. The Appellate Division stated: "We agree with the ruling below barring Dr. Veronen's testimony, both on the authority . . . of *State v. Bess*, and on the ground that its exclusion was not clearly capable of producing an unjust result, R. 2:10–2, and did not beyond a reasonable doubt lead the jury to a result it otherwise might not have reached, *State v. Macon*, 336 (1971)." *State v. Kelly*, No. A-2256-80-T4, slip op. at 4 (App. Div. July 6, 1982).

64. Brief of Amici Curiae, American Civil Liberties Union of New Jersey and New Jersey Coalition on Battered Women, *State v. Kelly*, 478 A.2d 364 (N.J. 1984); order of court granting leave to argue, *State v. Kelly*, No. 2256–80–T4 (App. Div. July 6, 1982) dated April 18, 1983; Brief of Amicus Curiae, American Psychological Association in Support of Appellate, *State v. Kelly*, 478 A.2d 364 (N.J. 1984). See Briefs of Amici Curiae, *State v. Kelly*, 478 A.2d at 364.

65. *State v. Kelly*, 370.

66. Id. at 372.

67. Id. at 372, 377.

68. Id. at 377.

69. Id. at 378.

70. Id.

71. Id.

72. In contrast, those courts that have rejected the admissibility of expert testimony have not focused on the woman's victimization. See, e.g., *People v. White*, 414 N.E.2d 196 (Ill. App. Ct. 1980). Cases in which the court adopted feminist perceptions include *Terry v. State*, 467 So.2d 761 (Fla. Dist. Ct. App. 1985); *Smith v. State*, 678; *People v. Minnis*, 209; *State v. Anaya*, 892.

73. See, e.g., *State v. Kelly*, 364, 371, discussed at notes 72–105 and accompanying text; *State v. Allery*, 312, 316.

74. See e.g., *State v. Kelly*, 364, 370; *Terry v. State*, 761; *People v. Minnis*, 209; *State v. Anaya*, 892; *State v. Allery*, 312; *People v. Torres*, 358, 362.

75. *State v. Kelly*, 364, 370; *People v. Torres*, 358, 362; *State v. Wanrow*, 559 P.2d 548, 558–59 (Wash. 1977). See also Franklin Zimring, Satyanshu K. Mukherjee, and Barrik Van Winkle, "Intimate Violence: A Study of Intersexual Homicide in Chicago," 50 *University of Chicago Law Review* 910, 920 (1983).

76. See generally MacKinnon, "Toward Feminist Jurisprudence," 34 *Stanford Law Review* 703 (1982); Phyllis Crocker, "The Meaning of Equality for Battered Women Who Kill Men in Self-Defense," 8 *Harvard Women's Law Journal* 121 (1988).

77. For the traditional view, see generally Barbara Brown, Thomas Emerson, Gail Falk, and Ann E. Freedman, "The Equal Rights Amendment: A Constitutional Basis for Equal Rights for Women," 80 *Yale Law Journal* 871 (1971); Wendy Williams, "The Equality Crisis: Some Reflections on Culture, Courts and Feminism," 7 *Women's Rights Law Reporter* 175 (1982). For challenges to that view, see generally Catharine A. MacKinnon, *Sexual Harassment of Working Women* (1979); Linda J. Krieger and Patricia N. Cooney, "The Miller-Wohl Controversy: Equal Treatment, Positive Action and the Meaning of Women's Equality," 13 *Golden Gate Law Review* 513 (1983); Ann C. Scales, "Towards a Feminist Jurisprudence," 56 *Indiana Law Journal* 375 (1981); Note, "Toward a Redefinition of Sexual Equality," 95 *Harvard Law Review* 487 (1981).

78. Compare Krieger and Cooney, "The Miller-Wohl Controversy," with Wendy Williams, "Equality's Riddle: Pregnancy and the Equal Treatment/Special Treatment Debate," 13 *New York University Review of Law and Social Change* 325 (1984–85). See also *California Federal Savings and Loan Corporation v. Guerra*, 479 U.S. 272 (1987); Samuel Issacharoff and Elyse Rosenblum, "Women and the Workplace: Accommodating the Demands of Pregnancy," 94 *Columbia Law Review* 2154 (1994).

79. Williams, "The Equality Crisis."

80. "Until such time as the effects of that history are eradicated, care must be taken to assure that our self-defense instructions afford women the right to have their conduct judged in light of the *individual physical handicaps which are the product of sex discrimination.*" *Wanrow*, 559 P.2d at 559 (emphasis added).

81. See Ann Jones, *Women Who Kill* 158–66 (1980); Elaine Showalter, *The Female Malady: Women, Madness and English Culture* (1985); "The Insanity Plea: For Women Only," *Psychology Today*, 16 (March 1985); see also sources cited in Schneider, "Equal Rights to Trial," 638, nn.82 and 83.

82. See generally George Fletcher, *Rethinking Criminal Law* 855–57 (1978); Kent Greenawalt, "The Perplexing Borders of Justification and Excuse," 84 *Columbia Law Review* 1897 (1984); Paul Robinson, "A Theory of Justification: Societal Harm as a Prerequisite to Criminal Liability," 23 *UCLA Law Review* 266 (1982).

83. Crocker, "The Meaning of Equality," 130–31; MacKinnon, "Toward Feminist Jurisprudence," 717, n.73.

84. This characterization may somewhat overstate the psychological description in

Kelly. In describing the expert's testimony, the court states that Dr. Veronen "described in general terms the component parts of the battered woman's syndrome and its effects on a woman's physical and mental health. The witness then documented, based on her own considerable experience in counseling, treating and studying battered women, and her familiarity with the work of others in the field, the feelings of anxiety, self-blame, isolation, and, above all, fear that plagues these women and leaves them prey to a psychological paralysis that hinders their ability to break free or seek help." *State v. Kelly,* 372–73. This psychological dimension has become even more developed in subsequent cases.

85. MacKinnon suggests that justification and excuse are correlated with a dichotomy of personal or individual versus universal and social. MacKinnon, "Toward Feminist Jurisprudence," 717, n.73. Greenawalt suggests that justification and excuse are correlated with dichotomies of objective-subjective and general-individual. Greenawalt, "Perplexing Borders," 1915.

86. MacKinnon, "Toward Feminist Jurisprudence," 717, n.73; Crocker, "The Meaning of Equality," 130–31.

87. Greenawalt, "Perplexing Borders," 1915.

88. For example, some courts have characterized the testimony as evidence of extreme emotional disturbance, misunderstanding the purpose for which the testimony was offered. See generally *Ledford v. State,* 333 S.E.2d 576 (Ga. 1985); *State v. Edwards,* 420 So. 2d 663 (La. 1982); *State v. Martin,* 895; *People v. Powell,* 102 Misc.3d 775 (N.Y. Co. Ct. 1980), *aff'd,* 83 A.D.2d 719 (N.Y. App. Div. 1981); *State v. Kelly,* 685 P.2d 564 (N.J. 1984); *State v. Hundley,* 475; *State v. Felton,* 161; but see also *People v. Torres,* 358 (battered woman syndrome specifically not offered for mental disease or defect).

89. See, e.g., *Neelley v. State,* 494 So.2d 669; *Ledford v. State,* 576; *State v. Edwards,* 663; *State v. Necaise,* 466 So. 2d 660 (La. Ct. App. 1985); *State v. Burton,* 421; *State v. Felton,* 161.

90. *Wanrow,* 559 P.2d at 559.

91. Of course, *Wanrow* did not involve the issue of the admissibility of expert testimony. But see *State v. Allery,* 312, 316 (where the Washington Supreme Court relies on *Wanrow* for the admissibility of expert testimony).

92. See. e.g., *Smith v. State,* 678, 683; *State v. Kelly,* 478 A.2d at 364, 379; *People v. Torres,* 358, 363; *State v. Allery,* 312, 316.

93. The court in *Wanrow* discussed the issue of the standard in the following way: "The second paragraph of instruction No. 10 contains an equally erroneous and prejudicial statement of the law. That portion of the instruction reads: 'However when there is no reasonable ground for the person attacked to believe that his person is in imminent danger of death or great bodily harm, and it appears to him that only an ordinary battery is all that is intended, and all that he has reasonable grounds to fear from his assailant, he has a right to stand his ground and repel such threatened assault, yet he has no right to repel a threatened assault with naked hands, by the use of a deadly weapon in a deadly manner, unless he believes, and has reasonable grounds to believe, that he is in imminent danger of death or great bodily harm.' In our society women suffer from a conspicuous lack of access to training in and

the means of developing those skills necessary to effectively repel a male assailant without resorting to the use of deadly weapons. Instruction No. 12 does indicate that the 'relative size and strength of the persons involved' may be considered; however, it does not make clear that the defendant's actions are to be judged against her own subjective impressions and not those which a detached jury might determine to be objectively reasonable. . . . The applicable rule of law is clearly stated in *Miller,* at page 105, 250 P. at page 645: 'If the appellants, at the time of the alleged assault upon them, as reasonably and ordinarily cautious and prudent men, honestly believed that they were in danger of great bodily harm, they would have the right to resort to self-defense, and their conduct is to be judged by the condition appearing to them at the time, not by the condition as it might appear to the jury in light of testimony before it.' " *Wanrow,* 559 P.2d at 558.

94. Given the blurred lines between objective and subjective standards of self-defense, the theory in *Wanrow* is applicable even where the standard is more objective. A critical aspect of sex bias in the law of self-defense is the notion of reasonableness in general as problematic for women. The more individualized the standard, the easier it may be for women. But it is possible that individualization may not go far enough because "while it considers individual characteristics, it may not recognize their significance." Crocker, "The Meaning of Equality," 125, n.11.

95. The *Wanrow* court emphasizes that sex discrimination is the social context in which the individual woman's experience is to be evaluated. The notion of individualization was not intended to discount social factors, because the circumstances of the act and the characteristics and perceptions of the individual defendant are shaped by social experience. For a discussion of the interrelationship of social and individual factors in these cases, see generally MacKinnon, "Toward Feminist Jurisprudence."

96. *People v. Humphrey,* 10. For cases that have admitted expert testimony on battered woman syndrome with a standard that the court has characterized "subjective," see *People v. Humphrey,* 1; *People v. Torres,* 358; *State v. Kelly,* 655 P.2d 1202 (1982); *State v. Allery,* 312. For cases that have admitted expert testimony with a standard that the court has characterized as "objective," see, e.g., *State v. Kelly,* 478 A.2d at 364. Some of the courts admitting expert testimony do not characterize their own standards of self-defense. See, e.g., *People v. Minnis,* 209; *State v. Anaya,* 438 A.2d 892 (Me. 1981), *aff'd* on other grounds, 456 A.2d 1255 (Me. 1983).

97. The trial court in *Kelly* held that the expert testimony was not relevant under New Jersey's objective standard of self-defense.

98. *State v. Kelly,* 478 A.2d 364; Appellant's Brief, *State v. Kelly* (Appellate Division), and Brief of Amici Curiae American Civil Liberties Union of New Jersey *et al.* in *State v. Kelly.*

99. *Malott v. Her Majesty the Queen,* 1998 Can. Sup. Ct. LEXIS 7, at 1, 28 (1998).

100. Md. Code Ann., Cts. & Jud. Proc., §10-916 (1999); Ohio Rev. Code Ann. §2901.06 (1999); Ohio Rev. Code Ann. §2945.392 (1999). The use of the term "battered spouse syndrome" is even more problematic than "battered woman syndrome" because it is questionable whether there is such a phenomenon. The Maryland statute appears to recognize this, as it defines "battered spouse syndrome" as the "psychological condi-

tion of the victim [of battering] recognized in the medical and scientific community as the battered woman syndrome."

101. Ohio Rev. Code Ann. §2945.392 (1999).

102. This is not to say that the statutes discussed herein intend to do this. Indeed, the Maryland statute specifically states that it "does not create a new defense to murder." Md. Code Ann., Cts. & Jud. Proc. §10-916 (1999). However, the presence of a separate statute with regard to some cases cannot help but create the impression that a separate defense or other "special" treatment has been created for those cases alone. The presence of language to the contrary within the statute seems to speak to those who are fearful that justice may be thrown to the wind to "make up for" past discrimination. See Fletcher, "Justification and Excuse," 576. In fact, these statutes attempt to deal with the acknowledged present unequal treatment that battered women face in the justice system. Recognition of unequal treatment by thoughtful legislators is welcome, and efforts to remedy that treatment may be well intentioned. Nevertheless, I am concerned with the impact these statutes may have on particular women's cases.

103. See, e.g., Maguigan, "Battered Women and Self-Defense"; Sue Osthoff, "Defending Battered Women."

104. Maguigan, "Battered Women and Self-Defense," 451–55. Maguigan carefully separates out the procedural strands of substantive self-defense standards (identified as reasonableness, imminence, proportionality of force, and duty to retreat) from evidentiary rules (history of abuse and expert testimony). She discusses the ways these aspects of the problem are interrelated and emphasizes that they must be analyzed together in assessing how a state's criminal law and procedural rules affect battered women charged with homicide.

105. Tex. Crim. P. Code Ann. §38.36 (1999); La. Code Evid. Ann. art. 404(A)(2)(a) (1999); Mass. Ann. Laws ch. 233, §23E (1999).

106. Maguigan, "Battered Women and Self-Defense," 432–33 (citing Chapper and Hanson, National Center for State Courts, 38); Parrish, "Trend Analysis," 86–87, 132–39.

107. Strickland v. Washington, 466 U.S. 668 (1984). Courts are strict about what kinds of claimed attorney error they will review. Furthermore, the standard of review is so high, few defendants can prove ineffective assistance. Even a breach of an ethical standard "does not necessarily make out a denial of the Sixth Amendment guarantee of assistance of counsel." Nix v. Whiteside, 475 U.S. 157, 165 (1986).

108. See Burger v. Kemp, 483 U.S. 776 (1987). Other areas where attorney incompetence is difficult to challenge because they require "hindsight" are: (1) claims based largely on the attorney's decision to pursue a particular line of defense over other possibilities, where the attorney appears to have investigated other defenses; (2) failure to call a witness who offers to give favorable testimony; (3) the attorney's decision to relinquish a certain defense right where he or she had exercised various other rights; and (4) failure to advance additional supporting arguments or rebut counterarguments to a legal objection the attorney had made and developed previously. Indeed, the difficulty of meeting the burden of proof to show ineffective assistance of counsel for defendants generally, and battered women particularly, is illustrated by the

fact that, of twenty-six reported cases from fourteen states and one federal jurisdiction in which ineffective assistance of counsel claims had been raised by battered women as of 1994 (see cases annotated at 18 A.L.R. 5th 871 [1994]), twice as many of the claims were denied as were successful. Battered women face particular difficulties in proving ineffective assistance of counsel, related to their unique experiences and to widespread ignorance about the phenomenon of intimate violence. In *Strickland,* for example, the Supreme Court noted that claims based on attorney failure to investigate must focus on the "information supplied [to counsel] by the defendant." *Strickland,* 691. Claims of ineffective assistance of counsel by battered women defendants collected in 18 A.L.R. 5th are divided into seven categories: (1) failure to investigate adequately; (2) improper legal advice (generally regarding plea bargaining or whether or not defendant should testify); (3) choice and application of defenses (frequently a focus on or misunderstanding of the law of self-defense that eclipses the attorney's exploration of provocation, heat of passion, or other available defenses); (4) faulty opening statements (often promising evidence of battering that is not adequately delivered); (5) failure to adduce evidence or examine witnesses at trial (almost always including a failure to present expert testimony on battering, and often a failure to present medical records, witnesses, and the defendant's own testimony that could have demonstrated the existence of domestic violence and its impact on the defendant); (6) failure to request jury instructions about battering (particularly in terms of how it is relevant to the law of self-defense); and (7) other acts or omissions (including failure to obtain exculpatory reports regarding battering, failure to object to prosecution's closing remarks, and advancing the interests of counsel over the client's interests in making tactical decisions). All but the last two categories of attorney ineffectiveness complained of by battered women are in areas where courts are loathe to find incompetence because investigation into and analysis of these actions or omissions by attorneys requires the "hindsight" discouraged in *Strickland.* For discussion of the particular problems of ineffective assistance of counsel in expert testimony cases, see Parrish, "Trend Analysis," 116–17.

109. For faulty advice, see, e.g., *State v. Scott,* 90613; *Larson v. State,* 261; *State v. Zimmerman,* 823 S.W.2d 220 (Tenn. Crim. App. 1991); *State v. Gfeller,* 1987 WL 14328 (Tenn. Crim. App. 1987). For the attorney's failure to adduce evidence or examine witnesses, see *People v. Day,* 916; *State v. Zimmerman,* 220; *Martin v. State,* 501 So. 2d 1313 (Fla. Dist. Ct. App. 1986); *Commonwealth v. Stonehouse,* 555 A.2d 772 (Pa. Super. Ct. 1989). Cases where ineffective assistance of counsel has been found also include complaints over the attorney's failure to investigate evidence of battering (*People v. Day,* 916), the attorney's choice and use of available defenses (*State v. Felton,* 161), the attorney's opening statements indicating a defense involving evidence of battering which was not followed with any such evidence (*State v. Zimmerman,* 220), and the attorney's self-interest interfering with the effectiveness of his or her performance (*Larson v. State,* 261).

110. See, e.g., *Commonwealth v. Singh,* 539 A.2d 1314 (Pa. Super. Ct. 1988).

111. Executive clemency is at the discretion of the governor or president. The executive may choose to grant a pardon (thus doing away with the conviction) or commute a

sentence. See Mary E. Greenwald and Mary-Ellen Manning, "When Mercy Seasons Justice: Commutation for Battered Women Who Kill," 38 *Boston Bar Journal* 3, 13 (1994). An advisory board, usually the parole board, may be authorized to advise and make recommendations to the executive officer. Typically, executive officers follow the recommendations of their advisory boards. Therefore, appeals to this body are an important part of the clemency process. Usually, the clemency process involves several levels. First, the petition must meet basic requirements or be changed to comply with such requirements. Second, an investigation is conducted into the petitioner's criminal, social, and institutional histories. Third, the advisory or parole board makes a recommendation to the executive officer, based upon which the officer makes a determination. Finally, where commutation is granted, there is usually a review conducted under the auspices of the executive officer, sometimes including another hearing. Because executive officers, as well as many executive advisory or parole board members, are elected to office, they are particularly susceptible to public opinion. Community education about battering and identifying support by the community are therefore also important parts of the clemency process. Cookie Ridolfi, who has assisted many battered women and contributed to women's self-defense work for the past two decades, has identified three situations in which clemency is appropriate: (1) situations where the convicted person is factually innocent; (2) situations in which the convicted person is technically guilty but mitigating factors exist that argue for leniency; and (3) situations in which the convicted person is technically guilty but morally innocent. She suggests that the third case is often hardest to argue, and frequently the most accurate description of what has happened to a battered woman who fought back against her batterer. Essentially, the argument is that, if not for imperfections in the law as it currently exists, or such trial factors as jury bias or improper jury instructions, the woman would have not have been convicted. See comments of Cookie Ridolfi in "Courtroom, Code and Clemency: Reform in Self Defense Jurisprudence for Battered Women" (panel discussion), 23 *Golden Gate University Law Review* 829, 833 (1994). Precise statistics and even anecdotal data regarding clemency petitions are difficult to document. Transcripts of clemency proceedings are rarely published. Groups that assist battered women with their clemency petitions are a patchwork of attorney-led organizations, battered women's lay advocacy groups, and other community organizations that do not necessarily share data on a regular basis.

112. See Linda L. Ammons, "Discretionary Justice: A Legal and Policy Analysis of a Governor's Use of the Clemency Power in the Case of Incarcerated Battered Women," 3 *Journal of Law and Policy* 1, 5 (1994); Christine N. Becker, "Clemency for Killers? Pardoning Battered Women Who Strike Back," 29 *Loyola Los Angeles Law Review* 297, 299 (1995); Greenwald and Manning, "When Mercy Seasons Justice," 14–15; Joan H. Krause, "Of Merciful Justice and Justified Mercy: Commuting the Sentences of Battered Women Who Kill," 46 *Florida Law Review* 599, 771–72 (1994); Sue Osthoff, "Clemency for Battered Women," reprinted in "Defending Battered Women," 5–6; "Developments in the Law: Legal Responses to Domestic Violence: Battered Women Who Kill Their Abusers," 106 *Harvard Law Review* 1574, 1591 (1993).

113. See Ammons, "Discretionary Justice," 4; Leslie F. Goldstein, *Contemporary Cases in Women's Rights* 276 (1994); Nancy Gibbs, "Til Death Do Us Part," *Time,* 41 (January 18, 1993); "Six Battered Women Win Clemency," *Arizona Republic* (December 31, 1998); Nancy Ehrenreich, "Battered Victims Who Kill Deserve Mercy," *Denver Post* (May 20, 1999); "Save Pamela Ramjattan; Stands Accused of Murdering Her Husband in Trinidad and Tobago," *Nation* 9 (April 19, 1999). A California statute permits the Board of Prison Terms to report to the Governor "from time to time" the names of prisoners they determine ought to be considered for clemency on the basis of several criteria, including "evidence of battered woman syndrome." This statute, though well-intentioned, also raises the special "legislation" problem discussed earlier. Cal. Penal Code §4801 (1996). There may be a connection between the decline in the granting of clemency and the rise of "special" legislation. For example, policy makers often think that legislation which makes expert testimony admissible in the trials of battered women who kill their batterers is the key to battered women's staying out of prison. Such measures can obstruct the possibility of clemency for women by creating the illusion that clemency is no longer necessary. "A statute allowing Battered Woman Syndrome evidence is not necessarily going to prevent convictions, but policy makers may feel that there is no longer a problem." Comments of Rebecca Isaacs in "Courtroom, Code and Clemency," 833. Moreover, the absence of "special" statutes is often cited in support of clemency. In Ohio, for example, Governor Celeste justified clemency for battered women by the fact that a state Supreme Court decision specifically barred such testimony until 1990 (when a statute permitting expert testimony on "battered woman syndrome" was passed). In Maryland, clemency activism was also based on the inadmissibility of evidence of battering; see also Rita Thaemert, "Till Violence Do Us Part," *State Legislatures,* 26 (March 1993) (noting that Florida's parole board has adopted a rule making "Battered Women's Syndrome" one of the criteria that may be considered in determining whether to grant clemency).

114. Statistics gathered by the National Clearinghouse for the Defense of Battered Women, Philadelphia (on file with author). It appears that only a small percentage of women accused of killing their batterers are acquitted at trial. Between 72 and 80 percent are convicted or accept a plea. Sue Osthoff, "Clemency For Battered Women," in *Double-Time* (National Clearinghouse for the Defense of Battered Women, 1990). Women who kill generally receive longer sentences than men who kill, serving an average of sixteen or seventeen years. Battered women who kill tend to receive even longer sentences. One statewide survey showed that 83.7 percent of these women received sentences ranging from twenty-five years to life. Linda L. Ammons, "Parole: Post Conviction Relief for Battered Women Who Kill Their Abusers," in "Defending Battered Women," 5.

115. Ammons, "Parole: Post Conviction Relief," 5. For example, the Georgia Department of Corrections in 1992 released a report indicating that 45 percent of the women incarcerated there for killing a husband or lover had been abused by that person. A 1989 Missouri study showed that of men and women incarcerated there for murdering partners, 89 percent of the women and 57 percent of the men reported that the

relationship was violent before the partner's death. Jane Totman, surveying women in a California state prison, found that of the thirty women there who had murdered partners, twenty-nine had been abused by them. See Angela Browne, *When Battered Women Kill,* 10 (1987). The National Clearinghouse for the Defense of Battered Women gathers statistics on this issue from around the country.

116. See, e.g., Gibbs, "Til Death Do Us Part," 44 (quoting psychologist Julie Blackman as saying "I've worked [with] battered women who have talked only briefly to their lawyers in the courtroom for 15 or 20 minutes and then they take a plea and do 15 to life . . . women who . . . don't speak English well, or women who are very quickly moved through the system, who take pleas and do substantial chunks of time, often without getting any real attention paid to the circumstances of their case"). See also Osthoff, "Defending Battered Women" (estimating that 72–80 percent of battered women who kill are convicted or accept a plea).

117. Jody Armour, "Just Deserts: Narrative, Perspective, Choice, and Blame," 57 *University of Pittsburgh Law Review* 525 (1996).

118. Donald Nicolson, "Telling Tales: Gender Discrimination, Gender Construction and Battered Women Who Kill," 3 *Feminist Legal Studies* 185 (1995). In this article, Nicolson details how English judges interpreted very differently the cases of two battered women who killed their assailants in similar factual contexts. In the case of Kiranjit Ahluwalia, the defendant was seen as passive and consequently treated by the court as mentally impaired. In the case of Sara Thornton, the defendant was treated as a "bad" woman and found guilty. Nicolson concludes that battered women who kill face the choice of being seen as "mad" or "bad," but either way their actions are not understood as rational.

Chapter 9: Motherhood and Battering

1. Martha Fineman, "The Neutered Mother," 46 *University of Miami Law Review* 653–54 (1992). See also Martha Fineman, *The Neutered Mother, the Sexual Family and Other Twentieth-Century Tragedies* (1995).

2. Martha Fineman, "Images of Mothers in Poverty Discourses," 1991 *Duke Law Journal* 274, 289–90; Martha Albertson Fineman, Preface, in *Mothers in Law: Feminist Theory and the Legal Regulation of Motherhood* (Martha Albertson Fineman and Isabel Karpin, eds., 1995).

3. Dorothy E. Roberts, "Motherhood and Crime," 79 *Iowa Law Review* 95, 97 (1993). See also Dorothy Roberts, *Killing the Black Body: Race, Reproduction and the Meaning of Liberty* (1997).

4. On the high correlation between pregnancy and battering, see Pauline Quirion, Judith Lennett, Kristen Lund, and Chanda Tuck, "Protecting Children Exposed to Domestic Violence in Contested Custody and Visitation Litigation," 6 *Boston University Public Interest Law Journal* 501 (1997) ("according to the Second National Family Violence Survey, the overall rate of domestic violence during pregnancy was fifteen percent in the first four months and seventeen percent during the remaining five months"). For the statistics given in the text, see Ann M. Delaney, "The

Time to Treat Domestic Violence as Serious Crime," *Indianapolis Star,* B4 (August 17, 1997). See also Evan Stark and Anne Flitcraft, *Women at Risk: Domestic Violence and Women's Health* 11 (1996) (noting that battered women are three times more likely to be injured during pregnancy than non-battered women); Kate Nicholsen, "Pregnancy and the Battering Taboo: Erasure (and Silencing) of Women in Legal and Social Contexts" (1992) (manuscript on file with author). There are other shocking statistics on this subject. The Chicago Department of Health reports that "4 percent to 17 percent of pregnant women are abused." Dr. Shireen Ahmad, "It Takes a Community to Prevent Domestic Violence," *Chicago Tribune,* 8 (May 4, 1997). In a *San-Diego Tribune* editorial, it was stated that "one woman in 12 is battered while she is pregnant." Key Daut Alvarez, "Education Is the Key to Curbing Abuse," *San-Diego Union-Tribune,* B9 (August 7, 1997). An *Arkansas Lawyer* article reports that it "is estimated that as many as 21% [of] pregnant women are being battered." Sandy Moll, "Letting an Old 'Family Secret' Out of the Closet," *Arkansas Lawyer,* 20 (Summer 1995).

5. Stark and Flitcraft, *Women at Risk,* 203; Delaney, "The Time to Treat Domestic Violence," B4. Stark and Flitcraft found a link between domestic violence and "poor pregnancy outcomes." Stark and Flitcraft, *Women at Risk,* xviii.
6. Jenny Knight, "Midwives and Physicians Focus on Domestic Abuse of Pregnant Women," *Milwaukee Journal Sentinel,* 19 (June 15, 1997). The article also notes that "violence is connected to low birth weight, an increase in stillbirths, miscarriages and pre-term delivery. Stress from abuse, including psychological abuse, may affect the supply of oxygen to the fetus."
7. See, e.g., "Inside the NFL: Boulware, Ravens Finally Get Together," *Chicago Tribune,* 10 (August 17, 1997).
8. "Police Report," *St. Petersburg Times,* 9 (February 17, 1997); "Metro Police Reports," *New Orleans Times-Picayune,* B2 (March 8, 1997); "Police Report," *Chicago Tribune,* 3 (May 15, 1997); "Police Log," *Orlando Sentinel,* 3 (May 22, 1997); "Police Log," *Orlando Sentinel,* K6 (June 1, 1997); "Metro Police Reports," *New Orleans Times-Picayune,* B4 (May 31, 1997); "Police Log," *Orlando Sentinel,* 3 (July 10, 1997); "Local Wanted," *Sun-Sentinel Ft. Lauderdale,* 4B (July 17, 1997); "Police Report, Metro Du Page," *Chicago Tribune,* 3 (July 23, 1997); "Local/State Palm Bay Map," *Florida Today,* 3B (August 1, 1997); "Community News," *Florida Times-Union,* 2 (August 2, 1997).
9. Kimberly Theidon, "Taking a Hit: Pregnant Drug Users and Violence," 22 *Contemporary Drug Problems* 4:663, 666–70 (1996).
10. Roberts, "Motherhood and Crime," 95, 115–16.
11. Evan Stark and Anne Flitcraft, "Woman Battering, Child Abuse and Social Heredity: What Is the Relationship?" in *Marital Violence,* 97 (Norman Johnson, ed., 1985). For other studies, see Nancy S. Erickson, "Battered Mothers of Battered Children: Using Our Knowledge of Battered Women to Defend Them Against Charges of Failure to Act," 1A *Current Perspectives in Psychological, Legal and Ethical Issues* 197, 200 (1991); Richard J. Gelles, 8 *The Myth of Battered Husbands and New Facts about Family Violence* 65–72 (1979); Jean G. Moore, "Yo-Yo Children: Victims of Matrimonial Violence," 54 *Child Welfare* 558–61 (1975) (describing the effect of the pattern of violence

on children); Evan Stark and Anne H. Flitcraft, "Child Abuse and the Battering of Women: Are They Related and How?" (paper presented at the National Family Violence Conference, Durham, N.H., 1984); Murray Straus, "A General Systems Theory Approach to a Theory of Violence Between Family Members," 12 *Social Sciences Information* 115.

12. See Stark and Flitcraft, "Woman Battering, Child Abuse and Social Heredity," 98–100 (offering statistical evidence that men — especially men who batter their wives — are more likely than women to batter their children). See also Coalition of Battered Women's Advocates, "Position Paper on Child Welfare," 467 (November 1988) ("It has been our experience that far too few child abusers are actually prosecuted and convicted by the courts; while too many battered women face child neglect charges").

13. See John Davidson, "It's Always the Mother," *Mirabella* 167 (May 1991); "Georgia Network Against Domestic Violence, Abused Mothers of Abused Children: A Perspective," *Network News* 1 (January 1990); Suzanne Groisser, "Battered Women and Their Battered Children: Criminal and Civil Allegations of the Woman's Failure to Protect," 3 (May 14, 1991) (manuscript on file with author).

14. Bernadine Dohrn, "Bad Mothers, Good Mothers and the State: Children on the Margins," 2 *University of Chicago Law School Roundtable* 1, 2 (1995).

15. Anna L. Tsing, "Monster Stories: Women Charged with Perinatal Endangerment," in *Uncertain Terms: Negotiating Gender in American Culture* (Faye D. Ginsburg and Anna L. Tsing, eds., 1990).

16. Sam Ehrlich, *Lisa, Hedda and Joel: The Steinberg Murder Case* 7 (1989) (quoting Gloria Steinem).

17. See Susan Brownmiller, "Hedda Nussbaum: Hardly a Heroine," *New York Times*, A25 (February 2, 1989).

18. Barbara Ehrenreich, "Susan Smith: Corrupted by Love," *Time*, 78 (August 7, 1995).

19. 515 A.2d 311 (Pa. Super. Ct. 1986).

20. *Matter of Christopher II*, 222 A.D.2d 900, 902 (N.Y. App. Div. 1995).

21. The issue of a battered mother's failure to protect has been accorded public attention not only in the Lisa Steinberg case but in other cases as well. In Houston, Robbi Boutwell pleaded guilty to manslaughter for the death of her son. See Groisser, "Battered Women and Their Battered Children," 30 (citing Barbara Whitaker, "Finding Levels of Victimization: Nussbaum, Cortez Abuse Cases Viewed Differently," *Newsday*, 9 [January 8, 1989]). Boutwell never struck her child, and she was beaten and had her life threatened when she told her batterer, Chris Zuiliani, not to bother the child. See Davidson, "It's Always the Mother," 167. Similarly, Abigail Cortez, a battered woman, was indicted for second-degree murder, second-degree manslaughter, and endangering the welfare of a child, in the same year and city as Hedda Nussbaum.

22. See Martha Minow, "Words and the Door to the Land of Change: Law, Language, and Family Violence, 43 *Vanderbilt Law Review* 1665, 1681 (1990).

23. On criminal liability, see Anne T. Johnson, "Criminal Liability for Parents Who Fail to Protect," 5 *Law and Inequality Journal* 359, 366–67 (1987); Groisser, "Bat-

tered Women and Their Battered Children, 26–29. On child endangerment, see, e.g., Del. Code Ann. tit. 11 §1102 (1996); Haw. Rev. Stat. Ann. §709-903.5 (West 1996); Iowa Code Ann. §726.6 (West 1996). Similar provisions exist in Illinois, Kansas, Maine, Missouri, Montana, New Jersey, New York, Ohio, Pennsylvania, Texas, and Wyoming. On injury to children, see, e.g., Cal. Penal Code §273a (West 1997); Conn. Gen. Stat. Ann. §53-21 (West 1997). On neglect, see, e.g., Ariz. Rev. Stat. Ann. §13-3619 (West 1997); Fla. Stat. Ann. §827.03(3)(a) (West 1997); Minn. Stat. Ann. §609.378 (West 1996). Similar provisions exist in Mississippi, Oregon, and Rhode Island. On child abuse, see, e.g., Fla. Stat. Ann. §827.03(1)(c) (West 1997); Nev. Rev. Stat. Ann. §200.508 (Michie 1995). Similar provisions exist in North Dakota, Utah, and Virginia. On battery to an unborn child, see 720 Ill. Comp. Stat. Ann. §5/12-3.1 (West 1997); N.D. Cent. Code §12.1-17.1-05 (1997); S.D. Codified Laws §22-18-1.2 (Michie 1997). See also 7 American Political Network, Abortion Report, no. 212 (1997), where Pennsylvania passed a feticide bill giving legal status to an unborn child under the Pennsylvania Crimes Code. Although North Dakota, South Dakota, and Pennsylvania specifically describe this crime as one of assault on a pregnant woman, women themselves are increasingly the targets of liability for acts they committed while pregnant, such as drug or alcohol abuse. See Dorothy Roberts, "Punishing Drug Addicts Who Have Babies: Women of Color, Equality, and the Right of Privacy," 104 *Harvard Law Review* 1419 (1991).

24. The Mississippi statute is Miss. Code Ann. §97-5-39 (1996); the Hawaii statute is Haw. Rev. Stat. Ann. §709-904 (Michie 1996).

25. See generally V. Pualani Enos, "Prosecuting Battered Mothers: State Laws' Failure to Protect Battered Women and Abused Children, 19 *Harvard Women's Law Journal* 229 (1996); Howard A. Davidson, "Child Abuse and Domestic Violence: Legal Connections and Controversies, 29 *Family Law Quarterly* 357, part 2 (1995); Audrey E. Stone and Rebecca J. Fialk, "Criminalizing the Exposure of Children to Family Violence: Breaking the Cycle of Abuse, 20 *Harvard Women's Law Journal* 205 (1997).

26. See Johnson, "Criminal Liability for Parents," 367 n.54 (citing Iowa Code Ann. §726.6.1e [West Supp. 1986]; Minn. Stat. §609.378 [1984]; Okla. Stat. Ann. tit. 21, §852.1a [Supp. 1990]).

27. *State v. Mott,* 931 P.2d 1046 (Ariz. 1997). Judge Feldman, in a lengthy dissent, accused the majority of depriving Ms. Mott of due process by refusing to admit evidence that might negate mens rea.

28. *Lane v. Commonwealth,* 949 S.W.2d 604 (Ky. 1997).

29. Iowa's child endangerment statute states that a person is guilty of the crime if the person "knowingly permits the continuing physical or sexual abuse of a child or minor. However, it is an affirmative defense to this subsection if the person had a reasonable apprehension that any action to stop the continuing abuse would result in substantial bodily harm to the person or the child or minor." Iowa Code Ann. §726.6 (West 1996). Minnesota provides a defense to its neglect or endangerment statute if "there was a reasonable apprehension in the mind of the defendant that acting to stop or prevent the neglect or endangerment would result in substantial bodily harm to the defendant or the child in retaliation." Minn. Stat. §609.378 (2) (1999).

30. See Erickson, "Battered Mothers of Battered Children," 200, 214 n. 26; Groisser, "Battered Women and Their Battered Children," 59.

31. For cases in which battered women are convicted of child abuse for failure to act, see *Commonwealth v. Cardwell*, 515 A.2d 211 (Pa. Super. Ct. 1986); *Commonwealth v. Howard*, 402 A. 2d 674, 678 (Pa. Super Ct. 1979); *State v. Williquette*, 385 N.W. 2d 145, 149–50 (Wis. 1986).

32. *In re ADR*, 542 N.E.2d 487, 490 (Ill. App. Ct. 1989); *In re Lonell J.*, 242 A.D.2d 58 (N.Y. App. Div. 1998); *In re Deandre T.*, 253 A.D.2d 497 (N.Y. App. Div. 1998); *In the Matter of Glenn G.*, 587 N.Y.S.2d 469 (N.Y. Fam. Ct. 1992); see also Kristian Miccio, "In the Name of Mothers and Children: Deconstructing the Myth of the Passive Battered Mother and the Protected Child in Child Neglect Proceedings," 58 *Albany Law Review* 1087 (1995).

33. *In the Interest of Betty J. W.*, 371 S.E.2d 326 (W. Va. 1988); *In the Matter of Aimee Janine Farley*, 469 N.W.2d 295 (Mich. 1991).

34. 931 P.2d 1046 (Ariz. 1997).

35. Id. at 1050.

36. Id. at 1057.

37. Id. at 1058.

38. Id. at 1060, 1064.

39. 482 S.E.2d 147 (W. Va. App. Ct. 1996).

40. Id. at 151, 152. Dr. Veronen was also the expert who testified in *State v. Kelly*, discussed in Chapter 8.

41. Id. at 157.

42. Id. at 158.

43. 574 N.E.2d 340 (Mass. 1991).

44. Id. at 345, 343.

45. Id. at 346.

46. Id. at 348.

47. Id. at 350.

48. 675 N.E.2d 1112 (Ind. App. 1996).

49. See Martha Mahoney, "Legal Images of Battered Women: Redefining the Issue of Separation," 90 *Michigan Law Review* 1, 44 n.198 (1991).

50. Martha Fineman, "Dominant Discourse, Professional Language and Legal Change in Child Custody Decisionmaking," 101 *Harvard Law Review* 727, 769, and n.166 (1988); see also Lenore Weitzman, *The Divorce Revolution* 230, 240 (1985) (noting that husbands spend even less time on child care when their wives are employed).

51. Mahoney, "Legal Images of Battered Women," 44.

52. For problems that women face in custody disputes generally, see Phyllis Chesler, *Mothers on Trial: The Battle for Children and Custody* (1986). For discussion of custody problems faced by women who are sexually active, see Maryland Special Joint Committee on Gender Bias in the Courts, *Gender Bias in the Courts* 35–37 (1989); "Report of the New York Task Force on Women in the Courts," 15 *Fordham Urban Law Journal* 1, 105–7 (1986–87). For discussion of how lesbian relationships adversely affect women's attempts to gain custody of their children, see Nancy Polikoff, "This

Child Does Have Two Mothers; Redefining Parenthood to Meet the Needs of Children in Lesbian-Mother and Other Nontraditional Families," 78 *Georgetown Law Journal* 459, 464–68 (1990). For problems battered women face in custody proceedings, see Naomi R. Cahn, "Civil Images of Battered Women: The Impact of Domestic Violence on Child Custody Decisions," 44 *Vanderbilt Law Review* 1041 (1991).

53. Mahoney, "Legal Images of Battered Women," 44–45.

54. Id. at 46.

55. Id.

56. Id. at 47.

57. See *Glasbrenner v. Sapio,* No. A-4263-88T5 (N.J. Super. Ct. App. Div. 1990), *cert. denied,* 584 A.2d 205 (N.J. 1990); Mahoney, "Legal Images of Battered Women," 45.

58. This issue was recently highlighted in the Simpson case. Although O. J. Simpson was acquitted in the criminal case, he was found liable for his wife Nicole's death in the civil case; nonetheless, he has been awarded custody of their two children. Cary Goldberg, "Simpson Wins Custody Fight for Two Children by Slain Wife," *New York Times,* A1 (December 21, 1996). However, in February 1999 the California Supreme Court ordered a new custody trial, finding that the judge failed to hear evidence that O. J. Simpson killed his ex-wife. As of October 1999, Simpson and the children's maternal grandparents were negotiating a custody settlement that would give Simpson permanent custody of the children. "O. J. to Retain Custody of the Children, Lawyer Says," *Desert News,* A10 (October 5, 1999). Other custody cases in which the father's killing of the mother was deemed irrelevant include *In re H.L.T.,* 298 S.E.2d 33 (Ga. Ct. App. 1981); *In re Lutgen,* 532 N.E.2d 976 (Ill. App. Ct. 1988); *Bartasavich v. Mitchell,* 471 A.2d 833 (Pa. Super. Ct. 1984). Cases in which the father's killing was taken into account include *In re Abdullah,* 423 N.E.2d 915 (Ill. 1981); *Viola v. Randolf W.,* 356 S.E. 2d 464, 470 (W. Va. App. Ct. 1987).

59. See Cahn, "Civil Images of Battered Women," 1055–78; Mahoney, "Legal Images of Battered Women," 345–46.

60. Many states have recognized that domestic violence affects the welfare of children, and have enacted legislation that makes violence by parents an issue to be considered in custody determinations. The strictest statues create a presumption against awarding custody to an abuser. N.D. Cent. Code §14-09-6.2(l)(j)(1999) ("if the court finds credible evidence that domestic violence has occurred, this evidence creates a rebuttable presumption that a parent who has perpetrated domestic violence may not be awarded sole or joint custody of a child"); Ariz. Rev. Stat. §25-403(B) (1999) ("the court shall consider evidence of domestic violence as being contrary to the best interests of the child"). Other states have similar statutes: Colo. Rev. Stat. Ann. §14-10-124(1.5)(m) (West 1999); Del. Code Ann. tit. 13, §705A (1999); Fla. Stat. Ann. §61.13(b)(2) (West 1999); La. Rev. Stat. Ann. §9:364(A) (West 1999); Minn. Stat. Ann. §518.17(2)(d) (West 1999); Okla. Stat. Ann. tit. 10, §21.1(D) (West 1999); Wash. Rev. Code Ann. §26.09.191(2) & (3) (West 1999); Wyo. Stat. Ann. §20-2-113(a) (Michie 1999). If there is evidence of domestic violence, some states require the court to make specific findings to support the custody decision. Mo. Rev. Stat. §452.375.11 (1999) ("the court shall make specific findings of fact to show that the custody or

visitation arrangement ordered by the court best protects the child and the parent or other family or household member who is the victim of domestic violence from any further harm"). Finally, other states simply require that evidence of domestic violence be considered as a factor in the custody determination. Mo. Rev. Stat. §452.375.2(5) (1999) ("the court shall determine custody in accordance with the best interests of the child and the court shall consider all relevant factors . . . including any history of abuse of any individuals involved"). See also Alaska Stat. §25.20.090 (Michie 1999); 750 Ill. Comp. Stat. Ann. §5/602(a)(6) (West 1999). For discussion of this issue, see Cahn, "Civil Images of Battered Women"; Catherine F. Klein and Leslye E. Orloff, "Providing Legal Protection for Battered Women: An Analysis of State Statutes and Case Law," 21 *Hofstra Law Review* 801, 950 (1993); Lynne R. Kurtz, Comment, "Protecting New York's Children: An Argument for the Creation of a Rebuttable Presumption Against Awarding a Spouse Abuser Custody of a Child," 60 *Albany Law Review* 1345 (1997); Jack M. Dalgleish, Jr., Annotation, "Construction and Effect of Statutes Mandating Consideration of, or Creating Presumptions Regarding, Domestic Violence in Awarding Custody of Children," 51 A.L.R.5th 241 (2000).
61. Mahoney, "Legal Images of Battered Women," 46.
62. See *Collins v. Collins,* 297 S.E.2d 901, 902 (W. Va. App. Ct. 1982).
63. See Cahn, "Civil Images of Battered Women," 1058, n.74 (discussing *Collins*).
64. Mahoney "Legal Images of Battered Women," 49.
65. See Christine A. Littleton, "Women's Experience and The Problem of Transition: Perspectives on Male Battering of Women," 1989 *University of Chicago Legal Forum* 23, 54 (1989).
66. See Cahn, "Civil Images of Battered Women," 1091 (citing Lenore E. Walker and Glenace E. Edwall, "Domestic Violence and Determination of Visitation and Custody in Divorce," in *Domestic Violence on Trial: Psychological and Legal Dimensions of Family Violence* 131 [Daniel J. Sonkin, ed., 1987]).
67. 664 N.E.2d 434 (Mass. 1996).
68. *Vaughan,* id. at 435–36.
69. Id. at 437.
70. Id. at 437–38.
71. Id. at 438–40.
72. Id. at 439.
73. Id. at 440, and n.12.
74. Ch. 179 (1998 Regular Session), Mass. House Bill No. 4951. In *Opinion of the Justices to the Senate,* 691 N.E.2d 911 (Mass. 1998), the Massachusetts Supreme Judicial Court held that this proposed act was constitutional.
75. See, e.g., N.D. Cent. Code 14-09-06.2 (1997); *Heck v. Reed,* 529 N.W.2d 155 (N.D. 1995).
76. 210 A.D.2d 741 (N.Y. App. Div. 1994).
77. *Pratt,* id. at 742.
78. Id. at 742–43.
79. 621 A.2d 267, 272–73 (Conn. 1993).

80. Dorothy Roberts, "Unshackling Black Motherhood," 95 *Michigan Law Review* 938 (1997); Dorothy Roberts, "The Unrealized Power of Mother," 5 *Columbia Journal of Gender and Law* 141 (1995); Dorothy Roberts, "Motherhood and Crime," 79 *Iowa Law Review* 95 (1993). See generally Marie Ashe and Naomi Cahn, "Child Abuse: A Problem for Feminist Theory," 2 *Texas Journal of Women and Law* (1993); Martha Fineman, "Images of Mothers in Poverty Discourses," 2 *Duke Law Journal* 274 (1991); Martha Fineman, "The Neutered Mother," 653; Stephanie M. Wildman, "The Power of Women," 2 *Yale Journal of Law and Feminism* 435 (1990).

81. See Lee Bowker, Michelle Arbitell, and J. Richard McFerron, "On the Relationship Between Wife Beating and Child Abuse," in *Feminist Perspectives on Wife Abuse* 164 (Kersti Yllö and Michele Bograd, eds., 1988).

Chapter 10: Engaging with the State

1. The phrase "engaging with the state" is from Nickie Charles, "Feminist Politics, Domestic Violence and the State," 43 *The Sociological Review* 617 (1995). See also Claire Reinelt, "Moving onto the Terrain of the State: The Battered Women's Movement and the Politics of Engagement," in *Feminist Organizations, Harvest of the New Women's Movement* 84 (Myra Marx Ferree and Patricia Yancey Martin, eds., 1995). As Deborah Rhode has observed, there are many dimensions to the term "the state." See Deborah L. Rhode, "Feminism and the State," 107 *Harvard Law Review* 1181, 1182 (1994). She notes that "most feminist work refers to 'the state' without defining it" and uses the term synonymously with central government. Some theorists, however, view the state more broadly, as all of the "administrative, legal, bureaucratic and coercive systems that structure social relations." Id. at 1182. Here, I use the term in the conventional sense of federal and state government.

2. For works on feminism and the role of the state, see, e.g., Margaret A. Baldwin, "Public Women and the Feminist State," 20 *Harvard Women's Law Journal* 47, 53–54 (1997); Judith Allen, "Does Feminism Need a Theory of 'The State'?" in *Playing the State: Australian Feminist Interventions* 21–22 (Sophie Watson, ed., 1990); Charles, "Feminist Politics," 619–20, 623.

3. Susan Schechter, *Women and Male Violence: The Visions and Struggles of the Battered Women's Movement* 94, 201 (1982). Schechter identifies the role of the state as an important issue for the battered women's movement and examines the movement's ambivalence toward the state in a number of different ways. Id. at 201.

4. Reinelt, "Moving onto the Terrain of the State," 91; Schechter, *Women and Male Violence,* 53–81.

5. Schechter, *Women and Male Violence,* 29–79.

6. Id. at 26. In this section, I am simplifying a complex story of different approaches within the battered women's movement, which Schechter describes in detail.

7. Id. at 185–89. See also Merle H. Weiner, "From Dollars to Sense: A Critique of Government Funding for the Battered Women's Shelter Movement," 9 *Law and Inequality Journal* 185, 277 (1991).

8. Schechter, *Women and Male Violence,* 201.

9. Catharine A. MacKinnon, "Feminism, Marxism, Method, and the State: Toward Feminist Jurisprudence," 8 *Signs: Journal of Women in Culture and Society* 635, 644 (1983). MacKinnon continues: "The law sees and treats women the way men see and treat women. The liberal state coercively and authoritatively constitutes the social order in the interests of men as a gender, through its legitimizing norms, relation to society, and substantive policies. . . . Substantively, the way the male point of view frames an experience is the way it is framed by state policy."

10. Carol Pateman, *The Sexual Contract* (1988).

11. Rosemary Pringle and S. Watson, "Women's Interests and the Post-Structuralist State," in *Destabilizing Theory: Contemporary Feminist Debates* 53–73 (Michelle Barrett and Ann Philips, eds., 1992). See generally Baldwin, "Public Women," 143–61; Michel Foucault, "Two Lectures," in *Power/Knowledge: Selected Interviews and Other Writings, 1972–1977* 78, 97 (Colin Gordon, ed., 1980), quoted in Steven L. Winter, "The 'Power' Thing," 82 *Virginia Law Review* 721, 797–98 (1996).

12. Foucault, "Two Lectures," 78, 97.

13. Kathleen J. Ferraro, "The Dance of Dependency: A Genealogy of Domestic Violence Discourse," 11 *Hypatia* 77, 89 (Fall 1996).

14. Id. See also Forum, "Mandating Prosecution in Domestic Violence," 7 *UCLA Women's Law Journal* 169 (1997). For discussion of various provisions of VAWA and how violence against women has become criminalized under VAWA through the creation of new crimes, longer prison sentences, mandatory arrests, and mandatory restitution, see George B. Stevenson, "Federal Antiviolence and Abuse Legislation: Toward Elimination of Disparate Justice for Women and Children," 33 *Willamette Law Review* 847, 851–52, 857–58 (1997). Several provisions of VAWA reflect its pro-criminalization stance. See 18 U.S.C. § 2247 (1994) (amended 1998) (providing increased criminal penalties for repeat offenders of any provision of the Act and amending sentencing guidelines); 18 U.S.C. § 2262(a)(1)–(2) (1994) (amended 1996) (creating criminal penalty for violation of interstate protection orders); 18 U.S.C. § 2261(a)(1) (1994) (creating criminal penalty for travel across state lines to commit acts of domestic violence); 42 U.S.C. § 13992 (1994) (allowing grants to the states to provide sensitivity training to better equip prosecutors and law enforcement officers to respond to domestic violence).

15. See Sheila James Kuehl, "Introduction to Forum: Mandatory Prosecution in Domestic Violence Cases," 7 *UCLA Women's Law Journal* 169 (1997).

16. For the range of VAWA Office of Justice Program grants, see www.ojp.usdoj.gov/vawgo/htm, visited June 1, 1999.

17. Many states and the District of Columbia have enacted mandatory arrest laws. See generally Marion Wanless, "Mandatory Arrest: A Step Toward Eradicating Domestic Violence, but Is It Enough?" 1996 *University of Illinois Law Review* 533, 554–57. For discussion of no-drop policies, see generally Cheryl Hanna, "No Right to Choose: Mandated Victim Participation in Domestic Violence Prosecutions," 109 *Harvard Law Review* 1849 (1996); Angela Corsilles, Note, "No-Drop Policies in the Prosecution of Domestic Violence Cases: Guarantee to Action or Dangerous Solution?" 63 *Fordham Law Review* 853 (1994).

18. See Linda G. Mills, "Intuition and Insight: A New Job Description for the Battered Woman's Prosecutor and Other More Modest Proposals," 71 *UCLA Women's Law Journal* 183 (1997).

19. See, e.g., Marion Wanless, "Mandatory Arrest," 533, 554–57; Joan Zorza, "Mandatory Arrest for Domestic Violence: Why It May Prove the Best First Step in Curbing Repeat Abuse," 10 *Criminal Justice* 2 (Fall 1995).

20. For a comprehensive analysis of the current debate surrounding no-drop policies and mandatory prosecution, see Hanna, "No Right to Choose." For a stand in favor of aggressive prosecution, see Donna Wills, "Domestic Violence: The Case for Aggressive Prosecution," 71 *UCLA Women's Law Journal* 173 (1995).

21. See Wills, "Domestic Violence."

22. For a general discussion on the problems of mandatory prosecution and no-drop policies, see Mills, "Intuition and Insight"; Donna M. Welch, "Mandatory Arrest of Domestic Abusers: Panacea or Perpetuation of the Problem of Abuse?" 43 *De Paul Law Review* 1133 (1994); Miriam H. Ruttenberg, "A Feminist Critique of Mandatory Arrest: An Analysis of Race and Gender in Domestic Violence Policy," 2 *American University Journal of Gender and the Law* 171 (1994).

23. See, e.g., Art Golab, " 'No-Drop' Rule on Abuse Puts Woman in Jail," *Chicago Sun-Times,* 1 (December 6, 1996); John Johnson, "Tougher Abuse Laws Bite on the Bitten; Mandatory Arrest for Domestic Violence Is Putting More Women in Jail, but the Evidence Is Controversial," *Guardian* (London) 11 (April 30, 1996).

24. Donna Coker, "Enhancing Autonomy for Battered Women: Lessons from Navajo Peacemaking," 47 *UCLA Law Review* 1, 48–49 (1999).

25. Linda Mills, "On the Other Side of Silence: Affective Lawyering for Intimate Abuse," 81 *Cornell Law Review* 1225, 1250 (1996).

26. Sally Engle Merry, "Wife Battering and the Ambiguities of Rights," in *Identities, Politics, and Rights* 271, 304 (Austin Sarat and Thomas R. Kearns, eds., 1995).

27. See Sally Goldfarb, "The Civil Rights Remedy of the Violence Against Women Act: Legislative History, Policy Implications and Litigation Strategy," 4 *Journal of Law and Policy* 391 (1996).

28. 8 U.S.C. § 1154(a) (1994) (funding for women's shelters); 42 U.S.C. § 10416(3)(2)(E) (1994) (domestic abuse hotline); 42 U.S.C. § 10418 (1994) (rape education and prevention programs); 42 U.S.C. §§ 13701, 13991, 13992, 14036 (1994) (training for federal and state judges).

29. For reforms for battered immigrant women, see, e.g., 8 U.S.C. § 1154(a) (providing self-petition by immigrant women for legally recognized status). As for other reforms, criminal sanctions will be imposed, for example, if a person crosses state lines with an intent to violate a protective order, or for causing injury to a spouse or intimate partner in the process of forcing that person to cross state lines by use of force, coercion, duress, or fraud. 18 U.S.C. § 2262(a) (1994). Punishment ranges from five years of imprisonment for violations that do not result in physical injury to life imprisonment in cases where the violation results in death. Fines may also be imposed. 18 U.S.C. § 2262(b). For the civil rights remedy, see 42 U.S.C. § 13981 (1994).

30. Statement of Sen. Biden, 1991 S. Hearing 369 at 2.
31. The civil rights remedy states, in pertinent part:

> (b) . . . All persons within the United States shall have the right to be free from crimes of violence motivated by gender. . . .
> (c) Cause of Action. A person (including a person who acts under color of any statute, ordinance, regulation, custom, or usage of any State) who commits a crime of violence motivated by gender and thus deprives another of the right declared in subsection (b) of this section shall be liable to the party injured, in an action for the recovery of compensatory and punitive damages, injunctive and declaratory relief, and such other relief as a court may deem appropriate. (42 U.S.C. § 13981 [1994])

32. On corroboration requirements, see Susan Stefan, "The Protection Racket: Rape Trauma Syndrome, Psychiatric Labeling and Law," 88 *Northwestern University Law Review* 1271, 1319 n.248, 1333 (1994). The cautionary instruction began in England in the seventeenth century. The three common elements of the cautionary instruction are: "(1) rape is a charge that is easily made by the victim, (2) rape is a charge that is difficult for the defendant to disprove, and (3) the testimony of the victim requires more careful scrutiny by the jury than the testimony of the other witnesses in the trial." A. Thomas Morris, Note, "The Empirical, Historical, and Legal Case Against the Cautionary Instruction: A Call for Legislative Reform," 1988 *Duke Law Journal* 154–55 (1988). On resistance "to the utmost," see Donald A. Dripps, "Beyond Rape: An Essay on the Difference Between the Presence of Force and the Absence of Consent," 92 *Columbia Law Review* 1780, 1783 (1992); see also Rosemary J. Scalo, Note, "What Does 'No' Mean in Pennsylvania? — The Pennsylvania Supreme Court's Interpretation of Rape and the Effectiveness of the Legislature's Response," 49 *Villanova Law Review* 193, 221 n.151 (1995).
33. See, e.g., Alabama Code § 12-21-203 (1999); New Jersey Statutes Annotated § 2A:84A-32.1 (West 1999); New Jersey Statutes Annotated § 2C:14-7 (West 1999); Ohio Rules of Evidence §404 (1999).
34. Senate Reports No. 138, 103d Cong., 1st Sess. 52 (1993) ("Judges and juries will determine motivation from the totality of the circumstances surrounding the event").
35. 28 U.S.C. § 534 (1994).
36. The White House Conference on Hate Crimes held on November 10, 1997, marked the attempt of the federal government to include gender bias in the federal hate crimes criminal statute. See the National Organization for Women Legislative Update, December 12, 1997. In addition, the Leadership Conference on Civil Rights prepared a report, "Cause for Concern: Hate Crimes in America," calling for violence against women to classify as a hate crime.
37. See Joseph M. Fernandez, "Bringing Hate Crime into Focus — The Hate Crime Statistics Act of 1990," Pub. L. No. 101-275, 26 *Harvard Civil Rights–Civil Liberties Law Review* 261, 285 n.129 (1991) (quoting *Federal Bureau of Investigation, U.S. Dep't of Justice, Uniform Code Reporting Summary Reporting System: Draft Hate Crime Data*

Collection Guidelines 2 [1990]); see also Marguerite Angelari, "Hate Crime Statistics: A Promising Tool for Fighting Violence Against Women," 2 *American University Journal of Gender and the Law* 63 (1994).

38. Hate Crimes Prevention Act, S. 622, 106th Congress (1999).

39. Reva Siegel, "The Rule of Love: Wife Beating as Prerogative and Privacy," 105 *Yale Law Journal* 2117 (1996).

40. See Senate Reports No. 545, 101st Cong., 2d Sess. 40–41 (1990).

41. *Brzonkala v. Virginia Polytechnic and State University,* 935 F. Supp. 779 (W.D. Va. 1996), *rev'd,* 132 F.3d 949 (4th Cir. 1997), *rev'd en banc,* 169 F.3d 820 (4th Cir. 1999), *cert. granted* 120 S.Ct. 605 (1999) *sub nom. United States v. Morrison, Brzonkala v. Morrison.* See Linda Greenhouse, "Justices Cool to Law about Women," *New York Times,* A18 (January 12, 2000) (reporting on oral argument in the Supreme Court in *Morrison*).

42. Only a few cases involving domestic violence have been litigated under the civil rights remedy; see *Seaton v. Seaton,* 971 F.Supp. 1188 (E.D. Tenn. 1997); *Doe v. Doe,* 929 F.Supp. 608 (D. Conn. 1996).

43. See *United States v. Bailey,* 112 F.3d 758 (4th Cir. 1997); *United States v. Wright,* 965 F.Supp. 1307 (D. Neb. 1997); *United States v. Casciano,* 124 F.3d 106 (2d Cir. 1997).

44. 132 F.3d 949, 952 (4th Cir. 1997). The Supreme Court has granted certiorari.

45. Jan Vertefeuille, "Judges Hear Violence Against Women Act Debated; Congress Found Courts Don't Treat Female Victims Fairly," *Roanoke Times,* A5 (June 5, 1997).

46. *Dolin v. West,* 22 F. Supp. 2d 1343 (M.D. Fla. 1998); *Kuhn v. Kuhn,* 1998 WL 673629 (N.D. Ill. 1998); *Ziegler v. Ziegler,* 28 F. Supp. 2d 601 (E.D. Wash. 1998); *Seaton v. Seaton,* 1188; *Doe v. Doe,* 608.

47. 22 F. Supp. 2d 1343, 1351 (M.D. Fla. 1998).

48. *Kuhn v. Kuhn,* WL 673629; *Ziegler v. Ziegler,* 601. In the other two cases, the District Courts have ruled that VAWA is constitutional, but neither court has yet addressed the sufficiency of the plaintiffs' allegations. See *Seaton v. Seaton,* 1188; *Doe v. Doe,* 608.

49. 1998 WL 673629 (N.D. Ill. 1998) at *1–*2.

50. 28 F. Supp. 2d 601, 606–7 (E.D. Wash. 1998).

51. *Kuhn v. Kuhn,* WL 673629 at *6.

52. *Ziegler v. Ziegler,* 607.

53. See, e.g., *Brzonkala v. Virginia Polytechnic and State University,* 935 F. Supp. 779, *rev'd,* 132 F.3d 949, *rev'd en banc,* 169 F.3d 820; *Anisimov v. Lake,* 982 F. Supp. 531 (N.D. Ill. 1997); *Mattison v. Click Corp. of America,* Inc., 1998 WL 32597 (E.D. Pa. 1998). Cf. *Wilson v. Diocese of New York of the Episcopal Church,* 1998 WL 82921 (S.D. N.Y. 1998) (alleging sexual assault of a male church musician by a priest).

54. See *Braden v. Piggly Wiggly,* 4 F. Supp. 2d 1357 (M.D. Ala. 1998) (the court declined to infer gender animus in a case in which the plaintiff alleged sexual assault by her supervisor at work, which resulted in hospitalization and severe emotional distress and trauma). But see *Anisimov v. Lake,* 531 (the court held that the plaintiff sufficiently pleaded gender animus under VAWA by averring that the defendant employer fondled her, grabbed her breasts, assaulted her, and attempted to rape her).

55. 132 F.3d 949, 964, *rev'd en banc,* 169 F.3d 820, *cert. granted,* 120 S. Ct. 605.

56. 132 F.3d at 964.

57. *Brzonkala,* 169 F.3d 820, 910.

58. Neil A. Lewis, "A Court Becomes a Model of Conservative Pursuits," *New York Times,* A1 (May 24, 1999).

59. *Ziegler v. Ziegler,* 606, 607 (citing S. Rep. No. 102-197, at 50 [1991]).

60. For a more detailed analysis of the "gender animus" requirement under VAWA, see Julie Goldscheid, "Gender-Motivated Violence: Developing a Meaningful Paradigm for Civil Rights Enforcement," 22 *Harvard Women's Law Journal* 123 (1999).

61. Siegel, "Rule of Love," 2202.

62. Reinelt, "Moving onto the Terrain of the State," 91.

63. HR 357, 106th Cong. §743 (1999). The Battered Women's Employment Protection Act provides unemployment insurance for victims of domestic violence who are forced to leave their jobs as a result of domestic violence, and entitles employed victims of domestic violence to take reasonable leave under the Family and Medical Leave Act of 1993 to seek medical help, legal assistance, counseling, and safety planning and assistance without penalty from their employers. H.R. 357, 106th Cong. § 743 (1999). The Victims of Abuse Insurance Protection Act provides that victims of domestic violence are protected against insurance discrimination. H.R. 357, 106th Cong. §423 (1999).

64. H.R. 357, 106th Cong. § 404 (1999); H.R. 357, 106th Cong. § 732 (1999).

65. The focus, instead, has been on criminalization. In an October 1995 proclamation declaring that month the first National Domestic Violence Awareness Month, President Clinton remarked that "Americans are fortunate that knowledge about domestic violence has increased and that public interest in deterrence is stronger than ever." http://www.usdog.gov/vawo/procla.htm, visited May 6, 1999. However, this "knowledge" and "interest in deterrence" were devoid of any recognition of the established link between domestic violence and welfare. Instead, the focus was on "the tough new sanctions" in the Violent Crime Control and Law Enforcement Act of 1994. In a radio address to the nation during this first annual National Domestic Violence Awareness Month, President Clinton related the story of a woman who was "battered and terrorized" by her husband for more than twenty years before "she got up the courage to leave the marriage and seek help," but he failed to recognize and address the economic restraints preventing many women from leaving their batterers. Instead, he touted laws "bann[ing] assault weapons from our streets and our schools," "impos[ing] tougher penalties for repeat offenders," and putting more police out on the streets. Id.; http://www.usdoj.gov/vawo/radio.htm, visited May 6, 1999. In 1996, the President recognized the need to "encourage all Americans to increase public awareness and understanding of domestic abuse as well as the needs of its victims," but the focus remained on criminal measures "with which to prosecute and punish criminals who intentionally prey on women and children." http://www.usdoj.gov/vawo/procla96.htm, visited May 6, 1999. In 1999, Janet Reno testified before the Senate Judiciary Committee about reducing domestic violence, also focusing on criminal measures. She noted six priorities identified by the Department of Justice in fighting domestic violence, including "the vigorous federal

prosecution of domestic violence . . . offenders under VAWA," and touted "new specialized prosecution and law enforcement units" that have sprung up around the country during the previous two years. http://www.usdoh.gov/vawo/ag796.htm, visited May 6, 1999.

66. The welfare legislation is Personal Responsibility and Work Opportunity Reconciliation Act of 1996, Pub. L. No. 104-193, 110 Stat. 2105 (1996) (eliminating the open-ended federal entitlement program of Aid to Families with Dependent Children and providing time-limited cash assistance for needy families through the creation of block grants to states). Research has established the link between domestic violence and welfare dependency. See Jody Raphael, Report of the Taylor Institute, *Domestic Violence: Telling the Untold Welfare-to-Work Story* (January 30, 1995). Taylor Institute's survey of welfare-to-work programs around the country found that domestic violence was one of the greatest obstacles in assisting program participants to move off welfare and into the labor market. See also Jody Raphael, "Domestic Violence and Welfare Receipt: Toward a New Feminist Theory of Welfare Dependency," 19 *Harvard Women's Law Journal* 201, 208 (1996); Lucie E. White, "No Exit: Rethinking 'Welfare Dependency' from a Different Ground," 81 *Georgetown Law Journal* 1961, 2000 (1993); Martha F. Davis and Susan J. Kraham, "Protecting Women's Welfare in the Face of Violence," 22 *Fordham Urban Law Journal* 1141 (1995).

67. As a result of the efforts of both violence and welfare advocates working together, the Personal Responsibility and Work Opportunity Reconciliation Act of 1996 allows states to adopt the Family Violence Option (FVO), which would allow them to exempt a family from the act's sixty-month cap on state benefits "if the family includes an individual who has been battered or subjected to extreme cruelty." 42 U.S.C. § 608(a)(7)(C)(i) (1996). Implementation of the FVO also allows states to waive time limits when a member of a family has been a victim of domestic violence or is at risk of domestic violence. 42 U.S.C. § 602(a)(7)(A)(iii). Jody Raphael, however, concludes that although the FVO is implemented in most states, it is unclear whether its main objective—to provide battered women with extra time and services in obtaining employment—is truly effective in assisting these women in making the transition from welfare to work. Jody Raphael, "The Family Violence Option," 5 *Violence Against Women* 449, 455–56, 465 (1999).

Chapter 11: Lawmaking as Education

1. Jane Gross, "Simpson Case Galvanizes U.S. about Domestic Violence," *New York Times*, A6 (July 4, 1994).

2. Jim Newton and Andrea Ford, "Ito Says Jury Can Hear Stalking, Abuse Claims," *Los Angeles Times*, 1 (Jan. 19, 1995).

3. *People of the State of California v. Orenthal James Simpson*, People's Motion to Introduce Expert Testimony Regarding Domestic Violence, filed Sept. 11, 1995.

4. Alan Dershowitz, *Reasonable Doubts*, 19 (1996).

5. Jeffrey Toobin, *The Run of His Life: The People v. O. J. Simpson* 54 (1997).

6. Id. at 245, 273.

7. Christopher Darden, *In Contempt,* 182–83 (1996).

8. Marcia Clark, *Without a Doubt,* 339, 244–49, 179–80 (1997).

9. Id. at 257, 179.

10. Vincent Bugliosi, *Outrage: The Five Reasons Why O. J. Simpson Got Away with Murder* 115 (1996).

11. Transcript #248, "Talk Back Live" (1:00 a.m. ET), October 9, 1995.

12. For a discussion of issues of race and gender in the O. J. Simpson case, see *Postmortem, the O. J. Simpson Case: Justice Confronts Race, Domestic Violence, Lawyers, Money and the Media* (Jeffrey Abramson, ed., 1996); Cheryl I. Harris, "Myths of Race and Gender in the Trials of O. J. Simpson and Susan Smith—Spectacle of Our Times," 35 *Washburn Law Journal* 225 (1996); Nancy S. Ehrenreich, "O. J. Simpson and the Myth of Gender/Race Conflict," 67 *University of Colorado Law Review* 931 (1996); Devon W. Carbado, "The Construction of O. J. Simpson as a Racial Victim," 32 *Harvard Civil Rights–Civil Liberties Law Review* 49 (1997).

13. "Judge in Simpson Trial Hands Defense Team Two Setbacks: Domestic Violence Testimony to Be Allowed," *Baltimore Sun,* September 18, 1996, at 4A. This Associated Press article was reprinted in a number of newspapers, including the *Dallas Morning News,* the *San Francisco Chronicle,* and the *Charleston Gazette.*

14. Id. See also Donn Esmonde, "Simpson Case Puts Domestic Violence at Center Stage," *Buffalo News* (December 7, 1996); Harriet Chiang and Susan Sward, "Jury Says Simpson Must Pay," *San Francisco Chronicle,* A1 (February 5, 1997).

15. See, e.g., Barry Shick, "Tried and True," *Newsweek,* 32 (February 17, 1997).

16. Id.

17. Matt Krasnowski, "Perturbed Sometimes Rambling O. J. Tries to Set Record Straight," *San Diego Tribune,* A1 (February 6, 1996).

18. For example, see the special report on domestic violence among athletes in *Sports Illustrated* (August 1995). More recently, a number of other college and professional athletes have been accused of domestic violence. In June 1999 Jim Brown, a former professional football player and Hall of Famer, was accused of threatening to kill his wife and destroying her car. Following the trial, he was convicted only of destruction of property and was sentenced to three years of probation, four hundred hours of community service, and one year of domestic violence counseling. "Jim Brown Draws Probation, Violence Counseling," *Seattle Post-Intelligencer* D2 (October 6, 1999). The problem of violence by athletes has become so widespread that an organization has been founded to try to stop the violence. Kathy Redmond, the founder of the National Coalition of Women Against Violent Athletes, was herself a victim of rape by a college athlete. Harvey Araton, "Sports of the Times; Isn't There Anyone Listening," *New York Times* D1 (December 23, 1999). See also Note, "Out of Bounds: Professional Sports Leagues and Domestic Violence," 109 *Harvard Law Review* 1048 (1996).

19. See Armanda Cooley, Carrie Bess, and Marsha Rubin-Jackson with Tom Byrnes, *Madam Foreman: A Rush to Judgment?* (1995); Marcia Clark, *Without a Doubt.*

20. Neil Websdale, Maureen Sheeran, and Byron Johnson, *Reviewing Domestic Violence Fatalities: Summarizing National Developments* (1999) on the Office of Vio-

lence Against Women web site at http://www.vaw.umn.edu./FinalDocuments/
fatality.htm.

21. Myrna S. Raeder, "The Admissibility of Prior Acts of Domestic Violence: Simpson
and Beyond," 69 *Southern California Law Review* 1463 (1996). See also Myrna S.
Raeder, "The Better Way: The Role of Batterers' Profiles and Expert 'Social Framework' Background in Cases Implicating Domestic Violence," 68 *University of Colorado Law Review* 147 (1997).

22. Raeder, "The Admissibility of Prior Acts," 1465. See also Donna Meredith Matthews,
"Making the Crucial Connection: A Proposed Threat Hearsay Exception," 27 *Golden
Gate University Law Review* 117 (1997); Karleen F. Murphy, Note, "A Hearsay Excep-
tion for Physical Abuse," 27 *Golden Gate University Law Review* 497 (1997).

23. Raeder, "The Better Way," 160–62; Benjamin Z. Rice, "A Voice from *People v. Simpson:* Reconsidering the Propensity Rule in Spousal Homicide Cases," 29 *Loyola Law
Review* 939 (1996).

24. Raeder, "The Better Way," 160–62.

25. B. J. Palermo, "A Rush to Reform," 83 *ABA Journal* 20 (April 1997); Brae Canlen,
"I'm O. J. — You're O. J.: How the O. J. Simpson Case Has Affected the Legal System," 17 *California Lawyer* 28 (1997); "Talk Back Live," Transcript #248, October 9,
1995; Esmonde, "Domestic Violence at Center Stage," C1; Jill Hudson, "Domestic
Abuse Cases Rise Sharply," *Buffalo Sun*, 18 (March 3, 1997). The O. J. Simpson trial
had an immediate effect on the law of evidence in California. After the trial, a law
was enacted that allows evidence of hearsay alleging domestic violence or threats.
In one of the law's first uses, diary entries of a woman who was allegedly murdered
by her husband were read to a jury in his murder trial. The diary entries describe
beatings by her husband during the last few weeks of her life. "Victim's Diary Read
in Court," *Sacramento Bee* A5 (May 28, 1997).

26. For child custody laws, see B. J. Palermo, "A Rush to Reform," 83 *April ABA Journal* 20 (1997). For exceptions to the hearsay rule, see generally Raeder, "The Better
Way"; Matthews, "Making the Crucial Connection"; Murphy, "A Hearsay Exception."

Chapter 12: Education as Lawmaking

1. Elizabeth M. Schneider, "Legal Reform Efforts for Battered Women: Past, Present
and Future" (1990) (manuscript on file with author).

2. Some of my recommendations in the Ford Foundation report were for meetings,
programs, and dissemination of materials that would bring the two communities
together and provide greater opportunities to make academic work useful to activists and activist experience useful to academics. Id. at 84–86.

3. The Battered Women's Advocacy Project was founded in 1988 by Sarah Buel and
Suzanne Groisser. Many Harvard Law School students have been actively involved in
the work of the project, which conducts a range of training programs for advocates
and educational programs on issues of violence against women.

4. In 1990 the Report of the Dean's Public Interest Advisory Committee of Harvard

Law School recommended the broader integration of clinical and classroom methodology within the law school curriculum for first-year required courses as well as
elective courses.

5. The 1990 Report of the Dean's Public Interest Advisory Committee of Harvard Law
School also emphasized the educational importance of this additional class hour for
clinical students, noting its future use in this course: "In passing, we note that direct faculty involvement in public interest clinical teaching can be increased in yet
another way. In second and third year courses, classroom teachers offering optional
clinical components to their courses should be urged to add one class hour per week
(i.e., classroom credit) in a seminar with their clinical students. . . . Visiting Professor Elizabeth M. Schneider will use this exact model for her Battered Women and
the Law course in the spring of 1991. Again, with fieldwork supervisors in attendance, the connection between class and placement would be deepened. The Committee feels that all parties — students, supervisors and faculty — would benefit from
the interaction." The clinical component of the class had a number of unique fea-
tures. First, the extra hour of class followed immediately after the two-hour class for
everyone, but it met in a different room. Part of the reason that I had the clinical
students move to a different classroom was to avoid the feeling of exclusion that the
"non-clinical" students might have experienced had we stayed in the same room
and appeared to continue discussion after they left. This turned out to be particularly important, both logistically and humanly, because as the semester continued,
many "non-clinical" students were sorry that they had not taken the clinical component and wanted to come to the clinic hour in order to continue discussion from
the previous two-hour class. Picking up and moving to a new room allowed me to
re-focus the clinical students on integrating theory with practice in their discussion
in the clinical hour. The aim of the additional clinical classroom hour was to focus
the clinical students on the specific ways the themes and issues that we had covered
in the previous class related to the work they were doing in their clinical placement.
The class was a two-credit seminar, and the clinical students also received from two
to four clinic credits: one clinic credit for each five hours of clinical work.

6. I had first come to know Sarah Buel in my work on the report for the Ford Foundation, and she had subsequently been a student in my class on gender discrimination at Harvard in the winter term of 1990. Sarah performed a multitude of roles in
the class on battered women and the law. She was the direct clinical supervisor of a
number of students who did not have clinical supervisors in their placements, and
a general troubleshooter to the rest. Students also consulted her on their papers.
Her experience as a formerly battered woman, battered women's activist in Massachusetts for the past ten years, and then a prosecutor handling domestic violence
cases, meant that she added a unique perspective to classroom discussion. I consulted with her regularly on all aspects of the class. Later she became supervisor
of domestic violence prosecutions in the Norfolk County District Attorney's Office,
Quincy, Massachusetts. She is now teaching a clinical program on domestic violence
at University of Texas Law School.

7. Mary Joe Frug, "Securing Job Equality for Women: Labor Market Hostility to Work-

ing Mothers," 59 *Boston University Law Review* 55 (1979); Mary Joe Frug, "Re-reading Contracts: A Feminist Analysis of a Contracts Casebook," 34 *American University Law Review* 1065 (1985).

8. The first edition of the casebook was published soon after Mary Joe's death under her own name. Mary Joe Frug, *Women and the Law* (1991). The second edition was published as Judith G. Greenberg, Martha L. Minow, and Dorothy E. Roberts, *Mary Joe Frug's Women and the Law* (2nd ed., 1998).

9. In order to protect the students' privacy, I do not use their names when quoting from their reflection pieces.

10. See, e.g., American Bar Association Commission on Women in the Profession, *Elusive Equality* (1996); Symposium, "Women in Legal Education—Pedagogy, Law, Theory and Practice," 38 *Journal of Legal Education* (1988). See also Mary E. Becker, "Obscuring the Struggle: Sex Discrimination, Social Security, and Stone, Seidman and Tushnet's *Constitutional Law*," 89 *Columbia Law Review* 264 (1989); Leslie Bender, "A Lawyer's Primer on Feminist Theory and Tort," 38 *Journal of Legal Education* 3 (1988); Jennifer Gerarda Brown, "To Give Them Countenance: The Case for a Women's Law School," 22 *Harvard Women's Law Journal* 1 (1999); Mary I. Coombs, "Crime in the Stacks, or a Tale of a Text: A Feminist Response to a Criminal Law Casebook," 38 *Journal of Legal Education* 117 (1988); Lucinda M. Finley, "Breaking Women's Silence in Law: The Dilemma of the Gendered Nature of Legal Reasoning," 64 *Notre Dame Law Review* 886 (1989); Ann E. Freedman, "Feminist Legal Method in Action: Challenging Racism, Sexism and Homophobia in Law School," 24 *Georgia Law Review* 849 (1990); Mary Joe Frug, "Rereading Contracts"; Kit Kinports, "Engendering Evidence," 1991 *University of Illinois Law Review* 413; Rosemary C. Hunter, "Gender in Evidence: Masculine Norms vs. Feminist Reforms," 19 *Harvard Women's Law Journal* 127 (1996); Vicki C. Jackson, "Empiricism, Gender and Legal Pedagogy: An Experiment in a Federal Courts Seminar at Georgetown University Law Center," 81 *Georgetown Law Journal* 461 (1994); Judith Resnik, "Changing the Topic," 8 *Cardozo Studies in Law and Literature* 339 (1996); Elizabeth M. Schneider, "Gendering and Engendering Process," 61 *University of Cincinnati Law Review* 1223 (1993); Elizabeth M. Schneider, Lucinda Finley, Carin Clauss, and Joan Bertin, "Feminist Jurisprudence—1990 Myra Bradwell Day Panel," 1 *Columbia Journal of Gender and Law* 5 (1991); Elizabeth M. Schneider, "Task Force Reports on Women in the Courts: The Challenge for Legal Education," 38 *Journal of Legal Education* 87 (1988); Carl Tobias, "Gender Issues and the Prosser, Wade and Schwartz Torts Casebook," 18 *Golden Gate University Law Review* 495 (1988); Morrison Torrey, Jackie Casey, and Karin Olsen, "Teaching Law in a Feminist Manner: A Commentary from Experience," 13 *Harvard Women's Law Journal* 87 (1990).

11. American Bar Association Commission on Domestic Violence, *When Will They Ever Learn? Educating to End Domestic Violence* (1997). I participated in one of these regional meetings in Washington, D.C., in September 1999. The creative and committed work of many law teachers who attended this meeting and the breadth of curricular work on domestic violence at many law schools were impressive and exciting. For discussion of other curricular possibilities, see Cynthia Grant Bowman and Eden

Kusmiersky, "Praxis and Pedagogy: Domestic Violence," 32 *Loyola of Los Angeles Law Review* 719 (1999); Naomi Cahn and Joan Meier, "Domestic Violence and Feminist Jurisprudence: Towards a New Agenda," 4 *Boston University Public Interest Law Journal* 339 (1995); Susan Bryant and Maria Arias, "Case Study: A Battered Women's Rights Clinic: Designing a Clinical Program Which Encourages a Problem-Solving Vision of Lawyering That Empowers Clients and Community," 42 *Washington University Journal of Urban and Contemporary Law* 207 (1992); Joan S. Meier, "Notes from the Underground: Integrating Psychological and Legal Perspectives on Domestic Violence in Theory and Practice, 21 *Hofstra Law Review* 1295 (1993).

12. Mithra Merryman, "A Survey of Domestic Violence Programs in Legal Education," 28 *New England Law Review* 383 (1993).

13. Clare Dalton and Elizabeth M. Schneider, *Cases and Materials on Battered Women and the Law* (Foundation Press, forthcoming). Two other law school casebooks that focus on domestic violence are Beverly Balos and Mary Louise Fellows, *Law and Violence Against Women: Cases and Materials on Systems of Oppression* (1994); and Nancy K. D. Lemon, *Domestic Violence Law: A Comprehensive Overview of Cases and Sources* (1996). For discussion about generic issues concerning teaching about violence against women, see Special Issue, "Teaching about Violence Against Women, International Perspectives," 27 *Women's Studies Quarterly* nos. 1 and 2 (Spring–Summer 1999).

14. Schneider, "Legal Reform Efforts."

15. See, e.g., Cheryl Hanna, "Ganging Up on Girls: Young Women and Their Emerging Violence," 41 *Arizona Law Review* 93 (1999); Cheryl Hanna, "Sometimes Sex Matters: Reflections on Biology, Sexual Aggression, and Its Implications for the Law," 39 *Jurimetrics* 261 (1999); Cheryl Hanna, "The Paradox of Hope: The Crime and Punishment of Domestic Violence," 39 *William and Mary Law Review* 1505 (1998); Cheryl Hanna, "No Right to Choose: Mandated Victim Participation in Domestic Violence Prosecutions," 109 *Harvard Law Review* 1849 (1996); Andrea Brenneke, "Civil Rights Remedies for Battered Women: Axiomatic and Ignored," 11 *Law and Inequality* 1 (1992); *Violence Against Women, Law and Litigation* (David Frazee, Ann Noel, Andrea Brenneke, and Mary C. Dunlap, eds., 1997); Merryman, "Survey of Domestic Violence Programs"; Valenda Applegarth, Laurie A. Freeman, Mithra Merryman, and Barbara H. Mitchell, "Safety and Protection Issues," in *Family Law Advocacy for Low and Moderate Income Litigants* (Massachusetts Continuing Legal Education, 1999); Ariella Hyman and Sarah Eaton, "The Domestic Violence Component of the New York Task Force Report on Women in the Courts: An Empirical Evaluation and Assessment of New York City Courts," 19 *Fordham University Urban Law Review* 201 (1992); Ariella Hyman and Dean Schillinger, "Laws Mandating Reporting of Domestic Violence: Do They Promote Patient Well-Being?" 273 *Journal of the American Medical Association* 1781 (1995); Pauline Quirion, Judith Lennett, Kristin Lund, and Chanda Tuck, "Protecting Children Exposed to Domestic Violence in Contested Custody and Visitation Litigation," 6 *Boston University Public Interest Law Journal* 501 (1997); Andree G. Gagnon, "Ending Mandatory Divorce Mediation for Battered Women," 15 *Harvard Women's Law Journal* 272 (1992);

Michele Lang, "Professionals, Activists, Crows: The Family Violence Program at Boston University School of Medicine" (Notes from the Field), 14 *Harvard Women's Law Journal* 222 (1991).

16. Lisa Sheehy, Melissa Reinberg, and Deborah Kirchwey, "Commutation for Women Who Defend Themselves Against Abusive Partners: An Advocacy Manual and Guide to Legal Issues" (1991) (available from the National Clearinghouse for Defense of Battered Women).

Chapter 13: Feminist Lawmaking, Violence, and Equality

1. The National Organization for Women estimated the number of demonstrators to be 250,000, making this the largest rally ever held protesting violence against women. Jennifer Gonnerman, "Lights, Camera, Protest," *Village Voice,* 14 (April 18, 1995).

Index

Abrams, Kathryn, 37, 84, 85
Abuse excuse, 112, 147, 264n1
Acquaintance rape, 47, 242n4
Affective privacy, 17
Agency. *See* Victimization-agency dichotomy
American Bar Association Commission on Domestic Violence, 105, 224
American Medical Association, 4
American Psychological Association, 127
Arizona Supreme Court, 158, 160–61
Arizona v. Mott, 160–62, 165
Armour, Jody, 147

Barbieri, Paula, 207
Barrett, Alice, 167
Barrett v. Indiana, 167
Battered spouse syndrome, 143, 276–77n100
"Battered woman survivor," 76
Battered woman syndrome: and female pathology, 6, 23, 24; Walker on, 23, 234–35n27; and expert testimony, 62, 80–81, 123, 125, 127–28, 132, 134, 137, 141, 143, 230; and victimization-agency dichotomy, 82, 131–32, 135; as defense, 115, 120, 124–25, 137, 143, 144, 163, 271n45, 277n102; and battered women who kill, 123–24; and reasonableness, 123, 137; and excuse-justification dichotomy, 135–36, 275n84; and bat-

tered women as mothers, 159, 160–61, 163–67, 168; and child custody, 168
Battered women: and law, 6, 9; complexity of experience of, 8, 18–19, 43–44, 59, 60, 62, 77, 79, 123–24, 136; in courts, 8, 49–53; experiences of, 9, 33, 34, 42, 62, 119, 122, 123, 147, 213, 259n32; vulnerability of, 12; Deutsch on, 20; psychological perspective on, 23–24; and right-wing organizations, 26; and feminist lawmaking, 34, 44; and rights claims, 44; requirement to leave, 51, 52, 53, 76, 77–79, 84; concept of battered woman, 60–62, 96, 120–21, 141, 247n22, 248n27, 267–68n25, 268n27; and essentialism, 62–65; and gender neutrality, 67; particularity and generality of, 72; and reasonableness, 76, 79–83, 154; agency of, 83–86; and resistant self-direction, 85; and public-private dichotomy, 88–89, 90, 91–97; and lawyers, 105, 106, 122, 145, 147, 187, 211, 219, 225, 226, 229; credibility of, 107, 108; misconceptions about, 113; and battered woman defense, 114, 115, 120, 124–25; and incarceration, 115, 146, 265n8, 280n114, 280–81n115, 281n116; and victimization-agency dichotomy, 149, 171; and mandatory arrest, 184–87; and Simpson case, 200; and legal education, 218

Physical abuse (continued)
and Violence Against Women Act,
192, 194
Planned Parenthood v. Casey, 3–4, 102,
228
Pleck, Elizabeth, 14, 20, 21, 27
Police practices: and battered women's
movement, 5; and battered women,
27, 50, 51; and feminist lawmaking,
30; and rights claims, 43, 44; and procedural remedies, 45; and courts, 50;
and battered women who kill, 80;
and public-private dichotomy, 88, 91–
92, 93; and process of proof, 107; and
mandatory arrest, 181, 184, 186–87;
and Simpson case, 201, 204, 206, 207,
209; and Violence Against Women Act
of *1994,* 240n34
Political action, 40–41
Political meaning, 6, 30, 45, 46
Political perspective: and heterosexual
intimate violence, 5; "personal is
political," 5–6, 35; dialectical interrelationship between rights and politics,
6, 34, 35, 37, 42, 54; and battering, 12,
27; and domestic violence, 15, 26, 48,
242n47; and chastisement, 16; and battered women's movement, 21, 22, 96;
and law, 30–31; and self-defense law,
32–33; and feminist lawmaking, 33–34;
and public-private dichotomy, 90, 92,
96–97
Pornography, 74, 75, 251n1
Postmodern theory, 62, 64, 183
Post-traumatic stress disorder, 24, 107,
123, 164
Power and control: power and control
wheel, 12; and battering, 12–13, 22, 46,
47, 65, 66–67, 198, 201; and violence,
24, 46, 115; and stalking, 48; and feminist theory, 59, 66; and woman abuse,
72; and public-private dichotomy, 78,
90; and domestic violence, 208; and

lesbian battering, 249–50n38. *See also*
Coercive control
"Power feminism," 75, 76
Pratt v. Wood, 176
Pregnancy: and discrimination, 29, 56;
and battered women as mothers,
89, 150–51, 281–82n4, 282n6; and
differences-sameness dichotomy, 134;
and drug use, 151
Privacy: and domestic violence, 9, 13;
family privacy, 13, 14, 17, 27, 87–90;
and victimization, 43; and mediation,
45; and racial or cultural issues, 64;
and law reform, 87; and denial, 90–91,
97. *See also* Public-private dichotomy
Process, 9, 35–37, 46
Proof: process of, 106–8; burden of, 143,
277n104
Psychological abuse, 4, 12, 47–48, 70, 78
Ptacek, James, 109
Public education: and gender bias, 6;
and Simpson case, 9, 199–201, 208–10;
and feminist lawmaking, 9, 199, 228;
and legal claims, 42; and definition of
battering, 66; and battered women's
agency, 85–86; and public-private dichotomy, 94–95; and gender violence,
190; and Violence Against Women Act
of *1994,* 240n34
Public-private dichotomy: and rights
claims, 42, 46, 240–41n38; and intimate violence, 48, 90, 182, 230; and
women's international human rights,
54; and family privacy, 87–90; and
battered women, 88–89, 90, 91–97;
and judges, 88, 92, 95, 109–10; and
mandatory arrest, 92, 93, 94, 182; and
marriage license fees, 93, 259n21; and
excuse-justification dichotomy, 136.
See also Privacy

R. v. Lavalee, 140–42
Raeder, Myrna, 209